Modernity, Memory and Identity
in South-East Europe

Series Editor
Catharina Raudvere
Department of Cross-Cultural and Regional Studies
University of Copenhagen
Copenhagen, Denmark

This series explores the relationship between the modern history and present of South-East Europe and the long imperial past of the region. This approach aspires to offer a more nuanced understanding of the concepts of modernity and change in this region, from the nineteenth century to the present day. Titles focus on changes in identity, self-representation and cultural expressions in light of the huge pressures triggered by the interaction between external influences and local and regional practices. The books cover three significant chronological units: the decline of empires and their immediate aftermath, authoritarian governance during the twentieth century, and recent uses of history in changing societies in South-East Europe today.

More information about this series at
http://www.palgrave.com/gp/series/15829

Vahram Ter-Matevosyan

Turkey, Kemalism and the Soviet Union

Problems of Modernization, Ideology
and Interpretation

Vahram Ter-Matevosyan
American University of Armenia
Yerevan, Armenia

ISSN 2523-7985   ISSN 2523-7993 (electronic)
Modernity, Memory and Identity in South-East Europe
ISBN 978-3-319-97402-6   ISBN 978-3-319-97403-3   (eBook)
https://doi.org/10.1007/978-3-319-97403-3

Library of Congress Control Number: 2018949317

This Palgrave Macmillan imprint is published by the registered company Springer Nature
Switzerland AG
The registered company address is: Gewerbestrasse 11, 6330 Cham, Switzerland

To Tigran, Hayk,
and
Anahit,
with all my love

PREFACE AND ACKNOWLEDGEMENTS

This book is the product of ten years of research. Since its inception, new insights, questions, and approaches have presented themselves. In spite of the varying pace of its progress, I never stopped believing that one day the text of the present research would be published. Throughout this period, I had the chance to share the findings of the research in different forums, conferences, workshops; and after each event, I became convinced that the topic is no less relevant today than it was a decade ago.

My interest in Turkish Studies started in February 1997 when Turkey experienced its fourth military intervention, known as a *"post-modern coup."* The Kemalist elite in Turkey was determined to reaffirm secular principles. To pursue that goal, they tasked the coalition government, headed by Necmettin Erbakan, to roll the country back to its Kemalist foundations. Then, in 1998, the Constitutional Court of Turkey closed down the Welfare Party for violating the secular principles of the Republic. The next few years were no less eventful—the earthquake in Izmit in 1999, the attainment of candidate status for EU membership in the same year, the economic downfall of 2001, and the victory of the Justice and Development Party in the 2002 snap elections. When discussing these developments the relevance of Kemalism was clearly visible in various forms and manifestations. It became obvious to me also that in order to understand Turkish history and politics, it was essential to understand the ideological foundations of Kemalism and its transformations.

This objective brought me to the University of Bergen, Norway, to pursue my doctoral degree, and to embark on the long journey to understand Turkey from within. The Centre for Middle Eastern and Islamic Studies at the University of Bergen with its rich facilities kindly welcomed me. I am very grateful to have had Professor Knut Vikør as my advisor. Thanks to him, I learned that what is needed in the study of history is hard work, precision, and consistency. He was always available to discuss, encourage, and support me in carrying out my research. I particularly value the independence that he granted me, being confident that I was on the right track. I also want to thank Professor Anders Bjørkelo, whose support and advice, particularly in the early stages of my research, was significant in choosing the correct methodological pathway.

Throughout the research process, I met many knowledgeable scholars and intellectuals whose support has been invaluable. I particularly want to thank Zafer Toprak, the late Hrant Dink, Etyen Mahçupian, Stein Ugelvik Larsen, Hakan Sıcakkan, Ståle Knudsen, Ayşegül Komsuoğlu, Doug Shumavon, Arpie Balian, and many others. Long and in-depth discussions about the Ottoman past and republican history of Turkey with Ruben Safrastyan, Stephan Astourian, and Ruben Melkonyan helped me to gain intellectual synergy. Their unconditional support, guidance, and invaluable hints on how to improve the research and explore the lesser known dimensions of Turkish history expanded my understanding of the subject. Reşat Kasaba, Isa Blumi, and Anne Katrine Bang, who served as members of the evaluation committee, read the text with utmost care and provided insightful comments, suggestions, and criticism. Their reassurance that the research was worthy of publication was instrumental in transforming it into a book. They all deserve special appreciation. I am also thankful to my colleagues at the Institute of Oriental Studies of the National Academy of Sciences of Armenia and the American University of Armenia for their assistance and for providing a supportive work environment to nourish my scholarly interests.

I am grateful to Palgrave Macmillan Commissioning Editor Molly Beck for guiding me through the review process. I also want to thank Catharina Raudvere, the series editor, who welcomed the project and encouraged me to improve certain parts of the text. I was fortunate to have Oliver Dyer as my Assistant Editor—he helped me immensely by embracing the project. Alina Gharabegian and Daniela Blei have read the entire manuscript and helped to make it better.

I cannot forget to mention all the people that I met during my end-less trips to Turkey. This research would have been impossible to complete without the generous hospitality of the Davitian family in Bergen. Constant inquiries by my close friends also helped me not to lose sight of my objective.

Without the constant encouragement of my wife, Anahit, and my parents, Hamazasp and Shoushan, I could never have completed this intellectual journey. My sons, Tigran and Hayk, helped to convince me of the necessity to complete this research to compensate for the long periods of my absence.

Yerevan, Armenia   Vahram Ter-Matevosyan

PRAISE FOR *TURKEY, KEMALISM AND THE SOVIET UNION*

"Kemalist ideology and its interpretations have generally been viewed, interpreted, and reconstructed within the Westernization paradigm. Ter-Matevosyan's sophisticated and far-reaching use of original material enables him to provide a multi-layered account of the half-a-century that he examines. This is a work of depth, narrative power, and substantive importance. It will remain as the standard book on the subject for the foreseeable future."

—Şükrü Hanioğlu, *Professor of Near Eastern Studies, Garrett Professor in Foreign Affairs, Princeton University, USA*

"This study of Kemalist Turkey sheds new light on an ideology that has irrigated the entire Turkish society to the present day, including the Erdogan regime. The examination of its historical links with the Soviet Union is the heart of this work which opens new historical perspectives and helps us to understand contemporary Turkey."

—Raymond H. Kévorkian, *Honorary Director of Research at Université Paris 8 Saint-Denis, France*

"This is an important, very instructive and innovative study. Ter-Matevosyan succeeds in carefully exposing the dizzying metamorphoses of Kemalism whose early genesis the Soviet Union had more attentively followed than self-absorbed Western powers."

—Hans-Lukas Kieser, *Associate Professor, University of Newcastle, Australia and Adjunct Professor, University of Zurich, Switzerland*

Contents

Abbreviations

ARF	Armenian Revolutionary Federation
CCCPSU	Central Committee of the Communist Party of the Soviet Union
CPSU	Communist Party of the Soviet Union
CUP	Committee of Union and Progress
DP	Democrat Party
FRP	Free Republican Party
JDP	Justice and Development Party
JP	Justice Party
MFA	Ministry for Foreign Affairs
NAP	Nationalist Action Party
NSC	National Security Council
NSP	National Salvation Party
NUC	National Unity Committee
PCFA	People's Commissariat for Foreign Affairs
PH	People's Houses
PRP	Progressive Republican Party
RAAO	(All)Russian Academic Association of Orientalists
RPP	Republican People's Party
SCS	Socialist Culture Society
SU	Soviet Union
TGNA	Turkish Grand National Assembly
TH	Turkish Hearths

Introduction

In 2023, the Republic of Turkey will celebrate its centennial. Like its predecessor, the Ottoman Empire, republican Turkey has been and remains a perplexing country, not only for its own citizens and others in the region, but also for most of the world. Followers of developments in modern Turkey realize that the country is undergoing a difficult period in its history, as notions of Erdoğan's Turkey and other "Turkeys" collide. One may be tempted to look at the current context for explanations, while others turn to history to find the root causes of existing problems.

Understanding the challenges that the Turkish state and society are currently facing requires examining the country's relationship to its ideological foundations. Throughout its existence, the key ideas, principles, and norms of Kemalism, the governing philosophy of republican Turkey named after its founding father, Mustafa Kemal Atatürk (1881–1938), have repeatedly emerged in politics, law, education, and public space. Eventually, Kemalism came to dominate the mentality, value system, and collective consciousness of Turkish society. Despite recurrent setbacks, Kemalism has remained an integral part of political and social processes, generating public debates about its place and role in the future of Turkey. In one way, everything about Kemalism became sensitive, given the polemics surrounding its protagonists, defenders, and critics. Just a few examples suffice to show the complexity of these discussions. Some

© The Author(s) 2019
V. Ter-Matevosyan, *Turkey, Kemalism and the Soviet Union,*
Modernity, Memory and Identity in South-East Europe,
https://doi.org/10.1007/978-3-319-97403-3_1

practitioners and observers loudly defend the synthesis of Islamism and Kemalism, pointing to the likelihood of compromise between these two conflicting creeds. Other scholars go beyond conventional assessments of the crisis of Kemalism, declaring its final demise. Still others claim that Kemalism is immortal. Recent developments have only added ambiguity to the existing debates. Since the 1980s, Kurdish nationalism, political Islam, and rising conservatism visibly weakened Kemalism and its followers' hold on power.

The results of the 2002 parliamentary elections are widely interpreted as a turning point between the past and the future of the Turkish Republic. The words of Muammar Kaylan, a veteran journalist and a former editor-in-chief of the Turkish daily *Hürriyet*, help to comprehend the significance of the election results for the Kemalists: "*On November 3, 2002… Kemalism and the secular reforms of my childhood years suffered a humiliating defeat in Turkey's 172.143 polling stations.*"[1] The electoral victory of the Justice and Development Party (*Adalet ve Kalkınma Partisi*—henceforth, JDP), led by Recep Tayyip Erdoğan, and consequent political, social, and cultural reforms, which, by and large, overhauled the Kemalist legacy, have led to a renewed interest in Kemalism. These developments indicate, once again, that understanding the structure and framework of Kemalism is not an easy task; its grip over the Turkish state and society has both tightened and weakened in the republican era. At any rate, it is reasonable to attribute many challenges in modern Turkey to interpretations and applications of Kemalism.

Against this backdrop, this study seeks to illumine another perspective, which, hopefully, expands the breadth and depth of existing knowledge about Turkey and its ideological construction. The primary purpose of this study is to determine existing problems and perspectives in interpretations of Kemalism.

The study pursues this goal by:

First, examining the evolution and internal dynamics of Kemalism. A lack of consensus about its structure, content, and form has always existed. Perhaps this explains why Kemalism was used and misused by different actors. The peculiarities of dominance and power are therefore discussed, providing a broader picture of the era that formed the foundations of Kemalism and shaped the behaviour of its followers. Kemalism, both as an ideological construct and a pattern of transformation, has given rise to numerous interpretations and perspectives. Although it is practically impossible to discuss them all, some major patterns are clearly discernible. It is through the study of these interpretations that several problems have emerged.

Second, examining existing problems and gaps in the study of Kemalism. This book deals with the significance of incorporating "non-Western" interpretations of Kemalism by examining how the Kemalist transformation, and particularly the ideology of Kemalism, were seen and interpreted by Soviet observers between the 1920s and 1970s. How Kemalism was perceived in the Soviet Union has not been an object of scholarly analysis. Instead, most researchers have concentrated on the complexities of bilateral relations between Turkey and the Soviet Union, their patterns of modernization, and geopolitical rivalry during the Cold War. Both Kemalism and the Kemalists, initially viewed as an ally in the struggle against the West, were later treated negatively by the Communist regime. In the 1960s and 1970s, the Soviet position returned to normalization. Looking at these shifts through the lenses of Soviet leaders, diplomats, Communist party functionaries, and scholars helps us grasp the underlying dynamics behind these changing attitudes. Placing them in the larger context of republican history—delineating phases in the Kemalist paradigm of development and discerning its various rises and falls—will enrich our knowledge of the transnational history of Kemalism.

"History cannot and does not aim to answer big questions about human destiny," posits historian Arthur Marwick. "To the contrary, its great value to society lies in the fact that by limiting itself to clearly defined manageable questions, it can offer succinct and well-substantiated answers."[2] Bearing this caveat in mind, this study tackles the following interrelated questions: *What are the major problems in existing interpretations of Kemalism, and how can the incorporation of Soviet perspectives enrich our understanding of Kemalism?* Posing these two questions raises additional ones: what are the major transformative stages of Kemalism and how are they differentiated from one another? How did different development stages of Kemalism influence interpretations of it? How significant is the incorporation of Soviet interpretations in studying Kemalism? What factors facilitated Soviet interest in Kemalism and domestic transformations in Turkey?

Turkey's Westernization model, this book argues, has powerfully shaped the historiography of Kemalism. By drawing on "non-Western"—in this case, Soviet perspectives on Kemalism, this book challenges and contributes to our understandings of republican Turkey and its history. Beginning in the 1920s, Soviet research institutions and scholars, together with Communist Party functionaries and diplomats, scrutinized power relations inside Turkey. Not only the concepts of Marxism–Leninism, but also geopolitical concerns influenced their critical views and interpretations of Kemalism. Identifying the meanings, virtues, and weaknesses of Kemalism, they insisted on the political significance of classes and class relations for understanding basic structural features of Turkish politics and society. They recognized early on the inherent contradictions of Kemalism's ideological hegemony and the inevitable social and political consequences. This rift curbed Kemalism's popularity and precluded the broad legitimacy that its advocates sought in society. This divide also portended the religious turn in Turkish politics that started in the 1950s and would come to dominate the conservative political parties.

This study's research method is qualitative. It relies on qualitative content analysis and document analysis. Primary sources include documents, speeches, and statements made by Mustafa Kemal, RPP programs, statutes, declarations, publications by the Turkish Grand National Assembly (*Türkiye Büyük Millet Meclisi*—henceforth, TGNA), and memoirs by Mustafa Kemal's supporters and opponents. This book also draws on archival materials, letters, and newspapers as well as statements, speeches, and analytical reports prepared by the Communist Party of the Soviet Union (henceforth, CPSU), and by leaders, functionaries, and observers of Turkey. Diplomatic cables by Soviet (Armenian and after December 1922, SU) Diplomatic Representatives to the People's Commissariat for Foreign Affairs (henceforth, PCFA) of the SU are used. Between 2004 and 2006, field research conducted in Turkey included ten in-depth interviews with scholars, reporters, and politicians who have written on Kemalism.

This study was conducted in several countries and at various research institutions: in Turkey, at Istanbul Bilgi University, Boğaziçi University, the Atatürk Centre for Modern History, the Turkish Economic and Social Studies Foundation (TESEV), and with local newspapers (*Milliyet, Agos, Marmara*), political party headquarters, and NGOs. In the United States, the list includes the Henry M. Jackson School of International Studies at the University of Washington in Seattle; the Institute of Slavic, East European, and Eurasian Studies at the University of California, Berkeley; and Duke University. In Switzerland, research was carried out at the University of Fribourg, and in the Russian Federation at the Russian State Library. In Armenia, the National Archives and the Institute for Oriental Studies provided important materials, too. Some of these research findings have been published in international and national peer-reviewed journals and presented at international conferences and workshops between 2007 and 2017. In 2008, a part of this research (on political Islam and its challenges to Kemalism) was published as a monograph.[3]

Even though Soviet interpretations and approaches are discussed mainly in the last two chapters, some Soviet positions and insights pertaining to specific events and developments in Turkey between the 1920s and 1970s are explored in the preceding chapters. This chronological order aims at providing the historical context for the existing interpretations of Kemalism before moving on to address Soviet interpretations of it. To analyse the latter, it is important to reflect upon some of the relevant political and historical developments in the Soviet Union, also. A separate examination of the discursive dimensions of Kemalism in Turkey and the Soviet Union will map out the core determinants of existing interpretations.

Because Russian authors usually write only the initial of their first name (followed by their surname), sometimes it was difficult to identify them, although painstaking efforts were made to trace their full names. In some cases, when authors used the initials of their first and last names on purpose, it was especially difficult to determine them or restore full names. The translation of texts and titles belongs to the author. Russian language sources are transliterated using the Library of Congress standard (without diacritic marks).

The first chapter in this study explores existing problems of definition and periodization of Kemalism and discusses the historiography of the research problem. It emphasizes the patterns and strands in the Kemalist historiography and how the incorporation of the Soviet research on Turkey can enrich the literature. It focuses also on the transnational scholarship on Kemalism. The second chapter begins by providing a historical assessment of the political and ideological consolidation of Mustafa Kemal's rule in the 1920s and 1930s. This chapter also examines the evolution of certain principles that came to constitute the core of the Kemalist system of thought. The third chapter considers the intellectual and contextual origins of Kemalism and the efforts by Kemalist elites to popularize the principles of Kemalism. The fourth chapter looks at the first efforts of refining the Kemalist system of thought in the post-Atatürk era in the 1940s and its transformative features during the era of multi-party democracy in the 1950s. The fifth chapter touches on the further transformation of Kemalist discourse, which includes the period between the 1960s and 1970s. The sixth chapter examines problems and perspectives of different interpretations of Kemalism. The last two chapters discuss how Kemalism and its advancement were seen and interpreted by Soviet observers from the 1920s to the 1970s. Chapter Seven explores the period of the 1920s, when the most active discussions about Kemalism were held in the SU. The final chapter addresses the period from the late 1920s to the late 1970s, when Soviet–Turkish relations started to deteriorate, and then slowly recovered over the course of the last two decades. These and all other related subjects examined in this book, while answering many questions, raise many others about the background of problems that modern Turkey still confronts.

NOTES

1. Muammar Kaylan. 2005. *The Kemalists: Islamic Revival and the Fate of Secular Turkey.* New York: Prometheus Books, 412.
2. Arthur Marwick. 2001. *The New Nature of History: Knowledge, Evidence, Language.* Basingstoke: Palgrave, 6.
3. Vahram Ter-Matevosyan. 2008. *Islamy Turkiaji Hasarakakan-Qakhaqakan Kyankum, 1970–2001 tt.* [Islam in the Social and Political Life of Turkey, 1970–2001]. Yerevan: Limush.

Problems of Definition and Historiography of Kemalism

While the literature on Kemal Atatürk is considerable, discussion of his revolutionary reforms and policies has been marked by a lack of consensus on relevant terminology. At the outset of the nationalist movement, different expressions emerged both in Turkey and abroad, *inter alia*—"Kemalists," "Kemalist movement," "Kemalist revolution," "Kemalist Turkey," and so on—which amounted to mere generalizations and descriptive terms. Later, when it became apparent that the Kemalist revolution was not limited to the struggle for independence, but also incorporated the internal affairs of the state, a new general term, "Kemalism," emerged. Many observers used this term as a synonym for describing the Kemalist revolution, with an emphasis on its political and socio-economic content. Thus, it took some time before Kemalism acquired ideological connotations.

Throughout subsequent decades, the principles and perceptions of Kemalism, deliberately or otherwise, went through transformation, reformation, and deformation. Politicians and observers alike have sought to attach new meanings and content to Kemalism. As a result, Kemalism was overstretched or narrowed to its core ideas. One of the profound implications of this pursuit was that it eventually acquired a second name: Atatürkism [*Atatürkçülük*]. This may seem confusing for observers both in Turkey and abroad.[1] For instance, Esra Özyürek defined Kemalism as a "more left-wing, nationalist, anti-Islamist and anti-neo-global interpretation of the principles of Kemal Atatürk,"

© The Author(s) 2019

V. Ter-Matevosyan, *Turkey, Kemalism and the Soviet Union,*
Modernity, Memory and Identity in South-East Europe,
https://doi.org/10.1007/978-3-319-97403-3_2

whereas, Atatürkism was "a more right-wing, authoritarian understanding of the ideology."[2] For some time, these two terms were used interchangeably. Since the 1960s and 1970s, however, certain ideological features were ascribed to each one, more or less in line with Özyürek's definition. While subsequent chapters address this issue, for the clarity of the analysis, "Kemalism" is preferred and Atatürkism will be applied when discussing or quoting specific authors.

These variations of approaches also challenged the traits of Kemalism. The literature on Kemalism is abundant with various characterizations: *a mere ideology, a state ideology, a soft ideology, an official ideology, a governing philosophy, a political philosophy, a system of thought, a system of beliefs, a dynamic force for social transformation, a political movement, a political platform, a modernizing ideology, a guiding vision, an ideological compass, a cultural tradition, an intellectual tradition,* etc. In addition to these definitions, many others exist which are addressed in more detail below. Although these formulations dominated the scholarship for decades, some contained limitations, contradictions, and outright problems. For the sake of analytical and terminological clarity, this research identifies Kemalism both as an ideology and as a system of principles. This study uses these two concepts interchangeably, depending on the period and context. Kemalism as an ideology is viewed as a normatively constructed collection of ideas and concepts, which are endorsed by a political party or by state institutions (armed forces, judiciary, etc.). Kemalism as a system (or a set) of principles implies an extensive application of circumstantially adjusted ideas, norms, values, and visions by different agents, which, however, failed to properly contextualize and elaborate the system.

This analysis refrains from depicting Kemalism as a single and unitary ideological construct or political project. This approach is based on the argument that since its inception, Kemalism underwent various transformations, both in form and content, and, subsequently, each period (marked by radical domestic and global shifts and challenges, military interventions, regime change, etc.) left its mark on the shape and essence of Kemalism and vice versa. But for the sake of analytical clarity, the key characteristics of Kemalism, specific to each period under discussion, will be provided. Another major drawback of previous approaches is that some scholars looked at Kemalism in a particular moment without acknowledging the features it inherited from previous periods and the implications the previous problems had for later decades.

Explaining the periodization and timeframe of Kemalism is also significant. A number of observers date the origins of some Kemalist principles to the eighteenth century,[3] while others point to the nineteenth, in particular, to the *Tanzimat* reforms (1839). Still others trace the roots of Kemalism to the constitutional endeavours of the 1870s. Mustafa Kemal himself used May 19, 1919 as the starting point for the nationalist Kemalist movement and his nation-building project. Others have picked different dates, like December 24, 1919, when Mustafa Kemal delivered an ideologically driven speech in Kırşehir.[4] Others claim that the history of Kemalism should be dated from October 29, 1923, when the Republic was proclaimed, since it signified a radical break from the Ottoman era, marking the birth of a different country. More conventional claims are that the birthdate of Kemalism is 1931, when its six principles were incorporated into the program of the ruling Republican People's Party (*Cumhuriyet Halk Partisi*—henceforth, RPP); or 1935, when the term Kemalism was first used in the party program, or 1937, when Kemalism gained legal status and was incorporated into the constitution of Turkey. Other scholars, such as Erik-Jan Zürcher, claim that contrary to popular opinion, it is irrefutable that both Kemalism and Kemalist policies constitute the last phase of the reforms initiated by the Ottoman Empire.[5] Still others offer a metaphorical interpretation, claiming that Kemalism was born with the Republic and subsequently reborn in different phases of the development of the Turkish state. In other words, there is no consensus on the beginning of Kemalism. Ambiguity also dominates later developments. Some claim that conventional Kemalism was over with the death of Mustafa Kemal Atatürk in 1938 because his followers would go on to distort the spirit of Kemalist thought and principles. Others have proposed that Kemalism is immortal as long as the memory of the reforms and deeds of Mustafa Kemal are alive.

This research will consider Kemalism as a specifically republican phenomenon with strong and vivid characteristics inherited from the Ottoman past. The following scheme of periodization is applied: (a) In the 1920s, the first efforts were made to conceptualize Mustafa Kemal's understanding of the Turkish modernization paradigm; (b) in the 1930s–1940s, after Kemalism was officially introduced, it was transformed into a hegemonic political platform controlled by party ideologues, state bureaucracy, and intellectuals; (c) the period of multiparty politics and intense ideological polarization in the 1950s–1970s significantly challenged the hegemony of Kemalism.

The book ends in the 1970s because this decade signified the plurality and manifestation of different facets of Kemalism. The 1980 military intervention was a deliberate effort to restore statist, republican, nationalist, and secular traditions. In the post-intervention era, the military tried to reinstate Kemalism according to its modified perceptions and interpretations. Therefore, Kemalism in the 1980s and in later decades was a structurally distinct construct. The reimposition of Kemalism onto society in the 1980s and 1990s was both desperate and anachronistic. Newly emerging political, economic, cultural, and social realities in the 1980s proved Kemalism even more incompatible and unprepared than it had been in the 1960s. Furthermore, increasing consolidation of political Islam, conservatism, and Kurdish nationalism fundamentally challenged the entire edifice of arguments championed by the Kemalists.

HISTORIOGRAPHY OF KEMALISM

The historiography of Kemalism has generated various explanations and approaches, perspectives, and considerations. Discussions on Kemalism evolved either around its core principles and supporting concepts or its ideological and practical applicability. Traditionally, Kemalism has been interpreted in line with its "Six arrows" (*Altı Ok*) or principles: nationalism, secularism, populism, republicanism, revolutionism, and étatism.[6] Other scholars have shown a more holistic approach, like Stanford Shaw and Ezel Kural Shaw, who defined Kemalism as Mustafa Kemal's "basic ideas and policies, developed in hundreds of speeches, programs, and laws from the early days of the nationalist movement to his death in 1938."[7] The US Department of State summarily defined Kemalism (referring to Atatürkism) as the ideological basis of modern Turkey, comprised of secularism, nationalism, étatism, and inspired by the West.[8] Metin Heper argues that previous studies have failed to capture "the gist of Atatürkism," and explores Atatürk's idea of the creation of a transient, moderate, transcendental state. They also did not distinguish, according to Heper, between Atatürk's strategies and tactics. Even Atatürk's opponents could pose as "genuine Atatürkists," because when necessary, they could find a quotation from Atatürk to support their point of view.[9] Robert Mantran differentiates a few elements for characterizing Kemalism: defence of Turkish territory and more generally, "Turkism," secularism, direct or indirect state control of the principal means of production, and social progress through the modernization and westernization of Turkey.[10] According to a general interviewed by Mehmet Ali Birand in the 1980s, Atatürkism fits the definition of ideology because it provides a framework for interpreting events and new developments. He shows that it is dynamic, not static, like communism, and has been applied in every field, including family and education.[11]

For some time, historians have distinguished between two distinct approaches in the historiography of Kemalism. The first, which presents "orthodox" views of Kemalist historiography, focuses on the reforms and achievements of the Atatürk era (1919–1938), and characterizes the period as a new beginning, a distinct departure from the Ottoman past. Based on that approach, many publications decoupled the republican present from the immediate Ottoman past. This view prevailed until the 1960s, when it was challenged within Turkey by politicians and then was taken over by scholars both from Turkey and abroad. Deriving from this standpoint, only a few would challenge the argument that Turkey in the 1920s and 1930s had been comprehensively studied. As a result, as Zürcher put it, literature on that period "completely dried up," which "must be considered a notable tribute to the effectiveness of the official historiography in establishing its version as an unchallenged truth."[12] The second approach perceives the Atatürk era more broadly, and ascribes transformational qualities to it. This approach situates Kemalism within a larger chronology, spanning at least two centuries, and thereby underscoring continuity between modern Turkey and its Ottoman predecessor.

Most twentieth-century studies of Kemalism have depicted the life of Kemal Atatürk and the history of his era by attributing a degree of mysticism and divinity to him. Thus, the *Kemalocentric* interpretation of republican history[13] became one of the characteristic features in the study of Kemalism. Kemalist historiography was a "metanarrative," in the words of Jean-Francois Lyotard, that provided meaning for past events, legitimating the actions of the existing power structure by presenting definitions of development, progress, nation, and democracy within narrow boundaries.[14] It must be stated that this trend was largely based on Mustafa Kemal's interpretation of his own deeds and actions, which culminated in a series of speeches, statements, and interviews in the 1920s and 1930s,[15] and were undoubtedly shaped by his famous six-day speech delivered in 1927.[16] Prominent Kemalist historians and intellectuals—Enver Ziya Karal, Tarik Zafer Tunaya, Şevket Süreyya Aydemir, Niyazi Berkes, Suna Kili, and many others[17]—covered the origins of the ideas and reforms of Kemal Atatürk. They shaped and sustained official Kemalist historiography, each leaving a profound mark on it. Some of the research contained little or no critical approach towards Kemal and his principles, while other studies, including those by Niyazi Berkes, a left-leaning Kemalist intellectual, traced the origins of Turkish modernization earlier than what was commonly believed, making an argument for continuity between the imperial and republican eras. Historians praised Atatürk's reforms by presenting them as a radical break from the Ottoman past. Along similar lines, most books and articles published in the West between the 1920s and 1950s bore the imprint of the Kemalist narrative of a radical break with the Ottoman era.[18] However, in later writings, some scholars accepted the lack of a comprehensive account of Kemalism per se.[19] Some studies of Kemalism argued against interpreting it separately from Atatürk's personality. Özlem Bagdonas' argument has amplified one of the dominant ideas in the field: "Atatürk's charisma … has turned Kemalism into a safe haven in Turkish political discourse. … the socially acknowledged appeal of Atatürk's charisma created a legitimate basis for justifying subsequent policy objectives in the name of Kemalism."[20]

A mild revision in the historiography of Turkey occurred in the 1960–1970s. Alongside evolving socio-political realities (the proliferation of leftist movements and the expanding activities of Islamic and liberal intellectuals), more scholars started to question the reliability of earlier interpretations of historical events. In particular, they questioned inconsistencies and misrepresentations of the formative years of the republic, which led them to challenge orthodox Kemalist interpretations.[21] Mete Tunçay and Doğan Avcıoğlu, who published extensively on leftist movements in Turkey, produced a few critical works during this period.[22] Two journals of the left, *Yön* and *Devrim*, have significantly contributed to the critical revision of the role and place of Kemalist ideology. Emerging critical views claimed that Atatürk alone should not be credited for victory in the nationalist movement. The publication of Mustafa Kemal's long-time political-ally-turned-opponent Kâzım Karabekir's forbidden memoir, "The War of Our Independence" (*Istiklâl Harbimiz*),[23] contributed to the expansion of revisionist trends.[24] In the same vein, the publication of works by other lifetime political opponents of Atatürk, Ali Fuat Cebesoy[25] and Hüseyin Rauf Orbay,[26] also contributed to the process of questioning established views on the formative years of the Republic.

The position of anti-Kemalist forces was strengthened by the policies of the RPP, which, after embracing Atatürk's ideals for three decades after his death, shifted its orientation to "left of centre," then towards social democracy, and finally, to something resembling socialism. Simultaneously, more intellectuals and observers in Turkey produced more critical works on Kemalism and on the Kemalist movement.[27] Staunch followers of Kemalism viewed these efforts with suspicion since, for them, these mutations were aimed to discredit Atatürk and his achievements. Recently, important studies have depicted the transformation of the RPP's course in general, and Kemalism in particular, as it evolved in the 1960s and 1970s.[28] Studies of this period also reveal that in the 1970s, no particular political group or party embraced "the orthodox Kemalism." Thus, in 1980, when the Turkish armed forces (TAF) staged a third military coup, they could not resort to the orthodox discourse of Kemalism. As a result, the TAF had to reinvent and reinterpret, and rebrand and rethink the official discourse of Kemalism to reformulate Kemalism according to the existing Kemalist vocabulary.[29]

Before the late 1980s, most existing accounts of Kemalism failed to see Kemalist reforms and ideas as stemming from the Ottoman era. These approaches carried with them well-known limitations, which eventually made it impossible to see characteristics of Kemalism that were borrowed from the Young Turks, if not from earlier currents of thought. This lacuna entailed conceptual problems, which were eliminated thanks to the valuable contributions, methodological and empirical, of Erik-Jan Zürcher. His research proved that the Kemalist era should be characterized as a continuation of the Ottoman past (Young Turk era) rather than as a rupture.[30] This depiction also helped explore the impact that fashionable European ideologies had on Young Turks and hence on Kemalists.

Another dominant trend in the historiography of Kemalism deals with whether Kemalism was an ideology, a set of principles, visions, or, as argued by Bagdonas, a chain of competing discourses.[31] Following the first military intervention in 1960, the ideologically driven deliberations of Kemalism became widespread. Suna Kili, a prominent republican historiographer, reflected on the events of the 1960s when open challenges to the hegemony of Kemalism became widespread. During this period, even Atatürk's fellow politicians questioned the efficacy of his reforms.[32] Instead, Kili asserts that the newly emerging political forces, as such, never questioned Kemalism, which, simply put, is a debatable claim. In fact, Kemalism became a subject of intense debate that shaped the politics of subsequent decades. Kili provided further explanations and systematizations of Kemalism. Yet, from the beginning, she added to the confusion by referring to Kemalism as an ideology of Turkish revolutionary politics of the 1920s and to subsequent reforms as a rapid and radical change of Turkish state and society.[33] She called the ideology of Kemalism a composite of ideas, actions, and Turkish national aspirations—an ideology that combines elements of realism and idealism and that grows over time without sacrificing its basic tenets. Through Kili's lens, Kemalism is benevolent and anti-imperialist; it is a progressive-radical-revolutionary ideology that finds a place for change in Turkish society.[34]

Kili refers to the period between 1918 and 1938 as the years of Kemalism's formation, and the period between 1938 and 1960 as the advancement of Kemalism. Deeply influenced by the 1960 "revolution," she emphasizes its impact in moving Kemalism forward. One gets the impression that "real Kemalism" emerged no earlier than 1961. Kili does not pay sufficient attention to intellectual and inter-elite debates on Kemalism that surfaced in the mid-1930s, nor does she analyse the ideological construct of the Kemalist state in the period between the 1920s and 1940s. Again, under the influence of the 1960 revolution, Kili urges her readers not to conceive of Kemalism as a mere concept that served its historical purposes, but as a panacea against political and ideological conflicts in Turkey.[35]

Along the same lines, İsmet Giritli defined Kemalism as "a democratic and non-dogmatic ideology of national modernization described by rationality and scientism." He further viewed it as "a flexible amalgam of secularism, realism, empirical rationalism, and nationalism," opposed to the "rigid ideologies" of Marxism and National Socialism.[36] By contrast, İsmet Tamkoç argues that if Atatürkism needs to be interpreted as an ideology, then it should be done with reservations, since it is fundamentally different from other "isms," in that it only calls on the Turkish people to look forward to the future, expressing full confidence in the capabilities of the Turks to fulfil their ever-expanding desires.[37] To Niyazi Berkes, Atatürkism lacks a doctrinal, dogmatic basis since it does not contain a blueprint for a perfect and prosperous Turkish society.[38]

Concerning the question of whether Kemalism was an ideology, Paul Dumont contends that in the 1920s and 1930s, Mustafa Kemal and his associates were guided by the necessities and circumstances of the moment. Hence, the rulers never initiated a truly great doctrine. They also maintained that Atatürk's socio-cultural and political revolution was guided by ideas and later on was codified, often loosely and often awk-wardly, by the ideologists of the RPP.[39] Sabri Akural regards Kemalism as "based on various compatible assumptions and that there does exist a certain harmony among its manifested goals."[40] By rejecting it as an ide-ology or a comprehensive manifesto, Metin Heper delineates Atatürk's thought as "a 'soft' ideology at best," or as "a technique for discover-ing the truth and dissolving illusions."[41] Şükrü Hanioğlu claims that Mustafa Kemal was interested in promoting his ideas "but was reluctant to develop... a full-fledged ideology."[42] He further argues that in spite of consistent efforts of his followers to turn his 1927 six-day speech (and other statements and arguments) into a foundational text, it was "virtu-ally impossible to find a *mise en abyme* in this dry and unadorned text" with the possible exception of his address to the Turkish Youth.[43] In the minds of many Kemalists, however, *Nutuk* came to signify a different view. Mustafa Akyol, a conservative contributor to *Hürriyet Daily News*, noted succinctly: "Whenever there is a political crisis, his devotees, the Kemalists, rush to his shrine in drones and present wreaths as offerings. One of our retired generals recently said, 'Whenever I despair, I read the Nutuk.' ... the spiritual power it transmits is apparently not too dissim-ilar to what the Bible gives to a devout Christian."[44] The comparison between the Bible with the Nutuk is telling, suggesting a symbolic and secure space that Nutuk created for the Kemalists. Deriving from this approach, Akyol argues: "The result of this strict mental blueprint is detachment from reality. That's why, despite all its rhetoric on 'science and reason' as guiding lights for society, Kemalism has become an irra-tional ideology. When its adherents are challenged by rational arguments, they respond by emotional reactions. They take extra tours to Anıtkabir and sing more anthems."[45]

Another observer of Turkey in the 1930s and a great admirer of Atatürk, Gerard Tongas, a Frenchman, distinguished "ultra-practical and ultra-popular" features of Kemalism, since the system aimed at "studying, elevating and civilizing the people," and inculcating notions of liberty and happiness.[46] In his efforts to find solutions to emerging political, eco-nomic, and social crises in Europe, he also claimed that "the new philos-ophy of Atatürk can play a mediating role between communism and the old social regimes."[47] Tongas also wrote that through "rapid evolution" and "disciplined training" Kemalism could be presented "to mankind as a model philosophy tested by experience: Kemalism has accomplished in ten years the work of ten centuries."[48] Rum Landau, who visited Turkey between 1936 and 1938, noted: "Kemalism is both a philosophy and a method of life, a political and a social system… It stands for all the political and material innovations brought about by Atatürk's reforms."[49]

Taken together, these views suggest that most of these authors (except Kili, Giritli, and a few others) do not consider "Kemalism" an ideology. Rather, they provide various arguments explaining the challenges of interpreting Kemalism as an ideology. For them, Kemalism is scientific and non-ideological pragmatism, democratic universalism, and something above or below ideology that bridged the gap between the ideal and reality. In other words, many observers and citizens of Turkey believe that Kemalism is not an ideology because an authentic ideology is coherent, even repressive. Conversely, they believe the Kemalist revolution unleashed a new beginning for modernization, secularism, and the westernization of Turkey, and offered a paradigm for an alternative democracy.

Another group of scholars has suggested examining Kemalism and its principles by looking beyond their established objectives to expand their meanings. Deriving from this approach, Andrew Mango established a list of principles that formed the axis of the Kemalist ideology: modernization; secularism; a nationalism compatible with peaceful foreign relations and with membership in international associations and alliances; the rule of law (these four principles were explicitly formulated and defended by Atatürk); and democracy and human rights (implicit in his legacy).[50]

Other scholars saw Kemalism as a primary reason for many of Turkey's problems. For instance, Stephen Salamone claims that Atatürkism must be understood as the root of many instabilities in Turkey since, as a working state ideology incorporated into its constitutions, it has failed to create a superstructure of governing principles that is intelligible and acceptable to a plural polity. Subsequent ideological confusion was a result of the Turkish state's extreme insecurity about age-old ethnic, religious, and territorial disputes that it inherited from the Ottoman Empire and that have been exacerbated by the monolithic ideology of Kemalism.[51] Ali Fuat Borovali argues that Kemalism was fused with the structures and machinery of the state for two obvious reasons, which were also causes of its vulnerability: cultural and political opposition from traditionalists and economic nationalism, which was a source of latent antagonism from the West.[52] Sabri Akural also asserts, "… neither the Kemalist principles nor Ziya Gökalp's conservative prescriptions are any longer at work as major forces in the processes of social change,"[53] yet Kemalism "remains an intellectual force of considerable importance," though maybe not "a dynamic force for social transformation."[54]

In the 1990s and 2000s, research on Kemalism entered a new critical phase. For the last two-three decades Kemalism has been studied through the lenses of civil–military and state–society relations, Turkey's EU accession process, political, social, and economic transformations, oppressed identities in Turkey, Kemalism's compatibility with political Islam and liberalism, expanding Ottomanism and social conservatism.[55] These new approaches presented new classifications of Kemalism (or resurfaced old ones) by labelling Kemalism anti-liberal, elitist, authoritarian, dictatorial, discriminatory, anti-intellectual, exclusionary, assertive, etc. More studies have shed light on the hegemonic features of Kemalism, which strived to erect an ethnically and culturally homogenous, centralized, and secular nation.

Since 1960, the Turkish military has played a central role in Turkish politics, resulting in five direct/indirect military interventions (1960, 1971, 1980, 1997, 2007). Studies in recent decades concentrated on the convergence of Kemalism with the Turkish military. William Hale, Nilüfer Narli, Mehmet Ali Birand, and Gerassimos Karabelias argue that the Turkish armed forces contributed immensely to the constant re-emergence of Kemalism in various forms.[56] For the Turkish armed forces, the legacy of Kemalism was the last compromise. Acting on behalf of Kemalism and its specific, strict interpretations, the TAF strived to safeguard and maintain Turkey's constitutional order as well as its political, economic, social, cultural, and ideological integrity. Inefficient civilian governments and their inability to oversee the military, together with unstable and fragile policy created fertile ground for the military's active engagement in politics, using the banner of Kemalism.

Kemalism's associations with conservatism, as it vehemently opposed the JDP and its reformist agenda, began in the mid-2000s.[57] With the consolidation of the JDP's power, other depictions of Kemalism emerged, which were labelled neo-Kemalist or neo-nationalist. Proponents of the former advocated for an anti-western, authoritarian, and elitist agenda, employing substantial anti-Islamic and pro-interventionist rhetoric, while the latter entailed the resurrection of ethnocentric nationalism, as displayed in the Ergenekon affair.[58] In addition to these depictions, Doğan Gürpınar viewed neo-Kemalism as an outcome of globalization. He singled out another strain of neo-Kemalism, arguing that the entire end-result of its promotion was the plebianization of Kemalist discourse.[59] Using different communication tools, he noted, a self-styled Kemalist intelligentsia fought against the JDP by championing extremely xenophobic, ideologically radical, and intellectually demagogic and redundant discourse.[60] Pro-JDP and liberal intellectuals further delegitimized Kemalism and its manifestations as an outdated and obsolete worldview. They also urged a revision of its policy of state-centrism and the abandonment of deep-rooted distrust towards society, Islam, and forces emerging from the national periphery. Kemalism was presented as vehemently opposing Turkey's democratization and the establishment of the rule of law.

Toni Alaranta's recent study of contemporary Kemalism advances another argument about its current phase. He points out that recently, liberal, leftist, and Islamic intellectuals have "mercilessly attacked" Kemalism, presenting it as anachronistic and harmful, inherently illiberal and anti-democratic, intolerant, and violent. Studying Kemalism from 1992 to 2012, through the writings of five Kemalist intellectuals, he argues against scholars claiming that Kemalism is dead.[61] Along the same lines, Bagdonas argues that even though Kemalism has been transformed domestically, it was too early to accept the notion that the Kemalist hegemony was dissolved. Instead, he differentiated between security- and democracy-centred interpretations of Kemalism.[62]

The headscarf debate, which has intensified since the late 1980s, resulted in the 2008 Constitutional Court decision to annul the JDP's and NAP's proposed changes to the two constitutional articles regulating the headscarf controversy, reignited criticisms of Kemalism for its inhumane treatment, discrimination of devout women, and strict application of laicism. Kemalist practices of a narrow interpretation of laicism and the entire modernization project of the 1920s and 1930s were criticized for interfering into education, cultural life, and the social and religious lives of citizens.[63] Studies by Emelie Olson, Nilüfer Göle, Elisabeth Özdalga, Ahmet Kuru, Merve Islam Kavakçı, and many others depicted the ideological and symbolic antagonism between republican Kemalist women and conservative, Islamist women trying to shed light on the root causes of the headscarf controversy.[64] These studies were also significant contributions in that they elevated discussions on Turkish secularism. Rightly, they argue that the Turkish model of "assertive secularism" and modernization projects not only transformed and westernized women but also damaged social harmony and the educational foundations of the state as well as its liberal and democratic basis.

Most of these studies interpreted Kemalism as a conservative and anti-modernization ideology. However, the JDP also started to promote its brand of conservatism, which shared common features with the centre-right parties of earlier decades, the Democrat Party in the 1950s, the Justice Party in the 1960s and 1970s, the Motherland Party in the 1980s, and all political parties associated with the "National Outlook" (*Milli Görüş*) movement.

Turkey's EU accession process also sparked investigations of Kemalism and its development paradigms as intolerably state-centred and illiberal.[65] Turkey's efforts to meet the Copenhagen Criteria opened different debates, which the Kemalist elite proved unprepared to address. Murat Hakkı, Paul Kubicek, Ioannis Grigoriadis, Şule Toktaş, and Bülent Aras argued that the initiation of EU accession talks unveiled different faces of the formerly little-known, unknown, or hidden problems inside Turkey.[66] They singled out the Kurdish question, the Armenian Genocide, the Cyprus problem, the Aegean Sea, Northern Iraq, and many other critical issues (surfacing of oppressed identities, expanding cultural and educational rights to ethnic and religious minorities, returning confiscated property), which the Kemalists had successfully managed for decades within the secular-republican and nationalist domains. Kemalists considered them hallmarks of their nationalist policies. As a result, the EU-driven democratization agenda made Turkey's Kemalist elite face formerly cloaked problems and oppressed identities. This prospect pushed some secular-republican Kemalist intellectuals and members of the military and bureaucracy to resist the possible redrawing of red lines and the reconsideration of Turkish national identity. As a reaction, some explicitly contested the JDP's reforms, while others championed Eurasianism as an alternative to pro-Western foreign policy orientation.[67] On the other hand, the JDP benefited from this self-imposed marginalization of the Kemalists and, as Joerg Baudner argued, managed to use the EU accession agenda as an additional resource and "external constraint" to eliminate the "domestic constraints" of the dominant Kemalist statist elite and Kemalist opposition.[68]

Efforts have been made to observe Kemalism from a comparative perspective as an ideology of "national developmentist" regimes much like several middle-income countries in the developing world.[69] Kemalist Turkey, like others in the "global south" (Mexico, Argentina, Egypt, Indonesia, Brazil, etc.), embraced the state-led development model and political modernization, but unlike them, failed to overcome low-level institutionalization and weak organization. The latter cost dearly to the overall integrity of Kemalism.[70]

"Kemalism has been superficially Western in form while remaining rigidly authoritarian and dogmatic in substance," argued proponents of Kemalism's anti-democratic classification. They also claimed: "Kemalism continues to stress republicanism over democracy, homogeneity over difference, the military over the civilian, and the state over society. Its quixotic quest to radically recast Turkish culture, history, and identity has ensured a permanent Kulturkampf against society," guaranteeing, ironically, Turkey's failure to transition to a Western-style liberal democracy.[71] In the words of Zafer Yörük, Kemalism, in essence, became a state religion, combining modern scientific discourses with racist fantasies— that is, a synthesis of the Enlightenment's "Religion of Reason" and Rousseau's project to replace Christianity with a "popular religion."[72] Ernest Gellner also critically noted that the Kemalist establishment became as "reactionary" and "dogmatic" in its redemptive mission as any religious orthodoxy.[73]

Until recently, there has been little interest in a comprehensive historiography of Kemalism. The second volume in the "Modern Turkish Political Thought" series, published in 2001, brought together around fifty prominent intellectuals to provide critical insights into the intellectual origins and dynamics of Kemalism.[74] It was a significant contribution to the historiography. The fact that in March 2015 it was published in its eighth edition attests to its success. This comprehensive volume, however, failed to address the missing link that is discussed in the present study.

The Missing Link in the Historiography of Kemalism: In the 1920s and 1930s, Turkey played a prominent role on the international stage. Its domestic transformations and the evolution of the Kemalist system of ideological and political principles were closely observed in Germany, France, Britain, the USA, and beyond, including several nations farther East. In recent years, scholarly interest in the transnational history of Kemalism has grown. A 2011 workshop at the French Institute of Anatolian Studies brought together participants to discuss local and international configurations of Kemalism, and incorporated perspectives from Bulgaria, Albania, Iraq, Cyprus, Egypt, and Bosnia.[75] Since then, scholars have invoked the "transnational history of Kemalism."[76]

Several studies published in 2014 only deepened the discussion. Looking at Germany, Stefan Ihrig, a German historian, examined how right-wing movements, mass media, and politicians—especially Adolf Hitler—perceived Turkey's Kemalist transformation.[77] For Hitler and the Nazi press, argues Ihrig, Turkey offered an example that bolstered German nationalist morale in the post-war period. The Weimar Republic's right-wing press drew parallels between anti-Western, anti-Entente, and anti-Greek sentiments in Germany and Turkey, touting Turkish political tactics as an example for Germany to emulate.[78] Alongside Turkey's successes, Mustafa Kemal and even İsmet İnönü garnered praise and admiration in Germany's nationalist pages.[79] Pınar Dost-Niyego's book probed the French perspective.[80] In the 1920s and 1930s, French observers reflected on their own ideas about France, using developments in Turkey. According to Dost-Niyego, the search for new ideological reference points in France fuelled a national fascination with Atatürk, who was portrayed as "a good dictator."

Roger Trask charted Turkey's interwar modernization through the eyes of American diplomats, missionaries, educators, traders, and others,[81] while Rıfat Bali published "US Diplomatic Documents on Turkey," a compilation of writing by US diplomats and Turkey-watchers in the 1920s and 1930s and 1950s and 1960s.[82] Trask and Bali unearthed insights and observations from an otherwise neglected group, but their work says little about the ideological sources of the Kemalist transformation—and American analyses of these sources—in the period under consideration in this book.

Some scholars have looked farther East—to Persia, Afghanistan, China, India, and other parts of the Muslim world—to assess the influence wielded by Mustafa Kemal and his modernization project.[83] Observers in these countries closely followed the making of modern Turkey, writing books and reporting in periodicals. Naeem Qureshi, a Pakistani historian, detailed the profound impact of the Kemalist movement and Mustafa Kemal for Indian Muslims in a 2014 study.[84] His discussion highlights the importance of two pan-Islamic and pro-Turkish Indian Muslim leaders, Muhammad Iqbal and Mohammad Ali Jinnah, who saw in both Mustafa Kemal and Turkey models to be emulated in India in the 1920s and 1930s. Writings in Urdu on Atatürk and Turkey, wrote Qureshi, were "very informative and analytical, and provide a deeper analysis of the contemporary Turkish scene."[85] A rare instance where Kemalist reforms are covered from a "non-Western" point of view, Qureshi's book contributes an important perspective to the transnational history of Kemalism. In his effort to analyse the impact of

Kemalism abroad, Jacob Landau has recently published a preliminary examination of the impact of Atatürk's reforms and his image on the Jewish community in British-ruled Palestine before the establishment of Israel in 1948.[86] Landau argues that the Hebrew press presented the developments in Kemalist Turkey with sympathy, excitement, and an undertone of admiration. He also notes that the architects of the State of Israel, particularly David Ben-Gurion, thought highly of Atatürk's reforms. In 1941, Ben-Gurion praised Mustafa Kemal for transforming "the rotten, subjugated and chained empire" into a national Turkish Republic, free and independent, progressive and youthfully vigorous.[87]

Works by Ihrig, Dost-Niyego, Qureshi, and Landau, explore perceptions of Kemalism that are mostly positive in their respective countries. These authors, whose contributions belong to the burgeoning literature on Kemalism, have provided few critical insights into Kemalism's evolution and its reception as an ideological project. Exploring the Soviet perspective will enrich and expand the transnational history of Kemalism.

Contextualizing the Soviet Literature on Kemalism: A decade after Abraham Bodurgil's 1974 bibliography featuring books and articles from the Republic's first two decades,[88] the Ministry of National Education of Turkey published the three-volume *Bibliography of Atatürk and his Reforms*, which listed all studies published before 1981.[89] In 1985, Kemal Karpat referred to more than 7,000 books and articles about Atatürk's personality, ideas, visions, and reforms; however, neither Karpat nor previous bibliographers paid any particular attention to Soviet sources.[90]

Oriental Studies thrived in the Soviet Union, even amid the peculiarities of Soviet humanities and social sciences.[91] Turkologists in Turkish Studies, which was part of Oriental Studies, examined Turkish history, politics, and social processes as well as ideological transformations. In 1979, the Institute of Scientific Information of Social Sciences (*Institut nauchnoj informatsii po obshestvennim naukam*) of the Soviet Academy of Sciences published *Kemalism*, a reference book.[92] Merely "For Official Use" (*Dlya sluzhebnogo pol'zovanija*), it included 450 titles and brief annotations of books published between 1930 and 1976 in Turkish, Bulgarian, Polish, French, and English that dealt with Atatürk, as well as ideological, political, and economic developments, and cultural reforms in Turkey. In 1982, *A Bibliography on Turkey* appeared as an extended version of the 1959 collection, published by the Institute of Oriental Studies of the Soviet Academy of Sciences.[93] Containing 18,000 entries in Russian, ranging from 1917 to 1975, it addressed a number of themes in Turkish history, culture, literature, geography, economy, and politics. The bibliography covered Soviet–Turkish bilateral relations, Turkish Communists and geopolitics, and included hundreds of publications on Atatürk and his reforms. More importantly for this book, it listed scholarly works on the ideological construction of Kemalist Turkey from a Soviet perspective.

A critical reading of Cold War history and Turkish–Soviet relations explains the lack of interest in Soviet perspectives of Kemalism on behalf of Turkish and Western scholars. Specifically, the role of Marxist and Leninist ideologies in Soviet interpretations, the incompatibility of research methodologies, and the prominence of other topics kept scholarly interest at bay.[94] Instead, Western and Turkish academics drew on Soviet scholarly contributions when discussing the formative years of the Turkish Republic, bilateral relations, Soviet assistance to Turkey in the 1920s and 1930s and 1960s and 1970s, and matters of trade, cooperation, cultural exchanges and geopolitics.[95] Despite being mostly descriptive with little critical interpretation of events, these works provide important contributions to the historiography of Soviet–Turkish relations. Beginning in the 1920s, Communist (Bolshevik) party functionaries, scholars, and journalists carefully watched developments in Turkey, reporting to Moscow and Soviet readers.[96] Their observations and insights gave Soviet readers a better understanding of Turkey. Soviet scholars in the 1920s paid close attention to research on Turkey. In a 1928 article, for example, Gurko-Kryazhin listed all primary and secondary sources on Turkey and the Kemalist movement, dating back to 1919.[97] Yet Kemalism hardly became an academic sub-discipline in the field of Turkish studies in the SU. With the exception of a short 1974 survey, discussed in greater detail below, neither Kemalism nor interpretations of it have been the focus of a single research project. The first two decades of ideological transformations in Turkey were the subject of most Soviet work on Kemalism. Only in the 1960s and 1970s did scholarly interest re-emerge. Soviet observers in the 1970s and 1980s examined the principles of Kemalism—mainly nationalism, populism, laicism, and étatism—and how these evolved and were applied. This implies a profound lack of interest on the side of Soviet observers in presenting or sharing their work on Kemalism to Western scholarship.

Soviet press and academic periodicals also followed domestic transformations in Turkey.[98] This study draws on a number of periodicals that

shed light on Soviet official, popular, academic, and journalistic perceptions of Kemalism in Turkey. Other periodicals belonged to Universities
and to the Academies of Sciences of Soviet Republics *Novij Vostok* (The
New East), *Narody Aziji I Afriki* (Nations of Asia and Africa), *Azija I
Afrika Segodnya* (Asia and Africa Today), or literary unions *Zvezda
Vostoka* (Star of the Orient), which reinforced the party line. Given the
nature of the Communist regime's strict censorship, participation in
these journals and institutions was mostly formal, since all of them had
to strictly adhere to party doctrine. This study will also discuss how
doctrinal transformations of the Communist party affected the fate of
these journals and their authors.

Reports dispatched to Moscow from the Soviet embassy in Ankara
and the consulate in Istanbul discussed the impact of domestic political,
social, cultural, and ideological reforms in Turkey. Soviet foreign policy
documents are no less important for understanding Soviet perceptions
of Turkish domestic transformations.[99] While focused on diplomatic and
political issues, these volumes illumine how Soviet diplomats perceived
ideological and socio-cultural shifts in Turkey and their implications for
Turkish–Soviet relations.

In the 1920s and 1930s, Soviet historians, reporters, and other
observers in Turkey hewed to the official Communist Party line, but
some differences in approach emerged. Openly critical of Turkey's
domestic reforms and foreign policy initiatives, most Soviet observers
called them insufficiently revolutionary for failing to meet the demands
of society.[100] Anatolij Miller, who also wrote under the nickname
Mel'nik (the English translation of "Miller"), was openly sympathetic to
the Kemalist cause and domestic reforms in Turkey, which led some in
the SU to label him a "Turkophile."[101] While working in the diplomatic
service between 1920 and 1938, Mel'nik/Miller studied various aspects
of Turkey and the Kemalist cause. He was Head of the First Eastern
Department by the time he left the PCFA, and later consulted the PCFA
and continued to study Turkey until his death in 1973.[102]

During the consolidation of Stalinism in the late 1920s and early
1930s, internal divisions appeared among Soviet observers regarding
various aspects of the Kemalist development paradigm. Publishing in academic journals, these observers harshly criticized one another for failing
to understand various aspects of Kemalism. Some labelled their opponents "bourgeoisie orientalists," for allegedly borrowing "imperialist
interpretations" while studying Kemalist Turkey. Boris Platonov, who

had several publications in *Blizhnij Vostok* (The Near East) and Ziya Feridov, writing in *Revolucionnij Vostok* (Revolutionary East), are especially prominent voices. Representing the "new school" of Orientalists, they harshly criticized scholars of the previous decade for neglecting Soviet ideology in their considerations of Kemalism.

After reviewing Soviet historiography, it is possible to identify distinct stages in the evolution of Kemalist studies in the SU. In the 1920s and the early 1930s, the Soviets focused on Turkey's domestic political, social, cultural, and economic transformations. While some scholars in the orientalist school of the SU deliberated over Kemalism and its ideological components, other Soviet observers published on the topic. Understandably, not every work was dedicated to political, socio-cultural, or ideological reforms in Turkey, since scholars mostly wanted to make sense of Turkish foreign policy, maintain Turkey's neutrality towards the Soviet Union, capitalize on Soviet assistance to Kemalists during the nationalist movement, and assess the prospects of class-based struggle, or the potential for anti-imperialist revolution. Through comparative study, a coherent picture of changing Soviet attitudes towards Kemalism emerges. Another minor but interesting aspect of this period is that some of its key observers (Irandoust and Gurko-Kryazhin), who contributed to the development of Turkish historiography, published similar work on Persia, which featured the same titles as monographs on Turkey.[103]

Soviet interest in ideological and domestic transformations in Turkey began to shift in the mid-1930s and continued to change until the late 1950s. One reason was the proliferation of racist and radical-nationalist movements in Turkey, whose members were often called fascists in Soviet media. Turkey's ruling regime was also sometimes described as fascistic.[104] Deteriorating bilateral relations contributed to declining interest in Kemalism as an ideological construct and Turkey's guiding philosophy. Soviet observers were primarily interested in Turkey's position during WWII and international geopolitics. The growing confrontational tone between the two states affected scholarly work, too.

Amid efforts to normalize relations in the 1960s and 1970s, interest in Turkey surged in the National Academies of the Union Republics of the Soviet Union (mainly in the Caucasus Republics, Russia, and Ukraine). Paying little or no attention to the complexities of the 1930s and 1950s, most studies praised Soviet-Turkish relations.[105] A few Soviet historians and intellectuals revisited Kemalism during the period, gauging the consequences of earlier political, social, and cultural

reforms. Some publications sought to re-examine Kemalism, reconsid-
ering earlier views on the founding years of the Turkish Republic.[106]
In 1974, Esmeralda Gasanova, a historian from Azerbaijan's Academy
of Sciences, presented a paper at a conference in Romania. Assessing
the study of Kemalism in the Soviet Union, Gasanova made a first
effort by a Soviet historian to offer a brief survey of the historiography of Kemalism in the Soviet Union.[107] Offering a concise description
of work by Soviet Turkologists in the 1920s (Pavlovich, Gurko-
Kryazhin, Astakhov, Youst, Butayev, Irandoust, Mel'nik), she argued
that although these scholars had unearthed the many ideological layers of Kemalism, they perceived Kemalism as the "anti-imperialist feature of national-liberation movement of Turkey" and shared "a set of
ideas about the ideological platforms of the Kemalist revolution."[108]
Gasanova addressed changing perceptions of Kemalism in the SU in the
1930s, citing only Abid Alimov, and concluding that in that decade,
Kemalism was regarded as "a development pathway of Turkey," or "the
combination of six principles of the RPP."[109] At the end of the short
paper, she noted that in the 1960s, "the concept of Kemalism appears
to be a synonym of national bourgeoisie ideology on the Turkish foundation."[110] While important in many respects, Gasanova's presentation
held fast to Soviet vocabulary and failed to consider the socio-political
layers of Kemalism, which were widely discussed in the works of
other Soviet scholars she neglected. In her discussion of mainstream
authors, Gasanova was also selective, failing to mention observers of
Turkey whose research was mostly critical of Kemalism. Aside from
Alimov and Miller, she ignored Soviet scholars who studied Kemalism
in the 1930s and 1940s. Discussing the Soviet scholarship on Kemalism
in the period between the 1960s and 1970s and mentioning the
name of Dmitrij Yeremeev, for instance, she cited two publications of
her own: one published in 1968, which dealt mainly with Kemalism's
ideological origins, and another, which had no relation to Kemalism.
Mentioning only a shortened version of the title, without mentioning
"*the period of Young Turks, 1908–1914*," she left the audience with the
mistaken impression that her earlier published book was also about
Kemalism.[111] As leftist movements in Turkey grew in the 1960s and
1970s, interest in Kemalism and the ideological transformations associated with it were somehow transformed.[112]

   Despite Marxism–Leninism's[113] dominance of the social sciences
in the 1960–1970s, Soviet scholarship on Turkey proved more

sophisticated than in previous decades. Scholars successfully contextualized their work within global academic research on Turkey and Kemalism. In the 1960s, Soviet scholars tried to place their research in a wider frame by identifying gaps in scholarly research on Turkey. In 1963, for example, Miller pointed to the absence of a reliable, balanced, and helpful biography of Atatürk. Most research on "democratic Western European and American authors" presented only Atatürk's "Westernism," he declared, and ascribed to him political ideas that the Turkish leader never believed. The Soviet approach to Atatürk, noted Miller, had been ignored or downplayed.[114] In 1966, he published a book containing speeches and statements to better present Atatürk to the Soviet people.[115] Yet the work of Soviet scholars and other observers was largely omitted from studies of Atatürk and his political ideas.

Weaving Soviet sources into the study of Kemalism requires a few clarifications. Soviet perspectives not only developed from a distance, but were also based on hands-on experience that came with interactions and cooperation with people in Turkey. While projects linked Turkey and the SU, beginning in the 1920s and continuing until the mid-1930s, exchanges, mainly from Turkey to the SU, took place in education, academia, sports, and arts. Soviet specialists provided technical assistance on industrial development projects in Turkey, and Soviet observers, including party functionaries, reporters, and scholars, engaged with Turkish scholars and intellectuals. Through cultural exchanges, both Soviet and Turkish writers, composers, actors, musicians, film directors, and artists established contacts. They visited or lived in both countries, experiencing the results of political, cultural, and social transformation. Despite fickle relations between the two nations, officials made regular visits in the 1920s and 1930s, and later in the 1960s and 1970s. The Soviet embassy in Ankara remained one of the largest Soviet representations abroad, a sign of the importance the Soviet government, in its formative decades, attached to Turkey. With respect to relations between official and academic sources, two points should be clarified. In the 1920s, the PCFA could shape policy directions with Turkey, while the Comintern pursued specific goals that sometimes conflicted with the official PCFA line. Reports and articles prepared by the two organizations reflected this contradiction. The PCFA and scholars cooperating with it were often critical of the Comintern, while scholars hewing to the Comintern line often did so at the expense of official policy directives. Soviet sources offer many examples that show this pattern.

Next, the relationship between scholars and the Communist party needs clarification. Soviet observers of Turkey demonstrated some degree of independence in their interpretations of Kemalism until 1926–1927, when a new pattern became evident. Under total institutional censorship, self-censorship, and terror (until the mid-1950s), most statements, articles, reports, and books adhered to official Communist Party positions. This implied focusing on the class-based nature of the Turkish transformation, maintaining Turkey's status as a friendly nation, and, when possible, reviving its anti-imperialist tendencies against the West. Soviet scholars were obviously constrained by Marxist–Leninist methodology. As a result, they employed Marxist-specific vocabulary in their work. Despite these problems, many Soviet observers furnished remarkably accurate analyses of Turkish domestic affairs. Since Soviet observers closely followed domestic politics, power relations, and ideological transformations in Turkey from the beginning, they could chart the making, development, and transformation of Kemalism.

NOTES

1. Akyaz Doğan. 2001. "Ordu ve Resmi Atatürkçülük." In *Kemalizm: Modern Türkiye'de Siyasi Düşünce*, cilt 2, edited by Murat Belge, 180–191. İstanbul: İletişim Yayınları; Levent Köker. 2001. "Kemalizm/Atatürkçülük: Modernleşme, Devlet ve Demokrasi." In *Kemalizm: Modern Türkiye'de Siyasi Düşünce*, edited by Murat Belge, 97–112. İstanbul: İletişim Yayınları.
2. Esra Özyürek. 2005. "Miniaturizing Atatürk Privatization of State Imagery and Ideology in Turkey." *American Ethnologist* 31 (3): 375.
3. Fatma Müğe Göçek. 2011. *The Transformation of Turkey: Redefining State and Society from the Ottoman Empire to the Modern Era*. London: I.B. Tauris, 2.
4. Andrew Mango. 1999. *Atatürk*. New York: The Overlook Press, 262.
5. Erik-Jan Zürcher. 2005. "Ottoman Sources of Kemalist Thought." In *Late Ottoman Society: The Intellectual Legacy*, edited by Elisabeth Özdalga, 14. London: Curzon.
6. Şevket Süreyya Aydemir. 1999. *Tek Adam: Mustafa Kemal (1922–1938)*, cilt 3, 16th ed. İstanbul: Remzi kitabevi, 421–434.
7. Stanford Shaw and Ezel Kural Shaw. 1977. *History of the Ottoman Empire and Modern Turkey*, vol. II: *Reform, Revolution, and Republic: The Rise of Modern Turkey, 1808–1975*. Cambridge: Cambridge University Press, 374–375.

8. *Turkey: Background Notes.* 1988. The United States Department of State Bureau of Public Affairs. March: 4.

9. Metin Heper. 1985. *The State Tradition in Turkey.* Hull: The Eothen Press, 11.

10. Robert Mantran. 2005. "Mustafa Kemal Atatürk." In *Turkey Today—A European Country?* edited by Olivier Roy, 130. London: Anthem Press.

11. Mehmet Ali Birand. 1991. *Shirts of Steel: An Anatomy of the Turkish Armed Forces.* London: I.B. Tauris, 55.

12. Erik-Jan Zürcher. 1991. *Political Opposition in the Early Turkish Republic: The Progressive Republican Party, 1924–1925.* Leiden: Brill, 2.

13. John Van der Lippe. 2005. *The Politics of Turkish Democracy: İsmet İnönü and the Formation of the Multi-Party System, 1938–1950.* New York: State University of New York Press, 3.

14. Van der Lippe (2005, 5).

15. *Atatürk'ün Söylev ve Demeçleri.* 2006. Atatürk Kültür, Dil ve Tarih Yüksek Kurumu, Atatürk Araştırma Merkezi, cilt 3.

16. It had a series of English translations. The first one was Mustafa Kemal. 1929. *A Speech.* Leipzig: K. F. Keohler. This study has used the following publication Ghazi Mustafa Kemal Atatürk. 2008. *The Great Speech (Nutuk),* 2nd ed. Ankara: Atatürk Research Center. For a detailed analysis of the 1927 speech in English see Hülya Adak. 2003. "National Myths and Self-Na(rra)tions: Mustafa Kemal's Nutuk and Halide Edib's Memoirs and The Turkish Ordeal." *The South Atlantic Quarterly* 102 (2/3): 509–527; Toni Alaranta. 2008. "Mustafa Kemal Atatürk's Six-Day Speech of 1927: Defining of Official Historical View of the Foundation of Turkish Republic." *Turkish Studies* 9 (1): 115–129.

17. Enver Ziya Karal. 1945. *Türkiye Cumhuriyeti Tarihi [History of Turkish Republic],* 1st ed. İstanbul; Tarık Zafer Tunaya. *Türkiye'de Siyasi Partiler (1859–1952)* [Political Parties in Turkey (1859–1952)]. İstanbul: Doğan Kardeş, 1952. A three-volume biography of Atatürk, Şevket Süreyya Aydemir. 1999. *Tek Adam: Mustafa Kemal, (1881–1919),* cilt 1, 18th ed., İstanbul: Remzi kitabevi; Şevket Süreyya Aydemir. 1999. *Tek Adam: Mustafa Kemal 1919–1922,* cilt 2, 17th ed., İstanbul: Remzi kitabevi. Şevket Süreyya Aydemir. 1999. *Tek Adam: Mustafa Kemal 1922–1938,* cilt 3, 16th ed., İstanbul: Remzi kitabevi; Niyazi Berkes. 1964. *The Development of Secularism in Turkey.* Montreal: McGill University Press; Suna Kili. 1969. *Kemalism.* İstanbul: Robert College; and Suna Kili. 1980. "Kemalism in Contemporary Turkey." *International Political Science Review* 1 (3): 380–404.

18. Henry Elisha Allen. 1935. *The Turkish Transformation: A Study in Social and Religious development.* Chicago: University of Chicago Press; Sir Harry Luke. 1936. *The Making of Modern Turkey: From*

Byzantium to Angora. London: Macmillan; Halide Edib. 1930. *Turkey Faces West: A Turkish View on Recent Changes and Their Origin.* New Haven: Yale University Press; Donald E. Webster. 1939. *The Turkey of Atatürk.* Philadelphia: The American Academy of Political and Social Science; Eleanor Bisbee. 1951. *The New Turks: Pioneers of the Republic.* Philadelphia: University of Pennsylvania Press; Berthe Georges-Gaulis. 1924. *La Nouvelle Turquie.* Paris: Colin; and Irfan Orga. 1958. *Phoenix Ascendant: The Rise of Modern Turkey.* London: Hale.

19. Karal (1997, 12).

20. Özlem Demirtaş Bagdonas. 2008. "The Clash of Kemalisms? Reflections on the Past and Present Politics of Kemalism in Turkish Political Discourse." *Turkish Studies* 9 (1): 101.

21. For an insightful analysis of the interpretation of Kemalism by the radical leftist movements in the 1960s see Özgür Mutlu Ulus. 2011. *The Army and Radical Left in Turkey: Military Coups, Social Revolution, and Kemalism.* London: I.B. Tauris.

22. Mete Tunçay. 1966. *Türkiye'de Sol Akımlar.* Ankara: Bilgi Yayınevi; Doğan Avcıoğlu. 1969. *Türkiye'nin Düzeni: Dün-Bugün-Yarın.* Ankara: Bilgi Yayınevi; and Doğan Avcıoğlu. 1974. *Milli Kurtuluş Tarihi 1838'den 1995'e.* İstanbul: Tekin Yayınevi. Avcıoğlu published extensively in the pages of "Yön" too.

23. Kâzım Karabekir. 1960. *İstiklâl Harbimiz.* İstanbul: Türkiye. Yayınevi.

24. For the detailed analysis about the impact of Karabekir book see, Erik-Jan Zürcher. 2010. *The Young Turk Legacy and Nation Building; From the Ottoman Empire to Atatürk's Turkey.* London: I.B. Tauris, Ch. 2.

25. Ali Fuat Cebesoy. 1960. *Siyasi Hatıralar* [Political Memoirs], 2 kısım. İstanbul: Doğan Kardeş.

26. Hüseyin Rauf Orbay. 1962–1963. *Hatıraları, Yakın Tarihimiz* [Memoirs. Our Modern History], cilt 2, 4. İstanbul.

27. For instance, between 1968 and 1974, Mahmut Goloğlu wrote seven monographs about the turning points of the republican history: "The congresses of Erzurum", "The Congress of Sivas", "The Third Constitutional Period—1920", "The Birth of the Republic 1921–1922", "Revolutions and Responses 1924–1930", "One Party Republic 1931–1938", "The Era of National Chief 1939–1945".

28. Sinan Ciddi. 2009. *Kemalism in Turkish Politics: The Republican People's Party: Secularism and Nationalism.* London: Routledge; Ulus (2011); and Yunus Emre. 2014. *The Emergence of Social Democracy in Turkey: The Left and the Transformation of the Republican People's Party.* London: I.B. Tauris.

29. Bagdonas (2008, 110).

30. Erik-Jan Zürcher. 1984. *The Unionist Factor. The Role of the Committee of Union and Progress in the Turkish National Movement 1905–1926.* Leiden: Brill; Erik-Jan Zürcher. 1992. "The Ottoman Legacy of the Turkish Republic: An Attempt at a New Periodization." *Die Welt des Islams* 32: 237–253; and Zürcher (1992, 2010).
31. Bagdonas (2008, 100).
32. Suna Kili. 1969. *Kemalism.* İstanbul: School of Business Administration and Economics, Robert College, 2.
33. Kili (1969, 2).
34. Kili (1969, 5–6, 132–133).
35. Kili (1969, 7).
36. İsmet Giritli. 1984. "Kemalism as an Ideology of Modernization." In *Atatürk and the Modernization of Turkey*, edited by Jacob Landau. Boulder: Westview Press, 251–253.
37. Metin Tamkoç. 1976. *The Warrior Diplomats: Guardians of the National Security and Modernization of Turkey.* Salt Lake City: University of Utah Press, 113.
38. Berkes (1964, 52).
39. Paul Dumont. 1984. "The Origins of Kemalist Ideology." In *Atatürk and the Modernization of Turkey*, edited by Jacob Landau. Boulder: Westview Press, 25.
40. Sabri Akural. 1984. "Kemalist Views on Social Change." In *Atatürk and the Modernization of Turkey*, edited by Jacob Landau, 125–152. Boulder, CO: Westview Press, 126.
41. Heper (1985, 64).
42. Şükrü Hanioğlu. 2011. *Atatürk: An Intellectual Biography.* Princeton: Princeton University Press, 187.
43. Ibid.
44. Akyol Mustafa. 2007. "The Gospel According to Atatürk". *Turkish Daily News*, Saturday, November 10.
45. Ibid.
46. Gerard Tongas. 1939. *Atatürk and the True Nature of Modern Turkey.* London: Luzac & Co, 24–25.
47. Tongas (1939, 24).
48. Tongas (1939, 27).
49. Rum Landau. 1938. *Search for Tomorrow: The Things Which Are and the Things Which Shall Be Hereafter.* London: Nicolson and Watson Limited, 243.
50. Andrew Mango. 2002. "Kemalism in a New Century." In *Turkish Transformation: New Century, New Challenges*, edited by Beeley Brian. Tallahassee: The Eothen Press, 23.

51. Stephen Salamone. 1989. "The Dialectics of Turkish National Identity: Ethnic Boundary Maitanance and State Ideology." *East European Quarterly* 23 (2): 231.
52. Ali Fuat Borovali. 1985. *Kemalist Tradition, Political Change, and the Turkish Military*. Unpublished dissertation, Queen's University, 162.
53. Akural (1984, 145).
54. Akural (1984, 126).
55. Soner Çağaptay. 2006. *Islam, Secularism and Nationalism in Modern Turkey: Who Is a Turk?* London: Routledge; Ciddi (2009); *Nationalism and Politics in Turkey: Political Islam, Kemalism and the Kurdish Issues*. 2010. Edited by Marlies Casier and Joost Jongerden. London: Routledge; Umut Azak. 2010. *Islam and Secularism in Turkey: Kemalism, Religion and the Nation State*. London: I.B. Tauris; Toni Alaranta. 2011. *Kemalism, Enlightenment, and Legitimacy; The Reproduction of Secularist National Identity in Turkey, 1930–1980*. Lambert Academic Publishing; Toni Alaranta. 2014. *Contemporary Kemalism: From Universal Secular-Humanism to Extreme Turkish Nationalism*. London: Routledge; Sena Karasipahi. 2009. *Muslims in Modern Turkey: Kemalism, Modernism and the Revolt of the Islamic Intellectuals*. London: I.B. Tauris; and Taha Parla and Andrew Davison. 2004. *Corporatist Ideology in Kemalist Turkey: Progress or Order?* Syracuse: Syracuse University Press.
56. William Hale. 1994. *Turkish Politics and the Military*. London and New York: Routledge; Gerassimos Karabelias. 2008. "Dictating the Upper Tide: Civil–Military Relations in the Post-Özal Decade, 1993–2003." *Turkish Studies* 9 (3): 457–473; Nilüfer Narli. 2000. "Civil-Military Relations in Turkey." *Turkish Studies* 1 (1): 107–127; and Birand (1991).
57. Çinar Menderes. 2006. "Turkey's Transformation Under the AKP Rule." *The Muslim World* 96 (3): 469–486.
58. Ioannis Grigoriadis and Irmak Özer. 2010. "Mutations of Turkish Nationalism: From Neo-Nationalism to the Ergenekon Affair." *Middle East Policy* 17 (4): 101–113.
59. Doğan Gürpınar. 2013. "The Reinvention of Kemalism: Between Elitism, Anti-Elitism and Anti-Intellectualism." *Middle Eastern Studies* 49 (3): 454–476.
60. Ibid., 457.
61. Toni Alaranta. 2014. *Contemporary Kemalism: From Universal Secular-Humanism to Extreme Turkish Nationalism*. Oxon: Routledge, 3.
62. Bagdonas (2008).
63. Nilüfer Göle. 1996. *Forbidden Modern: Civilization and Veiling*. Ann Arbor: University of Michigan Press.

64. Emelie Olson. 1985. "Muslim Identity and Secularism in Contemporary Turkey: The Headscarf Dispute." *Anthropological Quarterly* 58 (4): 161–171; Göle (1996); Elisabeth Özdalga. 1998. *The Veiling Issue. Official Secularism and Popular Islam in Modern Turkey.* Richmond: Curzon Press; Ersin Kalaycioğlu. 2005. "The Mystery of the Turban: Participation or Revolt." *Turkish Studies* 6 (2): 233–251; Dilek Cindoğlu and Gizem Zencirci. 2008. "The Headscarf in Turkey in the Public and State Spheres." *Middle Eastern Studies* 44 (5): 791–806; Ahmet Kuru. 2007. "Passive and Assertive Secularism: Historical Conditions, Ideological Struggles, and State Policies Toward Religion." *World Politics* 59 (4): 568–594; and Merve Kavakçi Islam. 2010. *Headscarf Politics in Turkey: A Postcolonial Reading.* New York: Palgrave Macmillan.

65. Menderes (2006, 480–482).

66. Murat Metin Hakki. 2006. "Turkey and the EU: Past Challenges and Important Issues Lying Ahead." *Turkish Studies* 7 (3): 451–471; Paul Kubicek. 2005. "Turkey's Assession to the European Union." *World Affairs* 168 (2): 67–78; Ioannis Grigoriadis. 2007. "Türk or Türkiyeli? The Reform of Turkey's Minority Legislation and the Rediscovery of Ottomanism." *Middle Eastern Studies* 43 (3): 423–438; and Şule Toktaş and Bülent Aras. 2009. "The EU and Minority Rights in Turkey." *Political Science Quarterly* 124 (4): 697–720.

67. Emel Akçali and Mehmet Perinçek. 2009. "Kemalist Eurasianism: An Emerging Geopolitical Discourse in Turkey." *Geopolitics* 14 (3): 550–569.

68. Joerg Baudner. 2014. "The Domestic Effects of Turkey's EU Accession Negotiations: A Missed Opportunity for Europe?" In *Turkey and the European Union: Facing New Challenges and Opportunities,* edited by Firat Cengiz and Lars Hoffmann, 178–194. London and New York: Routledge.

69. Berk Esen. 2014. "Nation-building, Party-Strength and Regime Consolidation: Kemalism in Comparative Perspective." *Turkish Studies* 15 (4): 600–620.

70. Ibid.

71. Hakan Yavuz and Mujeeb R. Khan. 2000. "Turkey's Fault Lines and the Crisis of Kemalism." *Current History* 99 (633): 34.

72. Zafer Yörük. 1997. "Turkish Identity from Genesis to the Day of Judgment." In *Politics and the Ends of Identity,* edited by Kathryn Dean, 117. Vermont: Ashgate.

73. Ernest Gellner. 1994. *Encounters with Nationalism.* Cambridge: Blackwell, 81–91.

74. Murat Belge, ed. 2001. *Kemalizm: Modern Turkiye'de Siyasi Düşünce*, cilt 2. İstanbul: İletişim.
75. Conference program. Paris. Workshop Towards a Transnational History of Kemalism Beyond Turkey. 2011. http://www.ifea-istanbul.net/index.php?option=com_k2&view=item&id=1390:workshop-towards-a-transnational-history-of-kemalism-beyond-turkey-08-09-12-2011&Itemid=286&lang=tr.
76. For instance, Erdal Kaynar used it in his review of Stefan Ihrig's book. Erdal Kaynar. 2015. "Review of Stefan Ihrig's "Atatürk in the Nazi Imagination", The Belknap Press of Harvard University Press, Cambridge, MA. *International Journal of Turkish Studies* 21 (1–2): 227–229.
77. Stefan Ihrig. 2014. *Atatürk in the Nazi Imagination*. Cambridge: The Belknap Press of Harvard University Press. For the book review see Vahram Ter-Matevosyan. 2015. "Review of Stefan Ihrig's "Atatürk in the Nazi Imagination", The Belknap Press of Harvard University Press, Cambridge. *International Journal of Armenian Genocide Studies* 2 (1): 87–92.
78. Ibid., 49.
79. Ibid., 113.
80. Pınar Dost-Niyego. 2014. *Le Bon Dictateur: L'image de Mustafa Kemal Atatürk en France (1923–1938)*. İstanbul: Libra Yayınevi.
81. Roger Trask. 1971. *The United States Response to Turkish Nationalism and Reform, 1914–1939*. Minneapolis: The University of Minnesota Press.
82. *"Turkish Students' Movements and the Turkish Left in the 1950's–1960's"*, "US Diplomatic Documents on Turkey" series, 2006, presented and annotated by Rıfat N. Bali, Istanbul, The Isis Press; *"The Turkish Cinema in the Early Republican Years"*, "US Diplomatic Documents on Turkey" series, 2007, presented and annotated by Rıfat N. Bali, Istanbul, The Isis Press; "Family Life in the Turkish Republic of the 1930's", A Study by G. Howland Shaw, "US Diplomatic Documents on Turkey" Series, 2007, presented and annotated by Rıfat N. Bali, Istanbul, The Isis Press; "New Documents On Atatürk: Atatürk as Viewed Through the Eyes of American Diplomats" Foreword by Andrew Mango, "US Diplomatic Documents on Turkey" series, 2007, presented and annotated by Rıfat N. Bali, Istanbul, The Isis Press; "The First Ten Years of the Turkish Republic Thru the Reports of American Diplomats", "US Diplomatic Documents on Turkey" series, 2009, presented and annotated by Rıfat N. Bali, Istanbul, The Isis Press; "Sports and Physical Education in Turkey in the 1930's", "US Diplomatic Documents on Turkey" series, 2009, presented and annotated by Rıfat N. Bali, Istanbul, The Isis Press.

83. Amin Saikal. 1982. Kemalism: Its Influences on Iran and Afghanistan. *International Journal of Turkish Studies* 2 (2): 25–32; Ali Kazancigil. 2001. "Anti-emperialist Bağımsızlık Ideologisi ve Üçüncü Dünya Ulusçuluğu Olarak Kemalizm." In *Kemalizm: Modern Turkiye'de Siyasi Düşünce*, cilt 2, edited by Murat Belge, 235–246. İstanbul: İletişim.
84. Naeem Qureshi. 2014. *Ottoman Turkey, Atatürk, and Muslim South Asia: Perspectives, Perceptions, and Responses.* Karachi: Oxford University Press.
85. Qureshi (2014, 184).
86. Jacob Landau. 2018. A Note on Kemalizm in the Hebrew Press of Palestine. *Middle Eastern Studies* 54 (4): 723–728.
87. Landau (2018, 727).
88. Abraham Bodurgil. 1974. *Atatürk and Turkey: A Bibliography, 1919–1938.* Washington: Library of Congress, Near East Section, Orientalia Division.
89. Muzaffer Gökman. 1981–1983. *Atatürk ve Devrimleri Tarihi Bibliyografyası* [Bibliography of the History of Atatürk and His Reforms], cilt 3. İstanbul: Milli Eğitimi Basımevi.
90. Kemal Karpat. 1985. "The Personality of Atatürk." [Review of *The Immortal Atatürk: A Psychobiography* by Vamik D. Volkan; Norman Itzkowitz.] *The American Historical Review* 90 (4): 894.
91. It needs to be stressed that since the 1890s Oriental Studies in Russia became the second largest area of research after Slavic Studies. The scholarly works of Victor Rozen and his students (Vaislii Bartol'd, Nikolay Marr, Sergei Ol'denburg, Fedor Shcherbatskoi) widely contributed to the development of Russian and Soviet Oriental Studies. For a detailed discussion of the development of Oriental Studies in Russia see Vera Tolz. 2008. "European, National, and (Anti-)Imperial: The Formation of Academic Oriental Studies in Late Tsarist and Early Soviet Russia." *Kritika: Explorations in Russian and Eurasian History* 9 (1): 53–81; Vera Tolz. 2011. *Russia's Own Orient: The Politics of Identity and Oriental Studies in the late Imperial and Early Soviet Periods.* Oxford and New York: Oxford University Press.
92. Ozherel'eva Z. (compiler). 1979. *Kemalizm (Ukazatel' Inostrannikh knig 1930–1976 gg (Po fondam bibliotek Moksvi, Leningrada i Baku))* [Kemalism (Index of Foreign Books 1930–1976 (Based on the Fonds of Libraries of Moscow, Leningrad and Baku)]. Moscow: Institute of Scientific Information for Social Sciences, National Academy of Sciences.
93. Bibliografija Turtsii (1917–1975) [Bibliography on Turkey (1917–1975)]. 1982. Collected by A. Sverchevskaja and T. Cherman, edited by A. Shamsutdinov. Moscow: Nauka.

94. In 1963, Mark Pinson, a doctoral candidate in Russian and Turkish history at Harvard University, discussed the writings of some of the Soviet authors who covered the early period of Turkish history. His article was one of the rare pieces of Western accounts which looked at the transformation of Kemalism from the perspective of Soviet historiography. Pinson, Mark. 1963. "Turkish Revolution and Reform and Soviet Historiography, 1919–1928." *Middle East Journal* 17 (4): 466–478.

95. *SSSR i Turtsija. 1917–1979* [USSR and Turkey. 1917–1979], edited by Gasratyan and Moiseyev. Moscow, Nauka. 1981. Harish Kapur. 1966. *Soviet Russia and Asia 1917–1927: A Study of Soviet Policy towards Turkey, Iran and Afghanistan.* Geneva: Geneva Graduate Institute of International Studies, Chs. 4, 5; Vladimir Danilov (1997). "Kemalism and World Peace." In *Atatürk: A Founder of a Modern State,* 2nd ed., edited by Ergun Özbudun and Ali Kazancigil, 103–126. London: Hurst and Company; A. Mel'nik. 1937. Turtsija [Turkey]. Moskva: Gosudarstvennoe Social'no-Ekonomicheskoe Izdatel'stvo; S. Kuznetsova. 1961. *Ustanovlenie Sovetsko-Turetskikh otnoshenij: K 40-letiju Moskovskogo dogovora mezhdu RSFSRi Turtsiej* [Establishing Soviet-Turkish Relations: The Fortieth Anniversary of the Moscow Treaty between RSFSR and Turkey]. Moskva: Izdatel'stvo Vostochnoj Literatury; P. Moiseyev and Yu Rozaliev. 1958. *K Istorii Sovetsko-Turetskikh Otnoshenij* [Towards the history of the Soviet-Turkish Relations]. Moskva: Gospolitizdat; A. Miller. 1948. *Kratkaja Istorija Turtsii* [A Short History of Turkey]. Moskva: Gosudarstvennoe izdatel'stvo politicheskoj literatury; Emel Akal. 2012. *Mustafa Kemal, Ittihat Terakki ve Bolşevizm Milli Mücadelenin Başlangıcında.* İstanbul: İletişim Yayıncılık; Bülent Gökay. 2006. *Soviet Eastern Policy and Turkey, 1920–1991: Soviet Foreign Policy, Turkey and Communism.* London and New York; Igor Chernikov. 1977. *V Interesakh Mira i Dobrososedstva: (O sov.-tur. otnoshenijakh v 1935-1970 gg)* [In the Interest of Peace and Friendly-Neighboring Relations: About Soviet-Turkish Relations, 1935–1970]. Kiev: Naukova Dumka; and Sverchevskaia Antonina. 1983. *Sovetsko-Turetskie Kul'turnye Sviazi, 1925–1981* [Soviet-Turkish Cultural Relations, 1925–1981]. Moscow: Nauka.

96. Ferdi. 1927. "Evoljutsija Kemalizma: Ot Natsional'noj Revoliutsii k Diktature Burzhuazii." [Evolution of Kemalism: From National Revolution towards the Bourgeoisie Dictatorship.] *Sputnik Kommunista* 10 (43): 30–38; T. Kross. 1930. "Vnutrennee Polozhenie Turtsii [Domestic Situation in Turkey]." *Mezhdunarodnaja Zhizn'* (NKID) (7–8): 57–66; Irandust. 1928. *Dvizhushchie Sily Kemalistskoj Revoljutsii* [Driving Forces of the Kemalist Revolution]. Moskva-Leningrad; and Konstantin Youst. 1926. "Pis'ma iz Turtsii: Novye puti i ih smysl." [Letters from Turkey: New Paths and Their Meaning.] *Krasnja Nov'* 174–186.

97. V. Gurko-Krjazhin. 1928. "Vozniknovenie Natsional'no-Osvoboditel'nogo Dvizhenija v Turtsii." [The Origins of the National-Liberation Movement in Turkey.] *Novij Vostok* 23–24: 268–275.

98. Recently, Rasim Örs, a Turkish researcher, published a short book with excerpts and photocopies from Soviet newspapers (two newspapers and three journals) of the 1920s. His objective was to present to the Turkish readers how the birth of the Turkish Republic and the character of Mustafa Kemal were covered in the Soviet Union through pictures and cartoons. See Rasim Dirsehan Örs. 2010. *Rus Basininda Kurtuluş Savaşı ve Atatürk*. Devrim Yılları. İstanbul. Cumhuriyet Kitapları.

99. *Dokumenty Vneshnej Politiki* [Foreign Policy Documents—USSR MFA]. 1963. Ministerstvo Inostrannyh Del SSSR, Gosudarstvennoe izdatel'stvo politicheskoj literatury, Moskva. For this research the volumes from five to twenty-two are considered.

100. P. Kitaygorodskij. 1927. "Zametki o Kemalistskoj Turtsii: Prichini Pobedi Natsional'noj Revoljutsii v Turtsii." [Notes on the Kemalist Turkey: The Causes of the Victory of the National Revolution in Turkey.] *Bol'shevik* 18: 41–50.

101. M. Lazarev. 2003. "Yubilej." [Anniversary.] In *Ot Stambula do Moskvi: Sbornik statei v Chest' 100-letija profesora A. F. Millera* [From Istanbul to Moscow: Collection of Articles Dedicated to the 100th Anniversary of Professor A. F. Miller]. Moscow: Muravej, 18. For the criticism of Miller's scholarly works by the Soviet scholars in the period between 1940s and 1960s, see Boris Potskhveria. 2003. "Chornije dni A. F. Millera." [Black Days of A. F. Miller.] In *Ot Stambula do Moskvi: Sbornik statei v Chest' 100-letija profesora A. F. Millera* [From Istanbul to Moscow: Collection of Articles Dedicated to the 100th Anniversary of Professor A. F. Miller]. Moscow: Muravej, 23–30.

102. For a detailed analysis of Anatolij Miller's bio and scholar works see M. Lazarev (2003, 11–22).

103. Irandoust. 1926. Zametki o Smene Rezhima v Persii [Notes on the Change of Regime in Persia]. *Novij Vostok* 15; Gurko-Kryazhin. 1925. *Kratkaja Istoriya Persiji* [Short History of Persia], Moscow.

104. V. Krimskij. 1944. "Panturkisti – fashistskaja agentura." [Pan-Turkists: Fascist Agents in Turkey.] *Bol'shevik* 10–11: 79–85; Ivan Samilovskij. 1952. *Turtsija – votchina Wall-Strita* [Turkey—Patrimony of the Wall Street]. Moscow: GosPolitIzdat; Anna Tveritinova. 1953. "Ot natsional-shovinizma k natsional-predatel'stvu." [From National-Chauvinism to National Treachery.] *Zvezda Vostoka* 8 (79): 70–87; and G. Akopyan. 1951. "Turtsija - Votchina Amerikanskogo Imperializma." [Turkey—A Patrimony of the American Imperialism.] *Propanagist i Agitator* 14: 23–31.

105. Igor' Chernikov. 1977. *V interesakh mira i dobrososedstva: (O sov.-tur. Otnoshenijakh v 1935-1970 gg.)* [In the Interest of Peace and

Friendly-Neighboring Relations: About Soviet-Turkish Relations 1935–1970]. Kiev: Naukova Dumka.
106. Esmeralda Gasanova. 1968. "Ob ideologicheskih osnovah kemalizma i ih sovremennom tolkovanii v Turtsii." [On the Ideological Foundations of Kemalism and Their Contemporary Interpretations in Turkey.] *Narody Azii i Afriki* 3: 24–35; Dmitrij Yeremeyev. 1963. "Kemalizm i pantjurkizm." [Kemalism and Pan-Turkism.] *Narody Azii i Afriki* 3: 58–60.
107. Esmeralda Gasanova. 1974. "Voprosy Ideologii Kemalizma v Trudakh Sovestkih Uchenykh." [Questions of the ideology of Kemalism in the works of the Soviet scholars.] In *Doklady i soobshhenija sov. Delegatsii. III Mezhdunar. S"ezd po izucheniju stran Jugo-Vostochnoj Evropy, Buharest,* 4–10 sentjabrja, 9 p., Moscow.
108. Gasanova (1974, 2).
109. Ibid., 6.
110. Ibid., 7.
111. Esmeralda Gasanova. 1966. *Ideologija Burzhuaznoj Natsionalizma v Turtsii v Period Mladoturok, 1908-1914 gg* [Ideology of bourgeoisie-nationalism in Turkey in the Period of Young Turks, 1908–1914]. Baku. Publication of National Academy of Sciences of Azerbaijani SSR.
112. Ingelab Alibekov. 1966. *Gosudarstvenii kapitalizm v Turtsii* [State Capitalism in Turkey]. Moscow: Nauka.
113. John Kautsky argues the importance of looking at Marxism and Leninism as two distinct ideologies. The author of this study shares that approach; however, the use of the Marxist–Leninist concept in this study, implies that it follows the dominant Soviet interpretation of the ideology, which saw not much difference between them. John H. Kautsky. 1994. *Marxism and Leninism, not Marxism-Leninism: An Essay in the Sociology of Knowledge*. London: Greenwood Press.
114. Miller (1963, 66–67).
115. Kemal Atatürk.1966. *Izbrannye Rechi i Vystuplenija* [Selected Speeches and Statements], edited by Anatolij Miller. Moscow: Progress.

REFERENCES

Akural, Sabri. 1984. "Kemalist Views on Social Change." In *Atatürk and the Modernization of Turkey*, edited by Jacob Landau, 125–152. Boulder, CO: Westview Press.
Bagdonas, Özlem Demirtaş. 2008. "The Clash of Kemalisms? Reflections on the Past and Present Politics of Kemalism in Turkish Political Discourse." *Turkish Studies* 9 (1): 99–114.
Berkes, Niyazi. 1964. *The Development of Secularism in Turkey*. Montreal: McGill University Press.

Birand, Ali Mehmet. 1991. *Shirts of Steel: An Anatomy of the Turkish Armed Forces.* London: I.B. Tauris.

Ciddi, Sinan. 2009. *Kemalism in Turkish Politics: The Republican People's Party: Secularism and Nationalism.* London: Routledge.

Gasanova, Esmeralda. 1974. "Voprosy Ideologii Kemalizma v Trudakh Sovestkih Uchenykh [Questions of the Ideology of Kemalism in the Works of the Soviet Scholars]." In *Doklady i Soobshhenija Sovetskoj Delegatsii. III Mezhdunar. s"ezd po izucheniju stran Jugo-Vostochnoj Evropy, Buharest, 4–10 sentjabrja*, 9 p. Moscow.

Göle, Nilüfer. 1996. *Forbidden Modern: Civilization and Veiling.* Ann Arbor: University of Michigan Press.

Heper, Metin. 1985. *The State Tradition in Turkey.* Beverley: Eothen Press.

Karal, Enver Ziya. 1997. "The Principles of Kemalism." In *Ataturk: Founder of a Modern State,* edited by Ergun Özbudun and Ali Kazancigil, 2nd ed., 11–36. London: Hurst and Company.

Kili, Suna. 1969. *Kemalism.* İstanbul: School of Business Administration and Economics, Robert College.

Landau, Jacob. 2018. "A Note on Kemalizm in the Hebrew Press of Palestine." *Middle Eastern Studies* 54 (4): 723–728.

Menderes, Cınar. 2006. "Turkey's Transformation Under the AKP Rule." *The Muslim World* 96 (3): 469–486.

Miller, Anatolij. 1963. "Formirovanije Politicheskikh Vzglyadov Kemal'a Atatürka (K 25-letiju so dnja ego smerti) [Formation of Political Ideas of Kemal Ataturk (25th year since his death)]." *Azija i Afrika Segodnya* 5: 65–85.

Pinson, Mark. 1963. "Turkish Revolution and Reform and Soviet Historiography, 1919–1928." *Middle East Journal* 17 (4): 466–478.

Qureshi, Naeem. 2014. *Ottoman Turkey, Atatürk, and Muslim South Asia: Perspectives, Perceptions, and Responses.* Karachi: Oxford University Press.

Tongas, Gerard. 1939. *Atatürk and the True Nature of Modern Turkey.* London: Luzac & Co.

Ulus, Özgür Mutlu. 2011. *The Army and Radical Left in Turkey: Military Coups, Social Revolution and Kemalism.* London: I.B. Tauris.

Van der Lippe, John. 2005. *The Politics of Turkish Democracy: İsmet İnönü and the Formation of the Multi-Party system, 1938–1950.* New York: State University of New York Press.

Zürcher, Erik-Jan. 1992. "The Ottoman Legacy of the Turkish Republic: An Attempt at a New Periodization." *Die Welt des Islams* 32: 237–253.

———. 2010. *The Young Turk Legacy and Nation Building: From the Ottoman Empire to Atatürk's Turkey.* London: I.B. Tauris.

(Trans)formation of Kemalism, 1920s–1930s

This chapter examines turning points in the first two decades of the Republic from its foundation until the death of Kemal Atatürk in 1938. It focuses on major phases of ideological consolidation and delineates their distinctive features. Exploring ideological layers of the RPP congresses in the 1920s and 1930s, it offers a comparative analysis of the party programs. RPP rule, pervasiveness of the state, enduring authoritarianism, crackdown on dissent, leader cult, demographic and social engineering, and imposition of a new secular-republican identity constituted the core of the Kemalist politics and political system. Overturning old practices, discrediting values and habits of the old regime, imposition of radical social, cultural, and economic changes puzzled many in Turkey, although many, especially the young, fervently embraced them. Many facets of socio-political organization in the new state were indeed new, while the roots of many ideological features extended at least 50 years back. Formative in many regards, the Kemalist era also constituted a transformative phase and a springboard for ideals and insights that had long existed in the Ottoman Empire.

FEATURES OF POLITICAL CONSOLIDATION IN THE 1920s

World War I was a disastrous adventure for the Ottoman Empire. The Committee of Union and Progress (henceforth, CUP) took the shattered empire to war, which ended in defeat in October 1918. A large and

© The Author(s) 2019
V. Ter-Matevosyan, *Turkey, Kemalism and the Soviet Union,*
Modernity, Memory and Identity in South-East Europe,
https://doi.org/10.1007/978-3-319-97403-3_3

growing body of literature covers the reasons and motivations for the Sublime Porte's participation in WWI.[1] Since the formative years of the Turkish Republic have also attracted ample attention,[2] this chapter does not deal with those developments but instead discusses how the ground was prepared for Kemalist political consolidation.

Alongside the decline of the Ottoman Empire, resistance movements emerged in different parts of Eastern and Central parts of Turkey. The arrival of 38-year-old General Mustafa Kemal in Samsun on May 19, 1919, was a departure point for nationalist forces to wage their concerted struggle for national resistance. Kemal initiated a series of congresses in Erzurum (July 23–August 6, 1919), Sivas (September 4–11, 1919), and elsewhere to mobilize and coordinate the activities of different movements.[3] Thanks to these initiatives, the "National Pact" (*Misak-ı Milli*) was drawn up on January 28, 1920 in Istanbul. Its six articles sought to determine official objectives and define the borders of the future state.[4] These became the driving force of the National Struggle (*Milli Mucadele*). The culmination of these efforts was the opening of the TGNA on April 23, 1920, which was followed by the reinforced occupation of Istanbul by Allied forces and the dissolution of the last Ottoman parliament. On January 20, 1921, the TGNA promulgated the Law on Fundamental Organization (*Teşkilat-I Esasiye Kanunu*), which was also known as the Constitutional Law. It was composed of twenty-three articles, which served as a de facto constitution for the Kemalist regime and governed the country for three years until the Republic of Turkey adopted its first constitution in April 1924.

Myriad circumstances paved the way for the rise and victory of Mustafa Kemal and his faction, Defence of Rights Group (*Müdafaa-I Hukuk Grubu*). Although it is rather difficult to capture its many orientations and groupings, Kemal and his loyal supporters were particularly uncomfortable with various factions in the Assembly, which he referred to as parties: The Union Party, the Independence Party, the Union for the Defence of the Rights Party, the People's Party, and the Reform Party.[5] Another widely known case of elite division occurred in the parliament on May 10, 1921, by the "First Group" (*Birinci grup*), led by Mustafa Kemal, and the "Second group" (*Ikinci grup*) led by opposition forces. The "First Group," consisting of 262 members, became the foundation of the ruling People's Party (*Halk Fırkası*) on September 9, 1923. "Republican" (*Cumhuriyet*) was added on November 10, 1924.[6] On October 29, 1923, Turkey was proclaimed a Republic at 8:30 in the evening, followed by the election of the first president (Mustafa Kemal) some fifteen minutes later.

After the establishment of the Republic, Mustafa Kemal initiated radical cultural and institutional reforms that had a major impact not only on the state's social composition but also on Turkey's ideological construction. One of his first acts, on March 2, 1924, was abolishing the Caliphate, the ministry for Islamic law (*Sharia*), and pious foundation (*wakifs*). Then, Koranic instruction in the countryside, at institutions like religious seminaries, were shut down, while religious high schools were placed under the authority of the Ministry of Education. On January 2, 1925, Muslim Friday was replaced by Sunday. On November 30, 1925, Sufi dervish orders were closed, and soon after, the fez, an important accessory for adult Muslim men, was declared illegal. The lunar calendar and clock were dropped and the country switched to the Gregorian calendar and solar clock. On February 17, 1926, a new civil code was approved to regulate matters of marriage, inheritance, divorce, and adoption. On October 4, 1926, *Sharia* courts were annulled, and Islamic law declared null and void. Finally, on April 10, 1928, Islam, as Turkey's state religion, was eliminated from the constitution (Article 2), thereby nominally separating religion from the state. Articles 16 and 38 introduced a new oath, which resembled oaths used in secular states, for Deputies and the President of the Republic, respectively. On November 1, 1928, Ankara announced that effective January 1, 1929, Turkey would drop the Arabic alphabet and switch to a new, Latin-based alphabet.[7] However, it soon became obvious for the republican elite that the cultural reforms of the 1920s, aimed at rational devotion to the republican cause, had not gone deep enough. As early as 1926, Arnold Toynbee and Kenneth Kirkwood wrote: "Turkey has taken a step forward – a great step – but the shadow of the past still overhangs the Republic. Neither individuals nor nations can completely escape from their inheritance, and Turkey, even in her new dress, cannot in a day, or even in a decade, change her character completely."[8]

By 1924, it became obvious that certain circles (clergy, conservative forces, sections of the military, etc.) were not satisfied with this course of events. As a result, on November 17, 1924, an opposition party, the Progressive Republican Party (*Terakkiperver Cumhuriyet Fırkası*—henceforth, PRP), was established, led by prominent wartime allies of Mustafa Kemal (Ali Fuat Cebesoy, Rauf Orbay, Refet Bele, and Kâzim Karabekir as well as politicians and intellectuals Adnan Adıvar, Mehmet Rahmi Eyüboğlu, and İsmail Canbulat, etc.). Soon, the opposition party managed to grow, expanding into various parts of Turkey by building supporters (around 40,000 members). In February 1925, an uprising by Kurdish leader Sheikh Sait was used as a pretext to put an end to the existence of the second party (June 3, 1925). Although an investigation was opened, the PRP's involvement in the rebellion was not proved.[9] Martial law was declared, the liabilities of the Independence Tribunals were reactivated, and, consequently, the PRP was closed down.[10] In 1926, Kemal carried out extensive political purges and trials against his political opponents, former members of the CUP and the PRP.[11] Thus, from 1925 to 1945–1946, the RPP ruled Turkey in the absence of an opposition party, except for the ninety-nine-day existence of the Free Republican Party (*Serbest Cumhuriyet Fırkası*—henceforth, FRP) in 1930.[12] Suna Kili argues that Mustafa Kemal's move to allow the establishment of another party in 1930 reflected a long-standing belief that a multiparty system would be the culmination of his reform program.[13] The Ambassador of the United States to Turkey, Joseph Grew, described the new party's short experience "as an experiment with a little bit of democracy." Neither Mustafa Kemal, nor Fethi Okyar or İsmet İnönü, he explained, knew the state of opinion in Turkey, as they "had no idea apparently of the strength of resentment which was gathering momentum underneath... [it] had become a clinical thermometer for taking the political temperature of the country and there could be no doubt of the fever which it registered."[14]

The Menemen incident in 1930,[15] as well as visible support for the short-lived Free Republican Party, indicated that there was increasing discontent and resentment towards the ruling party. Policy choices for the next few years proved that Mustafa Kemal was leaning from authoritarianism towards a system that resembled contemporary dictatorial regimes. Against this backdrop, Weiker argues that by considering the opinions of more liberal-minded party officials, Mustafa Kemal intended "to convert the RPP from rigidity to flexibility, from monolithic into a pluralistic body, from centralized to decentralized structure."[16] This claim is rather unusual when the policies that came later are analysed.

First Steps of Ideological Conceptualization

The forces that stood behind the national struggle and later entered the parliament were extensive and diverse. This alliance included army officers, state officials, lawyers, journalists, teachers, clergy (*ülema*), secular-minded intellectuals, merchants, businessmen, and landowners and magnates from the countryside. The parliament, which was rather multi-ethnic, was composed mainly of deputies who belonged to the defunct CUP. As its observers noted, Mustafa Kemal's first parliament was more multi-ethnic and plural than later parliaments of the republican period.[17]

Initially, the ruling People's Party had only nine guiding principles (*Dokuz Umde*),[18] which Mustafa Kemal elaborated on April 8, 1923. They were to serve as a platform for upcoming elections to the Second TGNA. For Kemal, these principles constituted a full-fledged party program "full of substantial and practical matters," which made "acts precede words and theories."[19] He understood that to be considered a classical party, he had to adopt "an orderly and detailed program … based upon the moral and material principles…[which] will be proposed for the peaceful discussion and approval by all its members."[20] The Nine Principles constituted more of a short-term policy platform than ideologically driven formulations. The first three principles, which pertained to national sovereignty, TGNA's supreme power, and national security, reflected priorities that had been essential. These principles, however incomplete or vague, remained in force until 1931, when the RPP adopted its first party program. It is interesting to note that even though the introduction of the Nine Principles promised an "orderly and detailed program," during the 1927 party congress, Kemal took a defensive line and slightly modified his argument. In his speech, he touched upon critiques, which in 1923 pushed for a more elaborate and long-term party program with clearly defined articles. He emphasized that he could write a book but it was time for action.[21] His arguments could have stemmed from the fact that the opposition, the Progressive Republican Party, adopted a comprehensive party program.

Since the start of the nationalist movement, Kemal and his associates introduced programs, manifestos, and declarations to communicate with the public. Kemal sought practical utility in his congress declarations (Erzurum, Sivas, etc.) and later in other documents: The National Pact of 1920, the Constitutional Law of 1921, the Nine Principles of the

RPP of 1923, the Three Descriptive Natures of the RPP in 1927, the Six principles of the RPP of 1931 confirmed the argument that during his management of the party and state affairs, Kemal harboured conceptual approaches and methods. Compared to the six principles of Kemalism, previous documents were practically instead of ideologically driven.

It needs to be emphasized that the initial growth of the RPP was rather slow until 1927, it was used as an office to formally legitimize, on behalf of the nation, the activities of parliament. The same was true with local branches. Kazimirskij, a Soviet orientalist who shared his observations about developments in Eastern Thrace between 1924 and 1925, mentioned that the RPP had only limited representation in the region. According to Kazimirskij, the RPP paid sporadic attention to the European part of Turkey by sending its members from Ankara to establish local party units. Instead, he reported that the ultra-nationalist organization "Turkish Hearths" had a wide presence in the region and was much more visible. In Adrianapol (*Edirne*) alone, it had 230 members who were actively involved in local social and cultural life.[22] Lüfti, another Soviet observer of Turkey, also noted in 1927:

> Although the RPP exists for already four years now and despite extremely easy entry conditions, it failed to bring together wide layers of merchants, intelligentsia, landowners and middle villagers… the real number of members, in fact, are rather insignificant, without even speaking of the party activists, which literally consists of individuals.[23]

Initially, the RPP did not pay enough attention to its growth as a mass party. It would take a few more years until Mustafa Kemal acknowledged the importance of expanding the party.

The First Congress of the RPP, known as the Great Congress (*Büyük Kongra*), was held in Sivas in October 1927. That congress was later named the Second Congress, since the RPP was considered the continuation of the Defence of the Rights Committee, which was founded in 1919. This congress is widely known for Mustafa Kemal's "Six-day speech," commonly known as "Nutuk."[24] At the congress the RPP adopted its first extensive party statute (*Cümhuriyet Halk Fırkası nizamnamesi*). For the first time, the first article mentioned the party's republican (*cümhuriyetçi*), populist (*halkçı*), and nationalist (*milliyetçi*) nature.[25] The rest of the document presented the governing bodies, decision-making, and organizational structures of the party in different territorial-administrative units of the country.[26]

Commentators who covered the 1927 congress rarely looked at its impact on immediate political developments. How did two Soviet observers from different schools of Oriental Studies (discussed in detail below) view it? Ol'ga Kameneva, sister of Lev Trotsky, who was the first head of the All-Soviet Society of Cultural Relations with Foreign Countries,[27] was paying a three-week visit to Turkey when the congress took place. After returning to Moscow, she referred to that political event as "the historically significant congress of the People's party of Turkey which was in the spotlight of the entire Turkish press."[28] In 1928, one year after the speech, Ziya Feridov, who published regularly in "*Revolucionnij Vostok*," provided insight concerning the importance of that congress and Mustafa Kemal's 36-hour speech. His interpretations were well-informed and different from what followed in his later work. Contrary to most analysis focusing on the speech, Feridov concentrated more on the congress and its implications for the Turkish political system. At the outset, he criticized the speech, considering it "rich material for historians, but in no way having an urgent character relevant to the period that [Turkey] is going through."[29] He singled out one element, that in the speech, "false modesty" on the part of Kemal "was completely missing."[30] Feridov noted that the statute of the party "formally confirmed the personal dictatorship of Kemal," thereby sidelining the RPP. The document and what followed, he noted, reaffirmed Kemal's distrust of the RPP.[31] The argument historians make about the 1935 congress as a watershed in merging the state and the party[32] was expressed by Feridov years earlier. Analysing Mustafa Kemal's speech and potential political implications, he concluded that the 1927 congress marked the beginning of the merger between the state and the party.[33] Feridov's analysis is also important because it was an early effort to view the cultural and educational reforms of the Kemalist regime as superficial and urban-centred. In 1928, Gurko-Kryazhin, another prominent Soviet commentator on Turkey, claimed that one might get an impression that "the political program of Kemal... was an irretrievable value, which was created as a result of political intuition, some kind of prophecy." Whereas in reality, he explained, Kemal's program-speech was "temporarily adopted to situational circumstances."[34]

Just two years after Mustafa Kemal's thirty-six-hour speech, Soviet Turkologists published a Russian translation of it. While the first volume came out in May 1929 under the imprint of the PCFA of the SU, another five years passed before the next three volumes appeared. These included a preface, footnotes, comments, maps, and notes that helped guide the reader, not only through the particulars of the project, but also through the text, making it easier to digest than other Turkish publications. Aiming at presenting a complete history of Kemalist Turkey through 1927, the project's title was also noteworthy. The Turkish original, "*Nutuk*," usually presented as "The Speech" or "The Great Speech", became "The Road of the New Turkey" (*Put' Novoj Turtsii*) in Russian. "Until this moment there is no single work in European literature," stated the preface, "which would provide the complete picture of the Turkish national-freedom movement. It also does not exist in Turkey."[35] In addition to the Russian version, the preface continued, "*Nutuk*" was translated into Turkish, French, German, and English.[36] The four volumes of *Put' Novoj Turtsii* became a major resource for generations of Soviet scholars of Turkish studies. In 1928, the first volume of the German translation of Kemal's speech appeared. Its title, *Der Weg Zur Freiheit* (The Road to Freedom), was a departure from the original version and Russian translations. Based on this, Gordlevskij explained that the Russian version had been translated from German.[37]

The term "Kemalism," with all its ideological connotations, was likely first used in 1929, according to most researchers, becoming widespread in the country shortly after.[38] But some observers point to Yakup Kadri Karaosmanoğlu, a former CUP member, who first employed the term in *Milliyet*, the national daily. Others cite language expert Ahmet Cevat, who used "Kemalism" in the journal *Muhit*,[39] or long-time Justice Minister Mahmut Esat Bozkurt.[40] Since Cevat and Bozkurt first invoked the term in the early 1930s, which was too late for its earliest introduction, it is unlikely that either coined it. Westerners and interviewers of Kemal "branded the movement 'Kemalist,'" wrote Josef Washington Hall in 1930. Since Kemal wished to establish a new Turkey, not "Kemalism, nor did he wish to incite the resentment of the Nationalists," he resented the term. It was Western authors who first invoked "Kemalism," argues Enver Karal.[41]

In 1922, French author Michel Paillarès published "*Le Kemalisme: Devant Les Alliès,*"[42] a history of the rise of Mustafa Kemal and the nationalist movement. In a few other instances in the 1920s, when Western observers invoked "Kemalism,"[43] most used it in holistic, episodic, and descriptive ways to depict anything related to Mustafa Kemal and the processes associated with him. However, as will be discussed, the external, particularly Soviet efforts to conceptualize the ideological construct and principles of Kemalism in the 1920s remained understudied.

THE 1931 CONGRESS OF THE RPP AND THE FIRST PARTY PROGRAM

After long deliberations, Kemal launched his new project aimed at restructuring the government and party. On March 3, 1931, he sent a letter to the RPP asking for new elections. On March 10, 1931, Recep Peker, a radical nationalist, was appointed the RPP's new Secretary General. On April 24, parliamentary elections were held, on May 4, the fourth term of the Parliament held its inaugural meeting, and on May 5, İnönü's sixth government was formed. The Third congress of the RPP, which was held in Ankara, in May 1931, adopted its first fully elaborated program after eight years of formal existence.

The Third congress revised the Nine Principles adopted in 1923. At the outset, the program stressed that the main principles were for the future.[44] Then it explained principles (*esaslar*) that included Fatherland (*Vatan*), Nation (*Millet*), Fundamental organization of the state (*Devletin esas teşkilatı*), and Public Law (*Amme hukuku*). The first part of the program defined the nation as a "political unit composed of citizens bound together with the bonds of language, culture, and ideal." This formulation reappears in later programs. Comparing the four principles of the first section to the first eight articles of the constitution, it is clear that they are an elaboration of the "Fundamental provisions" of the 1924 Constitutions.[45] These principles also appeared in subsequent programs.

The first article in the second part of the party program, "*Main Characteristics of the Republican People's Party*," mentioned six principles and briefly explained each principle. In addition to three principles mentioned in the 1927 party statute—Republican, Nationalist, and Populist—three more were added: Etatist (*Devletçi*), Secularism (*Lâyik*), and Revolutionism (*İnkilâpçilik*).[46] Most studies of Kemalism concentrated on the six principles of the RPP without giving enough credit to the four fundamental principles (*esaslar*) of the party program. Those fundamentals constituted the backbone not only of the party but also of the state. Since 1919, Mustafa Kemal frequently cited these terms during his public speeches and interviews. In later decades, these formative ideological concepts, along with explanations, became the constituent parts on which politicians, scholars, bureaucrats, and journalists who positioned themselves as true Kemalists drew. The term Kemalism was not officially coined in 1931. In a speech on September 24, 1931, Atatürk reiterated the six principles and backed the idea of building the future of the Republic on them. The RPP adopted a flag of "Six arrows" (*Altı Ok*) on a red background, like the Turkish flag. The adoption of the party flag and its omnipresence in public spaces were early deliberate steps by the RPP to intertwine party ideology and its symbolic prominence.

Debates on the introduction of a system of thought has long created intensive discussions among historians. For instance, Lord Kinross provides two reasons for Mustafa Kemal to introduce the party program, which he called a doctrine: of the complex problems that lay ahead and the importance of rejecting rising Fascism and Communism.[47] Neither reason sufficiently explains Mustafa Kemal's true motivations. He did not even specify to which period of the 1930s he referred. Andrew Mango's approach follows a slightly different logic. He argues that by introducing the party principles, Kemal drew a line between single-party rule and a full-blown totalitarian dictatorship.[48] Others argue that Mustafa Kemal felt that the RPP had lost touch with society and needed rebranding and restructuring. The literature has overlooked the problem of regime security. Most scholars agree that after 1926, Kemal ruled the country without tangible opposition. However, sources from abroad suggest that there were internal disagreements within the elite about development perspectives. Observers of Turkish politics of 1931 described it as a country ruled by a Triumvirate consisting of Mustafa Kemal, İsmet (İnönü), and Marshal Fevzi (Çakmak).[49] The same newspaper described Ghazi as "impulsive, supple and imaginative," İsmet Pasha as "dogged, included to be vindictive, and does not readily change either his friends or his ideas," and Fevzi Pasha as "a steady going Conservative, whose sole object is to make Turkish Army efficient and content." The article mentions financial and economic difficulties as well as violent campaigns conducted by "one or two Constantinople newspapers" as the Triumvirate's chief anxieties.[50] Examining how Soviet observers interpreted power relations within Turkey is also useful. Kross, a Soviet observer of Turkey, confirmed that factions within Kemalist revolutionary circles had deviated from the politics of the mid-1920s by the end of the third decade.[51] Kemalism's right wing (or pro-Western section) demanded a greater commitment to Western model in Turkish state building. The Left, meanwhile, called for a larger state role in the economy and daily life. Pan-Turkist circles initiated efforts to make Kemalism an official ideology and scientific doctrine, establishing the Museum of Kemalist Revolution and the Institute of Turkism, etc. Relying on peasants and the petty-bourgeoisie, the orthodox section promoted nationalism, republicanism, and laicism.[52] Bekar Ferdi, a Turkish Communist leader, contended that after five years of independence, factions had appeared within the ranks of the RPP, a symptom of which was the growing dissatisfaction of the masses. As a result, more people were leaving than joining the party.[53] The RPP never became a mass political party, argues Godes. Counting only 2000–3000 nominal members, it had even fewer real active members, a figure that did not exceed 500, across the entire country.[54] Hence, insights from Kross, Ferdi, and Godes indicate that Kemal had to prevent cracks in the ruling elite from growing. One of the best ways to consolidate his power was possibly the introduction of a system of principles, to strengthen the "imaginary relationship of individuals to their real conditions of existence,"[55] as proposed by Althusser, between the state, elites, and society, and to initiate a common cause among his associates. This political experiment seemed to work, since at the next congress, it was only sharpened. This was yet another indication that Kemal set a course for, what Ottar Dahl called "continuous discussion and change" (1996, 24) of his ideological project.

Among other short-term and mid-term reasons for the ideological inception was an intention to provide clear, vivid, patriotism-infused guidelines of the Revolution's future goals, around which the population, the relatively untouched peasantry might be rallied.[56] Weiker further argues that the new ideological initiative aimed "… to provide a set of basic tenets which would form a framework of outer limits which all would-be political groups would observe but within which debate on specific programs and policies would be as free as possible."[57]

By the early 1930s, M. Kemal and those in circles close to him acknowledged that the Kemalist regime and their cherished revolution were out of favour, which forced responsible elites to initiate measures to enhance the efficacy of the revolution. The world financial crisis of 1929 also played a role in these events. The Great Depression pushed the government to undertake countermeasures to cope with its effects, which were interpreted as the fatal outcome of the Western development model. Turkish ruling elites drew inspiration from the Soviet

Union, which had escaped the crisis owing to state control over the economy. Those who visited the SU and observed its economy had a major say in adopting Soviet economic planning.[58] Expressing its intention to play a greater role in the economy, the Soviet model was never entirely embraced in Turkey, although some of its features were incorporated into Turkish economic management. In 1932, Lev(on) Karakhan, Deputy Head of the PCFA of the SU, wrote in a letter to the SU's ambassador to Persia, Petrovskij, that "the Kemalists aspire to have a self-supporting path of development (neither capitalism nor communism)."[59] He also explained that given the negative consequences of the economic crisis, "the government of İsmet [i.e. İnönü] was under criticism because of his poor handling of the country's economic affairs."

FURTHER CONSOLIDATION OF KEMALISM AT THE 1935 CONGRESS

In 1934, the TGNA bestowed the president with the surname Atatürk. Translated literally, the full name of Mustafa Kemal Atatürk means "the Chosen Perfect Forefather of the Turks." On February 9, 1935, the parliamentary elections were held. Weeks later, İnönü formed his seventh government, and its program received Parliament's support after six days. Between May 9 and 16, 1935, the Fourth Congress of the RPP was held, the last attended by Atatürk. This party convention became its most important political event, since the ideological tenets incorporated into the text of the party program became more direct and elaborate.

During the third meeting of the Congress, on May 13, 1935, Secretary General Recep Peker announced: "after the new party program has been approved fundamental principles (characteristics) [*ana vasıfları*] of the party will become the principles of the new Turkish state."[60] The amended party program indeed stated: "The main lines of our intentions, not for a few years, but for the future as well, are here put together in a compact form. All the fundamentals, that the Party pursues, constitute the principles of Kemalism [*Kamâlizm*]."[61] In the first two of eight sections, the party program meticulously elaborated the principles (*esaslar*) and party's main (or essential) characteristics (*ana vasıfları*). As was the case in 1931, the principles (*esaslar*) included Fatherland (*Vatan*), Nation (*Ulus*), Principle foundation of the state (*devlet esas kuram*), and Public Rights (*Kamusal Haklar*).

Five organizational forms ascribed to the Turkish Republic—(nationalist (*ulusçu*), populist (*halkçı*), revolutionary (*devrimçi*), secular (*lâik*), and etatist (*devletçi*)—corresponded to the RPP's six main characteristics.[62]

The second part mentioned all six principles, with minor amendments. The names of the three principles, as mentioned in the 1931 program, remained unchanged, whereas the former *milliyetçi* was replaced by *ulusçu*, and *inkilapçı* was replaced by *devrimci*, just as *cümhuriyetçi* was replaced by *cumhuriyetci*.[63] These changes, like Kemal's new name, *Kamâl*, were related to extensive language reforms, which aimed to instil or restore "pure Turkish" (*öz Türkçe*) by abolishing non-Turkish components.[64] Another difference from the previous program was the extensive elaboration of each party principle. Analysing the first two sections in both versions of the program reveal that taking only the six principles of the RPP, which were mentioned as characteristics is utterly misleading. The Kemalist system of ideological and political principles was much more comprehensive and fundamental in the minds and deeds of the Turkish political elite.

The next noteworthy dimension of the program reflected the Party's perception of the social composition of the state. While rejecting the class-based nature of "the people of the Turkish Republic" and introducing "a community divided into various professions,"[65] the program envisaged that "the life and happiness of others and the community" depend on "the functioning of each of these groups."[66] This suggests a corporatist view of society, which was common in Europe in that decade. No less important for this analysis, the fifth part of the program dealt with national education. The education system was to train "strongly republican, nationalist, populist, etatist, and secular citizens in every degree."[67] It also urged the system to bring up Turkish youth "with the conviction that the defence of the Revolution and the Fatherland is its highest duty."[68]

Examining the first two sections confirms the merging of party and state, which began in 1927, as Feridov argued, and became more profound after the 1931 party congress. The trend of merging party ideologies, institutions, and cadres with the state was a defining feature of this period, and Turkey was no exception. Congress minutes also revealed no opposition among deputies to the proposed merger.[69] After the Congress, Peker emerged as a radical. He also emerged as the "party ideologue," claiming to have the full approval of Atatürk who was present at the Congress.[70] He also eulogized the head of the state and proposed to further strengthen the party's authority.

Between 1935 and 1936, the merging of the party and state was intensified as governors of the provinces became chairmen of local branches of the party, which increased the role of the Secretary General of the RPP, Recep Peker. It was apparent that Peker's making the party secretariat a major player in the decision-making process was detrimental to the party chairman. He fervently supported a rigid party ideology with a coherent philosophical core, which indicated his inclination to grasp the opportunity to further expand the highly concentrated power of the Kemalist authoritarian regime. However, on June 15, 1936, on İnönü's advice, Atatürk removed Peker from his position, since he was seen as a possible challenger to İnönü for the party's next chairman. Others interpreted his departure as a sign of Atatürk's increasing anxiety about Peker's desire to imitate German and Italian totalitarian regimes. Şükrü Kaya, the RPP's new Secretary General and long-time Interior Minister,[71] who previously played a central role in the deportation and massacre of Armenians in WWI, became actively involved in the party and state affairs. As a result, instead of the state merging into the RPP, as Peker wished, now it seemed that the RPP would merge into the state and be subjugated to its authority.[72] Weiker's explanation concerning Peker's 1936 resignation reflects the dominant rationale of the time. Weiker argues that when individuals or groups "threatened to exceed the allowable limits of power or doctrine", Kemal "did not hesitate to intervene personally."[73]

The government was also resolute in imposing certain forms of censorship. For instance, in August 1936, a permanent commission was established, composed of the Ministry of Education, Ministry of Interior, General Staff, and the General Direction of the Press. It was mandated to "prohibit the exhibition of political and religious propaganda films, or films which show colonies or Oriental countries in an inferior position, and any film which may be considered as an incentive to crime or subservice of discipline."[74]

The six essential characteristics of the RPP were added to the Constitution on February 5, 1937. Article 2 of the Constitution was amended to read: "The Turkish state is Republican, Nationalist, Populist, Etatist, Laic, and Revolutionary. Its official language is Turkish and its Capital is the city of Ankara." No further definitions or clarifications were provided on the meaning of these principles. First formulated in

1931 in the RPP program, the six characteristics were incorporated into the main legal document of the state six years later. In September 1937, upon Atatürk's recommendation, İnönü resigned and Celal Bayar was appointed Prime Minister. Thus, without the two key figures of his team, Peker and İnönü, and with the appointment of Bayar as the new PM, it seemed Atatürk wanted to support other sections within the party to pursue new economic endeavours. The death of Atatürk on November 10, 1938, did not bring an end to his ideas. Borovali argues that the real era of what he calls "radical Kemalism" was finished when after one year of tenure as Prime Minister, Peker resigned in 1947, signaling the final demise of the radical course, at least within the RPP.[75] From this perspective, Soner Çağaptay is correct in arguing that with the death of Atatürk, one period of "High Kemalism" ended, only to enter a new era under İnönü.[76]

Even though during the last two years of his life Kemal Atatürk was not actively involved in daily politics due to his deteriorating health, total control over the socio-political and ideological realms of the Turkish nation continued. Although from 1925 until 1938 almost seventeen different rebellions were suppressed in various parts of the country, general stability prevailed. There was no opposition, which fact was due to the unparalleled personal charisma and authoritative power of Kemal Atatürk and the system that came into existence, thanks to him. With the death of Atatürk, no obstacles remained, as Lewis explains: "… authoritarian and paternalistic mode of government degenerated into something nearer to dictatorship as the word is commonly understood."[77] Alkan has noted that in Atatürk's later period the outlook of elites changed, and in conjunction with an emphasis on the principles of the revolution, liberal tendencies disappeared.[78]

This chapter demonstrated that the production and accommodation of ideological constructs have proved as important as their interpretation and communication. This study of Kemalism's formative years reveals that its radical secular-modernization project underwent all the necessary phases of the operationalization circle. Another feature of the period was efforts by Kemalists to elaborate programs and adhere to them as much as circumstances allowed. From the outset, Turkish leaders communicated with the people using conceptual frames, approaches, and methods. The adoption of the party program in 1931, which could be interpreted as the culmination of previous efforts, was, therefore, a gradual process. Yet Kemalists did not stop there; in the 1930s, they continued to further crystalize and fine-tune many of the formulations that were reflected in the party statutes and programs. The incorporation of the six principles into the constitution was therefore a negative turning point, since it halted Kemalism's conceptual development for a decade or two.

NOTES

1. Altay Fahrettin. 2008. *10 Yıl Savaş ve Sonrası.* İstanbul: Eylem; Mahmut Boğuşlu. 1997. *Birinci Dünya Harbi.* İstanbul: Kastaş Yayınevi; Shaw and Shaw (1977); Stanford Shaw. 2006. *The Ottoman Empire in World War I.* Ankara: Turkish Historical Society; Taner Akçam. 2006. *A Shameful Act: The Armenian Genocide and the Question of Turkish Responsibility.* New York: A Holt Paperback; Mehmet Beşikçi. 2012. *The Ottoman Mobilization of Manpower in the First World War: Between Voluntarism and Resistance.* Leiden: Brill; Bedross Der Matossian. 2014. *Shattered Dreams of Revolution: From Liberty to Violence in the Late Ottoman Empire.* Stanford: Stanford University Press; and Sean McMeekin. 2014. *The Ottoman Endgame: War, Revolution, and the Making of the Modern Middle East, 1908–1923.* New York: Penguin Press.
2. Ryan Gingeras. 2009. *Sorrowful Shores: Violence, Ethnicity and the End of the Ottoman Empire 1912–1923.* Oxford: Oxford University Press; Hakan Özoğlu. 2011. *From Caliphate to Secular State: Power Struggle in the Early Turkish Republic.* Santa Barbara: ABC Clio; Şükrü Hanioğlu. 2008. *A Brief History of the Late Ottoman Empire.* Princeton: Princeton University Press; Zürcher (1984); Zürcher (1993).
3. It is noteworthy that as early as 1921 prominent Russian historian Mikhail Pavlovich (Vel'tman) considered it wrong to view "the congress of Erzurum" as the first in line. He claimed that it was preceded by two other congresses. The First congress, according to him, was held in Aydin under the slogan "De-annexation of Smyrna," and the second in Trabzon, under the slogan, "Defense of rights of Trapezund". Mikhail Pavlovich. 1921. "Kemalistskoje dvizhenie v Turtsii." [The Kemalist movement in Turkey.] *Krasnaja Nov'* (1): 218.
4. Erik-Jan Zürcher. 1993. *A Modern History.* London: I.B. Tauris, 144.
5. Ghazi Mustafa Kemal (2008, 495).
6. The spelling of the first term was changed to *Cumhuriyet*; it was not until May 9, 1935, that the CHF changed its name to the *Cümhuriyet Halk Partisi*, adopting the French term in place of the Arabic word *fırka*.
7. For more about cultural and institutional reforms see Zürcher (1993). Niyazi Berkes. 1964. *The Development of Secularism in Turkey.*

Montreal: McGill University Press; Carter Findley. 2010. *Turkey, Islam, Nationalism, and Modernity: A History, 1789–2007.* New Haven: Yale University Press; Umut Azak (2010). On the detailed account about the significance and implications of the language reform see Geoffrey Lewis. 1999. *The Turkish Language Reform: A Catastrophic Success.* Oxford: Oxford University Press.

8. Arnold J. Toynbee and Kenneth P. Kirkwood. 1926. *Turkey.* London: Benn, 186.

9. Zürcher (1984, 140).

10. For a detailed analysis of the emergence and closure of the PRP, see Erik-Jan Zürcher. 1991. *The Political Opposition in the Early Turkish Republic: The Progressive Republic Party, 1924–1925.* Leiden: Brill.

11. Zürcher (1984, 142–167).

12. Walter Weiker. 1973. *Political Tutelage and Democracy in Turkey: The Free Party and Its Aftermath.* Leiden: Brill.

13. Kili (1969, 119).

14. State Department Records, Decimal File 867.00/2049, From Grew to: Secretary of State, December 3, 1930 cited in Nur Bilgi Criss. 2009. "Shades of Diplomatic Recognition: American Encounters with Turkey (1923–1937)." In *Studies in Atatürk's Turkey: The American Dimension,* edited by George Harris and Nur Bilgi Criss. Leiden: Brill, 124.

15. The uprising, which was later known as the Menemen incident, took place on December 23, 1930, when a number of dervishes, led by Derviş Mehmet from the Nakşibendi order, ordered to take up arms and attack government soldiers in Menemen, a small city north of Izmir. One soldier was brutally murdered and the government's response was no less brutal; hundreds of people across the country were arrested on the assumption that they participated in the rebellion or were members of the Nakşibendi order. Many of them were tried in martial courts, and twenty-eight were executed.

16. Weiker (1973, 184).

17. Interview with Alin Taşçian. May 11, 2005. Istanbul.

18. For English translation of "*The Nine Principles*" see Zürcher (1991, 118–122).

19. Mustafa Kemal (2008, 591).

20. Cited in Zürcher (1991, 118).

21. Mustafa Kemal (2008, 591–592).

22. K. Kazimirskij. 1927. "Sovremennaia Evropejskaia Turtsija." [Contemporary European Turkey.] *Novij Vostok* (16–17): 187.

23. Lüfti (1927, 75).

24. For detailed analysis of *Nutuk* see Toni Alaranta. 2008. "Mustafa Kemal Atatürk's Six-Day Speech of 1927: Defining of Official Historical View

of the Foundation of Turkish Republic." *Turkish Studies* 9 (1): 115–129; Hülya Adak. 2003. "National Myths and Self-Na(rra)tions: Mustafa Kemal's Nutuk and Halide Edib's Memoirs and The Turkish Ordeal." *The South Atlantic Quarterly* 102 (2/3): 509–527.

25. *Cümhuriyet Halk Fırkası Nizamnamesi.* 1927. Ankara. 3.
26. Ibid., 7–51.
27. The Council of People's Commissaries of the Soviet Union established the All-Soviet Society of Cultural Relations with Foreign Countries (*Vsesoiuznoe Obshchestvo Kul'turnoi Sviazi s zagranitsei* (known by its initials 'VOKS')) in 1925 to promote cultural exchanges between the SU and other countries.
28. *The Central State Archive of the October Revolution, F. 5283, L. 4, C. 57, p. 59* cited in Sverchevskaia (1983, 18).
29. Feridov (1928, 25).
30. Feridov (1928, 25).
31. Feridov (1928, 27–28).
32. Mango (1999, 501).
33. Feridov (1928, 25–26).
34. Gurko-Kryazhin (1928, 274).
35. Mustafa Kemal. 1929. *Put' Novoj Turtsii* [The Road of the New Turkey]. Vol. 1. Moscow: Litizdat. NKID, XII.
36. Ibid., XII.
37. Vladimir Gordlevskij. 1968. "Izuchenije Turtsii v SSSR." [Research on Turkey in the USSR.] In *Izbrannije Sochinenie* [Selected Writings], edited by Vladimir Gordlevskij, vol. 4. Moscow: Nauka, 358.
38. Alec Macfie. 1994. *Atatürk.* London and New York: Longman, 152.
39. İsmet Giritli. 2001. "The Superiority of the Kemalist Ideology Over Dogmatic Ideologies." In *A Handbook of Kemalist Thought*, translated by Ayşegül Amanda Yeşilbursa, 125–136. Ankara: Atatürk Research Center, 125.
40. Hans-Lukas Kieser. 2006. "An Ethno-Nationalist Revolutionary and Theorist of Kemalism: Dr. Mahmut Esat Bozkurt (1892–1943)." In *Turkey Beyond Nationalism*, edited by Hans-Lukas Kieser. London: I.B. Tauris, 26.
41. Karal (1997, 11).
42. Michel Paillarès. 1922. *Le Kemalisme: Devant Les Alliès.* Constantinople, Paris: Bosphore.
43. Elbert Francis Baldwin. 1922. The Turco-Bolshevist Menace: Editorial Correspondence from the Lausanne Conference. *The Outlook*, December 20, 698; *Kemalism Totters in Turkey.* 1925. Current Opinion. April; and Oriens. 1926. The Crisis of Kemalism. *The English Review.* August, 162–165.

44. *C.H.F. Nizamnamesi ve Programi*. 1931. Ankara: T. B. M. M. Matbaası, 29.
45. For the text of 1924 constitution, see Edward Mead Earle. 1925. "The New Constitution of Turkey." *Political Science Quarterly* 40 (1): 73–100. Pages from 89–100 of that article contain one of the first translation of the 1924 text.
46. *C.H.F. Nizamnamesi ve Programi*. 1931. 30–31.
47. Kinross (1964, 457).
48. Mango (2002, 479).
49. *The Triumvirate in Turkey: Soldiers All*, September 1931, an excerpt from an unspecified British newspaper, Arshak Safrastian Unit (Articles on Turkey's Domestic and foreign policies). 38. Record group 412. L. 1. Case file 2025. National Archives of Armenia. Yerevan.
50. Ibid.
51. T. Kross. 1930. "Vnutrenee polizhenie Turtsii." [The Domestic Situation in Turkey.] *Mezhdunarodnaja Zhizn'* (7–8): 57–66.
52. Kross (1930, 59–61).
53. Ferdi (1927, 35).
54. Godes (1928, 35).
55. Louis Althusser. 1971. "Ideology and Ideological State Apparatuses." In *Lenin and Philosophy and other Essays*, edited by Louis Althusser. New York: Monthly Review Press as cited in Peter Burke (2005, 99).
56. Weiker (1973, 219).
57. Ibid.
58. Elisabeth Özdalga. 1978. *I Atatürks spår: Det Republikanska FolkPartiet och utvecklingsmobilisering i Turkiet från etatism till populism*. Lund: Dialog, 31.
59. *Pis'mo zamestitelja narodnogo komissara inostrannyh del SSSR polnomochnomu predstavitelju SSSR v Persii A. M. Petrovskomu*, May 31, 1932. 344–345 [Letter of the Deputy Foreign Minister of USSR to the Plenipotentiary Representative of the USSR to Persia, A. M. Petrovskij. May 31, 1932. 344–345. Ministry for Foreign Affairs of the USSR—Documents of USSR Foreign Policy]. Moscow: Izdatel'stvo Politicheskoi Nauki. 1969.
60. *C.H.P. Dördüncü Büyük Kurultayı Görüşmeleri Tutulgası*. 1935. Ankara: bolum 1, 45.
61. *C.H.P. Dördüncü Büyük Kurultayının Görüşmeleri Tutulgasi*. 1935. bolum 2, 77. In the original document it was referred to as "Kamâlizm" because after language reforms Kemal was "Turkified" and it became Kamâl meaning 'castle'.
62. *C.H.P. Dördüncü Büyük Kurultayının Görüşmeleri Tutulgasi*. 1935. bolum 2, 77–78.

63. *C.H.P. Programı.* 1935. Ankara: Ulus Basımevi, Mayis. 5–6.
64. Ilker Aytürk, 2004. "Turkish Linguists Against the West: The Origins of Linguistic Nationalism in Atatürk's Turkey." *Middle Eastern Studies* 40 (6): 1.
65. *C.H.P. Programı.* 1935. 6–7.
66. Ibid.
67. *C.H.P. Programı.* 1935. Beşinci kısım, Milli Talim ve terbiye.
68. Ibid.
69. *C.H.P. Dördüncü Büyük Kurultayının Görüşmeleri Tutulgasi.* 1935. bolum 2.
70. Ali Fuat Borovali. 1985. *Kemalist Tradition, Political Change and the Turkish Military.* Unpublished dissertation. Queen's University, 84–85.
71. It needs to be added that until 1942 the General Secretaries of the RPP simultaneously held the position of the Minister of Interior except Refik Saydam.
72. Soner Çağaptay. 2003. *Crafting the Turkish Nation: Kemalism and Turkish Nationalism in the 1930s.* Unpublished dissertation. PhD Yale University, 88.
73. Weiker (1973, 239).
74. Film Censorship in Turkey. August 1936, National Archives of Armenia, F. 412, L. 1, Case, 2025 (Articles on Turkey's Domestic and Foreign Policies). 64
75. Borovali (1985, 86).
76. Soner Çagaptay. 2006. *Islam, Secularism, and Nationalism in Modern Turkey: Who Is a Turk?* London: Routledge, 56.
77. Bernard Lewis. 1968. *The Emergence of Modern Turkey.* London: Oxford University Press, 304.
78. Alkan Türker. 1980. "Turkey: Rise and Decline of Political Legitimacy in a Revolutionary Regime." *Journal of South Asian and Middle Eastern Studies* 2 (4): 46.

REFERENCES

Azak, Umut. 2010. *Islam and Secularism in Turkey: Kemalism, Religion and the Nation State.* London: I.B. Tauris.
Borovali, Ali Fuat. 1985. *Kemalist Tradition, Political Change and the Turkish Military.* Unpublished dissertation, Queen's University.
Burke, Peter. 2005. *History and Social Theory*, 2nd ed. Cambridge: Polity Press.
Dahl, Ottar. 1996. "The Historical Study of Ideologies." In *Societies Made Up of History: Essays in Historiography, Intellectual History, Professionalization, Historical Social Theory and Proto-Industrialization*, edited by Björk Ragnar, Thorsten Nybom, and Rolf Torstendahl, 17–28. Stockholm: Edsbruk: Akademitryck AB.

Ferdi, Bekar. 1927. "Evolutsija Kemalizma: Ot Natsional'noj Revoljutsii k Diktature Burzhuazii." [Evolution of Kemalism: From National Revolution Towards the Bourgeoisie Dictatorship.] *Sputnik Kommunista* 4 (10 [43]): 30–38.

Feridov, Ziya. 1928. "Nekotorie Voprosi Sovremennoj Turtsii." [Some Questions of Contemporary Turkey.] *Revolutsionnyi Vostok* (6): 24–41.

Godes, Mikhail. 1928. *Chto Takoye Kemalistskij Put' i Vozmozhen li on v Kitae?* [What Is a Kemalist Pathway and Is It Possible in China?] Leningrad: Priboj.

Gurko-Kryazhin, Vladimir. 1928. "Vozniknovenie Natsional'no-osvoboditel'nogo Dvizhenija v Turtsii." [The Origins of the National-Liberation Movement in Turkey.] *Novyj Vostok* (23–24): 268–275.

Karal, Enver Ziya. 1997. "The Principles of Kemalism." In *Ataturk: Founder of a Modern State*, edited by Ergun Özbudun and Ali Kazancigil, 2nd ed., 11–36. London: Hurst and Company.

Kemal, Ghazi Mustafa. 2008. *The Great Speech (Nutuk)*, 2nd ed. Ankara: Atatürk Research Center.

Kili, Suna. 1969. *Kemalism*. İstanbul: Robert College, School of Business Administration and Economics.

Kinross, Lord. 1964. *Atatürk: The Rebirth of a Nation*. London: Weidenfeld and Nicolson.

Kross, T. 1930. "Vnutrennee Polozhenie Turtsii." [The Domestic Situation in Turkey.] *Mezhdunarodnaja Zhizn'* (NKID) (7–8 [57–66]): 57–66.

Lüfti. 1927. "Turtsija Segodnya." [Turkey Today.] *Za Partiju* ("Pravdi Vostoka") (4): 66–76.

Mango, Andrew. 1999. *Atatürk*. New York: The Overlook Press.

Mango, Andrew. 2002. "Kemalism in a New Century." In *Turkish Transformation: New Century, New Challenges*, edited by Beeley Brian, 22–36. Tallahassee: The Eothen Press.

Shaw, Stanford, and Ezel Kural Shaw. 1977. *History of the Ottoman Empire and Modern Turkey, vol. II: Reform, Revolution, and Republic: The Rise of Modern Turkey, 1808–1975*. Cambridge: Cambridge University Press.

Sverchevskaia, Antonina. 1983. *Sovetsko-Turetskie Kul'turnye Sviazi 1925–1981* [Soviet-Turkish Cultural Relations 1925–1981]. Moscow: Nauka.

Weiker, Walter. 1973. *Political Tutelage and Democracy in Turkey: The Free Party and its Aftermath*. Leiden: Brill.

Zürcher, Erik-Jan. 1984. *The Unionist Factor: The Role of the Committee of Union and Progress in the Turkish National Movement 1905–1926*. Leiden: Brill.

———. 1991. *Political Opposition in the Early Turkish Republic: The Progressive Republican Party 1924–1925*. Leiden: Brill.

———. 1993. *A Modern History*. London: I.B. Tauris.

Popularization of Kemalism: Intellectual, Contextual, and Popular Considerations

This chapter examines the policies that the Kemalist elite and intellectuals undertook to support and with which they disseminated Kemalism in the first three decades of its rule. Kemalists were quick to recognize that the adoption of party principles was not enough to earn popular support. This chapter discusses the several steps that were taken to reach that objective. The revolutionary modernizing ideological project of Kemalism had to be simplified and popularized among certain societal groups (intellectuals, youth, and urban residents) to secure its sustainability. At the same time, a number of concepts, ideas, and visions that Kemalism employed were either new or inherited from the late Ottoman era, and therefore had to be placed into a new context and adjusted according to changing social and political circumstances.

INTELLECTUAL FRAMEWORK

Ideological discourses starting in the Tanzimat period (1839–1876) and subsequent ideological currents such as Pan-Islamism, Ottomanism, Pan-Turkism, and Westernism (*Garbcılık*) pursued two primary objectives—the preservation and empowerment of the Ottoman Empire. However, they also constituted fertile ground for the development and further empowerment of Kemalist principles. Alongside the dissemination of ideological concepts, the Ottomans were exposed to Western-style schools, newly formed professional and social organizations, secret societies, Western

© The Author(s) 2019
V. Ter-Matevosyan, *Turkey, Kemalism and the Soviet Union,*
Modernity, Memory and Identity in South-East Europe,
https://doi.org/10.1007/978-3-319-97403-3_4

and Ottoman books and periodicals, reading rooms, and public libraries that paved the way for the emergence of "the cultural environment [and] Ottoman 'civil society' within which this alternate Ottoman vision acquired meaning."[1] Ottoman intellectuals, whom Göçek refers to as a "new social group,"[2] also played an important role in nourishing Western ideas and transplanting them into the Ottoman context. The Turkish masses, however, remained indifferent to the popular intellectual discources of the time. Divergent ideological currents and intellectual movements had limited popular involvement and, because of the absence of sophisticated and efficient organizations, did not leave elitist circles.[3]

At the turn of the century, active members of Turkish émigré centres in Europe played a key role in transforming the intellectual and political climate in the declining empire. A score of nineteenth-century European intellectuals and thinkers influenced the ideas, thoughts, and writings of Turkish nationalists and intellectuals. According to Berkes, "the suppressed [i.e. Hamidian] generation read European literature indiscriminately, like hungry children… the ground was being prepared for rebellion."[4] The list of European celebrities who influenced Turkish writing, according to Berkes, included "Schopenhauer, Hauckel, Büchner, Darwin, Draper, Renan, Taine, Herbert Spencer, Gustave Le Bon, Poincare, Th. Ribot, Balzac, Charles Richet, Flamarion, John Stuart Mill, Flaubert, Zola, and a score of less important personages."[5] Late Ottoman intellectuals were profoundly shaped by positivist and materialist philosophical currents. Key members of the Young Turks, such as Ahmed Rıza, Tekin Alp, Ziya Gökalp, Mehmet Emin, Abdullah Cevdet, Halide Edib (Adıvar), Mehmed Fuat (Köprülü), and Ahmet Hikmet implanted the European cult of scientism in the Ottoman milieu.[6] Muslim immigrants from Russia, most of whom received a modern education in Russia and Western Europe, like Yusuf Akçura (from Simbirsk on the Volga), Ahmet Ağaoğlu (from Shushi), İsmail Gasprinski (from the Crimea), Mehmed Reşit Şahingiray (from the North Caucasus), Hüseyinzade Ali (from Baku), and Halim Sabit Şibay (from Kazan)—transferred Russian radical and revolutionary outlooks (nihilism, utopianism, positivism, and materialism) and transplanted the fashionable ideas of Russian revolutionary movements and writers (Chernishevskij, Bakunin, Herzen, Turgenev, Belinski, Tolstoy, Dostoyevskij) to the Turkish context, thereby influencing the Turkish national movement.[7] Akçura and Ağaoğlu (along with many others) produced the most influential texts[8] in the history of Turkish nationalism by bringing an ideological framework to Turkism. The same Russian émigrés—Akçura, Ağaoğlu, Gasrpinsky, and Ali—became members of the founding committee of one of the most important nationalist organizations in the Ottoman Empire and Turkey: *Türk Ocakları* (the Turkish Hearths).[9] Shissler has called Russian émigrés "sophisticated observers with substantial exposure to the West," who were deeply affected by their Russian background. Their emotional distance from the Ottoman Empire allowed them to view history from a national perspective, apart from Ottoman pre-commitments.[10]

These are a few names among many who made an important impact on the Young Turks, the late Ottoman state, and republican ideological currents. Some of these preachers were radical nationalists who were well integrated into the CUP power system, while others held key administrative positions in government and in the regions, or were the members of CUP's Central Committee (*merkez-i umumi*), like Gökalp, Ali, Gasprinski and Ağaoğlu, giving them practical leverage to implement their ideals. Understandably, they had different perspectives on most urgent issues that the Ottoman state faced at the time: minority questions, nationalism, religion, etc. Many of these names are widely known to the students of the Armenian Genocide, too. Still, their ideas were instrumental in shaping the fundamentals of the Unionist and, particularly, Kemalist worldviews in matters related to nation-building and the construction of national identity. Many of these names reappeared in the republican era and became central figures of the political elite or intellectual milieu.

In the last two decades of the Ottoman Empire, a number of ideologies became more popular with CPU members and leading intellectuals. Espousal of strong Turkish nationalism, as well as Ottomanism and Pan-Islamism, sometimes interchangeably, served the supreme political goal of the Young Turks: saving the empire.[11] Despite the emerging importance of the above-mentioned ideologies and outlooks, intellectuals and European powers at the time frequently misunderstood, confused, and misused them. The Young Turks were also not confident about the right ideology until Pan-Turkism took precedence over others. This, however, did not imply that Pan-Islamism or Ottomanism were rejected or abandoned. Rather, the CUP leadership adopted a policy line that included features from all of these ideologies. For instance, a Pan-Islamist foundation served as the ideological basis for Ahmet Ağaoğlu to develop works on Turkish nationalism. In his writings between 1894 and 1919,

Ağaoğlu followed Jamal ad-Din al-Afghani's notions of Islam's rational interpretation and the importance of forming bonds of unity within and among different Muslim nations.[12] In some instances, especially during WWI, the Pan-Turkic CUP used Pan-Islamism for propaganda purposes.[13] Obvious contradictions existed not only on the political level, but also in ideological discourse. Prophets of Turkish nationalism were torn between their patriotic feelings and their Islamic heritage.[14]

Devastating defeats in the Tripolitanian War (1911–1912) and the Balkan Wars (1912–1913) fuelled the Turkish revanchist and militaristic nationalism of the early 1910s. Prior to WWI, the Ottoman Empire had lost North Africa and 83% of its European territories, resulting in political, socio-economic, and migration problems, as well as psychological wounds. This in turn provoked religious prejudice against the infidels and the notion of the racial superiority of Turks, which became the source of a number of disastrous endeavours. The Armenian Genocide, meticulously planned and executed by the CUP leadership, was one of the painful outcomes of radical Turkish nationalism. Using WWI as a pretext, the Armenian population of the Ottoman Empire was deported, massacred, and exterminated. The widespread conviction of the treachery of the Armenian population, as well as envy and greed regarding the Armenians' relative economic success were other motivations that elicited the participation of various levels of society in the mass murders. Driven by racial, religious, and material hatred, the mass killings of Armenians, as well as Assyrians and Greeks, were not concluded until the early 1920s. The genocide of the Armenians was carried out not only in the territory of the Ottoman Empire, but also in the borderlands of Russia, Armenia, and Persia, as Turkish troops moved back and forth between 1918 and 1921.[15]

The Second Constitutional Period (1908–1918) provided the necessary conditions for the Young Turks to implement their long cherished reforms. While some earlier initiatives were implemented by the CUP government, the former stance of the Young Turks on a number of issues was abandoned. In this regard, Hanioğlu notes that the years leading to the revolution were transformative for the Young Turks, as political ideas started to shift "from grand theories aimed at reshaping the world order to simpler and more narrowly political doctrines and tactics."[16] After the revolution, the CUP leadership gradually sidelined and then abandoned "its earlier yearning for a society shaped by scientific doctrines," the "theory of Darwinism," "positivism," and "natural laws"[17] to pursue more pragmatic political and ideological objectives. Many reforms that the Young Turks had sought to implement were left behind. Meanwhile, Mustafa Gündüz argues that republican era reforms originated in the intellectual movement of the Second Constitutional Period.[18]

The transition from the Ottomans to the republicans, regarding policies, ideas, and ideologies, was not a linear process. In some spheres, Kemalists continued where Unionists left off, while in others, republican policies constituted a clean break with the ideas of the previous era and sometimes even demonstrated unprecedented radicalism.[19] For fifty years, intellectuals, ideological currents, and "native intelligentsia" had prepared the ground for political, legal, cultural, and economic transformations that influenced the Kemalists.[20] The Kemalist republican elite not only witnessed, but also had hands-on experience with these past policies. The Kemalists recognized the utility of those ideologies and principles, which proved effective during the Second Constitutional Period. Indeed, they embraced Turkish nationalism, making it one of the core principles of the state's ideological construction. In public statements, Kemalist leaders despised Pan-Turkism, seeing it as a source of Turkey's many problems. Even the concept "Türkçülük," which implied both Turkism (Turkish nationalism) and Pan-Turkism, was replaced with *milliyetçilik* (nationalism). It later dominated Kemalist programs and became one of the core principles of Kemalism. Its provisions persisted in three republican constitutions (1924, 1961, and 1982) with the same formulation: "Everyone bound to the Turkish State through the bond of citizenship is a Turk." It was also preserved in a variety of legal, practical-political, and socio-cultural forms.

While discussing the impact of popular European authors (historians and anthropologists) and their writings on the formulation of certain republican ideas and concepts—science, race, social-Darwinism, progress, etc.—Hanioğlu presents a long list of authors who also influenced Mustafa Kemal. Among them were Wells, Alfred Cort Haddon, George Montandon, Eugene Pittard, and many others.[21] There have also been consistent efforts to trace the origins of Kemalism to Emile Durkheim, Jean-Jacques Rousseau, Auguste Mignet, and particularly the positivism of Auguste Comte.[22]

A cursory discussion illustrates the impact of three key thinkers of the period: Gökalp, Ağaoğlu, and Cevdet. An influential figure in his day, Ziya Gökalp played a critical role in formulating some of the key principles of Kemalism.[23] Here, it will suffice to say that he transplanted certain Western ideological currents to the Turkish intellectual tradition. Deeply influenced by French sociologist Durkheim, he was one of the first intellectuals to synthesize European elements and Ottoman Muslim civilization. He was particularly inspired by Durkheim's ideas on the supremacy of society over the individual, but differed in emphasizing the "nation" instead of "society."[24] Taha Parla singles out Gökalp's corporatist thinking, which he claims provided "the paradigmatic worldview for the several dominant political ideologies and public philosophies in Turkey," including Kemalism.[25]

Ahmet Ağaoğlu[26] was another central figure who fervently nurtured popular ideas and visions. For nearly five decades, he advanced Turkish nationalism and zealously supported the CUP, Kemalist revolutionary deeds, and Westernization efforts. In the 1930s, he opposed Kemalist authoritarianism.[27] During his education in Petersburg, he became a follower of the Russian radical Narodnik movement.[28] Later, when he moved to Paris, two prominent French Orientalists, Darmesteter and Renan, helped him shape his views on the role of history, the cult of heroic figures, Romantic individualism, and the French Revolution. Later, he would declare that the Kemalist Revolution was an Eastern counterpart of the "liberal" French Revolution.[29] As a faculty member at the Darülfünun, he frequently contributed to *Türk Yurdu* (Turkish Homeland) and *Islam Mecmuasi* (Islamic Review), one of the central nationalist journals of the later Ottoman Empire, established by Yusuf Akçura. Ağaoğlu was also the editor-in-chief of *Tercümân-i Hakikat* (The Interpreter of Truth), the mouthpiece of the CUP in the 1910s.[30] In 1915, he became a member of the Ottoman Parliament. In his writings, Ağaoğlu discussed the underprivileged position of the Turks in the Ottoman Empire and promoted the importance of saving Islam by intertwining it with nationalism.[31] Yet, in his earlier writings, he preached to liberate Turkish nationalism from the grip of Islam.[32] Kevorkian notes that Ağaoğlu was not merely a theoretician since he was the only CUP member who had played a direct part in a clash with Armenians in the Caucasus and got his hands dirty.[33] In his writings, Ağaoğlu argued that the Ottoman Empire was ethnically too diverse, too different to constitute a sound basis for the nation-state, which he viewed "as the most modern form of political and social organization towards which the history of humanity was moving."[34]

Abdullah Cevdet was another distinguished figure of the late Ottoman and early republican period. Creel claims that significant elements of

Kemalist ideology have clear roots in the writings of Cevdet, and some outstanding features of Kemalist ideology are historically inexplicable without referring to his ideas. Creel questions the dominant theory of primacy, or Gökalpism, on Kemalism.[35] Cevdet was one of the original founders of the CUP in the Royal Medical Academy in 1889, and later played a consequential role in the Young Turk movement. From September 1904 to November 1932, Cevdet published the journal "*Ictihad*," first in Geneva, and later in Cairo and Istanbul. In this journal, he articulated his views on modernization, which later were found in one form or another in the deeds of Mustafa Kemal. As early as 1891, explains Creel, Cevdet claimed the importance of abandoning the Arabic script and Arab metaphysics, by stressing the need for a Turkish language based on Latin script. He was concerned with education, the continuation of religious orders (whom Cevdet named "a bunch of blockheads"), and economic restructuring.[36] Cevdet played a pivotal role in the organization of the *Garbcılık* (Westernization) movement (1908–1918), which embraced Ottoman intellectuals who promoted publications designed to revise the role of Islam. The ideas of this movement made a considerable impact on Kemalism. Like many of his contemporaries, Cevdet believed that religion was one of the greatest obstacles to social progress and should be replaced with science. He began with a moderate stance and advocated the view that "science is the religion of the elite, whereas religion is the science of the masses."[37] Later in the 1910s, he became an outspoken opponent of religion. In various articles, he openly criticized many Islamic customs, such as fasting, women's veiling, the performance of *namaz*, and even hospitality, and urged Muslims to substitute European manners for their own outdated ones.[38]

PROPAGATION OF THE RPP PRINCIPLES

After the gradual introduction of the guiding principles in the late 1920s and 1930s, Kemal's close disciples were certain that a distinct bureaucratic and intellectual elite was formed, capable of teaching society the essence of Kemalism and the importance of the nation-building project. After 1931, the RPP expanded the number of organizations and strived to attract more young people under its banner. On October 16, 1931, Recep Peker voiced the RPP's commitment to the basic principles at a conference, speaking to university students in Istanbul (*Darülfünun*). He elaborated on a number of key issues concerning non-Muslims, the ethno-religious shape of the nation, and non-Turkish Muslims' position vis-à-vis the nation.[39]

Until 1942, Recep Peker, along with other key Kemalist ideologues, Yusuf Hikmet Bayur, Yusuf Kemal Tengirşek, İsmet İnönü, and Mahmut Esat Bozkurt, initiated a series of lectures aimed at injecting the newly developed course of "The History of Turkish Revolution" in the Turkish universities of Istanbul and Ankara as well as the War Academy. İnan Süleyman has discussed the importance that the Kemalist leadership attached to this initiative.[40] He claims that these courses developed a theoretical framework for the revolution and functioned as "revolutionary training."[41] He also argues that the lectures were seen as a necessary tool in the hands of the RPP "to prevent its people from being influenced" by totalitarian ideologies emanating from Germany, Italy, and Russia.[42] However, he does not elaborate on how exactly these lectures were going to stop the infiltration of totalitarian ideologies. In fact, in the decade of the 1930s, there were no efficient barriers to prevent the proliferation of totalitarian models. In the Turkish context, there were other instigators to embarking on an extremely radical course. Peker, for instance, was openly sympathetic to fascism and, if circumstances were right, he could have openly promoted that line, too.

Between October 28 and 30, 1933, as a part of a propaganda campaign launched by the RPP, the Republic celebrated its tenth anniversary. Webster examined mass media coverage surrounding the event. A book published by the General Executive Committee of the RPP, bearing the title "10," contained a chronology starting from May 19, 1919, and a meticulous account of the attainments and reforms of the Kemalist regime, commencing with the birth of the Republic and culminating in events prior to the celebration. It also provided an overview of how each sector emerged and functioned in the republican system. Webster claims that the content of the brochure was calculated to inspire increasing faith and loyalty in all who read it.[43] The same year, the book was translated into French as "10 Years of the Republic."[44] This book can be considered a supplement to *Nutuk* in several respects. If the latter signified Mustafa Kemal's interpretation of his political struggle and wars, "10" was reporting to citizens and the world about the achievements of the Kemalist regime since 1923. Many developments occurred between 1927, when *Nutuk* was delivered, and 1933, making the publication of the book an opportune occasion to conclude as well as use the past and prepare a ground for the advance of Kemalism.

Revision of History and Purification of Language

In the minds of Kemalists, the nation-building process and the homogenization of identities and visions around the core of Kemalism could not succeed without a radical revision of history and sweeping language reforms. The founder of the Turkish Republic, Mustafa Kemal Atatürk, once said: "Writing history is as important as making history" [*Tarih yazmak, tarih yapmak kadar mühimdir*].[45] The statement signifies the utility and political weight that Mustafa Kemal ascribed to history.

In the 1910s, deliberate efforts began to obliterate the Ottoman historiographical tradition by portraying the East as "the barbaric homeland of the bloodthirsty Mongols." The Young Turks turned to the Mongols and the Tatars of Russia for inspiration to shape a more flattering image of the Turks.[46] Two decades later, this policy of rethinking the past was revisited. The period between the 1920s and 1930s also marked the era of quasi-scientific enterprises. The aim of the Kemalists was to find extra sources for national consolidation and for developing a sense of common fate and destiny. The Kemalist government certainly saw language and history as critical tools to popularize its state-building and nation-state formation policies.

The Kemalist elite regarded the writing of history textbooks as a chance to "rewrite" Turkish history in a way that glorified the ancient past of Turks, leading in a linear progression to the establishment of the Republic and onto a bright republican future.[47] During the 1930s, ethnocentric nationalism and racial concepts, put forward by the "Turkish History Thesis" were additional manifestations of the Kemalist regime's ultra-nationalism. The "Introduction to the General Themes of Turkish History" included the following ideas: (1) Turks were a great and ancient race belonging to the Aryans; (2) their mission was to civilize the rest of the world; (3) the Turkish race was a creator of civilizations in many lands; (4) European languages derived from Turkish.[48] The Kemalist revision of history omitted the Ottoman era, and through a pragmatic, revolutionary and "crude positivist approach built the materialistic bridge between the Neolithic age of the Anatolian past and the Kemalist Revolution."[49] The reintroduction of the past, mostly in a glorious light, was fashionable in newly formed nation-states. Anthony Smith's observation is helpful: "In order to create a convincing representation of the 'nation', a worthy and distinctive past must be rediscovered and appropriated. Only then can the nation aspire to a glorious destiny for which its citizens may be expected to make some sacrifices."[50] Key provisions of the new historical concepts pertaining to the ethnic origins of Turks gained official status and were popularized.[51]

It was not a coincidence that the "Turkish History Thesis" was produced in the most intense phase of anti-Kurdish repressions and was partially aimed to contain Kurdish identity.[52] Some observers claim that after Atatürk's death, many radical and outlandish assertions of the "Turkish History Thesis" were abandoned; however, a brief look at the dominant public discourse of the later decades proves the opposite. Atatürk and his key ideologues initiated a trend that was later imprinted on the intellectual and academic circles of the Republic. Kemal's desire to shape an elitist monochromatic historiography resonated in the minds of many historians and social and political scientists. This strategy not only stagnated the critical development of the social sciences but also negatively affected future generations. The drive to prescribe certain sacred characteristics to the founding years of the Republic continues today.

The foreign press also was interested in this endeavour. Much has been written about facets of the neologism that new historians tried to impose. In this regard, it is important to quote *The Daily Telegraph*'s account, which recorded Mustafa Kemal's determination "to probe deep into the past and reconstruct the real and complete history of the Turkish race."[53] The primary objective was "to clear up as many as possible of the obscure points in Turkish history, with the hope of setting before the world a record of events which will span the ages, to prove the role that Turkish civilization has played in the world's history."[54]

In the late 1920s, a new public campaign popularized and expanded the use of the Turkish language. In his observations from Eastern Thrace, Kazimirskij reports that on May 10, 1925, the local periodical, "*Paşa Ili*," which was more of a leaflet than a journal, published an article, "Hegemony of the Turkish language." "All the conversations in Turkey, which are other than Turkish, should be seen as offensive." In the same vein, it further claimed, "those co-citizens, who speak Spanish, live French and think Jewish, make money and always stay away from the fusion with the Turks."[55] In an explicit reference to the Jewish citizens of Eastern Thrace, an excerpt illustrated the sporadic local practices that asserted the dominance of the Turkish language over local minorities long before this became state policy. One widely discussed public appeal was the "Citizen, speak Turkish" (*Vatandaş, Türkçe konuş*) campaign, the legacy of which has imprinted itself on Turkey. This rather short campaign implied that many young people and students merged into groups, wandered in non-Turkish populated areas of Istanbul, Izmir, and elsewhere, and urged non-Turkish minorities to speak only Turkish in public areas. The Ministry of Interior granted permission to a campaign that aimed to instil in the minds of minorities the notion that "speaking in a language other than Turkish meant not recognizing Turkish law and sentiments."[56] This movement of linguistic homogenization indicated that in parallel to the republican elite's perceptions and practices of nation-state formation, there were other important socio-cultural dimensions supported by diverse "social actors, who considered themselves the missionaries of the new regime."[57] What stands out in Aslan's analysis is that although she agrees with Zürcher's list of people (writers, teachers, doctors, other professionals, and students) that the Kemalist leadership had inspired,[58] she provides enough evidence to argue that the Kemalist cause attracted support from ordinary citizens, too. Indeed, what Zürcher refers to as the "'noblesse oblige' attitude of the Kemalist elite"[59] appealed to many people in Turkey, often gaining greater acknowledgement than initially planned, as was the case with many non-Turkish intellectuals who supported Kemalism in the 1930s.

Popularization of the Turkish language had other manifestations, too. The famous language purification campaign, which was launched in the beginning of the 1930s, stressed the importance of public support. Much has been written about the radical nature of reforms that aimed to purge the Turkish language of Persian and Arabic words.[60] As we saw in the case of the RPP principles in 1935, these changes affected even the name of Mustafa Kemal, mentioned as Kamâl. In the same issue of the *Daily Telegraph* the author of the article cited one example to demonstrate the steadfastness of Turkish historians. It quoted the example of "adam" and "ev," the Turkish words for man and house, respectively, to sufficiently prove that "the first two people on earth were Turks."[61]

While some Soviet observers were particularly critical of Kemalist historians who followed the "illiterate delusion of their leader" to invent a "Turkified world history,"[62] there were also prominent Soviet scholars who participated in languages congresses. Anna Tveritinova, among critics, not only saw obvious continuities between Ziya Gökalp and the Kemalist version of nationalism, but also argued that after considerable change, the latter had become more chauvinistic, outrageously racist, and unequivocally fascist.[63] Miller had a different perspective on the Turkish nationalism of the period. He praised Atatürk because "for the first time in Turkish history… he was able to disentangle Turkish nationalism - Turkism, not only from the Pan-Ottoman and Pan-Islamic quasi-nationalism of 'new Ottomans,' but also from the Pan-Turkism of the 'Young Turks,' which, although it had identical social roots to Turkism, essentially possessed anti-nationalist character."[64]

Nikolay Marr, Vice-President of the Soviet Academy of Sciences, and language theoretician of the Stalinist era, visited Turkey on the invitation of the Turkish government to participate in the Turkish Language Congress in 1932. He delivered lectures in Ankara and Izmir and proposed a thesis that was warmly received by Turkish revisionist scholars and politicians who were seeking external legitimization for their claims of shared roots with Turkish and Indo-European languages. Marr considered the Turks of Asia Minor autochthonous, "with deep Mediterranean roots," believing "there is no Mediterranean without Turks."[65] In 1936, Aleksandr Samojlovich, Director of the Institute of Oriental Studies of the National Academy of Sciences of the SU, participated in the Third Turkish Language Congress. He shared his impressions of his third visit to Turkey—the previous two trips were in 1900 and 1911—in an article. Speaking on behalf of Soviet linguists, Samojlovich claimed that an "anti-scholarly Sun language theory" was unacceptable since "it turned the history of language, hence, the history of human society, upside down."[66]

The Role of the Turkish Hearths and People's Houses

As the next step towards the popularization of party principles and the ideological mobilization of society, the Kemalist regime suppressed those social and cultural institutions in the country that had the imprint of the past or voiced opposition to Kemalism. As part of a larger propaganda campaign, a number of institutions had been established since the end of the 1920s (National Schools, the Public Orators' Institution of the Republican People's Party, the Turkish Historical Society, the Faculty of Language, History and Geography, and People's Houses).[67] The People's Houses (*Halkevleri*—hereafter, PH) were established in 1931 for disseminating Kemalist ideas. It is noteworthy that some of the previous studies on Kemalism drew attention to the activities of the PH, while neglecting the significance of the Turkish Hearths (*Türk*

Ocakları—hereafter, TH), which were also not included in Şimşek's list of "reaffirmed and consolidated institutions." The reason for omitting them could be TH's affiliation with the previous regime and the Kemalists' possible concerns about their true intentions. Observers who concentrated on the PH mainly thought of it as the brainchild of Mustafa Kemal and did not pay sufficient attention to the TH. In reality, the TH played no less an important role in the 1920s when the Kemalist ideological framework was still vague.

The Turkish Hearths were the forerunners of the People's Houses, established in 1911 for formulating and inculcating the Unionist ideology of radical nationalism: Turkism along with its expansionist variations of Pan-Turkism and Pan-Turanism. The TH aimed at awakening cultural, linguistic consciousness and a feeling of cultural unity among all people belonging to the Turkish race, including those living in foreign countries, to create a united homeland. Aleksandr Kolesnikov, a Soviet historian, added the fourth component to the three-tier structure of the Young Turk's radical nationalism: Pan-Islamism.[68] Many observers dismissed its importance, along with Ottomanism (Pan-Ottomanism), after the Young Turks came to power in 1908. These four pillars constituted the ideological bases for the Young Turks, which extended assistance to all organizations, unions, and journals that endorsed them. In its formative years, the TH was greatly influenced by the writings of popular nationalists (Akçura, Ağaoğlu, Gökalp, Gündüz, Hikmet, etc.). The journal "Türk Yurdu" became the official mouthpiece of TH, a platform for expressing the nationalist worldviews of radical intellectuals.[69] Before the outbreak of WWI, there were twenty-eight branches of TH in different cities of the Empire. By 1930, the number of branches had increased only slightly.[70] Before and during the war, TH organized conferences, meetings, and cultural events, published books, and brochures and used every opportunity to share its interpretation of the three-tier ideological structure.[71] However, the Kemalist nationalist movement provided new ideas, opportunities, and a new philosophical framework, which was contrary to the Hearths' basic ideological construct.[72] They consequently failed to stick to one well-defined ideological framework. After the establishment of the Republic, they lost touch with the new interpretation of Kemalist nationalism, which did not openly endorse the Young Turks' convictions of Pan-Turanism, Pan-Turkism, and Pan-Islamism. Initially, the Kemalist elite was also not very much positively inclined towards them. However, in 1924, TH were officially reopened, since the RPP sought to use it to spread its version of nationalism. Kazimirskij reported that TH branches in Eastern Thrace were actively engaged in the everyday life of people. It had branches in the region's small towns and was led by the head of the local police. He claimed that TH served as a platform for educating the local population, offering lectures on patriotism, Pan-Turkism, history, nationalism, and literature.[73] This case indicates that TH continued to play an important role for the newly established republican regime; however, as the list of subjects illustrates, the RPP did not have effective control over the nature of its activities.

In 1927, TH adopted new by-laws that defined the aim of the organization: "… to strengthen the national consciousness and develop culture, hygiene, and national economy." Article 3 underlines TH's affiliation and endorsement of the RPP policy: "Hearths, having the ideal of the Republic, nationalism, new civilization, and democracy, are in compliance with the RPP policies in implementing these ideals. In scientific, cultural and social spheres they struggle for the popularization of these objectives."[74] Despite efforts to enjoy the RPP's support, TH failed to secure full assistance and consequently was not successful in reaching out to the wider public. It was not a mass organization, since its branches were mainly in large cities with no or small representation in rural areas, where 80% of the population resided. The Kemalist elite had different plans, and TH was obviously not part of them.

On April 10, 1931, TH was finally disbanded, its property was transferred to the RPP, and a decision was made to establish People's Houses. Atatürk's establishment of People's Houses elicited several interpretations. In 1948, Tanrıöver, former leader of TH, accused Atatürk of having feared the TH as a possible source of opposition.[75] Others claimed the closure was the result of "a stream of complaints flowing from the Soviet embassy,"[76] which viewed with alarm the "spread of Turkish national conscience beyond borders into their own country."[77] The closure of the TH had political and ideological sources, too. On the other hand, since 1927, the RPP had been slowly consolidating its ideological base and needed a more reliable partner. The new organization was supposed to serve as the RPP's proxy in remote areas of Turkey. Both Lüfti and Feridov agreed that despite the fact the RPP was the only legal and, besides, the ruling party, it was not a mass party.[78] Feridov sees the RPP more as a "system of political clubs," which were run by "special inspectors appointed by the centre and consisting of the administrative and military elite and more active parts of the local bourgeoisie and intelligentsia."[79] He noted that the real influence on the masses was sought through numerous societies and public and professional organizations, the "Turkish Hearths" the most prominent among them. He also pointed out that sometimes it was difficult to observe "where 'Turkish Hearths' ends and the party starts and vice versa."[80] Until 1931, it remained a party of city dwellers with a limited presence in the periphery.

The introduction of a new party program at the 1931 Congress was a result of long deliberations as it aimed to change the process of political and social engineering. The party leadership was well aware that a revitalized RPP and possession of a party program were not enough to circumvent political and social upheavals. At this juncture, the RPP could not reach its objectives with an organization inherited from the Ottoman past. The new organization was to be created anew, drawing on the new objectives of the Kemalist revolution. Another reason for the adoption of the program was possibly connected to the centre's desire to control the periphery. In this regard, Mardin claims: "... between 1923 and 1946 the periphery – in the sense of the provinces – was suspect and because it was considered an area of potential disaffection, the political centre kept it under close observation."[81] This observation explains another dimension of the ideological expansion of Kemalism in the 1930s.

On February 19, 1932, in various cities throughout Turkey, fourteen People's Houses went into operation. For the next few years, the number of People's Houses increased rapidly, reaching 373, which was two times more than TH in its twenty years of existence.[82] In 1950, there were almost 500 People's Houses in Turkey, and one was operating in London. People's Houses had nine sections: Language and Literature, Fine Arts, Drama, Sports, Social Assistance, Classes and Courses, Library and Publications, Village Development, and History and Museum.[83]

Although they aimed at being independent entities, TH immediately became an integral part of the RPP. The party leadership closely followed the activities of the Houses, and during each congress a report was prepared and delivered about their achievements. People's Houses paid particular attention to RPP party principles and fundamentals. For instance, they had underlined the concept of populism to signify "national unity."[84] Thus, the People's Houses served their initial purposes, since they were able to become the agency to inculcate Kemalist visions of progress and modernization as well as educating the masses. Already in 1935, during the opening of the Fourth Congress of the RPP, Atatürk noted: "Because of the People's Houses, our party became accessible to all our compatriots, it implemented social and cultural revolution in the country."[85] Article 48 of the RPP's 1935 program stated: "The State shall protect with all possible means the People's Houses which are working to this end."[86]

EVERYDAY KEMALISM: SYMBOLISM AND IMAGES

Stephen Salamone identifies four distinctive approaches to the uniform incorporation of official Turkish identity: (a) secularization of Turkish society through autocratic paternalism; (b) bureaucratic coercion; (c) educational elitism; and (d) strong principled resistance to the incorporation of religious or ethnic groups.[87] Sidney Verba argues that in addition to participating as physical and legal members in any political system, psychological membership is no less important because it "legitimizes the activities of national elites and makes it possible for them to mobilize the commitment and support of their followers."[88] This suggests that the effectiveness of Kemalism, its capacity for activation and for arousing and unleashing energies, did not reside in the ideological mentality as such, but required "ideological heating," as well as emotional involvement and ideological passion.[89]

Other studies have advised against relying on the abstract concept of ideology, favouring a pragmatic look at Kemalism. Gary Alan Fine and Kent Sandstrom have proposed considering ideology as a combination of interactions, emotions, symbols, affections, and behaviour.[90] That approach implies that people connect seemingly abstract ideologies to their everyday interests by following simple metaphors and images attached to them. Thus, individuals become part of the operationalization of ideologies by creating shared experiences and expectations.[91] Understanding the process by which an ideological concept becomes a functional tool requires considering the means through which state and society interact, accommodate, and internalize ideological constructs. Therefore, considering the techniques proposed by Fine and Sandstrom helps us look at the channels of interactionism between the producers of Kemalism and its consumers. Some studies, which have examined ideological constructs and applications, have neglected the fact that there are real people on each side of the ideology producing-consuming circle. Dahl claims that ideologies are located in individual persons, as thoughts and attitudes expressed in words and actions. They also exist in innumerable individual varieties, more or less fragmented and idiosyncratic.[92]

The other analytical tool that may help to explain why Kemalists popularized RPP principles through symbols and images has to do with the concept of security. Although widely used in political science, the term also has analytical value for historical research. In security studies, there are two views of security dimensions: wideners and traditionalists.[93] Turkey's political challenges, irrespective of their proportions, have been dealt through the lens of security concepts defined by the Kemalist elite. The concept of "ideological security" can serve as an alternative framework for the security discourse. Over time, the securitization of sacred domains of the state's structures became a prevailing and dominant consolidating device. The investigation of these authoritative realms, which helped to preserve and safeguard Kemalism, constitutes a pivotal part of this study. Securitization theory is espoused as a methodological and analytical dimension for uncovering the substance of Kemalist discourse. In some cases, securitization has become institutionalized, contrary to ad hoc cases. "Institutionalized" signifies cases where a particular threat is persistent or recurrent, eliciting an institutionalized response and sense of urgency.

There are two other important dimensions of security discourse: the threshold and significance/size of a given threat. Different societies have different thresholds for threat definitions, and the significance and size are essentially an intersubjective matter. Buzan et al argue "... individuals cannot determine alone whether an issue is a security issue or not. Hence, securitization is intersubjective and socially constructed."[94] This approach downplays the importance of dominative securitization theory, which argues in favour of a hegemonic insistence on the security agenda and does not need the consent of an audience. The same authors also state: "security should be seen as negative, as a failure to deal with issues as normal politics. Ideally, politics should be able to unfold according to routine procedures without this extraordinary elevation of specific 'threats' to a pre-political immediacy."[95] The application of these analytical tools may help us construct the framework or matrix that rationalizes the underlying reasons for the proliferation of Kemalist imagery and symbolism in Turkey.

Already in the mid-1930s visitors to Turkey observed an omnipresent reverence for Kemal and his deeds. Hanioğlu even argues that Mustafa

Kemal, albeit unintentionally, became a prophet and founder of a new religion based on the twin pillars of its preaching: scientism and nationalism.[96] This insight resonates with the dominant paradigm of the era, expressed by a school inspector to Grace Ellison, who visited Turkey: "Our prophet is our Ghazi: we have finished with that *individual* from Arabia. The religion of Mohamet was all very well for Arabia, but it was not for us."[97] Rum Landau, an Englishman who visited Turkey between 1936 and 1938, viewed Kemalism as "a reformation of Islam."[98] There were also other instances when close associates of Atatürk contributed to the creation of the personality cult of Atatürk. The founder of "Kadro,"[99] Karaosmanoğlu, who was a close supporter of Kemal and his cause, expressed his loyalty to Atatürk in the following way: "Dear Atatürk, it is a great honour to be even a simple pawn in your hands."[100] Former PM Celal Bayar stated in 1950, "To love Atatürk is a national cult."[101]

Kemalism largely utilized schools for disseminating, maintaining, and developing its legitimacy and a new political identity for republican youth. The first population census of October 28, 1927, revealed that 86% of the male and 95% of the female population were illiterate. By February 1929, there were over one million people studying in schools, including a few thousand women. While education became compulsory, the results were not satisfactory, since out of one million students, only 412,000 obtained certificates of completion of alphabet courses.[102]

A statement made by the Minister of Education in 1929 reveals the main features of Kemal's drive to educate the masses:

> ... To learn to read in Turkish formerly required five years; now with the Latin characters, six months are sufficient. For good administration and progress, a nation must be literate. In our country, there are regions composed of twelve villages where not a single person could be found who could understand a governmental decree or information about better ploughing or childhood diseases. Today ... in these schools 441,000 students learn history and geography, they know where Paris and New York are...[103]

Both the 1931 and 1935 party programs stressed the importance of national education. As Childress succinctly put it: "the purpose of the republican government was to shape the society rather than to reflect it." She refers to the case of Zekiye Süleyman, a Turkish woman who—funded by the Ministry of Education—studied at Smith College in the US and completed a Master's thesis on Turkish education in 1934. Süleyman observed that Atatürk and his followers advocated the centralization of the educational system because they feared that in the hands of local administrators, opportunities and quality of education would differ greatly among geographical locations.[104] The Kemalists consciously institutionalized their ideology as hegemonic at all levels of the education system, including the universities and the People's Houses. The 1931 program places extraordinary importance on the cultivation of the national citizenship perception.[105] The 1935 the RPP program goes even further, stressing the importance of a "clean ethics," "a high love of Fatherland and Revolution," "sacrifice[ing] everything in order to fulfil this task," and "strict discipline."[106] In general, by the end of the 1930s, it was taken for granted that educational policy was on the right track and showed progress, but the task was so great that almost two-thirds of Turkish children remained without elementary schooling. Although the law made education compulsory, there were not enough schools to meet growing demand.

Türker Alkan examined depictions of the Basic Principles of the Kemalist Revolution, Kemalism, Turkism, and Atatürk (henceforth, BPKR) in primary schoolbooks from 1924 and 1969. The BPKR included twelve categories: secularism, nationalism, populism, revolutionism, étatism, republicanism, purification of the Turkish language, changes in men's and women's dress, changes in calendar and time zone, change of alphabet, women's rights, and changes in education. He found, contrary to expectations, that "Atatürk" was used more in the multiparty period, while the principles of Atatürk were emphasized less. It is noteworthy that while the BPKR started to decline in the period of the DP, Atatürk as a person gained the highest score.[107] In the İnönü period, attempts at political socialization became more systemized and internally consistent in the textbooks, while revolutionary principles and concepts were defined more clearly. Some tendencies of the previous era were gone, and there was less and less criticism directed towards social, political, and economic life. Alkan further argues that BPKR reached its peak in 1949 and experienced a sharp decline thereafter.[108]

The Kemalist paradigm of development relied heavily on symbols. All political ideologies and systems of thought engage in symbolic communication. However, symbolic components of Kemalism in the late 1920s and 1930s had distinctive features reminiscent of single-party regimes of the era. Friedrich and Brzezinski contend that symbols are important for orientation and they refer to Charles Merriam who urges limiting the meaning of symbols to meta-rational signs (memorial days and monuments, songs, flags, decorations and uniforms, ceremonials and rituals, mass demonstrations and parades, and ceremonialism).[109] All these meta-rational signs were/are ubiquitous in Turkey, and some are examined below.

Pierre Bourdieu's concept of "symbolic violence" is helpful to comprehend the essence of Atatürk's cult. The new Republic experimented with a variety of symbols, some successful and some not, which represented principles, events, and personalities important to the state. The cultural, political, ideological, and intellectual hegemony of Kemalism was achieved through various practices that captured the entire spectrum of political and social life. Already in 1924, the year after the establishment of the Republic, the first stamps with Mustafa Kemal's image were issued. In 1927, banknotes were printed with his portrait.[110] Seven years later, in 1931, some twenty-two stamps were issued bearing his portrait.[111] In 1926, Mustafa Kemal's first statue was erected in Istanbul, which was followed by hundreds of monuments, sculptures, busts, and masks presenting him as a saviour and devout soldier of Turkey. These were placed in central squares, parks, public institutions, schools, and classrooms. In 1953, after nine years of work, the construction of Atatürk's mausoleum at Anıtkabir in Ankara was completed. On November 10, 1953, on the fifteenth anniversary of his death, Atatürk's coffin was transferred from the Ethnographic Museum in Ankara, which served as a temporary tomb since his death in 1938, to the newly completed mausoleum.[112] This venue became an important symbolic destination for state bureaucrats during anniversaries of Atatürk's death and part of state protocol. Later, in times of crisis, as described by Mustafa Akyol, Kemalists and followers of Kemal Atatürk used this space to gather and pledge their dedication to the cause of the founder of the Turkish Republic.

The walls of the public buildings and offices were embellished with his famous quotations. Buildings he visited and rooms he stayed in were turned into museums. Lilo Linke, a German who travelled to Turkey in 1935 and whose valuable insights are not widely shared among scholars, provided a succinct description of Atatürk's cult: "There is not a room and hardly a private house in Turkey without a picture of the Ghazi. I found it later even in remote cottages high up in the mountains, in cottages which were almost bare of furniture so that the cheap print completely dominated the room."[113] Well aware of the German experience with rising National Socialism and certain parallels to "Hitlerism," she warned: "I understood the reason – they needed a symbol around which they could rally the nation in its struggle for modernization – but I knew too well the excesses to which such attempts might lead."[114]

While discussing the importance of Atatürk's image in contemporary Turkey, Melih Aşık opined that in past decades, to have the portrait of Atatürk was to have a secular passport.[115] In an interview conducted by this author, Professor Cüneyt Akalın was no less descriptive: "Kemal is everywhere in Turkey... Kemal is unfortunately like a saint, and just as other saints, he does not harm anyone, like the ones in Christianity. They don't do any good or bad things."[116] Walter Denny asserts that there is scarcely a major event in Atatürk's life without a photograph to commemorate it. Photographic images such as Atatürk asleep on the snow, on horseback, or chalk in hand, writing the Latin alphabet formed a set of traditional images of the President of the Republic in which he embodies his extraordinary reforms.[117] Özyürek's comprehensive account of proliferation, transformation, and accommodation of Atatürk's images in the 1990s provides interesting insights into continuities in Atatürk's public representations.[118]

Speaking of Atatürk's images, Gilman noted in 1939: "Atatürk's photographs mainly showed him in evening dress, immaculate, handsome in a Mephistophelian way. While he lived he was an idol already, his bust or photograph was in every shop and almost every home. His statues were always overhead. Like the Russians with their Lenin and unlike Americans with their Washington, the Turks did not wait for Atatürk's death for the enshrinement."[119] Unlike Italian, German, and Soviet leaders, he rejected the military uniform, wore formal dress to show Westerners his elegance, sophistication, and learning, while setting an example for close associates and the whole nation. Many pictures of Atatürk overemphasize the blueness of his eyes and, in pictures from his youth, his blond hair. In Atatürk's time, these physical attributes were considered part of the overall image of Turks as European (light complexioned, with blond hair, and blue eyes) and not Middle Eastern (olive complexioned, with dark hair and eyes). Thus, in the early decades of the Republic, Atatürk's image was used as a model of Turkish physiognomy. The same story characterized Atatürk's life, which became more legendary as the years progressed, and was cited as a model of intelligence and perseverance.[120] Akşin claims that Atatürk is the symbol of the Republic and its revolution because he is the complete success story. He goes on: "whilst the French Revolution has its symbol the motto 'liberty-equality-fraternity,' Atatürk is himself a symbol."[121]

His name was used with superlatives to create a quasi-religious atmosphere: "Eternal chief" (*Ebedi Şef*); "Grand" (*Büyük*); "Our Forefather" (*Bizim Atam*); "Genius" (*Dahi*); "Peerless" (*Eşsiz*); "Saviour" (*Haláskar*); "Deliverer" (*Münci*); "Great" (*Ulu*); "Creator" (*Yaratıcı*); "Exalted" (*Yüce*); and "Wonder of Humankind" (*Beşeriyet Harikasi*).[122] One remarkable instance of the symbolic presence of Kemal's personality was the oath ceremony at primary schools, which was introduced in 1933 by a Board of Education and Instruction decree. Written by the Minister of Education, Reşid Galib, between 1932 and 1933, the Pledge (*Andımız*) of Turkish children to the nation and Mustafa Kemal was to remind students of their unitary national identity:

> I am a Turk. I am honest. I work hard. I have a principle – to protect my juniors, to respect my seniors, to love my country and my nation more than myself. I have an ideal – to rise and go forward. [should this be a new paragraph?] Great Atatürk! I swear to march without stopping on the road you have opened, to the end you have chosen. May my existence be a gift to the common existence of the Turks. Happy is the one who calls himself/herself a Turk.[123]

Children and adolescents were required to attend a number of routine ceremonies at schools (singing the National Anthem—*Istiklal Marşı*, reciting the Pledge, and the raising and lowering of the flag). The lyrics of the National Anthem and the "Address to the Youth" not only hung in every classroom next to Mustafa Kemal's portrait but were also included in textbooks from elementary through high school.[124] *Arev*, an Armenian newspaper published in Egypt, cited a French correspondent in Istanbul:

> Turkey's entire future depends on one man and this is the first challenge. That is why, there is not a single Turk, be it an opponent or critical of him, who does not wish a long-life to the president of the Republic. Because they understand very well that in case he dies, without finishing his job, not only his reforms will be threatened, but his close circle will not be able to secure the same level of prestige. His achievements will fall back and the story with Alexander's general will be repeated.[125]

A few studies conducted in Turkey in the 1960s shed light on political and intellectual elites who believed that Atatürk dominated the list of heroes and symbols of Turkish society in the republican era. In 1962, Frey launched a public survey in Turkey to assess how household members viewed Atatürk. The methodology and results were articulated in two articles published in 1963 and 1968.[126] Thirty-six per cent of village husbands named Atatürk as the person they admired most and as a symbol of national awareness. But only 17% of their wives had similar attitudes towards Atatürk. City couples did a little bit better—51% of husbands and 22% of wives admired him as a national symbol.[127] Another survey was carried out by Ozankaya in the late 1960s in four villages in Turkey—two in the northeast and two in the centre. According to the survey results, between 30% and 40% of men chose Atatürk as their most preferred person, with preferences for other national Turkish leaders ranging between 40% and 55%, while most of the women did not express their preference.[128]

There was a marked increase in the number of public monuments to Atatürk after 1969—a sign of the importance that the new regime attached to Atatürk's image to underscore the significance of his political, social, and cultural reforms.[129] However, amid the flourishing of identity politics in the 1960s, Atatürk's image became too narrow a symbol, contends Yörük. The flag and national anthem replaced Atatürk's likeness as the primary symbols of Turkish identity, widening the conception of Turkishness to include nationalist and Islamist connotations. New images and discursive markers indicated a shift in Turkey's political community, which began drawing the boundaries of Turkish identity by emphasizing its differences from Kurdish separatism and "Western imperialism." These changes provided Turks with a new subjectivity that was based on identification with a community that embraced a new concept of Turkishness.[130]

This chapter focused on policies that Turkish political and intellectual elites pursued in the 1930s in order to bolster the popularization and securitization of Kemalism. Some of these initiatives were radical, both in essence and objectives, while others were superficial without a solid intellectual base. The government took advantage of existing (and inherited) human and institutional resources and utilized them to advance and "secure" the Kemalist cause. Those efforts took place alongside the growing omnipresence of secular-republican symbols, which instilled ideas about and visions of a new Turkey in the minds of the people.

NOTES

1. Fatma Müğe Göçek. 1996. *Rise of the Bourgeoisie, Demise of Empire: Ottoman Westernization and Social Change*. Oxford: Oxford University Press, 117–118.
2. Ibid.
3. Jacob Landau. 2004. *Exploring Ottoman and Turkish History*. London: Hurst & Company, 23–24.
4. Berkes. 1998. *The Development of Secularism in Turkey*. New York: Routledge, 292.
5. Ibid.
6. Şükrü Hanioğlu. 2006. "Turkism and the Young Turks, 1889–1908." In *Turkey Beyond Nationalism: Towards Post-Nationalist Identities*, edited by Hans-Lukas Kieser. London: I.B. Tauris, 10–11; Hans-Lukas Kieser. 2008. *Türklüğe Ihtida: 1830–1939 İsviçre'sinde Yeni Türkiye'nin Öncüleri*. Istanbul: İletişim.
7. Hans-Lukas Kieser. 2011. "World War and World Revolution: Alexander Helphand-Parvus in Germany and Turkey." *Kritika: Explorations in Russia and Eurasian History* 12 (2): 401; Hilmi Ozan Ozavci. 2015. *Intellectual Origins of the Republic: Ahmet Ağaoğlu and the Genealogy of Liberalism in Turkey*. Leiden: Brill; Hans-Lukas Kieser. 2011. "From 'Patiotism' to Mass Murder: Dr. Mehmed Reşid (1873–1919)." In *A Question of Genocide: Armenians and Turks at the End of the Ottoman Empire*, edited by Ronald Suny, Fatma Müğe Göçek, and Norman M. Naimark. Oxford: Oxford University Press, 127.
8. Yusuf Akçura. 1976. *Üç Tarz-I Siyaset*. Ankara: Türk Tarihi Kurumu Basimevi; Ahmet Ağaoğlu. 1927. *Üç Medeniyet*. Ankara: Türk Oçakları Merkez Heyeti Matbaası.
9. Ozavci (2015, 80).
10. Holly Shissler. 2002. *Between Two Empires: Ahmet Ağaoğlu and the New Turkey*. London: I.B. Tauris, 184.
11. Hanioglu (2001, 296).
12. Ozavci (2015, 88–89).
13. Hanioğlu (2001, 25–29).
14. Kevorkian (2011, 194).
15. Norman Naimark. 2011. "Preface." In *A Question of Genocide: Armenians and Turks at the End of the Ottoman Empire*, edited by R. G. Suny, F. M. Gocek, and N. Naimark. Oxford: Oxford University Press, xiii–xix.
16. Şükrü Hanioğlu. 2001. *Preparation for a Revolution: The Young Turks, 1902–1908*. Oxford: Oxford University Press, 289.
17. Hanioğlu (2001, 289–290, 294).

18. Mustafa Gündüz. 2009. "Sociocultural Origins of Turkish Educational Reforms and Ideological Origins of Late Ottoman Intellectuals (1908–1930)." *History of Education* 38 (2): 197.

19. Erik-Jan Zürcher. 2005. "Ottoman Sources of Kemalist Thought." In *Late Ottoman Society: The Intellectual Legacy*, edited by Elisabeth Özdalga. London: Curzon, 16, 18.

20. Kohn (1943, 254).

21. Hanioğlu (2001, 160–198).

22. Enver Ziya Karal. 1997. "The Principles of Kemalism, 2nd ed." In *Atatürk: Founder of a Modern State*, edited by Ergun Özbudun. London: Hurst & Company, 11–36; Robert Spencer. 1958. "Cultural Process and Intellectual Current: Durkheim and Atatürk." *American Anthropologist* 60 (4): 640–657.

23. On Ziya Gökalp see Taha Parla. 1985. *The Social and Political Thought of Ziya Gökalp 1876–1924.* Leiden: E.J. Brill; Uriel Heyd. 1950. *Foundations of Turkish Nationalism: The Life and Teachings of Ziya Gökalp.* London: Luzac; Markus Dressler. 2015. "Rereading Ziya Gökalp: Secularism and Reform of the Islamic State in the Late Young Turk Period." *International Journal of Middle East Studies* 47 (3): 511–531.

24. Parla (1985).

25. Parla (1985, 7).

26. Born in Shushi in 1868, until WWI he used a name of Russian origin—Aghayeff or Agaiev.

27. Ozavci (2015, 11).

28. Ozavci (2015, 38).

29. Ozavci (2015, 24, 46–53).

30. Ozavci (2015, 78–79).

31. Ozavci (2015, 80).

32. Raymond Kevorkian. 2011. *The Armenian Genocie: A Complete History.* London: I.B. Tauris, 194.

33. Ibid., 194.

34. Shissler (2002, 183–184).

35. Frank Creel. 1980. "Abdullah Cevdet: A Father of Kemalism." *Journal of Turkish Studies* 4 (9): 9.

36. Ibid., 10–17.

37. Şükrü Hanioğlu. 1997. "Garbcılar: Their Attitudes Toward Religion and their Impact on the Official Ideology of the Turkish Republic." *Studia Islamica* 86 (2): 135.

38. Hanioğlu (1997, 141–142).

39. Recep [Peker]. 1931. *RPP Programinin Izahi* [Explanation of RPP's program]. Ankara: Ulus Matbaasi, 3–16, cited in Çağaptay (2003, 66).

40. İnan Süleyman. 2007. "The First 'History of the Turkish Revolution' Lectures and Courses in Turkish Universities (1934–1942)." *Middle Eastern Studies* 43 (4): 593–609.
41. Süleyman (2007, 607).
42. Süleyman (2007, 593).
43. Webster (1939, 184).
44. "10 ans de République: Résumé du guide, publié, par le Parti Républicain du Peuple, à l'occasion du X. anniversaire de la République: 1923–1933." 1933. Ankara.
45. Hasan Cemil Çambel. 1939. T.T.K. Belleten, Cilt 3. 10. 272. cited in *Türkiye Cumhuriyeti Kültür ve Turizm Bakanlığı,* http://www.kultur. gov.tr/TR,25417/tarih.html.
46. Kevorkian (2011, 193).
47. Childress (2001, 163).
48. Çağaptay (2002, 69–70) and Ersanlı (2002, 340).
49. Ersanlı (2002, 340).
50. Anthony Smith. 1997. "The 'Golden Age' and National Renewal." In *Myths and Nationhood,* edited by Geoffrey Hosking and George Schöpflin. London: Hurst, 36.
51. Anush Hovhannisyan. 1989. "Turkiajum «Nor Patmakan Kontseptsiayi» mshakman hartsi shurdj, XX d. 30-akan tt." [About the Elaboration of the 'New Historical Concepts' in Turkey, 1930s.] *Merstavor yev Mijin Arevelki Yerkrner yev Zhoghovurdner* [States and Nations of the Middle and Near East], 15: 5–13.
52. İsmail Beşikci. 1977. *Türk Tarih Tezi ve Kürt Sorunu* [Turkish Historical Thesis and the Kurdish Question]. İstanbul: Doz, 187–192, 219–237.
53. J. H. Walton. 1932. Was Adam a Turk? Angora's Historians' New Claim. *The Daily Telegraph,* Friday, September 9, 1932.
54. Ibid.
55. Kazimirskij (1927, 188).
56. Senem Aslan. 2007. ""Citizen, Speak Turkish!': A Nation in the Making." *Nationalism and Ethnic Politics* 13 (2): 251.
57. Aslan (2007, 246, 268).
58. Aslan (2007, 246).
59. Zürcher (1993, 189).
60. Lewis (1999); Soner Çağaptay. 2002. "Reconfiguring the Turkish Nation in the 1930s." *Nationalism and Ethnic Politics* (8) 2: 67–82.
61. Walton (1932).
62. Tveritinova (1953, 80, 85).
63. Ibid., 80.
64. Anatolij Miller. 1963. "Formirovanije Politicheskikh Vzglyadov Kemal'a Ataturka (K 25-letiju so dnja ego smeri)." [Formation of Political Ideas

of Kemal Atatürk (25th year Since His Death).] *Azija I Afrika Segodnya* [*Asia and Africa Today*] (5): 65.

65. Marr's visit to the Mediterranean was described in his work "About the linguistic visit to the Eastern Mediterranean" (1934). Gordlevskij briefly discussed Marr's visit to Turkey in his 1942 note which was published in 1968. See Gordlevskij (1968, 356–399).

66. Aleksander Samojlovich. 1936. "Stambul'skie vpechetlenija." [Impressions from Istanbul.] *Zvezda* 12: 167.

67. Sefa Şimşek. 2005. "'People's Houses' as a Nationwide Project for Ideological Mobilization in Early Republican Turkey." *Turkish Studies* 6 (1): 71.

68. Aleksandr Kolesnikov. 1984. *Narodnye Doma v Obshhestvenno-Politicheskoj i Kul'turnoj Zhizni Tureckoj Respubliki* [People's Houses in the Socio-Political and Cultural Life of the Turkish Republic]. Moscow: Nauka, 58.

69. Esmeralda Gasanova. 1959. "K istorii zhurnala 'Tyurk Yurdu'." [On the History of the 'Türk Yurdu' Journal.] *Izvestija Akademii Nauk Azerbajdzhanskoj SSR, Serija Obshhestvennyh nauk* (6): 132–134.

70. Hamdullah Suphi Tanrıöver. 1931. *Dağyolu*, 2nd ed. Ankara, 85–104.

71. Kolesnikov (1984, 61–62).

72. Kemal Karpat. 1963. "The People's Houses in Turkey: Establishment and Growth." *Middle East Journal* 17 (1): 57.

73. Kazimirskij (1927, 187).

74. Kemal' Mustafa. 1929–1934. *Put' Novoj Turtsii.* tom 3 [Kemal—The Road of the New Turkey, vol. 3]. Moscow, 263.

75. *Hareket.* November 1948, 10.

76. Ilker Aytürk. 2011. "The Racist Critics of Atatürk and Kemalism: From the 1930s to the 1960s." *Journal of Contemporary History* 46 (2): 328.

77. *Türk Yurdu.* November 1954, 170, 331.

78. Lüfti. 1927. "Turtsija segodnya." [Turkey Today.] *Za Partiju* [For the Party] ("Pravdi Vostoka") (4): 75; Feridov (1928, 29).

79. Feridov (1928, 29).

80. Ibid., 29.

81. Mardin (1973, 182).

82. Kolesnikov (1984, 79).

83. Karpat (1963, 60).

84. Kolesnikov (1984, 115).

85. Atatürk'ün Söylev ve Demeçleri (2006, 217).

86. C.H.P. Program (1935, 30).

87. Stephen Salamone. 1989. "The Dialectics of Turkish National Identity: Ethnic Boundary Maintenance and State Ideology." *East European Quarterly* 23 (2): 33–61.

88. Sidney Verba. 1965. "Conclusion: Comparative Political Culture." In *Political Culture and Political Development, Studies in Political Development*, edited by Lucian W. Pye and Sidney Verba. Princeton: Princeton University Press, 529.

89. Sartori (1969, 403).

90. Gary Alan Fine and Kent Sandstrom. 1993. "Ideology in Action: A Pragmatic Approach to a Contested Concept." *Sociological Theory* 11 (1): 21–38.

91. Ibid., 21.

92. Ottar Dahl. 1996. "The Historical Study of Ideologies." In *Societies Made Up of History: Essays in Historiography, Intelectual History, Professionalization, Historical Social Theory and Proto-Industrialization*, edited by Björk Ragnar, Thorsten Nybom, and Rolf Torstendahl. Stockholm and Edsbruk: Akademitryck AB, 26.

93. Barry Buzan, Ole Waever, and Jaap de Wilde. 1998. *Security: A New Framework for Analysis*. Boulder: Lynne Rienner.

94. Buzan et al. (1998, 31).

95. Buzan et al. (1998, 29).

96. Hanioğlu (2011, 192–193).

97. Grace Ellison. Turkey To-Day. 187 cited in Hanioğlu (2011, 192–193).

98. Rum Landau. 1938. *Search for Tomorrow: The Things which Are and the Things Which Shall Be Hereafter*. London: Nicolson and Watson Limited, 275.

99. The periodical "Kadro" (*cadre*) was aimed to prepared revolutionary cadres for the Kemalist cause.

100. Karaosmanoglu (1978, 42).

101. Celal Bayar'in Söylev ve Demeçleri, 1, 1921–1938. 1955. *Ekonomik Konulara Dair*, edited by Özel Şahingiray. Ankara: Doğuş Ltd. Ortaklığı, 241.

102. Kross (1930, 65).

103. Caleb Gates. 1931. "The New Turkey under Mustafa Kemal." *Current History* 34 (3): 393.

104. Childress (2001, 32).

105. Parla and Davison (2004, 122).

106. C.H.P. Program (1935).

107. Alkan (1980, 39–41).

108. Ibid., 43–46.

109. Charles Merriam. 1935. *Political Power, Its Composition and Maintenance*. New York. McGraw-Hill Book Company, 104–105 cited in Friedrich and Brzezinski, "Totalitarian Dictatorship and Autocracy," 103.

110. Hanioglu (2011, 186–187).

111. Walter (1982, 3).
112. For a detailed account on the history, architecture, and symbolism of the Anıtkabir mausoleum see Christopher Samuel Wilson. 2007. "Remembering and Forgetting in the Funerary Architecture of Mustafa Kemal Atatürk: The Construction and Maintenance of National Memory." Unpublished dissertation, Middle East Technical University, Ankara; Christopher Samuel Wilson. 2011. "The Persistence of the Turkish Nation in the Mausoleum of Mustafa Kemal Atatürk." In *Nationalism in a Global Era: The Persistence of Nations*, edited by Mitchell Young, Andreas Sturm, and Eric Zuelow. London: Routledge Press, 93–114.
113. Linke (1937, 19).
114. Ibid., 220, 319.
115. Interview with Melih Aşık, May 27, 2005.
116. Interview with Cüneyt Akalın, May 16, 2005.
117. Walter Denny. 1982. "Atatürk and Political Art in Turkey." *Bulletin of the Turkish Studies Association* (Turkish Studies Association) 6 (2): 18.
118. Esra Özyürek. 2005. "Miniaturizing Atatürk Privatization of State Imagery and Ideology in Turkey." *American Ethnologist* 31 (3): 374.
119. Gilman (1939, 388).
120. Childress (2001, 225).
121. Sina Akşin. 1999. "The Nature of the Kemalist Revolution." In *The Turkish Republic at Seventy-Five Years*, edited by David Shanland. Huntingdon: The Eothen Press, 14–28, 15.
122. Hanioğlu (2011, 187).
123. This oath-taking ceremony lasted until 2013 when it was removed as a result of the "Democratization package" introduced by the government of the JDP.
124. Hale Yılmaz. 2013. *Becoming Turkish: Nationalist Reforms and Cultural Negotiations in Early Republican Turkey, 1923–1945*. New York: Syracure University Press, 202–203.
125. "*Turkey's Future.*" 1928. "Arev." *Journal Armenien*, Wednesday, April 25, 3.
126. Frederick Frey. 1963. "Surveying Peasant Attitudes in Turkey." *Public Opinion Quarterly* 27 (3): 335–355; Frederick Frey. 1968. "Socialization of National Identification of Among Turkish Peasants." *The Journal of Politics* 30 (4): 934–965.
127. Frey (1968, 942).
128. Özer Ozankaya. 1971. *Köyde Toplumsal yapi ve siyasal kultur; iki grup köyde yapılan karşılaştırmalı bir araştırma*. Ankara: Sevinç Matbaası, 191–192.

129. Gültekin Elibal. 1973. *Atatürk ve Resim-heykel.* İstanbul: Türkiye İş bankasi Kültür Yayınları, 121.
130. Zafer Yörük. 1997. "Turkish Identity from Genesis to the Day of Judgment." In *Politics and the Ends of Identity,* edited by Kathryn Dean. Vermont: Ashgate, 129.

REFERENCES

Alkan, Türker. 1980. "Turkey: Rise and Decline of Political Legitimacy in a Revolutionary Regime." *Journal of South Asian and Middle Eastern Studies* (4) 2: 37–48.

Aslan, Senem. 2007. "'Citizen, Speak Turkish!': A Nation in the Making." *Nationalism and Ethnic Politics* 13 (2): 245–272.

Buzan, Barry, Ole Waever, and Jaap de Wilde. 1998. *Security: A New Framework for Analysis.* Boulder: Lynne Rienner.

C.H.P. Programı. 1935. *Mayis.* Ankara: Ulus Basımevi.

Çağaptay, Soner. 2002. "Reconfiguring the Turkish Nation in the 1930s." *Nationalism and Ethnic Politics* 2 (8): 67–82.

———. 2003. "Crafting the Turkish Nation: Kemalism and Turkish Nationalism in the 1930s." Unpublished PhD dissertation, Yale University.

Childress, Faith J. 2001. "Republican Lessons: Education and the Making of Modern Turkey." Unpublished PhD dissertation, University of Utah.

Ersanlı, Büşra. 2002. "History Textbooks as Reflections of the Politicsl Self: Turkey (1930s and 1990s) and Uzbekistan (1990s)." *International Journal of Middle East Studies* 34 (2): 337–349.

Feridov, Ziya. 1928. "Nekotorie Voprosi Sovremennoj Turtsii." [Some Questions of Contemporary Turkey.] *Revolutsionnyi Vostok* (6): 24–41.

Frey, Frederick. 1968. "Socialization of National Identification of Among Turkish Peasants." *The Journal of Politics* 30 (4): 934–965.

Gilman, William. 1939. "Turkey Offers Her Own Ism." *The South Atlantic Quarterly* 38: 377–391.

Gordlevskij, Vladimir. 1968. "Izuchenije Turtsii v SSSR." [Research on Turkey in the USSR.] In *Izbrannije Sochinenie* [Selected Writings], edited by Vladimir Gordlevskij, vol. 4, 356–359. Moscow: Nauka.

Hanioğlu, Şükrü. 1997. "Garbcılar: Their Attitudes Toward Religion and Their Impact on the Official Ideology of the Turkish Republic." *Studia Islamica* 86 (2): 133–158.

———. 2001. *Preparation for a Revolution: The Young Turks, 1902–1908.* Oxford: Oxford University Press.

———. 2011. *Atatürk: An Intellectual Biography.* Princeton: Princeton University Press.

Karaosmanoğlu, Yakup Kadri. 1978. *Diplomat Ponevole: Vospominanija i nabljudenija [A diplomat against his will: Recollections and Observations]*. Moscow: Mezhdunarodnye Otnoshenija.

Karpat, Kemal. 1963. "The People's Houses in Turkey: Establishment and Growth." *Middle East Journal* 17 (1): 55–67.

Kazimirskij, K. 1927. "Sovremennaja Evropejskaja Turtsija." [Contemporary European Turkey.] *Novyj Vostok* (16–17): 178–189.

Kevorkian, Raymond. 2011. *The Armenian Genocide: A Complete History*. London: I.B. Tauris.

Kohn, Hans. 1943. *Revolutions and Dictatorship*, 3rd ed. Cambridge: Harvard University Printing Office.

Kolesnikov, Aleksandr. 1984. *Narodnye Doma v Obshhestvenno-politicheskoj i kul'turnoj zhizni Tureckoj Respubliki* [People's Houses in the Socio-Political and Cultural Life of the Turkish Republic]. Moscow: Nauka.

Kross, T. 1930. "Vnutrennee Polozhenie Turtsii." [The Domestic Situation in Turkey.] *Mezhdunarodnaja Zhizn'* (NKID) (7–8): 57–66.

Lewis, Geoffrey. 1999. *The Turkish Language Reform: A Catastrophic Success*. Oxford: Oxford University Press.

Linke, Lilo. 1937. *Allah Dethroned: A Journey Through Modern Turkey*. London: Constable & Co. Ltd.

Mardin, Şerif. 1973. "Centre-Periphery Relations: A Key to Turkish Politics?" *Daedalus: Journal of the American Academy of Arts and Sciences* 102 (1): 169–190.

Ozavci, Hilmi Ozan. 2015. *Intellectual Origins of the Republic: Ahmet Ağaoğlu and the Genealogy of Liberalism in Turkey*. Leiden: Brill.

Parla, Taha. 1985. *The Social and Political Thought of Ziya Gökalp, 1876–1924*. Leiden: Brill.

Parla, Taha, and Andrew Davison. 2004. *Corporatist Ideology in Kemalist Turkey: Progress or Order?* Syracuse: Syracuse University Press.

Sartori, Giovanni. 1969. "Politics, Ideology and Belief Systems." *The American Political Science Review* 63 (2): 398–411.

Shissler, Holly. 2002. *Between Two Empires: Ahmet Ağaoğlu and the New Turkey*. London: I.B. Tauris.

Süleyman, İnan. 2007. "The First 'History of the Turkish Revolution' Lectures and Courses in Turkish Universities (1934–1942)." *Middle Eastern Studies* 43 (4): 593–609.

Tveritinova, Anna. 1953. "Ot Natsional-Shovinizma k Natsional-Predatel'stvu." [From National-Chauvinism to National Treachery.] *Zvezda Vostoka* 8 (79): 70–87.

Walter, Denny. 1982. "Atatürk and Political Art in Turkey." *Bulletin of the Turkish Studies Association* (Turkish Studies Association) 6 (2): 17–24.

Walton, J. 1932. "Was Adam a Turk?: Angora's Historian's New Claim." *The Daily Telegraph*, September 9.

Webster, Donald E. 1939. *The Turkey of Atatürk*. Philadelphia: The American Academy of Political and Social Science.

Zürcher, Erik-Jan. 1993. *Turkey: A Modern History*. London: I.B. Tauris.

Transformation of Kemalism's Hegemony in the Post-Atatürk Era, 1940s–1950s

The period between 1938 and 1960 was critical for Kemalism and its supporters. WWII and post-war geopolitical challenges on the one hand and rising domestic problems on the other were significant factors for Kemalism as its supporters pushed it onto a course of constant adjustments. Kemalist principles and visions that were at the core of the policies of previous decades now entered the spotlight. A number of ideological beliefs and practices that were believed to be deeply entrenched came under widespread critical scrutiny. The policy of the Democrat Party in the 1950s significantly accelerated the process by allowing a clash between the rising tide of conservatism and the paradigm of Kemalist modernism to occur. The subject of this chapter is the discussion of these developments and their implications for Kemalist ideology.

KEMALISM WITHOUT MUSTAFA KEMAL

Atatürk died in office on November 10, 1938. Sometime before Atatürk's death, the names of a few possible candidates for the presidency were circulated: İsmet İnönü; Celal Bayar; Fevzi Çakmak; Tefvik Rüştü Aras; Şükrü Kaya; or Fethi Okyar. Çakmak and Okyar were not interested in running for the presidency. Besides, neither was a member of Parliament or the ruling RPP. Instead, Bayar's, and to a greater extent İnönü's, names were circulated prior to Atatürk's death. Both candidates emerged "from the inner sanctum of the system"[1] and had a deep

© The Author(s) 2019   95
V. Ter-Matevosyan, *Turkey, Kemalism and the Soviet Union,*
Modernity, Memory and Identity in South-East Europe,
https://doi.org/10.1007/978-3-319-97403-3_5

understanding of how it worked. Rumours held that Atatürk personally favoured Celal Bayar as a loyal politician and gifted economist. Two members of the Kemalist elite, Foreign Minister Tefvik Rüştü Aras and Minister of Interior Şükrü Kaya, who were opposed to İnönü, supported Bayar's candidacy. Yet Atatürk's death did not set off a succession struggle, as one might assume. External movements initiated a low-grade struggle to reinstitute former caliph Abdülmecid and/or Prince Sami, a nephew of the last sultan Vahdeddin. These rumours started to circulate around the early 1930s and continued as Atatürk's health deteriorated. Even though several Muslim Congresses (1924, 1926, 1931, and 1935) could not select a new caliph, Abdülmecid was convinced that the death of Atatürk might instigate internal strife among his associates, and that he could seize the opportunity to return to his former position. Appeals to British and American diplomats from Prince Sami and Abdülmecid for assistance to execute their plans were met with a cold response.[2]

On the morning of November 11, the parliamentary group of the RPP convened to vote on its nominee for president. Later that day, İnönü was elected the second President of the Republic. In his speech, he sought to dispel expectations that Atatürk's reforms would be revised and mentioned the importance of maintaining state security. Eleven days later, speaking to the foreign press, İnönü stated: "… the characteristic feature of Kemalism is continuity."[3] Others argued that since Atatürk made fundamental changes, İnönü, with his skills as an organizer and administrator, was "precisely the type of leader and example" that the Turkish people needed.[4] One month after Atatürk died, İnönü declared the deceased the "Eternal Chief" (*Ebedi Şef*) and himself the "National Chief" (*Milli Şef*).[5]

The succession of İnönü (particularly its peaceful nature) has not been duly examined in academic circles. Cemil Koçak describes it "as an unexpected and extraordinary development," because after being removed from power and virtually condemned to total solitude, İnönü's return deserves more study.[6] Kemalism had a few interpreters in the mid-1930s, and İnönü was not the strongest among them. In addition to these factors, Behlül Özkan notes that the fact that in less than thirty-six hours, İnönü was able to complete his plan to win the presidency and eliminate opponents "with stunning clockwork efficiency" attests to his total control over Parliament, key bureaucrats, and party members, while prime minister for twelve years.[7] What came after Atatürk's death proved that his close associates put aside differences and supported İnönü, thereby securing not only the deeds of the founder of the state, but also preserving their status and the entire system. That move proved to be justified since, unlike his associates, Atatürk died rather soon, while others kept significant positions as late as the 1970s. They played important roles by further consolidating Atatürk's visions and principles. The majority of them also remained loyal to his cause—another feature of Kemalism.

Some observers were sceptical of İnönü, arguing that it would be wrong to think of him as another Atatürk; he embodied only the voice of Kemalism. And yet, it was obvious that Atatürk's death did not automatically bring the death of his creature, Kemalism.[8] İnönü also made another surprising move by calling back into politics members of the "old political opposition" who had been forced out of politics in the mid-1920s and accused of misconduct, including plotting to kill Atatürk. İnönü imposed the condition, however, that there would be no arguments whatsoever regarding Atatürk. The old opposition was asked to abide by this condition, and most agreed and were given positions at the top levels of government.[9] İnönü also made sure that Aras and Kaya, who served in the government for a decade, did not have ministerial seats in the newly formed government of Bayar created in November 1938.[10]

The Fifth Congress[11] of the RPP took place between May 29 and June 3, 1939. At the first general Congress without Atatürk, there was a common belief that no major changes would be initiated in the party program. However, along with the general changes that İnönü initiated since assuming the presidency, the changes touched also the party program. The principles and fundamentals introduced in 1931 were brought back into the 1939 party program. This was seen as a departure from the language reform that had been fashionable only a few years ago. Another noteworthy innovation was presented in the program's introduction. While mentioning the party documents from previous decades (1927 and 1931 by-laws and declarations), the introduction skipped the 1935 party program, which was the peak of the Atatürk era. No less important was the fact that this introduction did not mention Kemalism (*Kemalizm*) or Kamâlism (*Kamâlizm*) as the name for party principles, as had been the case in the 1935 program. Instead, rather confusingly, this program introduced a general concept: "the path of Kemalism" ("*Kemalizm yolu*"), with "Kemalism" in brackets.[12] Furthermore, the concept "Kemalism" (*Kemalizm*) stood in the margins of the text, parallel to the concept "the path of Kemalism."

During this convention, an Independent Group (*Müstakil Grup*) of twenty-one deputies was formed under Ali Rana Tarhan's leadership within the assembly to play the role of a controlled loyal opposition and critic of the government. This recalled past experiences with independent parties in 1924 and 1930. Unlike previous cases, the Independent Group never posed a serious challenge and never played the role it aimed for until its elimination in 1946.[13] In the meantime, İnönü continued his administrative restructuring by separating the RPP's apparatus from the state, which was introduced in 1936 by Recep Peker who combined the positions of Secretary General of the RPP and Minister of Interior. In ideological matters, İnönü remained deeply devoted to the six principles of the party and supported a number of excessive and unpopular measures, such as the intensification of secularist policy (mosques were sometimes closed and used as storage rooms). As mentioned above, before the 1931 Congress, Mustafa Kemal was critical about the low level of infiltration of the RPP in society; it had limited membership and was concentrated in major cities. However, due to ideological and structural changes, as well as activities by the People's Houses, RPP membership significantly increased. In 1940, it was reported that nearly one in twelve citizens, or 1.3 million, belonged to the RPP.[14] This figure, most possibly presented during the 1939 Congress, was an indication of the RPP's transformation into a mass party.

In September 1939, the People's Houses movement was expanded into villages through the People's Rooms (*Halkodaları*), which were designed to be active in places the People's Houses had not reached. The number of Rooms grew from 141 in 1940 to 4332 in 1950. Between 1947 and 1950, only 278 Rooms were opened, although the initial goal was 10,000. The target number was not achieved because they came under attack after in 1945–1946, with the emergence of opposition parties.[15] Another remarkable event in 1939 was the commemoration of the centennial of the Tanzimat reforms,[16] which contrasted the Kemalist approach of the previous two decades, which neglected the Ottoman *ancien régime*.[17] However, after Kemal's death, the Ottoman past was reintroduced and popularized. İnönü's image temporarily replaced Atatürk's on banknotes and stamps.[18]

The outbreak of WWII presented Turkey with a major challenge. Even though Ankara tried to follow a policy of "active neutrality," in wartime, the country remained sympathetic to Germany and the German cause.[19] Therefore, Turkey's position was coined "pro-German neutrality"[20] or "active neutrality."[21] Until 1944, Germany kept its status as an important trading partner for Turkey, as the latter kept supplying it with chrome ore. Herbert Reginbogin, a scholar of WWII-Turkey, suggests that Turkish deliveries of chrome helped Germany prolong WWII. Without it, the loss of the Balkans could have ended the war in ten months.[22]

Turkey's main domestic problem was coping with wartime social and economic hardship. Poverty in rural Turkey, the country's rigid taxation system (especially the "Wealth Tax" (*Varlık Vergisi*)) imposed on non-Muslim citizens, the corruption of the bureaucracy, and lack of effective state management exacerbated the situation. The National Defence Law, which was adopted in December 1940 and remained in force until June 1, 1945, granted the government extensive rights, which the government misused on numerous occasions. From 1939 until his death on July 7, 1942, Refik Saydam, a military doctor, served as PM. He was followed by Şükrü Saracoğlu who stayed in office until August 1946. Recep Peker was back in government in August 1942 to assume the position of Minister of Interior for the second time in his political career.

The Sixth Congress of the RPP in June 1943 adopted the next party program.[23] It shared the same introduction as the 1939 program, except that no references were made to the 1927 and 1931 Congresses, by-laws, or declarations. The concept of "the path of Kemalism" and the parallel mentioning of "Kemalism" were also excluded. All the party principles and fundamentals remained the same as in the 1939 version, with one exception: it introduced the principle of *"yurttaş hakları"* (citizen rights) to replace the concept of "amme hukuku," present in the 1931 and 1939 editions of the program.[24]

ESTABLISHMENT OF THE MULTIPARTY SYSTEM

The post-war atmosphere pushed the state to focus on continuing reforms after a seven-year hiatus. However, the old guard, hardline Kemalists, who became deeply unpopular by the end of WWII, wanted to retain the single-party state, arguing that the multiparty system could jeopardize sustainable development and put the brakes on the reform program. In the atmosphere of widespread domestic discontent and resentment, as well as under the external pressure (the Soviet territorial demands in north-eastern Turkey and bases in the Bosphorus and the American political and military support), İnönü moved to initiate a process of political liberalization.[25] Several opposition parties emerged, the most prominent among them, the Democrat Party (DP) (January 7, 1946), which was headed by former key figures of the RPP: Celal Bayar, Refik Koraltan, Ali Fuat Köprülü, and Adnan Menderes. Prior to the establishment of the party, there was speculation concerning its name—a potential *Kemalist Democrat Party* was discussed. The DP's program was very much influenced by the Constitution, and hence the RPP's principles. Furthermore, Democrats adopted the six principles of Kemalism, although they interpreted them differently. In this regard, Feroz Ahmad argued: "[the DP] was virtually compelled to adopt these principles: not to have done so would have been a technical violation of the constitution and would certainly have provided ... the pretext to close down the new party."[26] Kemal Karpat wrote that during his interview with İnönü, rumours came up about İnönü having set conditions for allowing the establishment of an opposition party. İnönü responded to Karpat that he had told Celal Bayar that his group would be free to debate and challenge any principle of the ruling party except the Kemalist tenets of republicanism and secularism.[27] This indicates once again that the urgency for securing Atatürk's principles varied not only from period to period but also from principle to principle. Özkan sees more practical reasons for allowing opposition parties to operate. He argues that İnönü was eager to end Turkey's isolation in the international arena and "to rehabilitate his public image domestically and internationally, especially as American and British diplomats considered İnönü an authoritarian leader who had flirted with the Nazis during the war."[28]

On various occasions, İnönü reiterated the importance of the multiparty system. Despite his statement, the potential for political openings remained constrained, and a new system was developed in accordance with the Kemalist spirit, with its stress on the centrality of state power to achieve development and progress. Discourse remained limited to the best ways to interpret and enact the Kemalist program. Groups on the left and right that proposed alternatives to Kemalism were silenced, reflecting both the possibilities and limitations of the Cold War.

On July 21, 1946, parliamentary elections were held. Prior to portraying the results, it is noteworthy to observe the rhetoric of the election campaign, which became conventional in later decades. The opposition parties had always been reminded of critical times confronting Turkey, about the troubled constraints of foreign powers and the danger of irresponsible behaviour, which would eventually harm national unity.

Reflecting on actions by the opposition that allegedly harmed national security, İnönü asserted: "To this, I will give no chance. I am a revolutionary and a nationalist. We brought this state from nothing to the level it has today. We will not turn it over to a few plunderers. What we are doing is an experiment. If we are successful, that is great. If not, we will give up and continue a few more years under the old system. After that, we will try again."[29]

DP leaders, in turn, tried to maintain the image and personality of Atatürk by mentioning that they "go along the path designated by Atatürk in domestic and foreign policies."[30] The election results revealed that the DP had a long way to go to win the majority of votes; the party received only sixty-two seats out of 465, while the RPP gained 395 seats. After the elections, the parliament reelected İnönü as President of the Republic with 388 votes.

The 1947 Congress of the RPP

The RPP continued but was obviously in jeopardy. According to different media reports and general public opinion, the first parliamentary elections in the multiparty system were not conducted fairly, as the ruling party had used unrestrained administrative resources against the DP. Massive vote rigging by RPP members, imperfect electoral procedures, a lack of guarantee of secrecy during the actual voting, as well as the impossibility of checking the actual ballots, which were destroyed after the elections, left no doubt as to the scale of the fraud.[31] Hence, the election results did not reflect the shifting political aspirations of the people. After the elections, the DP grew stronger by the day. Aspirations for more democratic reforms characterized almost every sphere of public and political life. On the other hand, the RPP's single-party identity was steeped in a bureaucratic mentality. On November 17, 1946, the RPP opened its Seventh Congress, which lasted twenty-four days. At the convention, "hardliners" and "moderates" made public their differences concerning the party organization and its platform. "Hardliners" who retained considerable influence in the party were opposed to reforms that they believed would mean the abandonment of the Kemalist platform in favour of appeasing the opposition parties or conservative voters. "Moderates," many of whom were local party officials, defended the need for organizational reforms and opposed the centralist stance of the "hardliners." At the Congress, they emphasized the need to reassess the six principles, as part of an effort to appease the people and opposition forces. Hence, the emphasis on the revolutionary-radical aspect of the principle of "*inkilâpçılık*" (revolutionism) was reduced, while evolutionary development was stressed, implying gradual change with respect to existing circumstances, including the changing needs of the people.[32] Ahmad thinks of this step as a gesture to indicate that reforms would no longer be imposed from the top; only those acceptable to the people would be implemented in the future.[33]

On the second day of the Congress, the draft of the new party program was circulated. The new introduction stated that the RPP came into being through the transformation of the Society for the Defence of the Rights of Anatolia and Rumelia into a political party.[34] The main principles of the program derived from "Kemalism's path" (*Kemalizm yolu*). As before, Article 5 mentioned linguistic, cultural, ideological, and historical unity of the party with the Turkish nation.[35] As a result, several restrictive measures, which resulted from the excesses of nationalism in the past, were gradually eased. A less biased Ottoman history slowly received greater attention in schools. On the question of laicism, Article 13 of the party program draft stated: "Our party considers that [all laws] … must correspond to the requirements of modern civilization … and that the exclusion of religious ideas from the secular affairs of government and politics constitute the main factor of success, progress, and development."[36] This definition and subsequent measures were interpreted as the party's new policy to revise its radical position against Islam. The concept of "laicism" was relaxed, which led to some "religious liberalization," which in its turn ended the days of "militant secularism."[37] Similar changes occurred with the principle of étatism (*devletçilik*), which became more flexible, to reduce discrimination against private enterprise with the understanding that the state would continue to play a major role in heavy industry.[38]

Ahmad believes that the RPP's move was influenced by a desire "to bring the party even closer to the doctrine of the Democrats, meet many of their criticism, and regain the people's confidence."[39] It is obvious that in line with other motivations, religious initiatives were aimed at segregating the DP and the Nation Party, founded in 1948 by former members of the DP, which appealed to the nation by relying on religious symbols.

As a matter of fact, in 1947, Professor Joseph Roucek had used the term İnönüism to invoke the second phase of Kemalism, when analysing the post-Atatürk period in Turkey.[40] VanderLippe states that the İnönü era should be critically observed to understand that the central tenets of Kemalism were challenged by İnönü himself, who moved away from it or beyond it to pursue his own "İnönü-ist" program.[41] He went on to state that during this period, the limits of discourse were redefined by new acceptable margins of deviation from Kemalism that were mandated by the ruling party. In this context, a new Kemalism emerged, updated for the Cold War, under which acceptable mainstream political parties rallied to claim the legitimacy of their own interpretations of Kemalist discourse. Meanwhile, socialist and communist discourses were conceptualized as dangerous to the state, demonstrating the emerging geopolitical dynamics of the Cold War.[42]

It is safe to say that İnönü's impact on socio-political life and the ideological construct of the state is ambiguous. First, since he had always worked with Atatürk, he sought to stick to the reforms initiated by Atatürk and did his best to make sure that there would be no radical breaks or reversals vis-à-vis those reforms. To that end, he created a model of trustful Kemalism, since he had no desire to leave the fate of the reforms to people who might not be ardent defenders and guardians of Westernization in Turkey, and might have alternative visions for Turkey's future, and who would dare question the rationale of key principles of Atatürk's legacy. Future political leaders and elites followed İnönü and did whatever it took to look like better Kemalists, which led to the dominant notion that the state had primacy over democracy. In the same vein, İnönü wanted every Turkish citizen (even foreigners) to respect Atatürk so that Atatürk could exercise his 'much needed' authority, according to İnönü. İnönü's son, Erdal İnönü, elaborated on his father's respect for Atatürk and efforts to protect Atatürk from others. The rationale was as follows: "From the day my father became a president until he died, for him respect for Atatürk became a political principle as well as a way of life. ... his respect for Atatürk was a basic condition and guarantee for the Turkish Republic to continue as a modern state based on Atatürk's reforms."[43]

Heading Towards the 1950 Parliamentary Elections

As the 1950 elections approached, the religious question surfaced with unprecedented intensity. During debates in the Parliament preceding the general elections, some MPs argued that in the modern West, religious life was unrestricted, even encouraged by governments. Furthermore, they claimed that formal religious education would combat ignorance and religious fanaticism, while a lack of formal instruction would leave people exposed to teachings hostile to the Republic.[44] Under these influences, and following the provisions of the 1947 General Congress, İnönü restored religious instruction in the schools. In January 1949, the government introduced optional courses on Islam in public primary schools. These courses followed two objectives: providing religious training in accordance with the principles of secularism and preventing the spread of religious obscurantism and fanaticism. After school hours and voluntary, these courses required the written permission or request of parents for students to enroll.[45] Lessons were to be taught from a book prepared by the Directorate of Religious Affairs and approved by the Ministry of Education (in 1950 the Democrat Party made courses mandatory, unless parents requested their children not to participate).[46] Furthermore, in May 1949, the Preacher and Prayer-Leader Schools (*İmam-Hatip okulları*) were reestablished (they were closed in 1933), and the Faculty of Divinity was opened in 1949 to prepare students to teach religion.[47]

Meanwhile, religious, ultra-nationalist, and reactionary groups, which were antagonistic to Atatürk and his reforms, seized upon any opportunity to criticize and downplay his achievements. Some of these groups questioned Atatürk's contributions to the nationalist movement, claiming that other generals, like Kâzim Karabekir, should take credit for the victory. Moreover, Atatürk was accused of being a "second-class Turk," an outsider allegedly of a Greek or Jewish descent.[48] These currents remained marginal and were suppressed by authorities or counter-propaganda. In response to these groups, the government passed a law asserting that republicanism (*cumhuriyetçilik*), the political regime of the country, would be imposed on all political parties. Suspicion that any discussion regarding the country's political regime would lead to a debate on the restoration of the monarchy and the Caliphate led to the law's passage. By reflecting the dominant belief of the time, Karpat argues that surviving religious groups, anxious to regain their old privileges and supremacy, would try, purposely, to debate the country's political regime to prepare for the restoration of the Caliphate.[49]

The DP focused on the political potential of rural Turkey. Steinbach refers to this shift as the "Anatolization of politics," since it allowed the East/periphery of the country to get engaged in political affairs and become increasingly active in shaping Turkey's political landscape.[50]

In fact, the vote of the peasants, who still comprised from seventy-five to eighty per cent of the population, was an important consideration in multiparty politics, and it was widely believed that peasants wanted more religious freedom. From 1938 to 1950, challengers to the moral validity of state-sponsored development, legal policies, and power structures became more outspoken. Reforms during İnönü's presidency deepened the gap between the political system and various social forces.[51] In addition, signs of crisis in the RPP ideology became more visible, which led to the weakening of the party's image in the eyes of society.[52]

In the meantime, dissent within the RPP between moderates and radicals became unmanageable as the country moved closer to elections scheduled for May 14, 1950. There were speculations about radicals in the party who were intent on splitting it and forming a new "Kemalist Party."[53] The election results came as a total surprise both in Turkey and for international observers. The DP received fifty-three per cent of the votes and, thanks to the winner-takes-all principle of the electoral system, secured 408 seats in parliament. In other words, the RPP's actual popular support was stronger than it appeared, given that it received more than 3.1 million votes (sixty-nine seats), against 4.2 million votes (408 seats) for the DP out of a total 7.9 votes cast.[54] The fact that the RPP was able to pull a majority in only eleven of Turkey's sixty-seven provinces showed the magnitude of the defeat.

The politicians and observers of Turkey debated extensively the significance of these elections. Bernard Lewis addresses the importance of the 1950 election results: "The electoral defeat of the RPP was its greatest achievement—the second revolution, complementing and completing that earlier revolution out of which the party itself had sprung."[55] Lewis was paraphrasing a statement of İnönü's regarding the elections: "My biggest defeat is my biggest victory."[56] There has been much speculation about why İnönü allowed free elections to take place in 1950. Some say that he did not really conceive of the possibility of the RPP's defeat, although this is likely inaccurate. Several witnesses who spoke to an American senator before the election supported the notion that İnönü was sincere when he asserted: "I have been a General, Foreign Minister, Prime Minister and President. All that remains is to be a leader of the Opposition."[57] Rumours circulated that after the elections, military commanders approached İnönü with an offer "to intervene and annul the results of the election," thereby preventing the DP from taking power.[58]

İnönü denied the rumours, claiming: "They could not have come to me with such an offer, nor I could have approached them to ask such a thing."[59]

The change of government was also conditioned by the attitudes of a large peasant population. In this regard, James Bell has claimed that in the 1950 elections "long-neglected Anatolian peasants ... found their good will sought and their needs catered to. It was a new experience for peasants who formerly had been asked merely to die in wars, starve in peace."[60] Some coined the DP's victory a "White revolution," a bloodless overthrow of the existing regime and its replacement by a democratically elected government of the people. Some even argue that the DP's victory was in essence the victory of the counter-elite, or periphery, over the centre.[61] Frey summarizes the elite vs. counter-elite dilemma in the context of the possible impacts of the 1950 election results in the following way:

> ... The key conflict ... is the conflict between the residual national elite, basically found within or in support of the RPP (perhaps until recently), and the new breed of local politicians, basically found in the DP and its successor. The local politicos, however, now have obtained strong representation, even dominance, in all parties. The nationalist politicians, with strong external support from some of the military, the bureaucracy and generally from intellectuals, want to continue intensive Turkish development under strong central surveillance as seems politically feasible...[62]

The 1950 defeat fundamentally challenged the foundations and party structure of the RPP. As a result, the rank-and-file shifted to the ruling DP, while others actively questioned changing party leadership and preparing the ground for young, new cadres. The issue of an eventual successor assumed utmost importance. At the 1950 Eighth Congress of the RPP, Kasım Gülek was elected the Secretary General of the party, a post he retained until 1959. Sunar contends that the RPP had been created not to compete in mass politics but to hold onto central power to transform culture and society.[63] After twenty-seven years of continuous RPP rule, now it was the DP's turn to implement their ideas and transform Turkey into "a little America." Without going into the details of the DP years in power, the rest of this chapter will discuss the ideological debates that two major parties conducted on the meaning and future of Kemalism.

A NEW ROLE FOR THE RPP

Observers have aptly mentioned that at the outset, İnönü's personality and charisma largely constrained the DP from radical moves. The latter treated İnönü as a symbol of "vigilant forces" led by the army and bureaucracy.[64] However, soon the situation changed. In 1953, the RPP's assets were confiscated "on the grounds that they had been illegally acquired with public funds during the single-party period."[65] In 1955, RPP Secretary General Kasım Gülek was arrested for "insulting the moral personality" of the government. The same year, Metin Toker, a journalist and son-in-law of İnönü, was jailed. The RPP organ "*Ulus*" was suspended, and the journal "*Halkçı*" became the temporary official organ of the RPP.[66] During all its years in power, the DP rigidly intensified pressure, not only on RPP leaders and its rank-and-file, but also on anyone sympathetic to the RPP, such as judges, journalists, civil servants, and academics. Weiker argues that the DP's "intensified militancy," directed against "urban elites" was one of the major causes of the 1960 military intervention: "The status of the armed forces, bureaucracy, and intellectuals had been seriously reduced both politically and materially, leading to a return of much of these groups to the RPP and increasing their complaints about what were now being called programmatic betrayals of Kemalism."[67] The formula provided by Frey allows us to clearly distinguish emerging features of peculiarities in the Turkish political culture. A deep suspicion towards opposition forces, representatives of the party-state bureaucracy, and the army was the driving force of governments and regimes in Turkey. The demonization of the opposition and hostile attitudes towards its representatives continued to prevail. A constant sense of insecurity was another element of the new multiparty regime in Turkey. On the other hand, the DP's members formerly belonged to the RPP, its leaders were trained by Atatürk's ideas, and their perceptions of reality bore the imprint of Atatürk.

One significant characteristic of the DP's governing period was that some sections of society became more vocal in their demands for the restoration of Islamic practices in Turkey. The growth of self-assertiveness of religious functionaries, the rise of mosque attendance, the proliferation of religious books and pamphlets, as well as Arabic texts in public places, as described by Lewis in 1952,[68] were undeniable indications that Kemalist policies of radical secularization had only a marginal effect on large sections of society that lived in rural areas. Already in 1954,

Howard Reed presented measures of the DP government that aimed at containing the activities of reactionary movements.[69] Both Lewis and Reed argued that one of the visible outcomes of the rise of Islamic practices was the appearance of religious brotherhoods (*tarikat*), which, after remaining underground for almost a quarter century, emerged with their prestige almost intact and with a new self-confidence. They mentioned at least six names of *tarikat*-s (Ticani, Nakşibendi, Mevlevi, Kadiri, Halveti, and Bektaşi) that had restored their activities in the early 1950s while heavily persecuted by the police.[70] The Malatya incident in 1952[71] and the increasing influence and visibility of the *Nurcu* movement of Said Nursi, with its links to the DP, emboldened the fears of the Kemalist political and intellectual elite about the Islam-driven violence against the secular principles of Kemalism. A creeping *irtica* (reactionary Islam or religious fanaticism) made them uneasy about the prospects of Kemalism.[72] Migration from rural areas to cities has also increased the visibility of traditional Islam (for instance, women wearing *çarşaf*) in the big city centres. As Azak contends, the "Westernized" Kemalist elite felt disappointed and even betrayed when they faced the gap between the Kemalist ideal of civilization and the reality of the people.[73]

Some local authorities became outspoken about their intention to abolish Kemal's reforms of the 1920s. A resolution was introduced at the 1951 Konya convention of the DP to abolish the hat and introduce the fez, restore the veil and Arab letters, destroy existing statues, and reestablish the *Şeria* and polygamy. Hüseyin Nabat, a deputy from Afyon, requested that Islam be restored as the state religion[74]—a demand that would resurface repeatedly in the next few decades. Early in the 1950s, the Islamic activists launched more open activities, which concerned the RPP and the bureaucratic elite of the country. Reports of mutilations or decapitation of busts of Atatürk appeared in Turkish newspapers. At first, no information was given about the culprits who were generally described as "dark forces" or "vandals," and only occasionally as "reactionaries." In May 1951, the government introduced a bill inflicting penalties on anyone who insulted the memory of Atatürk. But the bill had little immediate effect. On the night of June 17, 1951, the head of the marble statue of Atatürk in the Republic Park at Turgutlu, Manisa province, was severed, and on June 26, another in front of the officers' club in Ankara was the victim of a similar "outrage."[75]

Soon the identities of the perpetrators, who belonged to the Ticani religious brotherhood, were made public, and the DP came under heavy criticism for its tolerance towards religious uprising. PM Adnan Menderes replied to these charges on July 15, 1951, by pointing out that his government had provided an antidote in the shape of the law to defend the memory of Atatürk. The government took proper actions for protecting Atatürk's statues and initiated investigations against violators. The DP passed an act popularly known as the Atatürk Law, "A law on the crimes against Atatürk" (*Atatürk aleyhine işlenen suçlar hakkında kanun*), on July 25, 1951, designed to protect Atatürk's memory, statues, busts, monuments, and his mausoleum, and to set a severe punishment against those who violated these provisions.[76] Two years later, on July 24, 1953, in the face of the increasing violations of the 1951 Law, the TGNA intensified penalties for the use of religion for political purposes.[77]

The general trend of the DP was to ascribe dynamic qualities to Kemalism, leading towards a new Turkey, rather than a fixed development scheme or a final aim for political, social, cultural, and economic development. In the meantime, although DP leaders called themselves Kemalists when necessary, they could not disguise any longer their antipathy towards the old Kemalist bureaucratic elite, in particular towards its representatives in the RPP and the army. Against this backdrop, Smogorzewski analysed the economic achievements of the DP between 1950 and 1954 and came to the following conclusion: "Democrats have achieved all this [i.e. economic development and foreign trade] by revising one of the six fundamental principles ... statism or *étatisme*.... Their victory of 1954 means that the great majority of the people does not view statism as being sacrosanct."[78]

Concurrent to the DP's ascent, the overall socio-political climate became worrisome. A deliberately inflated notion of social cohesion and harmony started to disintegrate. As deepening socio-political polarization became the norm, the governing elite started to emulate the experience of the RPP by utilizing the tools of mass socialization specific to the RPP style. By that time, the armed forces, with huge assistance from the United States, embarked on a large-scale technical modernization, justifying its role in the political life of Turkey. To support its intention for playing a larger role in Turkey, the army began citing Atatürk and his deeds on various occasions, thereby displaying existing disagreements with the DP.

For three years after the defeat, the RPP did not discuss the future of the ideology of Kemalism or matters concerning the amendment of the program. During this period, the primary objective of the RPP was to keep the party intact. The Ninth and Tenth Congresses, held in November 1951 and in June 1953, respectively, aimed to boost confidence in the party and bring back unity and harmony.[79] At these Congresses, party leaders conceded to past mistakes. Some principles of Kemalism were slightly modified, too. For instance, étatism was revised. From that point onwards, the state was to be engaged in spheres where private entrepreneurs were not able to cope with possible challenges and where state interests prevailed, while in other cases private initiatives were encouraged.[80] The Tenth Congress revealed the RPP's intention to introduce a bolder revision of the RPP program, which, according to Ahmad, had direct bearing on the ideology of Kemalism. For instance, the program introduced the concept "Atatürk's path" (*Atatürk Yolu*) instead of *Kemalizm Yolu*.[81] However, these modifications were in form rather than substance, and it was still too early to expect society and the state bureaucracy to appreciate the RPP's minor ideological revision. Although Ahmad argues that the RPP had already compromised itself over some of its fundamental principles from 1946 to 1950,[82] society seemed unwilling to go back and extend its support to the RPP. Kili also contends that from 1953 onwards, "Atatürk's way" and "Atatürkism" replaced the term "Kemalism."[83] But although different congresses of the RPP made amendments, or changed the emphasis on subjects that fell under the heading of Kemalism, the term was still widely used, more or less in line with its original meaning. "Atatürk's way," or even "Atatürkism," never completely replaced Kemalism, and as a result, Kemalism remained a more popular term. This ambiguity was further deepened in the coming decades, as will be discussed below. During the same Congress, the terms "social" and "economic" were also inserted into the program to stress the party's growing concern with such issues. Indications of a new socio-economic orientation became visible as the party began to stress the necessity of securing social justice and social security. The six principles of Kemalism, towards which the party had been lukewarm during its last years in power, as well as concepts like national unity, independence, and unconditional sovereignty of the people were given greater emphases.[84]

In the 1954 general elections, the RPP received 3.2 million votes (31 seats) against the 5.3 million votes of the DP (503 seats); the National Party received 480,000 votes (5 seats) out of a total 9.1 million votes cast.[85] During and after the 1954 elections, the RPP maintained its old posture as the party "representing the entire nation" and the sole guardian of Atatürk's legacy and reforms. Although the Eleventh Congress of the RPP, held in July 1954, produced amendments concerning political, judicial, and constitutional questions, it largely failed to resolve questions concerning productive party organization. It also failed to provide alternatives to the crisis within party leadership; as a result, more members of the RPP left it for the DP. After 1954, the RPP began incorporating new strategies by identifying itself with a new generation of intellectuals and their radical definition of economic statism.[86] Overall, the RPP remained a personality party—the party of İnönü. By 1955, Turkey was still not a country in which ideas and programs gave direction to political trends. The fate of the political parties depended on leaders and on the influence of local elite groups on the voters. İnönü made little effort to alter this situation, and the RPP remained a top-down party.[87]

The Twelfth Congress was held in May 1956 and brought new visions to the party's struggle for power. It proposed important reforms: forming a Senate with the structure of the Assembly, initiating a proportional election system, granting autonomous rights to universities, freedom of press, and the independence of judges.[88] Some of these ideas were later incorporated in the new constitution. Because of İnönü's deliberate efforts aimed at rejuvenating the party, he secured critical support from the intelligentsia.[89] Meanwhile, the political and social coalition, which had supported the DP since 1950, started to crumble.[90] In the 1957 general elections, the RPP's representation increased from thirty-one to 173 seats, while the DP's votes decreased from 490 to 424 out of a total 610, despite an increase in the total number cast (3.7 million votes of the RPP against 4.4 million votes of the DP).[91] Karpat contends that the electoral results of 1957 convinced RPP leaders that furthering Kemalist-secularist ideology and incorporating new socio-economic ideas promised future success and the reinstatement of their party to power.[92]

INCREASING ANTAGONISM AND ITS IMPLICATIONS

By the end of the 1950s, it became obvious that the RPP had transformed into a party that was dangerously intolerant of the DP and its leaders and that it would utilize every possible opportunity to regain power. The mounting unpopularity of the DP was another factor capable of pushing the RPP towards more radical measures. Backing from the army became increasingly significant. On the other hand, DP leadership considered the RPP a conspiratorial organization, an attitude that sharp-ened between 1957 and May 1960.[93] Menderes promised to be even harsher and to close down the RPP. Karpat argues that Menderes' fatal mistake was using the army against demonstrators with the aim of show-ing the RPP and İnönü that the DP had full control of the military.[94] İnönü counterattacked and, it is believed, openly called the army to intervene with the goal of "saving democracy" from the wrath of DP leadership.

It became increasingly obvious that the DP was in a deep ideologi-cal crisis, as its decade-long policy of capitalizing on anti-RPP campaigns and populist political agenda ceased to be productive or persuasive. Party leaders did not promote initiatives for revising RPP ideological constructs to meet the growing challenges of the period. Its policy of reaching out to the newly educated masses was considered out of fash-ion and inappropriate. Again, in 1959, Fahri Ağaoğlu, a Deputy from Konya, presented a motion before Parliament, seeking an amendment to the Constitution to the effect that Islam would be a religion of the State. This proposal also failed to win enough support.[95] Between 1951 and 1959, according to various calculations, around 25,000 mosques were built in Turkey, which could not have been done without encouragement from DP leaders. In 1959, the Islamic Institute was founded in Istanbul, where graduates of the *Imam-hatip* schools enjoyed easy admission.[96]

The January 1959 Fourteenth Congress of the RPP produced the par-ty's "Declaration of Priority Tasks" (*Ilk hedefler beyannamesi*).[97] In it, the RPP promised to eliminate "anti-democratic laws" and replace the con-stitution with the current understanding of modern democracy and social justice. The party Congress condemned the "partisan methods" of the rul-ing DP, while the latter's derivation from Atatürk's principles was regarded as treasonous.[98] As DP policy became intolerable for the new generation of RPP members, RPP leaders proclaimed the beginning of a new phase in the struggle against the DP. After the second half of the 1950s, many young people rallied back to the RPP because they were the product of the party's education program, which greatly emphasized continuing rapid social reforms. Groups that did not particularly like the RPP joined it merely because it was the only alternative to the Freedom Party in 1957.[99]

Against this history of a decade-long confrontation between the DP and the army, Karpat still thought that relations between them were not too antagonistic to allow the military to initiate a takeover.[100] In real-ity, the antagonism between the party and the army reached a peak at the end of the decade. Observers of this period agree that since 1959, various groups had emerged in the military with the aim of ousting the DP from power. Between 1959 and 1960, a few attempts at military intervention were reported. Karpat gave another explanation when he claimed that the general atmosphere was calm, and no one could have foreseen the possibility of intervention.[101]

Collaboration between the RPP and the military led to Turkey's first military coup on May 27, 1960. The coup confirmed the volatile nature of Turkish democracy and heralded the end of the First Republic (1923–1960) and the beginning of the Second Republic (1961–1980)—a widely accepted periodization which, however, is not unproblematic. With the blessing of statist intelligentsia, the military intervened, proclaiming that its venture reflected the desires of the entire military and Turkish nation. It claimed to safeguard democracy and the state while protecting the ideas and legacy of Atatürk.

The DP's decade-long reign and concurrent ideological and sociopolitical realities are an important moment in the study of Turkish republican history. This period can be evaluated as a commencing phase, which led to the rupture of the classical Kemalist interpretation of social reality. It proved a period of vital discourse between proponents of elitist-Kemalists and conformist-Kemalists. Speaking of the discourse and seeds of future conflicts, Zafer Toprak told this author in an interview: "From the 1950s onwards, the conflict became much more vital than consensus and concepts. Turkish democracy is a democracy of conflict or a conflict democracy, not consent politics. That is why the social-democracy was never understood."[102] Umut Azak views the 1950s as a decade of the Kemalist civil activism which emerged to protect the secular regime against reactionary Islam.[103] Akşin calls the events of the 1950s a partial counter-revolution. He argues that the Kemalist movement was frozen, and instead, great emphasis was placed on "ceremonial Kemalism" when Kemal's anniversaries were commemorated with increasing fervour and Atatürk's iconography filled every corner of public life. He further asserts that the RPP was somehow unable, or unwilling to conduct opposition based on the demand for a return to the Kemalist Revolution.[104] Karpat argues that the 1960 intervention, which he and many others referred to as "military revolution" or "revolution" was, among many other reasons, the outcome of the long struggle between traditional and secular nationalism. The latter, according to his account, won the fight and "completed the dichotomous evolution with Turkish nationalism."[105] His interpretation of the 1960 intervention is not unique, as many of his contemporaries thought of it:

as a watershed between the past and future of Turkey. In general, the 1950s also marked a moment when Atatürk's image, personality, deeds, achievements, and overall contributions to the modernization project of Turkey were presented in a different light from the practice of the previous decades, mostly because of an emerging plurality of voices and views.

Suna Kili, referring to the emerging views of the Turkish intelligentsia and university students, argued that establishment of the multiparty system and constitutional regime between 1945 and 1960 were "the ultimate culmination of Kemalism." In the same vein, she claimed that in contrast to 1923–1938, when Kemalism was treated as a theory of complete modernization, between 1945 and 1960, "Kemalism was used in the name of democratic political liberties and not of social reform."[106] Kili offers another perspective, contending that between 1945 and 1960, the ideology of Kemalism was not satisfactorily systematized, because more urgent socio-economic problems attracted ever-growing attention from the Turkish people.[107] Here, once again, we observe that Kili's analysis is based on the assumption that the Kemalist elite, or what remained of it after Kemal's death, did not systematize reforms. She thereby downplays the challenges of multiparty politics that made the dominance of the Kemalist system of principles more challenging.

This chapter examined ideological transformations after 1938. The RPP, under İnönü's leadership between 1938 and 1950, and the DP, under the leadership of Bayar and Menderes between 1950 and 1960, had to adjust and adapt Kemalism to new circumstances. The post-WWII international order, as well as opportunities emerging as a result of multiparty democracy, allowed political and social actors to revise earlier radical Kemalist policies. By formally embracing Kemalism, both parties moved away from "high Kemalism." Some of the revisions could be seen as too radical, which allowed observers to refer to the 1940s as a period of İnönüism—an indication of a clear departure from Kemalism. The DP moved even further by creating a space for the rise of conservatism in Turkey, which went against the secular-modernization drive of Atatürk's era.

NOTES

1. Friedrich and Brzezinski (1956, 55).
2. Criss (2009, 127–129).
3. Documents on International Affairs. 1938. Vol. 1. London, New York, and Toronto: Oxford University Press, 1942, 300.

4. John Parker and Charles Smith. 1940. *Modern Turkey*. London: George Routledge and Sons, 60.
5. Hanioğlu (2011, 197).
6. Cemil Koçak. 2004. "Some Views on the Turkish Single-Party Regime During the İnönü Period (1938–1945)." In *Men of Order: Authoritarian Modernization Under Atatürk and Reza Shak*, edited by Touraj Atabaki and Erik-Jan Zürcher. London and New York: I.B. Tauris, 116.
7. Behlül Özkan. 2012. *From the Abode of Islam to the Turkish Vatan: The Making of a National Homeland in Turkey*. New Haven and London: Yale University Press, 160.
8. Gilman (1939, 379–380).
9. VanderLippe (2005, 34–35).
10. Özkan (2012, 160).
11. Since 1927, the party congresses were given the epithet—the Great (*Büyük*). However, the word for 'congress' changed a few times, again following the logic of language reforms. The 1927 congress was named (Büyük Kongra), the 1931—Büyük Kongre, the 1935—Büyük Kurultay, the 1939—Büyük Kurultay.
12. C.H.P. Program. 1939. Ankara: Ulus Basımevi, 3.
13. VanderLippe (2005, 39).
14. Parker and Smith (1940, 69).
15. Karpat (1963, 63).
16. Hanioğlu (2011, 195).
17. Doğan Gürpınar. 2015. "Turkish Radicalism and Its Images of the Ottoman Ancien Régime (1923–38)." *Middle Eastern Studies* 51 (3): 395–415.
18. Hanioğlu (2011, 197).
19. Rita Korkhmazyan. 1977. *Turetsko-Germanskije Otnoshenije v Gody Vtoroj Mirovoj Voiny* [Turkish-German Relations During the Second World War]. Yerevan: NAS Armenia SSR Press.
20. Şaban Çalış. 1997. Pan-Turkism and Europeanism: A Note on Turkey's 'pro-German Neutrality' During the Second World War. *Central Asian Survey* 16 (1): 103–114.
21. Selim Deringil. 1989. *Turkish Foreign Policy During the Second World War: An "Active" Neutrality*. Cambridge: Cambridge University Press.
22. Herbert R. Reginbogin. 2009. *Faces of Neutrality: A Comparative Analysis of the Neutrality of Switzerland and Other Neutral Nations During WWII*. Berlin: Lit Verlag, 159.
23. C.H.P. Program. 1943. Ankara: Zerbamat Basımevi.
24. Ibid.
25. Erik-Jan Zürcher. 2017. *Turkey: A Modern History*. 4th ed. London and New York: I.B. Tauris, 208–211.

26. Feroz Ahmad. 1977. *The Turkish Experiment in Democracy, 1950–1975.* London: C. Hurst & Company, 13.
27. Kemal Karpat. 1988. "Military Interventions: Army-Civilian Relations in Turkey Before and After 1980." In *State, Democracy and the Military*, edited by Metin Heper and Ahmet Evin. Berlin: Walter de Gruyter, 138.
28. Özkan (2012, 179–181).
29. Metin Toker. 1970. *Tek Partiden Çok Partiye (1944–1950).* İstanbul: Bilgi Yayınevi, 99–104; Metin Heper. 1998. *İsmet İnönü: The Making of a Turkish statesman.* London: Brill, 185–186.
30. *Cumhuriyet* (1946, haziran 30).
31. Zürcher (2017, 214).
32. Kili (1969, 160–61).
33. Ahmad (1977).
34. *C.H.P. Yedinci Büyük Kurultayı.* 1947. Ankara: TBMM, 49.
35. Ibid.
36. *C.H.P. Yedinci Büyük Kurultayı.* 1947. Ankara: TBMM, 50.
37. Borovali (1985, 88).
38. *C.H.P. Yedinci Büyük Kurultayı.* 1947. 50.
39. Ahmad (1977, 26).
40. Joseph Roucek. 1947. *Governments and Politics Abroad.* New York: Funk & Wagnalls Company, 524–525.
41. VanderLippe (2005, 5).
42. Ibid., 5–6.
43. *Erdal İnönü* cited in Heper (1998, 112).
44. Mehmet Yaşar Geyikdaği. 1984. *Political Parties in Turkey: The Role of Islam.* New York: Praeger Publishers, 66–67.
45. Bernard Lewis. 1952. "Islamic Revival in Turkey." *International Affairs* 28 (1): 41.
46. Geyikdaği (1984, 67).
47. Lewis (1952, 41).
48. Karpat (1959, 246–247).
49. Karpat (1959, 249).
50. Steinbach (1984, 80).
51. VanderLippe (2005, 3).
52. Dmitrij Vdovichenko. 1967. *Bor'ba Politicheskih Partij v Turtsii (1944–1965)* [The Struggle of Political Parties in Turkey (1944–1965)]. Moscow: Nauka, 94.
53. Karpat (1959, 220).
54. K. Smogorzewski. 1954. "Democracy in Turkey." *The Contemporary Review* 186: 81.
55. Lewis (1968, 303).

56. "Baba İnönü'den Erdal İnönü'ye Mektuplar." [Letters from Father İnönü to Erdal İnönü.] By Sevgi Özel. 1988. Ankara: Bilgi Yayınevi, 149.

57. Walter Weiker. 1963. *The Turkish Revolution 1960–1961: Aspects of Military Politics*. Washington, DC: The Brookings Institution, 85.

58. Ahmad (1977, 150).

59. Metin Toker. 1990. *DP'in Altın Yılları, 1950–1954* [The DP's Golden Years, 1950–1954]. Ankara: Bilgi Yayınevi, 23–24. Cited in VanderLippe (2005, 204).

60. James Bell. 1952. *Turkey: Strategic and Tough. Readers Digest* [Condensed from *Time*], February, 100. National Archives of Armenia, F. 412, L. 1, case 1958.

61. Özbudun (1993, 255).

62. Frederick Frey. 1965. *The Turkish Political Elite*. Cambridge: Massachusetts Institute of Technology, 195–197.

63. İlkay Sunar. 2004. *State, Society and Democracy in Turkey*. Istanbul: Bahçeşehir University Publication, 75.

64. Ahmad (1993, 111).

65. Weiker (1963, 10).

66. Vdovichenko (1967, 183).

67. Walter Weiker. 1981. *The Modernization of Turkey: From Atatürk to the Present Day*. New York: Holmes and Meier, 183.

68. Lewis (1952, 42–43).

69. Howard Reed. 1954. "Revival of Islam in Secular Turkey." *The Middle East Journal* 8 (3): 267–282.

70. Reed (1954, 274–275) and Lewis (1952, 43).

71. In November 1952, Ahmet Emin Yalman, a famous journalist and the editor of *Vatan*, who opposed all efforts to revise Kemalism, survived an assassination attempt in Malatya. The Kemalist elite saw the religious fanaticism as the main driver for the incident and drew parallels with the Menemen incident in 1930. For details see Azak (2010, Ch. 4).

72. Azak (2010, Chs. 4 and 5).

73. Azak (2010, 112–113).

74. Cahiers (1951, XXIII. 114–115).

75. Emile Marmorstein. 1952. "Religious Opposition to Nationalism in the Middle East." *International Affairs* 28 (3): 346.

76. "*T.C. Resmi gazette*", 28.VII. 1951. http://www.mevzuat.adalet.gov.tr/html/956.html.

77. During the fieldwork in Istanbul, Emre Nuhoğlu, a political scientist, touched upon that law. He provided an interesting interpretation of it: "*Turks like to have heroes, it does not matter which centuries they are*

coming from. But unlike the heroes of the Ottoman period, we protect the main hero of the Republic with a special law, which, to me, needs to be changed. You do not make one heroic by putting his name in the law. Aside from Atatürk, there have been no less prominent figures like İnönü, Menderes, Özal, etc." Interview with Emre Nuhoğlu. August 18. 2004. Istanbul.

78. Smogorzewski (1954, 83).
79. Ahmad (1977, 108).
80. *Spetsial'nyj Bjulleten'* [Special Bulletin]. 1966. Akademija nauk SSSR. Institut Narodov Azii. no. 72, 39.
81. Ahmad (1977, 108–109).
82. Ahmad (1977, 108).
83. Kili (1969, 171).
84. Ahmad (1977, 113).
85. Smogorzewski (1954, 81).
86. Karpat (1988, 139).
87. Ahmad (1977, 113).
88. Special bulletin (1966, 42).
89. Ahmad (1977, 116).
90. Sunar (2004, 76).
91. The combined opposition had 186 seats and 4,758,000 votes, hence, the opposition had more votes than the DP. *Forum*, November 1, 1957, 3.
92. Karpat (1988, 139).
93. Şevket Süreyya Aydemir. 1975. *Ikinci Adam*. Cilt 3. İstanbul: Remzi Kitabevi, 355–449.
94. Karpat (1988, 140).
95. Muhammad Rashid Feroze. 1976. *Islam and Secularism in Post-Kemalist Turkey*. Islamabad: Islamic Research Institute, 123–124.
96. Vdovichenko (1967, 189–190).
97. Ahmad (1977, 117).
98. Special bulletin (1966, 42).
99. Weiker (1963, 86).
100. Karpat (1988, 141) and Ahmad (1977, 147–160).
101. Ibid.
102. Interview with Zafer Toprak. May 11, 2005. Istanbul.
103. Azak (2010, 104).
104. Akşin (1999, 26).
105. Karpat, Kemal. 1973. "Ideology in Turkey After the Revolution of 1960." In *Social Change and Politics in Turkey: A Structural-Historical Analsysis*, by Kemal Karpat. Leiden: E. J. Brill, 333.
106. Kili (1980, 393).
107. Kili (1969, 179).

REFERENCES

Ahmad, Feroz. 1977. *The Turkish Experiment in Democracy 1950–1975*. London: C. Hurst & Company.

———. 1993. *The Making of Modern Turkey*. London & New York: Routledge.

Akşin, Sina. 1999. "The Nature of the Kemalist Revolution." In *The Turkish Republic at Seventy-Five Years*, edited by David Shankland, 14–28. Cambridgeshire: The Eothen Press.

Azak, Umut. 2010. *Islam and Secularism in Turkey: Kemalism, Religion and the Nation State*. London: I.B. Tauris.

Borovali, Ali Fuat. 1985. Kemalist Tradition, Political Change and the Turkish Military. Unpublished dissertation, Queen's University.

Criss, Nur Bilgi. 2009. "Shades of Diplomatic Recognition: American Encounters with Turkey (1923–1937)." In *Studies in Atatürk's Turkey: The American Dimension*, edited by George Harris and Nur Bilgi Criss, 97–144. Leiden: Brill.

Friedrich, Carl, and Zbigniew Brzezinski. 1956. *Totalitarian Dictatorship and Autocracy*. Cambridge: Harvard University Press.

Geyikdaği, Mehmet Yaşar. 1984. *Political Parties in Turkey: The Role of Islam*. New York: Praeger Publishers.

Gilman, William. 1939. "Turkey Offers Her Own Ism." *The South Atlantic Quarterly* 38: 377–391.

Hanioğlu, Şükrü. 2011. *Atatürk: An Intellectual Biography*. Princeton: Princeton University Press.

Heper, Metin. 1998. *İsmet İnönü: The Making of a Turkish Statesman*. London: Brill.

Karpat, Kemal. 1959. *Turkish Politics*. Princeton: Princeton University Press.

Karpat, Kemal. 1963. "The People's Houses in Turkey: Establishment and Growth." *Middle East Journal* 17 (1): 55–67.

Karpat, Kemal. 1988. "Military Interventions: Army-Civilian Relations in Turkey Before and After 1980." In *State, Democracy and the Military*, edited by Metin Heper and Ahmet Evin, 137–158. Berlin: Walter de Gruyter.

Kili, Suna. 1969. *Kemalism*. İstanbul: School of Business Administration and Economics, Robert College.

Kili, Suna. 1980. "Kemalism in Contemporary Turkey." *International Political Science Review* 1 (3): 380–404.

Lewis, Bernard. 1952. "Islamic Revival in Turkey." *International Affairs* 28 (1): 38–48.

Lewis, Bernard. 1968. *The Emergence of Modern Turkey*. London: Oxford University Press.

Özbudun, Ergun. 1993. "State Elites and Democratic Political Culture in Turkey." In *Political culture and Democracy in Developing countries*, edited by Larry Diamond, 247–268. Boulder & London: Lynne Rienner Publishers.

Özkan, Behlül. 2012. *From the Abode of Islam to the Turkish Vatan: The Making of a National Homeland in Turkey*. New Haven and London: Yale University Press.

Parker, John, and Charles Smith. 1940. *Modern Turkey*. London: George Routledge and Sons.

Reed, Howard. 1954. "Revival of Islam in Secular Turkey." *The Middle East Journal* 8 (3): 267–282.

Roucek, Joseph. 1947. *Governments and Politics Abroad*. New York: Funk & Wagnalls Company.

Smogorzewski, K. 1954. "Democracy in Turkey." *The Contemporary Review* 186: 80–85.

Steinbach, Udo. 1984. "Atatürk's Impact on Turkey's Political Culture Since World War II." In *Atatürk and the Modernization of Turkey*, 78–88. Boulder: Westview Press.

Sunar, İlkay. 2004. *State, Society and Democracy in Turkey*. İstanbul: Bahçeşehir University Publication.

VanderLippe, John. 2005. *The Politics of Turkish Democracy: İsmet İnönü and the Formation of the Multi-Party System, 1938–1950*. New York: State University of New York Press.

Vdovichenko, Dmitrij. 1967. *Bor'ba Politicheskih Partii v Turtsii (1944–1965)* [The Struggle of Political Parties in Turkey (1944–1965)]. Moscow: Nauka.

Weiker, Walter. 1963. *The Turkish Revolution 1960–1961: Aspects of Military Politics*. Washington, DC: The Brookings Institution.

Zürcher, Erik-Jan. 2017. *Turkey: A Modern History*, 4th ed. London: I.B. Tauris.

Kemalism in the Second Republic, 1960s–1970s

The first successful military *coup d'état* in Turkey in 1960 made possible the emergence of fundamentally new trends in the political culture. It prepared a ground for new approaches and radical solutions to old political challenges that had existed long before the intervention. Between 1960 and 1980, interactions between various ideological currents gained momentum in Turkey. Efforts to reform and reconsider Kemalism took a decisive turn. Known as a period of ideological liberalization and radicalization, these two decades saw deepening social, political, and ideological cleavages in the country. This chapter delineates measures taken by the RPP to broaden its appeal and its move towards "the left of centre". In the 1950s, the RPP leadership had observed that in order to gain popular support and win in contested elections, the party needed to revise its ideological traction. The change of the party leadership and the shifting of the party position on several domestic socio-political issues changed the RPP's course. This chapter also discusses the Kemalist elite's perception of its role in the context of ideological polarization in the 1960s and 1970s.

THE KEMALIST PRINCIPLES IN THE SECOND CONSTITUTION

On the night of May 26, 1960, Turkey's armed forces took power, ending the decade-long reign of the Democrat Party. The coup was executed by a group of thirty-eight army officers who were later called the

© The Author(s) 2019
V. Ter-Matevosyan, *Turkey, Kemalism and the Soviet Union,*
Modernity, Memory and Identity in South-East Europe,
https://doi.org/10.1007/978-3-319-97403-3_6

National Unity Committee (NUC) (*Milli Birlik Komitesi*). The National Assembly and government of Adnan Menderes were dissolved, and the president, prime minister, ministers, and majority of DP members were arrested. Capitalizing on the image of guardianship, the military implemented its "veto coup"[1] to prevent "a further appeal of the government to the more religious minded and conservative rural masses."[2] Nuri Eren describes this first intervention: "Surely history will applaud this act of the military. They remained faithful to their involuntary thrust to power, refusing to emulate all other military regimes in a forceful perpetuation of their authority."[3]

Soon after the takeover, coup organizers elaborated on their ideological motivations. In September 1960, the U.S. Joint Publications Research Service published interviews with members of the coup. The opinions provide a framework of dominating views among the officers concerning Kemalism in general and Atatürk in particular. For a long period, these interviews were not widely discussed in Turkish academic circles, even though they offered many valuable insights, which are important for the present study. "I am convinced that the [Atatürk] reforms retrogressed during the period now behind us," said the head of the NUC and the president of Turkey, General Gürsel, by adding: "In fact, this was the greatest evil."[4] Colonel Alparslan Türkeş, a key figure in the coup, stated that thanks to the "May 27 revolution," the Atatürk spirit has been re-animated.[5] According to Colonel Sami Küçük: "This revolution [May 27] was carried out because Atatürk's reforms had been attacked. This [revolution] is a continuation of Atatürk."[6] He also noted that the revolution took its first point of action from Atatürk.[7] Major Orhan Erkanlı was convinced that "Atatürk is the greatest person whom the Turkish race has produced up to the present time. He is the symbol of Turkism. The first word of every Turk born on this soil must be Atatürk and his last word must be Atatürk... to say more is superfluous."[8] Captain Irfan Solmazer was also of the view that "[The DP] retrogressed a great deal. The reforms strayed from their basic routes. They were betrayed. The Turkish people were left destitute and wretched."[9] Keen to interpret the link between military intervention and Atatürk, Captain Numan Esin explained: "Atatürk and the May 27 revolution are linked in the sense of both being national unity movements. More correctly, they are a sequence of movements, one of which completes the other."[10] Lieutenant Colonel Orhan Kabibay claimed: "The May 27 revolution was a rising-up of the present generation trained by the revolutionary spirit of Atatürk with a view of protecting and rescuing the revolution of the great Atatürk from those who, during the last ten years, wanted to upset and destroy it out of a thirst for power."[11] Colonel Haydar Tunçkanat elaborated on the same question: "We are children of the Republic, at the same time, children of Atatürk. Our attainments come from him. We are indebted to him for everything we have, everything we have learned. Atatürk is the beginning of everything for us. From this point of view, there is a close, very close link between Atatürk and May 27."[12] Muzaffer Karan expressed his view of Atatürk: "Spurred by the inspiration we received from Atatürk, we, as the generation of his period, have gotten rid of those who betrayed that trust. Those who betray Atatürk's reform will always be doomed to suffer the same fate."[13] Opinions and statements expressed in the interviews stressed the importance of Atatürk and his reforms to the integrity of the Turkish state. They heavily criticized the past policies of the DP which deviated from the path of Atatürk and his reforms. The statements also reflected the dominant mindset of emerging militancy and radicalism in the Kemalist interpretations in the 1960–1970s.

In these interviews, generals and officers also voiced concerns about the exploitation of religion for political gain, the widespread use of head-scarves, and other issues of the day. Küçük made it clear that he resented efforts to exploit religion and opposed any intermediary coming between Allah and his servant.[14] To Captain Solmazer, "*charşaf* is not a religious garb. Religion has no dress. The exploitation of religion is irreligiousness. We shall never permit it."[15]

These statements illustrate that at least some members of the military attached the utmost ideological importance to their mission. Acting as the vanguards of Atatürk and his reforms, they not only legitimized their actions but also protected them under the aegis of Atatürk's reputation and authority. This was a double-sided process, since by acquiring legitimacy for their actions, the military prolonged the existence of Kemalism.

The Constituent Assembly convened in late 1960. Former DP members and even DP sympathizers were prevented from taking part in creating the new Constitution. Thus, the 1961 constitution was largely created by the RPP. The transition to democracy took fourteen months, and on July 9, 1961, a new Constitution was submitted to a national referendum. It was adopted with 61.7% approval. The Constitution[16] created an unprecedented atmosphere of political liberalization.

Fundamental principles in the Preamble underlined the "full dedication ... to the reforms of Atatürk." Comparing the document to the 1924 constitution with all its amendments, it becomes clear that six principles of Kemalism, as formulated in Article 2 of the previous constitution, were not present in the new 1961 version. The concept of Kemalism was also missing in the new document. Article 2 of the 1961 Constitution[17] defined the characteristics of the Turkish Republic: national (*millî*), democratic (*demokratik*), secular (*lâik*), and social (*sosyal*).[18] Only one out of six Kemalist or RPP principles was explicitly mentioned in Article 2. The "nationalist" (*milliyetçi*) principle of the previous constitution was transformed into "national" in Article 2 of the new constitution, although the official English translation kept the term "nationalistic." Article 9 stressed: "the form of the state as a Republic shall not be amended," which was the essence of Kemalism's republicanism principle.[19] Thus, three of the six basic principles of Kemalism, namely populism, étatism, and revolutionism, were not explicitly mentioned in the document.

When discussing the new constitution, Clement Dodd contends that it was less democratic and less republican, and while it showed a continued secularist drive, it was more etatist. But whether the constitution was more nationalist or revolutionist was a difficult question to answer.[20] While he did not comment on the new shape of populism, new shifts clearly affected politics in the Second Republic. Özbudun and Gençkaya agreed that a Kemalist notion of *étatism* that had more leftist and ideological terms was incorporated into the 1961 constitution while the state retained its leverage over socio-economic issues.[21] In contrast, Weiker indicates that in comparison to the previous constitution, the new one was more specific regarding revolutionism, since it provided eight specific "Reform laws."[22] Weiker referred to laws mentioned in Article 153, which aimed at "raising the Turkish society to the level of contemporary civilization and at safeguarding the secular character of the Republic:" (1) the unification of education; (2) the Hat Law forbidding the fez; (3) the closing down of dervish convents and mausoleums; (4) civil marriage; (5) the adoption of international numerals; (6) the new Turkish alphabet; (7) abolition of titles and appellations; and (8) the prohibition against wearing religious garments in public. Thus, Article 153 brought the key secular reform laws passed between 1924 and 1934 under constitutional protection.

In the new constitution, the old polarization of the centre against the periphery assumed a new form. Deposed president Bayar commented that the constitution legitimatized the bureaucracy and intellectuals as one source of sovereignty, in addition to the Turkish people, who had served as the only source of sovereignty in Kemalist ideology.[23] Heper contends that the new constitution's clear intention was to maintain Atatürkian thought as a political manifesto. He argues that the state elite thus propagated a juridical concept of state, placing greater faith in the rule of law (*Rechsstaat* or *l'etat de droit*) than in the rule of parliament.[24]

The constitution provided for extensive economic and social modernization programs. It also institutionalized the multiparty system. Now parties could be formed freely and function unhindered without violating constitutional principles and threatening Turkish democracy (Articles 56 and 57). The TGNA was now composed of two bodies: the National Assembly had 450 members and the Senate 165 members (Articles 63, 67, 70). One prominent feature of the new constitution was the creation of the National Security Council (hereafter, NSC) (Article 111). It soon became a legal mechanism to assure the voice of the military to "communicate the requisite fundamental recommendations to the Council of Ministers with the purpose of assisting in the making of decisions related to national security and coordination."[25] In later decades, the NSC played an instrumental role, not only in domestic politics by orchestrating military interventions, but also in contributing to the interpretation of Kemalism. In particular, its military wing made itself responsible for matters of security, domestic, and foreign policy issues. That role persisted until the middle of the first decade of the twenty-first century.

The various interpretations of the constitution and its characteristics reflected the inherently different nature of the new constitution, which wrote the rules of Turkish politics for the next two decades. One group of observers referred to it as a "revolution," as organizers of the coup saw it. This view was promulgated in the Preamble of the Constitution: "Revolution of May 27, 1960." Professor Enver Ziya Karal, chair of the Constitutional Committee, maintained: "It is a revolutionary constitution ... because it includes and gives legal value to the reforms of Atatürk ... and has brought the principles that will clear the way for our nation's tendency and aptitude to move forward."[26] Others regarded it more critically, pointing to its problems and conflicts. For instance, Yavuz distinguished two competing principles in the new constitution: (a) depoliticization of the society at the expense of increasing the power of bureaucracy; and (b) deepening associationalism, which reduced the monopoly on political life enjoyed by political parties.[27]

The prevailing trends in the post-intervention period were commonly called "a return to Atatürkism," or "neo-Kemalism"—the term that would reappear in later decades, with varying and mostly conflicting interpretations. In fact, for Andrew Mango, Clement Dodd, Frederick Frey, and a few other observers of Turkey, the 1960 coup was the triumph of what has been called neo-Kemalism. Its proponents were referred to as "neo-Kemalist officers."[28] This depiction of "neo-Kemalism" differed from the "neo-Kemalism" of the 2000s, discussed in this book's literature review.

The return to Kemalism, urged by some of the intelligentsia, had little in common with the concept in the single-party period. Orthodox Kemalists claim that the progressive social and economic values, nationalism, and laicism of true Kemalism had been perverted by privileged groups, confined to a narrow political dogma. Landau agrees with Türkkaya Ataöv, who stated that the 1960 military intervention was essentially "a revolution that shook but did not change her [Turkey's – Landau] political body,"[29] meaning that the NUC refrained from creating a new political system. In reality, political trends and ideological developments following the 1960 military intervention proved the opposite. The new constitution remade the state structure by empowering different social actors with institutionalized access to the government. Military intervention was also a turning point in Turkey's ideological development, as divisions between the centre and periphery grew more politicized as new social classes emerged. The challenge initiated by the DP was taken over by other political movements in the 1960–1970s.

In the general elections of October 1961, the RPP gained only 36.7% of votes, while the newly established Justice Party (*Adalet Partisi*—henceforth, JP) received 34.8% of national votes. To many observers, the results dealt a significant blow to the RPP and its image. Weiker attributes several factors to this narrow victory: (a) the RPP was identified with the repressive deeds of the military regime; (b) the overthrown DP retained many supporters, who would under no circumstances vote for the RPP; (c) the internal situation of the RPP; and (d) difficulties of simultaneous rapid reforms and free multiparty government.[30] Weiker underestimates the importance of the social and political developments of the previous decade. No less important was the fact that the ousted DP made the periphery a critical stakeholder in politics. It could not disappear from the forefront of politics where it found itself. Political movements and forces defending the interests of the periphery became vocal players in subsequent debates. Key players at the centre also acknowledged the critical importance of the periphery when building their political plans.

The generals were openly disappointed with the results of the general elections, since the RPP did not achieve the anticipated majority of votes. The military threatened to annul the results and seize power once again if certain conditions were not met, which put pressure on the JP. İnönü was asked to form a government in October 1961, which he did, returning to that position after twenty-four years. However, the RPP faced numerous socio-political challenges and constant ideological conflicts from both the left and right. Observers of Turkey agree that during the 1960s, for the first time in the country's history, movements on the right and the left came to full fruition. For our analysis, it is more important to observe the evolution of Kemalist discourse among these proliferating movements.

KEMALISM AND THE LEFT

In the 1960s, the Turkish left was striving to have "… a revised Kemalism," which would bear the name Atatürkism (*Atatürkçülük*). The trend "to genuine-*ise* the Kemalist thought" was first described by Faruk Güventürk, a Turkish general who wrote a book, *Genuine Kemalism* (Gerçek Kemalizm) in 1964.[31] His formulation referred to "the struggle against American imperialism and against foreign monopolies and capital."[32] Periodicals of the Turkish left, such as "*Yön*" (Direction), "*Sosyal adalet*" (Social Justice), "*Devrim*" (Revolution), "*Ant*" (Pledge), "*Türk yolu*" (Turkish path), and a dozen more were not only arguing for a return to Atatürkism, but also stressed the need to reform it.[33] Because of these galvanizing efforts, a new trend in political thought emerged, which later would be called "left Kemalism" (or left-Atatürkism). A few principles of Kemalism, such as revolutionism, were revived and became a powerful ideological tool in the hands of leftist groups.

A few journals stood out for their visible impact on Kemalist discourse in the 1960–1970s. One was *Yön*, established by a group of leftist intellectuals (Doğan Avcıoğlu, Mümtaz Soysal, Ilhami Soysal, İlhan Selçuk, Sırrı Hocaoğlu, Hamdi Avcıoğlu, and Cemal Reşit Eyüboğlu). Besides the main founders and contributors, *Yön*'s philosophy was also shaped by old-Kadrioists or leftists of the 1920s such as Şevket Süreyya Aydemir and Yakup Kadri Karaosmanoğlu.[34] From the outset (December 1961), *Yön*'s circulation reached thirty thousand copies in 1963—a figure higher than most popular dailies. It was particularly popular among young people.

Yön tried to redefine Kemalism as an anti-imperialist and "nationalist liberation" ideology by using a taboo word—"socialism."[35] In addition to promoting socialism as the only reliable model for Turkish development, *Yön* espoused radical interpretations of Kemalist ideals and used Marxist class analysis to approach the issues on which it concentrated. Scholars agree that *Yön*'s perspective on Turkish and world politics differed little from those advocated by the Kadrioists and their 1930s leading spokesman, Aydemir, who tried to make a doctrine out of Kemalism. Some argued that *Yön* had more radical character than the *Kadro* movement. By contrast, Özgür Mutlu Ulus argues that *Yön*'s principles were not completely new, but were modest and aimed at sparking debate. Its content and the personalities of its authors contributed to its popularity.[36]

Yön's propagation of revolutionary change through radical Kemalism and socialism and strong criticism of government policies agitated the government, conservatives, and liberals alike. *Yön* rejected charges of "leftist dogmatism" and "provocation of class conflict" from cabinet members Turhan Feyzioğlu and Bülent Ecevit. The journal argued that neither socialism nor Kemalism were dogmas; they were action-oriented doctrines aimed at the removal of the class differences dividing Turkish society.[37] The monthly *Barış dünyasi* assailed *Yön* for its challenge to Atatürk's étatism and stated that Atatürk had no intention to create a collective system but aimed at developing the private enterprise.[38]

Hoping to bring a new content to Kemalism, *Yön* reinterpreted some of its key concepts, among them: (a) *yeni-devletçilik* (neo-étatism), theory to propagate against rich feudal landlords in Turkey's east against the urban upper-middle class, and eventually against the West; and (b) *Türk sosyalizm* (Turkish socialism), which was very different from communism and was based on Kemalism.[39] Furthermore, the journal claimed that Kemalism was the embodiment of socialism, which itself was an advanced form of Kemalism.[40] *Yön*'s contributors, together with other leftists during the two İnönü coalition governments (1961–1963), were able to give wide currency to what they defined as Kemalist principles with republicanism and secularism remaining in the background. They tried, with some success, to give the remaining four principles new socio-economic content, promoting class-consciousness in Turkish society. It was therefore *Yön*'s Kemalist principles that opened the way to socialism for leftists.[41] The establishment of the "Socialist Culture Society" (SCS) by *Yön* contributors in 1963 gave greater popularity to ideas promoted in the journal. During panel discussions and conferences in several Turkish cities, the SCS developed some earlier interpretations of Kemalism that were reflected in previous issues of *Yön*. It distinguished three out of the six RPP principles—namely populism, étatism, and revolutionism, as building blocks in the transition to socialism.[42]

By 1967, *Yön*'s popularity decreased and it was closed down, only to reappear under a different name, while adopting a more radical drive and aggressive tone. In 1969, the founders of *Yön* established *Devrim*, a journal that aimed at attracting the military to back up its ideas. *Devrim* considered Kemalism "a semi-successful national democratic revolution," which degenerated after 1945. According to contributors to the journal, it was the historical duty of Kemalists to continue the Kemalist revolution by attaching importance to full independence and civilization.[43] The radicalization of *Devrim* led to the militarization of its activities. Retired General Cemal Madanoğlu, who planned to carry out a leftist coup, was particularly active. He set up a group composed of high-ranking military officers called the National Democratic Revolutionists modelled on the Committee of Union and Progress. He also enjoyed the support of Avcıoğlu, Soysal, and Selçuk. The group aimed to establish a broad base of patriots, and its members were obliged to swear an oath to the flag, Atatürk, and the rifle.[44] *Devrim*, along with affiliated organizations on the "extreme left" and "extreme right" were closed down because of the 1971 military intervention.[45]

Contributors to *Türk Solu*, which used to be a radical leftist-revolutionary weekly, took the "nationalism" of Atatürkism as a guiding idea and preached that all "nationalists" fight colonial exploitation in Turkey.[46] In essence, promoting these principles, which were rather far from the original conception of Kemalism, had only one objective: to acquire legitimacy in the eyes of the public.

Meanwhile, orthodox interpreters of Kemalism agreed that for three decades it had been mixed with traits from various ideological currents, which muddled its worldview. In Ankara in 1967, members of the Regional Cooperation for Development met to commemorate the anniversary of Atatürk's death. Hamdi Başar delivered a speech, "The distinction between Atatürk and Atatürkism cannot be made" (*"Atatürk ve Atatürkçülük ayrımı yapılamalıyor"*). During the presentation, he argued that academics of the highest level of specialization had not yet fully explained the differences between the two. He concluded that this disorganization had allowed the extreme left and right to unite in hostility against Kemalism; the "extreme right" attacked it as "the order of infidels," while the "extreme left" derided it as "the order of the bourgeoisie."[47] Periodicals published in November 1967, commemorating the death of Atatürk, questioned Kemalist discourse and Atatürk's image. The right-wing newspapers, *Yeni İstanbul* and *Son havadıs* insisted that Atatürk was a steadfast anti-Communist.[48] In an article published in *Milliyet*, Metin Toker warned the public about the danger of exploiting the name of Atatürk by the left and right. He stated that Atatürk was neither pro-*sharia* nor pro-communist, but was rather a proponent of Western civilization and nationalism.[49] Since a discussion of the Turkish Worker's Party (TWP) and its contribution to the evolution of Kemalist discourse would take this analysis in another direction, it suffices to claim that it brought new radical perspectives to the interpretation and development of Kemalist thought. The six principles of Kemalism, while embraced, were considered under the guise of socialist thought.

THE RPP'S NEW IDENTITY

The 1960s became known as the decade when socio-economic issues began shaping politics to an unprecedented extent. The political parties came under increasing pressure to define their position vis-à-vis social problems in clear and plain terms. The RPP did not remain unaffected and became increasingly concerned with the proliferating discourses of the time—social justice, the welfare state, and planned economic development—and subsequently had to revise its socio-economic platform. The Fifteenth Congress of the RPP, held in August 1961, surfaced existing disagreements within the party. Former Secretary General Gülek heavily criticized İnönü and his associates for closing their eyes in the face of grave problems in the country and for trying to establish a dictatorship within the party. The RPP must stop acting as if voters had a duty to put it in power, he declared, and should start living up to the name "People's Party."[50] Despite a tide of criticism, İnönü was re-elected as party chairman, and İsmail Rüştü Aksal was elected Secretary General. In September 1962, Aksal resigned in favour of Kemal Satır.[51]

Bülent Ecevit, a former journalist who had initially enjoyed İnönü's support, became a firm proponent of the RPP's ideological reorientation.

In 1965, the new concept of "left of centre" (*ortanın solu*) went public. Ince and Olson claim that Ecevit, together with Turan Güneş,[52] proposed "left of centre" as early as April 1962.[53] Yunus Emre situates the origins of the phrase in the 1950s, when debates took place within the party about its course in a multiparty political system.[54] In any account, that proposal facilitated Ecevit's elevation to the position of Secretary General of the RPP at the Eighteenth Congress in October 1966. Speakers there famously stated that the left of centre had been the core of the RPP since its foundation, and Ecevit added that those who opposed it were mainly against Atatürkism.[55] The final declaration of the congress emphasized the six principles of the RPP, but stressed the populism (*halkçılık*) principle. It interpreted the shift towards the left of centre as a requirement of populism.[56]

Some conservative intellectuals, the ruling JP, and opponents within the RPP met this turn with suspicion, calling Ecevit a bolshevik and communist. At a provincial party meeting in February 1967, İnönü responded to Ecevit in the following way:

> I have been the first to use the term 'left-of-centre'.... The RPP seemed to be outdated and stagnant vis-à-vis social problems... I stated with courage that the RPP was a left-of-centre Party both as regards its foundation and its forty-year-old program. I wanted the RPP to demonstrate its reformist and progressive character ... [and] that, through its populist and reformist principles, the RPP was the principal party of social justice.[57]

This assurance did not satisfy the party's old guard who denied the necessity of a new interpretation of Kemalism. These developments led to a major rift within the RPP's leadership ranks, which was resolved during the Fourth Extraordinary Congress in April 1967. Thanks to İnönü's neutral stance, or support, Ecevit's position gained the upper hand, which made eight more prominent party members, led by the veteran Turhan Feyzioğlu, to leave the party.[58] Observers agree that the new slogan was designed to undermine pressure from the Marxist Workers' Party of Turkey, which resided to the left of the RPP. Later, the "left of the centre" policy was transformed into an ideological concept despite the fact that it lacked proper historical and theoretical foundations. Ecevit began to promote the liberal social and political rights embodied in the constitution as the ideology and *raison d'etre* of the party. Eventually, Ecevit sharpened his own rhetoric and put forth another demand: "*Bu düzen değişmelidir*" (This system must be changed).

Ecevit's first book, *Ortanın solu*, was published in 1966, which was followed by two more in 1969: "*Atatürk ve Devrimcilik*" (Atatürk and Revolutionism) and "*Bu düzen değişmelidir*" (This system should be changed).[59] Both projected leftist inclinations that can be more clearly understood against the backdrop of *Yön*. Ecevit attempted to develop a conceptual framework based on economic nationalism and populism by reinterpreting Kemalist principles. He held the view that Turkish national development had no resemblance to that of the West and the Third World; hence, Turkey was neither developed nor underdeveloped and would have to find its own model of national development.[60] This approach strongly resonated with similar discussions among members of the Kemalist elite in the 1930s.

The party's internal clashes were among the reasons the RPP gained the lowest votes ever (27.4%) in the 1969 parliamentary elections (the JP gained 46.5% and 256 seats), which heated up intra-party debates. At a 1969 meeting, Ecevit criticized Atatürk, and gradually ceased to use the term "*Türk milleti*" (Turkish nation), adopting "*Türkiye halkı*" [The people of Turkey], instead.[61] Thus, Ecevit further challenged the principles of Kemalism. Already in 1970, Ecevit had announced that the RPP should renounce its old claim to mass party status; instead, it should define itself as an organization on the side of "workers, the poor, the oppressed and those who could not claim their rights," and to fight for realization of their dreams.[62] Ahmad argues that while criticizing Atatürk, Ecevit claimed to be a Kemalist, but "made it a secret that Kemalism ought to be updated."[63]

At the Twentieth Congress of the RPP, held in 1970, Ecevit's group consolidated its hold on the party, moving their members into key positions. In his speech, Ecevit stated that the RPP's perspective on the Kemalist principle of "revolutionism" had changed and was now to be understood as "infrastructural revolutionism."[64] The outcome of this dispute between RPP leaders took place in May 1972 at the Fifth Extraordinary Congress, when Ecevit-backed candidates won party elections over İnönü and his group. By then, İnönü wanted to oust Ecevit and his group from key positions and replace them with Kemal Satır, who had lost to Ecevit at the 1970 Congress. In his speech, Satır criticized Ecevit and his group for capturing control of the party in bad faith and for renouncing the heritage and accomplishments of the Kemalist era. Ecevit was accused of engaging in a "Marxist critique of Atatürk" and for its open invitation to communism. Ecevit denied all the charges, claiming that he had simply rehabilitated "Atatürk's concept of auto-criticism."[65] Ecevit was re-elected Secretary General, and İnönü resigned from the party chairmanship—a position he had held since 1938. At the Twenty-first Congress in July 1972, Bülent Ecevit, aged forty-seven, was elected a chairman of the RPP (826 votes out of 913), by invigorating the dissemination of his ideas among citizens. Rising tensions between Ecevit and traditionalists in the party had repercussions for the RPP's 1973 election manifesto, where Atatürk's name was mentioned only twice: once in a brief historical introduction, and then in the foreign policy Section [66] Continuing its ideological reorientation, the RPP soon became a member of the Socialist International (Socintern).[67]

The RPP's lean to the left, its revision of Kemalist principles, and inclusion of sensitive and potentially explosive issues (Ecevit openly supported Kurds and called Alevis an "oppressed" minority) alienated the military from the RPP in general, and from Ecevit in particular. In addition, groups that had separated from the RPP outspokenly criticized Ecevit's leftism. That job was done more vigorously by the Republic Security Party (*Cumhuriyet Güvenlik Partisi*—RSP), which was headed by Turhan Feyzioğlu. As a matter of fact, the ideology of the RSP and its interpretation of the Kemalist revolution and nationalism are considered the rebirth of the republican conservative ideological current; that is, contrary to the left-Kemalism of the late 1960s, right-Kemalism gained importance. As expected, right-Kemalism condemned left-Kemalism for falsifying important historical and political events. Right-Kemalism came to play an essential role in national politics at the end of the 1960s and throughout the 1970s.[68]

THE 1971 INTERVENTION:
RADICALIZATION OF DOMESTIC POLITICS

Although the military, bureaucrats, and intellectuals retained unity in the 1950s and collaborated closely for some time in the 1960s, the liberal atmosphere of the post-1960 period challenged its unity. As a result, by the end of the 1960s, the traditional RPP-army-bureaucracy alliance had almost completely broken down as many prominent RPP members whose brand of Kemalism was in line with the army high command, left the party.[69] Ahmad observes that because of left-of-centre policy, the alliance between the RPP and the leadership of the armed forces was abandoned.[70] The same policy could have also undermined the RPP's reputation among high-ranking officers. Kemalism, once the omnipotent binding feature and essence of officialdom, ceased to be a unifying factor, and instead became subject to various and often conflicting interpretations. Many observers agreed that the 1961 constitution, which aimed to address problems in state and society, had failed. By January 1971, urban guerrilla activity, bank robberies, kidnappings, and student demonstrations reached unprecedented levels. There was also a sustained propaganda campaign in the leftist press, depicting the armed forces as "allies with the bourgeoisie" and in the "service of US imperialism."[71]

On March 3, 1971, General Tagmaç held a gathering of all active generals in the country (almost 300) and announced that Turkey was in a dangerous situation. On March 12, 1971, commanders of the three armed forces issued an ultimatum, which marked the beginning of a second military intervention carried out through a memorandum. The first clause of the "March 12 Memorandum" (*12 Mart Muhtırası*) explained that the inept policies of Parliament and the government had brought the country to the brink of anarchy, civil war, and social and economic unrest, which had caused the public to lose hope in Atatürk's goals.[72] Soon, constitutional amendments that involved specific limitations on civil rights and freedoms enjoyed by the press and associations were initiated. Restrictions on individual and associative freedoms were applied to suppress organized political-ethnic or political-religious movements. Personal freedom was not to jeopardize the "integrity of the state and nation, public order, national security...."[73]

Thus, for the second time in a decade, the army attempted to restructure the country along Kemalist-statist lines. However, it became obvious that the imposition of solutions had become more problematic than before. Observers generally agree that the army's image suffered considerable damage. Even sections of the intelligentsia, particularly those who had formerly backed the army, began to view it as blocking the "forces of progress." Alongside the interventionist spirit of the time, Kemalism itself has become the major normative value to be defended and expanded. In June 1971, a special commission on the principles of Atatürk was created, its task to perpetuate the image of Atatürk and spread "Atatürkism" as the ideology of Turkey.[74] The NSC returned power to civilians in 1973. Analysing the period of the two-year interregnum, Borovali claims: "The 1971–1973 regime raised, perhaps for the last time, the question whether Kemalist development strategies were compatible with pluralist democracy. The question seemed to have been answered before the regime had run its full course."[75]

In October 1973, parliamentary elections were held and the army nominally announced its withdrawal from civilian affairs. The RPP won 185 seats (33.3%), but remained forty-one seats short of the simple majority, the JP came second with 149 seats (29.8%), while the National Salvation Party (NSP) (*Milli Selamet Partisi*—MSP) gained forty-eight seats (11.8%). Electoral success granted Ecevit the image of Turkey's potential saviour. Within a short period, he managed to inspire trust and confidence, and was seen as the man who was capable of changing the course of politics and leading the nation to "Bright days" (*Ak günlere*), as the title of the RPP's election manifesto suggested.[76] Ecevit's simple and direct style caught the imagination of voters, and earned him the moniker "*Halkçı Ecevit*" (People's Ecevit). The RPP began to be identified with and personified by Ecevit. RPP supporters described themselves as *Ecevitçi* (Ecevitist) and carried huge banners declaring "Ecevit is our hope." An English journalist reporting on the October election reported to his paper: "The Turkish election has been won by a party called Ecevit."[77]

The 1970s marks one of the most complex and difficult moments in Turkish history. In parliamentary elections held in 1973 and 1977, no political force was able to secure a clear majority to form a single-party government. Until 1980, both the RPP and JP had to rely on coalitions to form governments. These coalitions proved politically unstable and triggered deep structural, social, and ideological divisions within society. After the 1973 elections, the RPP chose the NSP as its partner to form a government, and the coalition government did not emerge until January 25, 1974. That venture came as a total surprise to politicians and society, since the party that claimed to have eradicated the influence of Islam in Turkey's political life had now established an alliance with a party that vindicated the idea of enhancing Islam's role in politics. Many scholars expressed their astonishment with this "anti-historical coalition." For instance, Suna Kili equates this move with "political heresy... since the decision to form such an alliance was contrary to the very essence of a political institution that had been the vanguard of a radical reform movement carried out to modernize the country."[78]

While on the surface this coalition looks odd, scholars have not paid sufficient attention to the fact that the RPP of 1973 was not the RPP of earlier years. Karpat correctly urges observers not to forget that by then, the RPP and NSP had shared a great deal on social and economic matters. Both parties were against capitalism and struggled for social justice, opposed the West while defending modernization, and favoured friendly relations with Third World countries.[79] Moreover, their views on industrialization strategies and Turkey's rural development had many common features. Both parties were reacting to rapidly changing social realities. Ahmad argues they were completely secular, with little regard for Islamic values, which they considered anachronistic. But as students of contemporary Turkish society, they appreciated the significance of religious sentiments for most Turks and the role these could play in elections. Thus, the RPP abandoned militant laicism for which it was known under İnönü, and Ecevit made it clear that the party's hostility to Islam was a thing of the past.[80] If the RPP and the NSP had common traits, however, their differences were equally great, and perhaps fundamental. Their positions on the social order and cultural development were of utmost significance.

This short-lived coalition broke down in November 1974, three months after the July 1974 Cyprus invasion, when Ecevit felt secure enough to call for an early election to form a one-party government. Ecevit failed, however, to gain support in parliament. In March 1975, Erbakan joined the first "national front" (*Milli Cephe*) government with the JP and Nationalist Action Party (NAP), which lasted until June 1977. It was during this time that both the NSP and the Nationalist Action Party (*Milliyetçi Hareket Partisi*—NAP) infiltrated various government offices with their own members. This reinforced the trend for parties in power to subvert and use government offices for their own ideological purposes. One characteristic feature of the 1970s was the undeniable importance of religion in shaping many aspects of everyday politics. Although this had been a consistent feature of Turkish politics from the 1950s onwards, many observers at the time argued that the role of religion was diminishing. They viewed it as a fragmentary phenomenon that had yet to come of age in Turkey.[81]

Throughout the 1970s, Bülent Ecevit used every opportunity to make the party's leftist inclination reappear in party programs. For instance, on November 29, 1976, the RPP's Twenty-Third General Congress adopted a new party program. It once again confirmed Kemalism's six principles, which were interpreted as complimentary characteristics to the six objectives supported by the party's democratic leftism: freedom (özgürlük); equality (eşitlik); solidarity (dayanışma); priority of labour (emeğin üstünlüğü); integrity of development (gelişmenin bütünlüğü); and democratization with efficiency (etkinliği ile demokratikleşme).[82] The RPP obtained 41.4% (213 seats in total, thirteen seats short of a majority) at the parliamentary elections in June 1977 (the highest percentage since 1946), but again failed to form a government. The JP (thirty-seven percent—189 seats), the NSP (twenty-four seats), and the NAP (sixteen seats) formed the second "national front" government, minus the RRP (Republican Reliance Party). The results of the elections made Ecevit believe that society now favoured leftist policy turns. Consequently, he moved further to the left and became utterly merciless in attacking political enemies.[83] One surprise in the 1977 elections was the success of the radical right NAP. Headed by the former NUC member, Alparslan Türkeş, the party transformed into a highly disciplined, hierarchal, nationalist group. The populist nationalist stance of NAP, based on the doctrine of *Dokuz Işık* (Nine Lights) of the party leader Türkeş, opposed communism, Marxism, and capitalism, and vindicated the radical interpretation of Kemalist national-secularism that espoused Islam to gain support in eastern and central Turkey.[84] Türkeş often positioned himself as the only politician who correctly interpreted Atatürkism. The ethnonationalism of this radical right party and extremism of its members—*ülkücü*-s (idealists)—widely contributed to violent polarizations in the Turkish political climate of the 1970s.[85]

The second national front lasted only five months, since in January 1978, Ecevit managed to form a government. Meanwhile, social and economic problems grew, while political violence and armed struggles between leftists and rightists manifested existing public discontent. In the autumn of 1979, the RPP was defeated in partial elections, and then Süleyman Demirel established a minority government, which introduced an economic stabilization program in January 1980. That program was, in fact, the most far-reaching economic reform program ever introduced in Turkey. He failed, however, to impose political stability. Thus, between 1973 and 1980, Ecevit and Demirel played a "game of musical chairs" due to intense ideological polarization.[86] Some have attributed the inability of the two parties to come together to the personal animosity between party leaders.

In the midst of this national calamity from 1978 to 1980, army generals had begun discussing a possible intervention already in 1977. The consensus was that the only possible solution out of political deadlock was another military intervention. On December 27, 1979, the High Command issued a letter to the president, demanding all political parties to unite in the direction of the principles of the constitution and Kemalism.[87] The same letter contained a reference to the Internal Service Code of the Turkish Armed Forces, particularly Article 35: "The duty of the Armed Forces is to protect and safeguard the Turkish land and the Turkish Republic as stipulated by the Constitution."[88]

However, not everyone agreed; for instance, Karpat believed that there was only one alternative to halting army intervention: a mobilizing ideology or force. For this, he assumed, Erbakan's NSP, as a carrier of commonly accepted ideological concepts, was the ideal candidate for reconciling the conflicting parties.[89] Yavuz defends this view: "Islam proved to be socially embedded in various forms of social life and was more conducive to mass mobilization than either nationalism or socialism, because of its flexible network system, norms, and symbolic values."[90]

The history of the Turkish Republic in the 1970s is regarded as its most violent, ideologically divided, and paralyzed decade. After the 1971–1973 hiatus, instability and political turmoil soon resumed with clashes between right- and left-wing militants. The fragmentation of society reached a dangerous point. In the 1970s, Turkey offered a prime example of a cleavage between centre and periphery, new and old, modernity and tradition. Students and youth, in particular, formed large, marauding gangs that roamed the streets and entered universities, beating up those who did not immediately identify themselves as sympathizers. Killings gradually spread, from targeted assassinations to widespread, indiscriminate raids on coffee houses, public meetings, market squares, and shops.[91] Starting from mid-1979, on average twenty citizens were killed each day. One of the underlying reasons for the state's failure to cope with the political extremism was the fact that the police and the security forces were heavily infiltrated by the diehard supporters of Türkeş's NAP. While, leftist movements emerged more fractioned and divided, the NAP provided support and protection to various rightist terrorist groups.[92] It was the case not only during the Nationalist Front governments, but also under Ecevit's government.[93] For the first time in many decades, the state's authority was partially collapsed in several parts of the country. In addition to the "liberated zones" in Ankara and Istanbul city neighbourhoods, which were controlled by terrorist groups, entire towns in various regions of Turkey (Çorum, Yozgat, Elazığ, Kars, Fatsa) had fallen under the virtual control of terrorist and radical left-wing organizations.[94]

The events in the Black Sea town of Fatsa, located some 400 km away from the Soviet Union border, were particularly extraordinary, as the left-wing local leadership of the *Devrimci Yol* movement rejected the central authority and declared a commune free from government control.[95] The economic crisis also, coupled with the rising price for energy, import restrictions, and high inflation rates, have undermined the government's credibility in society. Karpat's summary of the events in the 1970s is rather influential: "the entire political edifice erected by the Constitution of 1961 had deteriorated beyond repair."[96]

In addition to right-left cleavages, there were also instances of radicalization between dominant Sunnis and religious denominations. During the 1970s, some scholars—Çamuroğlu, Doğan among them—argued that Alevi identity had been assimilated by mainstream secular Turkish nationalism and was on the wane.[97] Communal massacres against Alevis in five major cities (Tokat, Çankırı, Çorum, Sivas, and Kahramanmaraş) between 1977 and 1980 challenged this perception and further deepened the connections between party affiliation and ethnoreligious identity. This communal conflict ended with 106 deaths (mostly Alevis), 176 injured, 210 homes destroyed, and seventy stores ruined.[98]

External powers were also concerned with NATO's southern ally's domestic upheavals. Major concern also came from Iran, where the Islamic Revolution brought new Islamic-oriented forces into power in 1979. Washington, concerned about the possible duplication of the Iranian scenario in Turkey, saw a threat to its regional interests, and encouraged the Turkish military to execute its historical duty and stabilize the country.

It is worth mentioning that not everyone in Turkey shared the opinion that the political system was facing a major crisis at the end of the 1970s. A prominent Turkish historian, Binnaz Toprak, even emphasized that the 1970s was a critical age for Turkish pluralist democracy.[99] It is indisputable that in comparison to the First Republic (1923–1960), the second constitution promoted pluralism of opinions and movements; however, it was incapable of building consensus between rising radical trends and mutually exclusive approaches. Moreover, the figures that later were provided by the army leadership should be cited: according to the army, anarchy and violence between 1977 and 1980 took 5421 human lives and injured 14,152 civilians, among them prominent and distinguished journalists, political figures, university lecturers, and human rights activists.[100] Turkish society paid an exorbitant price for its experiment with the "pluralist democracy."

Prior to the next intervention, parliament reached a stalemate. As a consequence, it failed to elect a president, despite 100 rounds over a three-month period. The minority government of Demirel, formed in the fall of 1979, was unable to handle the crisis. Given the circumstances, the army decided to act, and on August 12, 1980, set a date for the third intervention operation, which was code named "Flag Plan." It was carried out a month later, on September 12.

The foregoing discussion implies that in the 1960s and 1970s, the ideological construct of the Kemalist state proved too narrow to incorporate newly emerging social forces. Some observers argue that Kemalist thought was no longer regarded as a source of all public policies. New state elites used Atatürkist thought as a technique, not a political manifesto. Kemalist thought started to serve, however, as a justification for rejecting radical ideologies of both left and right. Capturing this complexity, Frey claimed in 1975 that the Kemalist paradigm was exhausted and had no accepted successor in sight.[101]

During the same period, various observers, trying to find the role and place of Kemalism in Turkey's growing ideological polarization, developed a number of approaches. For instance, in 1978, Mardin pointed out that Kemalist ideology lost its great potential and eroded, whereas it could have reshaped world views from candidates to elite.[102] In the same vein, speaking of the 1970s, Karpat noted: "… much of Kemalism, born from the demands of a rising national state, has become outdated by economic and social pressures though still the predominant political ideology."[103] Another argument, shared by Heper, Harris, and Karpat is that in the 1960s and thereafter, Kemalism served as a cover for other ideas or ideologies; each and every group, including radicals, interpreted Kemalism to suit their purposes.[104] In 1969, Kili cited multifaceted perceptions and interpretations of Kemalism that were dominant in the late 1960s: "… Some read into Atatürk's statements meanings which are not really there. Others try to develop a whole theory based on a few statements he made. There are also groups which claim allegiance although they are for the most part aware that some or almost all of their convictions and principles are in direct opposition to the principles of Kemalism."[105]

Atatürk's image and maxims, as in the previous decades, were everywhere during the 1960s and 1970s, as politicians tried to exploit the internalized hegemonic cult of the hero for their electoral purposes. Yet there were also efforts to construct parallel heroes by revising early republican history. Tarla and Davison explain:

Exalting Atatürk's ego was a way of exalting oneself subjectively, but it was effectively a self-abnegation because Atatürk, as all know, had no equal. In this persisting power relation, no independent role emerged, no autonomous personality development occurred, and hence, no political exchange between equal citizens took place. Under Kemalism, Turkish political life seemed permanently committed to apolitical, infantilist relations of hierarchical subordination.[106]

This chapter looked at a critical period for the RPP and Kemalism. The 1961 constitution broadened the political space that allowed different social actors and political parties to have a say in ideological reconfigurations. For the first time since the days of "high Kemalism," the key principles of the founding philosophy of Turkey were radically modified and interpreted, not only by social and political movements, but, more importantly, by the RPP. The latter had to position itself according to the demands of new social and political realities and adjust its ideological premises to meet demands to create a more egalitarian economic system. Within six to seven years of Ecevit becoming Secretary General of the party, he brought new insights and orientations to the RPP, which sidelined conservatives and inevitably changed the party's appeal. After taking over the party's leadership, the RPP won two consecutive parliamentary elections, but fell short of forming stable one-party majority governments. The new constitution also broadened the space for different interpretations of Kemalism. Emerging leftist movements were particularly vocal in their efforts to revise and repackage the principles of Kemalism. The Turkish armed forces' efforts to act on behalf of Kemalist principles also positioned them as vanguards of Kemalism.

Notes

1. Samuel Huntington. 1968. *Political Order in Changing Societies.* New Haven: Yale University Press, 221.
2. Jacob Landau. 1974. *Radical Politics in Turkey.* Leiden: Brill, 7.
3. Nuri Eren. 1963. *Turkey Today and Tomorrow: An Experiment in Westernization.* London: Frederick A. Praeger, 69.
4. *Interviews with Members of Turkey's National Unity Committee.* 1960. (by Cevat Baskut, Yasar Kemal, and Ecvet Guresin) New York: U.S. Joint Publications Research Service, 1–2.
5. Ibid., Interview with A. Türkeş, 9.
6. Ibid., Interview with S. Küçük, 20.

7. Ibid., 21.
8. Ibid., Interview with Orhan Erkanlı, 26.
9. Ibid., Interview with Irfan Solmazer., 40.
10. Interview with Numan Esin, 59; more on Numan Esin's views see Numan Esin. 2005. *Devrim ve Demokrasi, Bir 27 Mayısçının anıları.* İstanbul: Doğan Kitap.
11. Interview with Kabibay, 66.
12. Ibid., Interview with Col. Tunçkanat, 75.
13. Ibid., Interview with Muzaffer Karan, 109.
14. Ibid., Sami Küçük, 21.
15. Interview with Irfan Solmazer, 40.
16. For the English text see *Constitution of the Turkish Republic.* 1961. Translated for the Committee of National Unity by Sadık Balkan, Ahmet Uysal and Kemal Karpat. Ankara.
17. Constitution was promulgated as Law number 334 of July 9, 1961 in the Official Gazette number 10859 of July 20, 1961.
18. Constitution of the Turkish Republic (1961, 3).
19. Ibid.
20. Dodd (1979, 101).
21. Ergun Özbudun and Ömer Faruk Gençkaya. 2009. *Democratization and the Politics of Constitution-Making in Turkey.* Budapest: Central European University Press, 16–17.
22. Weiker (1963, 73).
23. Mardin (2006, 314).
24. Metin Heper. 1988. "State and Society in Turkish Political Experience." In *State, Democracy and the Military.* Berlin: Walter de Gruyter, 7.
25. Article 111. The Constitution of the Turkish Republic. 1961.
26. *Cited in* Suna Kili. 1971. *Turkish Constitutional Developments, Turkish Constitutional Developments and Assembly Debates on the Constitutions of 1924 and 1961.* Istanbul: Robert College Research Center, 71–72.
27. Hakan Yavuz. 2003. *Islamic Political Identity in Turkey.* Oxford: Oxford University Press, 63.
28. Nurhan Ince and Robert W. Olson. 1980. "Yön and Its Influence on the Leftist Movement in Turkey and on Foreign and Domestic Policy: 1960–1964." *Turcica: Revue d'Etudes Turques.* Tome XII: 174.
29. Landau (1974, 13).
30. Weiker (1963, 89).
31. Faruk Güventürk. 1964. *Gerçek Kemalizm.* İstanbul: Okat Yayınevi.
32. Ilhan Selçuk. 1966. *"Atatürkçü Antiemperyalist Cephe Kurulamadıkça".* Yön. 11.11.
33. See Landau (1974, 66–76).
34. Ince and Olson (1980, 175–176).

35. Özgür Mutlu Ulus. 2011. *The Army and Radical Left in Turkey: Military Coups, Social Revolution and Kemalism*. London: I.B. Tauris, 21.
36. Ulus (2011, 22).
37. Feyzioğlunun Görüşleri. "*Yön.*" ağustos 22, 1960. 4.
38. Ahmet Hamdi Başar. 1962. *Ne liberalizm, ne sosyalizm, fakat Kemalizm.* "Barış dünyasi", nisan 4–8; Başar. 1962. *Niçin sosyalizm değil de Kemalizm*, "Barış dünyasi". eylül.
39. See Landau (1974, 56).
40. Ulus (2011, 22).
41. Ince and Olson (1980, 186).
42. Ulus (2011, 32–33).
43. Ulus (2011, 51–54).
44. Ulus (2011, 59–60).
45. Ulus (2011, 62).
46. Landau (1974, 107).
47. Giritli (2001, 125).
48. Bulletin of the Turkish Press. 1967. The Ministry for Foreign Affairs of the USSR, November 10.
49. *Milliyet.* November 10, 1967.
50. Weiker (1963, 93).
51. Special bulletin (1966, 45–46).
52. Turan Güneş played an important role in making left of centre ideology a working political principle in Turkey; he wrote extensively on prospects of the leftist and social democracy in line with the Kemalist interpretation of socio-political modernization.
53. Ince and Olson (1980, 185).
54. Emre (2014, 82).
55. Cited in Yunus Emre, 98–99.
56. The Declaration of the 18th Congress of the RPP translated by Yunus Emre, see Emre (2014, 234–236).
57. Quoted in Suna Kili. 1969. *Kemalism*. Istanbul: Robert College, 192.
58. Sabri Sayari. 1990. "Bülent Ecevit." In *Political Leaders of the Contemporary Middle East and Africa*, edited by Bernard Reich, 159–166. Westport, CT: Greenwood.
59. Bülent Ecevit. 1968. *Ortanın Solu*. Ankara: Tekin Yayınevi; Bülent Ecevit. 1969. *Atatürk ve Devrimcilik*. Ankara: Tekin Yayınevi; and Bülent Ecevit. 1968. *Bu Düzen Değişmelidir.* Ankara: Tekin Yayınevi.
60. Ince and Olson (1980, 186).
61. Karpat (2004, 320).
62. Ibid.
63. Ahmad (1977, 260).

64. Borovali (1985, 119).
65. Borovali (1985, 114–115).
66. *Ak Gunlere: Cumhuriyet Halk Partisi 1973 Secim Bildirgesi.* 1973. Ankara. 217.
67. Kili (1980, 390).
68. Tanıl Bora and Taşkın Yüksel. 2009. "Sağ Kemalizm." In *Kemalizm, Modern Türkiye'de Siyasi Düşünce, cilt 2*, edited by Murat Belge, 529–545. İstanbul: İletişim Yayınları.
69. The RPP-army-bureaucracy relations are extensively discussed in Dankwart Rustow. 1966. "Development of Political Parties in Turkey." In *Political Parties and Political Development*, edited by Joseph La Palombara and Myron Weiner, 107–133. Princeton: Princeton University Press.
70. Ahmad (1977, 261).
71. Borovali (1985, 123).
72. For the most recent discussion of the 1971 March 12 Memorandum see Türkiye Büyük Millet Meclisi Darbe ve Muhtarıları Araştırma Komisyonu. Kasım 2012. Mercis Araştırma Komisyonu Raporu. Ankara.
73. Geoffrey Lewis. 1977. "Political Change in Turkey Since 1960." In *Aspects of Modern Turkey*, edited by William Hale, 9–20. London: Bowker in Association with the Center for Middle Eastern and Islamic Studies of the University of Durham; Richard F. Nyrop. 1973. *Area Handbook for the Republic of Turkey*. Washington: U.S. Govt. Print. Office, 198.
74. Tamkoç (1976, 112).
75. Borovali (1985, 129).
76. Ahmad (1977, 319); *"Ak Günlere"*. 1973. Cumhuriyet Halk Partisi 1973 Seçim Bildirgesi. Ankara: Ajans-Türk Matbaacılık Sanayii.
77. Ahmad (1977, 330).
78. Suna Kili. 2003. *The Atatürk Revolution: A Paradigm of Modernization*. Istanbul: Türk Iş Bankası, Kültür Yayınları, 401.
79. Karpat (2004, 323).
80. Ahmad (1977, 334).
81. Kili (1980, 394–396).
82. C.H.P. Program. 1976. Ankara: Ajans-Türk Matbaacılık Sanayi.
83. Kili (1980, 399–400).
84. Sultan Tepe. 2000. "A Kemalist-Islamist Movement? The NAP." *Turkish Studies* 1 (2): 63.
85. For more information on the NAP, see Hugh Poulton. 1997. *Top Hat, Grey Wolf and Crescent: Turkish Nationalism and the Turkish Republic*. New York: New York University Press.

86. Here is the list of the PM after 1974: B. Ecevit (January 25–November 7, 1974), S. Irmak (November 13, 1974–March 30, 1975), S. Demirel (March 31, 1975–June 21, 1977), B. Ecevit (June 21, 1977–July 21, 1977), S. Demirel (July 21, 1977–January 5, 1978), B. Ecevit (January 5, 1978–November 12, 1979), S. Demirel (November 12, 1979–September 12, 1980).

87. *12 September in Turkey: Before and After.* Ankara: The General Secretatiat of the NSC, 160–161.

88. Ibid., 224.

89. Karpat Kemal. 1981. "Turkish Democracy at Impasse: Ideology, Party Politics and the Third Military Intervention." *International Journal of Turkish Studies* 2 (1): 2–3.

90. Hakan Yavuz. 1997. "Political Islam and the Welfare (Refah) Party in Turkey." *Comparative Politics* 30 (1): 65.

91. Mehmet Ali Birand in his book *Shirts of Steel*, gives a detailed description of the events which led to the military intervention of September 12, 1980.

92. Sabri Sayari. 2010. "Political Violence and Terrorism in Turkey, 1976–1980: A Retrospective Analysis." *Terrorism and Political Violence* 22 (2): 199.

93. Zürcher (2017, 266).

94. Sabri Sayari (2010, 210) and Zürcher (2017, 267).

95. Clement Dodd. 1983. *The Crisis of Turkish Democracy.* Beverley: The Eothen Press, 20.

96. Karpat (1988, 148).

97. Izzettin Doğan. 2000. *Alevi-Islam Inanci, Kültürü ile Ilgili Görüş ve Düşünceler.* İstanbul: Cem.; Reha Çamuroglu. 1998. "Alevi Revival in Turkey." In *Alevi Identity: Cultural, Religious and Social Perspectives,* edited by Tord Olson, Elisabeth Ozdalga, and. Catherine Raudvere, 79–84. Istanbul: Swedish Research Institute in Istanbul.

98. Yavuz (2003, 68).

99. Binnaz Toprak. 1981. *Islam and Political Development in Turkey.* Leiden: Brill, 123.

100. John McFadden. 1985. "Civil-Military Relations in the Third Turkish Republic." *The Middle East Journal* 39 (1): 70.

101. Frey (1975, 70).

102. Şerif Mardin. 1978. "Youth and Violence in Turkey." *European Journal of Sociology* 19 (2): 246–247.

103. Kemal Karpat. 1982. "Introduction to Political and Social Though in Turkey." In *Political and Social Thought in the Contemporary Middle East,* edited by Kemal Karpat, 298. New York: Praeger.

104. Heper (1985, 110); George Harris. 1972. *Troubled Alliance: Turkish-American Problems in Historical Perspective.* Washington, DC: American Enterprise Institute for Public Policy Research, 96; and Karpat (1982, 347).
105. Kili (1969, 3).
106. Parla and Davison (2004, 186).

REFERENCES

Ahmad, Feroz. 1977. *The Turkish Experiment in Democracy 1950–1975.* London: C. Hurst & Company.

Borovali, Ali Fuat. 1985. Kemalist Tradition, Political Change and the Turkish Military. Unpublished dissertation, Queen's University.

Dodd, Clement. 1979. *Democracy and Development in Turkey.* Beverley: The Eothen Press.

Emre, Yunus. 2014. *The Emergence of Social Democracy in Turkey: The Left and the Transformation of the Republican People's Party.* London: I.B. Tauris.

Frey, Frederick. 1975. "Patterns of Elite Politics in Turkey." In *Political Elites in the Middle East,* edited by George Lenczowski, 41–82. Washington, DC: American Enterprize Institute for Public Policy Research.

Giritli, İsmet. 2001. "The Superiority of the Kemalist Ideology Over Dogmatic Ideologies." In *A Handbook of Kemalist Thought,* translated by Ayşegül Amanda Yeşilbursa, 125–136. Ankara: Atatürk Research Center.

Heper, Metin. 1985. *The State Tradition in Turkey.* Beverley: The Eothen Press.

Ince, Nurhan, and Robert Olson. 1980. "Yön and Its Influence on the Leftist Movement in Turkey and on Foreign and Domestic Policy: 1960–1964." *Turcica: Revue d'Etudes Turques.* Tome XII: 174–186.

Karpat, Kemal. 1988. "Military Interventions: Army-Civilian Relations in Turkey Before and After 1980." In *State, Democracy and the Military,* edited by Metin Heper and Ahmet Evin, 137–158. Berlin: Walter de Gruyter.

Karpat, Kemal. 2004. *Studies on Turkish Politics and Society: Selected Articles and Essays.* Leiden and Boston: Brill.

Kili, Suna. 1969. *Kemalism.* İstanbul: School of Business Administration and Economics, Robert College.

Kili, Suna. 1980. "Kemalism in Contemporary Turkey." *International Political Science Review* 1 (3): 380–404.

Landau, Jacob. 1974. *Radical Politics in Turkey,* vol. 14. Leiden: Brill.

Mardin, Şerif. 2006. *Religion, Society, and Modernity in Turkey.* Syracuse: Syracuse University Press.

Parla, Taha, and Andrew Davison. 2004. *Corporatist Ideology in Kemalist Turkey: Progress or Order?* Syracuse: Syracuse University Press.

Sayari, Sabri. 2010. "Political Violence and Terrorism in Turkey, 1976–80: A Retrospective Analysis." *Terrorism and Political Violence* 22 (2): 198–215.

Tamkoç, Metin. 1976. *The Warrior Diplomats: Guardians of the National Security and Modernization of Turkey.* Salt Lake City: University of Utah Press.

Ulus, Özgür Mutlu. 2011. *The Army and Radical Left in Turkey: Military Coups, Social Revolution and Kemalism.* London: I.B. Tauris.

Weiker, Walter. 1963. *The Turkish Revolution 1960–1961: Aspects of Military Politics.* Washington, DC: The Brookings Institution.

Yavuz, Hakan. 2003. *Islamic Political Identity in Turkey.* Oxford: Oxford University Press.

Zürcher, Erik-Jan. 2017. *Turkey: A Modern History,* 4th ed. London: I.B. Tauris.

Problems and Perspectives of Existing Interpretations of Kemalism

After discussing major turning points in the evolution and transformation of Kemalism between the 1920s and 1970s and before shifting to Soviet perceptions, it is useful to establish existing interpretations of Kemalism and revisit certain established patterns. Since its inception, Kemalism produced divergent interpretations and schisms over its meaning, not only during its active period—what was called "high-Kemalism"—but also after its decline. Different interpretations of Kemalism and ways of referring to it (Atatürkism, İnönüism, left-Kemalism, right-Kemalism, neo-Kemalism, and post-Kemalism) can also be seen as indivisible features of many political ideologies. Different efforts to interpret Kemalism proceeded along its six principles or by taking more holistic approaches. This chapter, then, lays out a few perspectives, which can potentially enlarge the scope of Kemalist studies. One of these aspects concerns the existing disagreement in the scholarship over Turkey's experience with totalitarianism, and particularly with fascism. This chapter explores this generally overlooked dimension and argues that even the limited research on this subject has been mainly done from comparative perspectives. Furthermore, the chapter establishes that there is a compelling continuity of totalitarian ideological and political practices between the Young Turks and the Kemalists. The chapter concludes with an examination of popular interpretations of Kemalism in the first decade of the twenty-first century.

© The Author(s) 2019   149
V. Ter-Matevosyan, *Turkey, Kemalism and the Soviet Union,*
Modernity, Memory and Identity in South-East Europe,
https://doi.org/10.1007/978-3-319-97403-3_7

Perspectives on Kemalism in the 1930s

Most scholars contend that ideologies exist in a state of internal tension, demanding various forms of adaptation and revision. An ideology should, therefore, not be studied merely as a fixed system, but as a process characterized by continuous discussions and change.[1] The Turkish case confirms this assertion; with the passage of time, the key concepts of Kemalism were transformed. For decades, observers saw in Kemalism the formation and evolution of it as a linear process. That logic meant that Atatürk and his close allies had a clear vision of the role that Kemalism would play. In reality, examining the history of just the 1930s reveals that at least six interpretations or definitions of Kemalism were known. They were proposed and defended by Celal Bayar, İsmet İnönü, Recep Peker, and the journals *Kadro* and *Ulku*, which were run by a group of Bergsonians. The gradual withdrawal of Kemal Atatürk from daily politics and the strife of the elite to fill this gap brought various currents of Kemalism to the surface. The physical presence of Kemal who formulated or perhaps coordinated the emergence and elaboration of Kemalist ideas, principles, and programs prevented major splits. He, however, did not hinder different interpretations and approaches from emerging.

As in many parallel cases, in Turkey too, the party leadership and intellectual elite took ideology seriously: to manipulate it, change it arbitrarily to suit shifting policy lines, or adapt it genuinely and change it meaningfully.[2] In the Turkish case, we can see the combination of the three. Ertan Aydın distinguishes three versions of Kemalism presented by conservative modernists (republican conservatives), or the "*Ülkü*" and "*Kadro*" movements, which had a considerable impact on the evolution of Kemalist discourse.[3] Nazım İrem gives an even broader picture of an elite fragmentation within the ranks of ruling republican cadres. He identifies three major groups with an organizational basis in the ruling RPP. Hard-line statist republicans were gathered around Recep Peker. An influential pro-business liberal faction, known as the *affairists*, led by Celal Bayar, countered him. The last section was made up of moderate statist-bureaucratic elites supported by İsmet İnönü.[4] Thus, İrem excluded the influence of the Kadro group, which, in reality, played a key role in the initial conceptualization of the Kemalist system of thought.

The *Kadro* movement adopted its name from the journal with the same name. The periodical was published for two and a half years, starting in January 1932. Prominent members of the movement

(Karaosmanoğlu, Aydemir, Tökin, and Tör, among others) set out to promote serious discussions of ideology and economic development strategies. It was not simply that *Kadro* appointed itself to undertake the task of developing a theoretical framework to interpret the Turkish revolution and propose a development strategy. Key members of the movement (Aydemir, Tökin, etc.) had visited and some even studied in the Soviet Union and were well versed in Communist ideology in economic innovations like the "New Economic Policy" (NEP),[5] and the Soviet experience of radical modernization and development.[6] Harris even claimed that the *Kadro* movement filled an intellectual void previously occupied by the Communist elite, while most of its members did not deviate far from their earlier Communist ideas.[7]

According to the founder of the journal, Karaosmanoğlu, its goal was "the propaganda of ideological foundations of the revolution and integration of the Republican People's Party principles into a unified system."[8] They draw parallels between the anti-imperialist nature of the Bolshevik and Kemalist revolutions. The revolutionary theory of the *Kadro* movement was expected to convert Kemalism from an isolated nationalist ideology into a universal theory of anti-colonialism that would be a "viable alternative to communism and violent capitalism, a sort of third way."[9] *Kadro*'s contributors thought of it becoming "the first example of the liberation of a technologically backward semi-colony,"[10] which could also set "a model for the colonized peoples of Asia and Africa."[11] Hanioğlu argues that it also signified the first attempt in Turkish intellectual life to formulate a genuine theory of the Kemalist revolution through a loosely Marxist, historical materialist theoretical prism.[12] In fact, as will be observed in the analysis of Soviet sources, many of the concepts, phrases, and expressions in *Kadro*'s vocabulary were widely used by Soviet observers in the 1920s. *Kadro*, thus, developed an alternative vision, as many perceived it. However, it bears mentioning that *Kadro*'s anti-colonial position raises some obvious objections as it disregards the political sovereignty of the Ottoman past and the republican present. It also obscures certain historical facts by implying that Kemalism emerged from a colonial struggle. These objections may also serve as credible explanations for the anti-colonial discourse not finding deep intellectual roots in Turkey.

The *Kadro* movement was viewed with suspicion both by the RPP's elite and eventually by Atatürk, although he initially approved of this "intellectual experiment"[13] and, contrary to many claims, maintained good relations with Karaosmanoğlu. The Secretary General of the RPP led the campaign against the movement and the journal, arguing against the claims of its leader, Karaosmanoğlu. In the face of *Kadro*, the Peker faction saw a challenge to the party's monopoly over ideology by a group of outsiders. Peker made clear to Karaosmanoğlu that the task of promoting and interpreting ideology belonged to him. *Kadro* became associated with Soviet propaganda and was vulnerable to criticism from Peker's and İnönü's factions and was eventually less productive at articulating ideological principles. However, Harris acknowledges that it was under *Kadro's* influence that Turkey adopted its first five-year plan in 1934, which was greatly influenced by the Soviet experiment of state economic planning.[14]

Unlike the left-wing *Kadro* movement, the *Ülkü* (Ideal) journal, founded in February 1933, served as a platform where the right-wing dimension of the Kemalist system of thought was extensively discussed and promoted. The journal's founder, RPP Secretary General Recep Peker, and his associates were impressed by German National Socialism and Italian Fascism and wanted to model the RPP accordingly.[15] Based on the analysis of Peker's lectures and his disagreements with Mustafa Kemal, Hanioğlu posits that Peker was interested in imitating Stalin and exploited his position to become a powerful party secretary by imposing strict party domination in all aspects of political life.[16] Many, as mentioned, saw him as sympathetic to the regimes of Hitler and Mussolini.[17]

During the revolution, and in various lectures, Peker expressed his vision for Turkey's ideological construction. He widely shared his views in the journal that was published until August 1936. Along with Recep Peker, Şevket Kansu, and Nusret Köymen, among others, Peker proposed various ideas to promote the cult of Mustafa Kemal and his ideologies. For instance, Köymen suggested inventing "a science of Kemalism...through scientific methods and turn[ing] it into social engineering."[18] In the same vein, Şevket Kansu recommended: "This pure, masculine, and robust ideology that can be called 'National Kemalism' should use bio-sociology and even eugenics to shape the new solidaristic society."[19] However, soon Peker's role decreased, because of Mustafa Kemal's displeasure with his initiatives and increasing opposition from the core of the party. After his dismissal, his radical ideals were shelved. Although short-lived, the *Ülkü* interpretation of Kemalism left a significant impact on ideological developments in Turkey. The right-wing Kemalism of *Ülkü*, with its narrow and exclusivist interpretation of

Turkish nationalism and personality cult, were vigorously followed in later decades.

Henri Bergson's criticism of rationalism and liberal-progressive evolution greatly influenced the republican-conservative movement, which, until recently, was widely ignored in the literature. The key intellectuals behind this movement (İsmail Hakkı Baltacıoğlu, Peyami Safa, Ahmet Ağaoğlu, Hilmi Ziya Ülken, and Mustafa Şekip Tunç) elaborated a new blend of concepts, terms, themes, and motives that originated and circulated within the Kemalist power structure in the late 1920s and 1930s, not only for interpreting novelties brought about by the Republic, but also for providing new content to the term "conservative," which would be radical, modernist, and most significantly, secular.[20] These intellectuals opposed mechanical-deterministic European philosophy, seeing it as the main cause for devastation that followed WWI, and the positivist-materialism of Ziya Gökalp. Instead, they saw spiritualist-romanticism as a new theory for national integration and moral renewal, with its emphasis on irrationalism, anti-intellectualism, mysticism, and intuitionist philosophy. They supported Kemal's cultural and political reforms, treated Kemalism as a positive phenomenon, and, meanwhile, contrary to *Kadro*, aimed at driving Kemalism towards a national path of development, away from a universalist course. To them, Kemalism was a form of élan engineering, which derived its constituent principles from the necessities of life, not from a guidebook.[21] They also warned their contemporaries, "If Kemalism failed to consolidate the new national moral order, people deprived of any sense of national identity and morality could fall into the pit of moral confusion that would make them vulnerable to the religion-bound communities of the Ottoman Islamic past."[22]

The mid-1930s was replete with efforts to popularize the principles of Kemalism among the general population and to encourage the participation of as many leaders as possible at all levels in this work (Recep Peker,[23] Şeref Aykut,[24] Saffet Engin,[25] Mediha Muzaffer,[26] and Halil Nimetullah Öztürk[27]). Kemalism became the basis of hundreds of articles in party publications, the subject of countless speeches by both national and local leaders in the People's Houses, and the foundation for required courses in Turkish schools and universities.[28] Ruling elites began to follow the policy of recruiting new intellectual groupings to engineer a new republican consensus and broaden the support base of the Kemalist state. In 1937, Tekin Alp, another proponent of Kemalist ideology, published a book, "*Le Kemalisme*." He discussed the concept of the nation as well as principles of unity in language, culture, and ideas, by considering this unity a prerequisite for the construction of a new rational nationhood.[29] It is noteworthy that he was not dealing with some vague prescriptions for political, economic, and social development, but with a network of doctrinal options, which had already been the subject of numerous official and semi-official considerations.[30] To him, "Kemalism" was no longer uncertain, or merely a term to describe the contemporary revolutionary reality, but an ideology in charge of the fate of the Turkish nation and state. It designated the path to follow to ensure that the Turkish nation-state achieved its goals.[31] Kemalism was empowered by dynamics and vitality, stated Alp, and there was no room for dreaming in abstractions.[32]

Another important aspect of Kemalism's public outreach was printed media. Kemal highly encouraged the foundation and activities of republican newspapers. Between 1925 and 1926, 153 Turkish periodicals were published in Turkey.[33] Some, including *Akşam, Milliyet, Cumhuriyet, Vakit,* and *Hakimiyet-i Milliye* shaped Kemalist principles. Their chief editors and journalists were men devoted to Kemal. Falih Rıfkı Atay (1884–1971) was editor-in-chief of the RPP's official organ, *Hakimiyet-i Milliye,* which became *Ulus.* He was a staunch proponent of Kemalist reforms[34] and is remembered by his uncommon remarks concerning the ideological construction of Kemalism. The following assertions of Atay were widely known by his contemporaries: "Kemalism is reserved for Turkey," "We are neither communists, nor fascists, we are Kemalists," "Kemalism is as much ideological as fascism and communism."[35] Atay was active in politics as well, particularly in the late 1950s and 1960s. Among other prominent journalists that should be mentioned are Yunus Nadi, Necmettin Sadık Sadak, Hamdullah Suphi Tanrıöver, Hüseyin Rahmi Gürpınar, Kâzım Şinasi Dersan, and Avram Galanti. Yunus Nadi played a particularly important role in disseminating Kemalist views from the outset of the war. He had been editor-in-chief of three periodicals since 1918 (*Yeni Gün, Hakimiyet-i Milliye,* and *Cumhuriyet*). His memoirs contained important insights about the Kemalist movement and the Allied occupation of Istanbul. Besides newspaper activities, Necmettin Sadık Sadak (1890–1953) disseminated Kemalist ideology in schools and colleges. Later, Sadak was also actively involved in politics, serving as the Minister for Foreign Affairs of Turkey (1947–1950).

By the mid-1930s, principles of Kemalist thought that were described as techniques for finding truth, assumed substantive meanings.

Turkish bureaucracy bore an outstanding load, making Kemalism a dominant ideological current. Heper thinks that the bureaucracies, devoid of Atatürk's charisma, had only one way to legitimate their influential role: transforming Atatürkist thoughts and ideas into a political manifesto that would assume responsibility for carrying these out.[36] By that time, the strong bureaucracy, empowered by a detailed knowledge of Atatürk's thoughts and Kemalist interpretations of worldly affairs, acquired confidence and legitimacy to defend the deeds and the achievements of the Kemalist revolution.

ANALYSES ALONG THE KEY PRINCIPLES

Efforts to understand Kemalism also occurred as scholars decoded its core principles. Some students of Kemalism have problematized all six principles, finding similarities among them or examining them as distinct concepts. As is presented below, some scholars tried to find parallels between two or more principles, while others viewed them as mutually enforcing. Still others found one or two principles more problematic and important than the rest, or built a hierarchy of six principles based on their perceived significance and applicability.

Of the six principles, three (nationalism, republicanism, and laicism) are not, in Parla's view, theoretically problematic and have been established without much controversy. A fourth principle, revolutionism (which he calls transformationism) took root in Turkish political culture without any political disputation. The other two, étatism and populism, are both theoretically problematic and have been politically controversial, causing distortions in different ways and by different groups.[37]

Suna Kili separated reformism [i.e., revolutionism] and secularism from the six principles, arguing that they had particular importance in retaining Kemalism's dynamic quality. She saw the other four principles as instrumental in maintaining its open character and keeping it committed to a continuing process of modernization.[38] Later, Kili saw an intimate relationship between the six principles and Atatürk's drive to provide "unity," "authority," and "equality." She outlined a table, which highlighted Atatürk's formula of rendering the state's power and seeing modern society along the following principles: "Unity: Nationalism, Populism, Laicism, and Étatism; Authority: Republicanism, Nationalism, Laicism; Equality."[39]

Other observers regarded revolutionism, populism, republicanism, and nationalism as the ideological basis of the new political structuring, while secularism and étatism expressed policies that were to provide a philosophical framework for reforms.[40] Zürcher, in turn, separated republicanism and étatism from the other four. He did not see the first two as objects of Kemalist policy, rather he described them "dealing with instruments" while the other four he termed "the quintessence of the Kemalist ideology."[41] Özdalga claims that particularly in the case of étatism, it was obvious that it intended to be a policy tool for dealing with the negative results of the 1929–1930 economic crisis, rather than a thoroughly regulated economic and social development strategy.[42] Frank Tachau tried to treat the Kemalist principles based on their endurance: "...of the main tenets ... two remained unchallenged (republicanism and nationalism), two became somewhat controversial (populism and secularism) and two became a subject of heated debate and fundamental disagreement (statism and reformism)."[43] Baskın Oran argues that nationalism was the central tenet of Kemalism, on which its principles hinged.[44] VanderLippe asserts that republicanism and nationalism were generally accepted by the politically active elite by the 1930s, while populism and revolutionism were diluted enough to mean little more than an emphasis on solidarism and the avoidance of Bolshevik-style revolution. Étatism and laicism proved the principles subject to the greatest debate and disagreement, within and outside the RPP.[45]

In 1939, when Gilman listed the six principles, instead of the conventional use of laicism, he used "tolerance" and placed the six arrows in order of relative importance, so that it looked as follows: étatism; nationalism; populism; republicanism; revolutionism; and tolerance. He also urged other scholars to view that order as helping explain how the arrows fit with one another.[46] Darina Vasileva argues that the principles of populism and revolutionism remained practically unrealized and were used chiefly for their propaganda effect for Kemalist policy.[47] The principle of nationalism as the basic content of Kemalist ideology fulfilled a dual function in carrying out cultural policy; on the one hand, it dampened social conflict by proclaiming a unified national culture, and, on the other, it imposed the standards and achievements of Western culture in a super-structural way, disregarding the specifics of traditional culture. In a quantitative content analysis of selected sections from history textbooks from 1929, 1950, and 1986, Avonna Deanne Swartz analyses the degree to which the six tenets of Kemalism were elaborated. She concludes that except for populism, the six principles received equal coverage over time. Both Eskicumali and Swartz,[48] however, see this nationalist ideology as fully formed from the advent of the Republic, rather than as an organic work-in-progress.

The existence of different perspectives on Kemalism demonstrates the utmost difficulty that the principles created for the students of Turkish history. As discussed in the previous chapters, the RPP introduced the principles, gradually hoping to enrich them with content and objective. Yet no single principle can grasp or convey the meaning and objective of Kemalism. The synthesis in the above-mentioned assertions and analysis demonstrates that the RPP strategy worked well in the cases of republicanism, nationalism, and laicism, while it faced resurfacing difficulties when applying populism, étatism, and revolutionism. The first three principles were not entirely new to republican politicians and the intellectual elite. They were in circulation for several years if not decades before the official introduction, although variations of populism also had an earlier appearance. The last three principles, by contrast, lacked clarity, hence it was easy to manipulate them. The Kemalists added more ambiguity by instrumentalising the last three principles according to domestic political needs. As a result, the first group of principles were implemented, albeit with varying degrees of success, because of their deep ideological and historical roots. They were also able to deliver tangible results, which the Kemalists successfully capitalized, whereas the second group of principles continued their existence by zigzagging through political and ideological considerations. It bears mentioning, however, that *populism* required a different set of operationalizations. The Kemalist regime and the secular-republican-nationalist ethos could hardly succeed without ideas, notions, and visions embedded in populism.

WIDENING RANGE OF INTERPRETATIONS

The study of Kemalism has been approached from different theoretical perspectives. Some have been raised and discussed in the preceding chapters. Among other approaches, two are touched upon here. One that still raises questions and doubts is related to the applicability of the concept of fascism. Studying the fascistic traits of Kemalism is a research problem that requires further and lengthier examination, involving more empirical evidence and theoretical exploration. Hence, for the sake of presenting existing interpretations of Kemalism, previous efforts and prospects to decipher it alongside the ideological and political practices of fascism will be briefly discussed below.

The literature has so far showed consensus on this question. Scholars have argued that there is no compelling evidence to prove that in the first half of the twentieth century Turkey went through a process that resembled contemporary totalitarianism in Europe and elsewhere. Fikret Adanır, for instance, agrees with Mete Tunçay's claim that a "specific compound" that produces fascism did not exist in Turkey in the inter-war period.[49] He agrees with the applicability of "fascism," in essence, and accepts that the Kemalist political system of the inter-war years had a strong fascist content and paralleled fascism elsewhere.[50] He also demonstrates his inclination towards following Roger Griffin's claim to establish a "mythic core" of generic fascism. He propounds the following ingredients of "minimum fascism" and agrees, while reflecting on the Turkish context: (a) anti-liberal; (b) anti-conservative; (c) tending to glorify certain epochs in the nation's history; (d) inclined to charismatic leadership; (e) deifying such mythical concepts as the nation, the leader, national identity; and (f) idealizing homogeneity in the national community.[51]

Such an approach is not unique, and other scholars have delved into the subject, reaching more or less the same conclusions. Taha Parla and Andrew Davison prefer the analytical categories of "partly fascist," "partly totalitarian," and, more holistically, "rightist tendencies" to study specific parts of Kemalism, which they refer to as a solidaristic corporatist ideology. They refused to apply these categories without attaching the word "tendencies" to them. They further claim that even though some ideological aspects of Kemalism exceeded "the limits of the solidaristic corporative perspective," they were never full-fledged developments, but leanings.[52] The authors also claim: "Fascistic and totalitarian ideological tendencies do not dominate Kemalism, but they are present and were active so that fascistic tendencies could form themselves within and out of Kemalism, as the existence of deeply rightist, Kemalist tendencies in the history of the republic show."[53] Thus, they accept the presence and active nature of "rightist tendencies" but are reluctant to relate Kemalism to fascism or totalitarianism. Describing Mustafa Kemal's own discourse and certain judgments, however, Parla and Davison indicate that at the ideological level, fascism was visible.[54]

The historiography also includes approaches to Kemalism as a "Third Way" experience. Hamit Bozarslan, for instance, claims that between 1930 and 1938, the Kemalist regime was openly and self-consciously anti-liberal and anti-democratic, thereby projecting itself "as the third pillar of an anti-democratic world, Fascism and Bolshevism constituting the two other poles."[55] Gökmen lists a few features of the Kemalist regime between 1931 and 1945, which, according to him, overlapped with fascism: "a single party, a strong reaction against the old regime, the existence of solidarist and corporatist and later on, totalitarian tendencies, coalescence of state with party, adoption of a national leader system, and increasing state interventionism in the economy."[56] However, he does not fully support the idea of fascism in Turkey, since he claims that Kemalism was a pragmatic ideology and, unlike fascism, "it did not have thoroughgoing totalitarian pretensions" and did not possess "the complex compound that made fascism possible in Italy."[57] Others claimed that the Kemalist revolution secured far-reaching social changes, which made Turkey "free from sharp social cleavages and class conflicts" that existed in Germany and Italy.[58] In his discussions of the Kemalist religion, Dragos Mateescu describes as "naive" the comparisons between Kemalism and fascist and communist dictatorships. He explains that the Kemalist regime "falls in the democratic category," and therefore, "original Kemalism cannot be defined as authoritarian in itself, and it was far from totalitarianism."[59]

Thus, claims about the lack of "specific" or "complex compounds" of fascism in Turkey have long dominated the scholarship. As a result, previous efforts to study Turkey's possible experience with fascism have shared a few common features. One has been the fact that previous approaches failed to mitigate conceptual, semantic, methodological, and theoretical flaws. Most of the time, for instance, Turkey's possible experience with fascism was studied alongside various examples of fascist regimes, usually using Italian fascism and to a lesser extent Nazism as departure points. Another problem in the scholarship is the overwhelming focus on the inter-war period, and particularly the 1930s, when trying to find the fascist traits of Kemalism, while Kemalism, as a system of principles, was the outcome of developments that unfolded much earlier. Another dominant approach (not only with respect to Turkey) is the conviction, resulting from the writings of Ernst Nolte and Renzo de Felice, that since fascism was born in Europe, and since it had European intellectual, social, organizational, and political origins, perspectives of fascism outside Europe were treated with scepticism. Fascism in the inter-war period was largely seen as a European-epochal phenomenon that was alien to non-European political systems[60]—a generic argument which distracted from non-European manifestations of totalitarian/fascist movements and regimes. In addition, the temptation to establish "a generic definition that might apply across many times and places"[61] limited various scholarly undertakings.

Six basic features or traits of a totalitarian regime, suggested by Friedrich and Brzezinski, serve as helpful guidelines for identifying the essence of such a regime. For them the following "universally acknowledged ... features" are important to be termed totalitarian dictatorships: "a) an ideology, b) a single party typically led by one man, c) a terroristic police, d) a communications monopoly, e) a weapons monopoly, and f) a centrally directed economy" which altogether aim at the "total destruction and total reconstruction" of the state and society. They also warn that there might be others, "now insufficiently recognized."[62] Through effective control, indoctrination, and manipulation of the population, the totalitarian regimes strive to achieve socialization and ideological homogenization.[63] Thus, they possess a more radical program of change, deliberately mobilized masses, equipped with ideology, and "a quasi-religious philosophy with a claim of exclusivity."[64] The majority of scholars are inclined to claim that those regimes were anti-modernist and wanted to reassert the old community, whereas others insist that they were progressive forces interested in rapid development in all spheres of social and economic lives.[65] Totalitarianism has also been criticized for its wide variety of applications for different regimes and for being normative, analytical, and non-teleological.[66]

Discussing the classifications and common objectives of totalitarian regimes, Stephen Lee argues that at least four sectors—individual/societal, ideological, political, and economic—require total reorganization and control. On the individual/societal level, totalitarian regimes sought to create new men empowered by a radical change in attitudes and beliefs. These changes would ultimately subordinate "new men" through coercion, propaganda, indoctrination, and control.[67] Lee posits that totalitarian regimes aim to control man's and society's existence according to doctrinal goals. Describing the objectives of totalitarian regimes, Lee explains that they were composed of a single party backed by the army and aimed at mobilizing mass support, particularly among the youth. The political system is also characterized by the executive branch's control over the legislature, and a single party headed by a strong leader with clear inclinations towards building a personality cult.

Concerning the economic system, Lee argues, totalitarian regimes strove to have complete control over the economy and to provide "bureaucratic co-ordination of formerly independent corporate entities."[68] Confident that these are reliable criteria for differentiating between "strong and weak models of totalitarian systems," he arrives at two interdependent conclusions: (a) there has never been a strong totalitarian model[69]; (b) all other regimes in Spain (under Franco), Greece (under Metaxas), Poland (under Pilsudksi), Austria (under Dollfuss), Portugal (under Salazar) and Hungary (under Gömbös) were termed authoritarian regimes, and not even partly totalitarian, because "they lacked any consistent attempt to mobilize the masses behind the regime, some of them even relied upon traditional ideas and distrusted anything which was remotely radical and revolutionary, there were hardly any attempts at mass indoctrination."[70] Lee and others dealing with this subject do not consider Turkey (or, for that matter, any regime outside Europe) as a weak totalitarian or even an authoritarian regime.

It goes without saying that movements and ideas outside Europe with their regional, historical, social, and local features absorbed European models with certain modifications; therefore, fascism, like other ideological currents, could not appear as an exact copy in different contexts.[71] Based on this assumption, Stein U. Larsen urges scholars to acknowledge this difference in order to grasp "the essence of the [fascist] phenomena."[72] Examining the formation and application of late-Ottoman and early republican ideas and practices that were intended to create an organic nation by promoting ultra-nationalist and radical policies (expulsion, deportation, mass violence, mass mobilization, social engineering, ethnic cleansing, assimilation, conversion and forced marriage, expropriation, confiscation, plunder, and, certainly, genocide) can produce both consistent and starkly different manifestations when drawing comparisons to Italy, Germany, or elsewhere. The other approach, rejecting a checklist definition of fascism, entails embracing Roger Griffin's "synchronic-epochal and generic-diachronic" approaches.[73] Certain Kemalist principles (for instance, nationalism and populism) could be explored as components of theoretical frameworks, referred to as "global or universal fascism"[74] and "generic fascism."[75] Formation, ascendance, and application of fascism in Turkey constituted different experiences; therefore, the most important question remains: how consistent and different were the components of Kemalist Turkey from Italian Fascism, German Nazism, or other fascisms elsewhere.

Failure to integrate these theoretical considerations into previous analyses resulted in underestimating the problem. In light of the above, the ideological and political continuities between the Young Turks and the Kemalists during the first half of the twentieth century needs another framework of analysis. In many ways, the consequences of remarkable continuity would not become completely apparent until we look into radical transformation policies and political practices of the two regimes. Once in power, from 1908 to 1918 (with a brief interlude in 1912), and especially after 1913, the Committee for Union and Progress experimented with some of the constitutive elements of fascist ideology, even though the word would not emerge until a few years later. The political and social implications of the Balkan Wars, and most importantly WWI, served as historical opportunities to implement some of the ideological and political objectives that were proposed by members of various political and intellectual circles of the period. It would be an overstatement to claim that the political leaders of the CUP acted as if they represented fascist forms of government. However, the way some political objectives were carried out made no difference in European developments that would take place decades later. Moreover, the pace of the transformation of theoretical and scientific understandings into practice was short enough that it resulted in the spontaneous application of many policy features (Pan-Turkism, unification of all Turks to build the Turkish fatherland, expansionist ambitions, homogenization, assimilation, resettlement of population). Sternhell correctly claims that the constitutive elements of fascist ideology, elaborated prior to August 1914, reappeared in an almost identical form in the 1920s and 1930s, in Italy and elsewhere.[76] It may reasonably be supposed that all three levels of the fascist phenomenon that Sternhell identified, mentioned above (ideology, political movement, and form of government), were exemplified in Turkey between the 1910s and 1930s–1940s. A few interludes during these decades do not change the central argument.

Regarding the success of some policy objectives, which later were included in the fascist checklist, the Kemalists and their political fathers, the Young Turks, could well be considered "undisputed forerunners," taking into account their ultra-nationalism, expulsion, deportation, mass violence, mass mobilization, social engineering, ethnic cleansing, assimilation, conversion and forced marriage, expropriation, confiscation, plunder, and, certainly, genocide. In essence, Turkish nationalism was late-developing in exhibiting all its peculiarities and spontaneous features. It was also developed "amid pronounced and continuous anxiety over the Turks' future and their very existence."[77] Distinctive features of radical nationalism in Turkey, assimilation, and homogenization (Turkification), were executed long before fascist regimes came to power in Europe and elsewhere, and long after they were defeated in WWII. It began with the Armenian Genocide, then deportations of Kurds, massacres of Greeks, Assyrians, and Chaldeans. This policy of annihilation was followed by the assimilation of non-Turkish speaking Muslim immigrants through settlement policies that were enacted between 1923 and 1939, and followed by events in Thrace against Jews in 1934, atrocities in Dersim (1935–1938), and the Wealth Tax (*Varlik Vergisi*) in 1942, etc.

Payne's inclusion of "extreme elitism" as a defining feature of fascism was distinctly manifest during the CUP and the Kemalists. Both the Young Turks and the Kemalists had an elitist conception of society; they saw themselves as the nation's "social physicians," the only ones capable of enlightening the "masses."[78] Other definitions and fashionable currents of thought that defined different facets of fascism— biological materialism, positivism, social Darwinism, and the quest for magic formulas—were also incorporated by both regimes in Turkey.[79] These elements implied that both regimes regarded themselves as empowered by a supreme or historical mission. Nothing was to interfere with their ultimate objective of "saving the nation" (during the Young Turks) and "modernizing and Westernizing" it (during the Kemalists).[80]

The evidence supporting the existence and extensive application of components of fascism in Turkey is ubiquitous. Non-European or "global fascism" was as pervasive in the first half of the twentieth century as was the European blend of fascism. The mentioned definitional framework of totalitarian systems proposed by Friedrich and Brzezinski, Lee, and the "mythic core" of the generic fascism proposed by Griffin can further be employed as conceptual structures for the analysis of the Kemalist regime in the 1930s and 1940s. These three checklists complement each other and constitute the core of the totalitarian concept, although in the literature there are some slight variations and additions to that list (anti-Marxism, nationalism, racism, corporatism, etc.).

Interpretations of Kemalism by political and societal actors and the proliferation of various Kemalist organizations and movements necessitate another theoretical approach. There have been efforts to study how the interests and strategies of these movements transformed Kemalism into a social movement.[81] Applying social movement theory to study the activities, insights, motivations, and interpretations of these organizations can also enrich our understanding of Kemalism's decades-long popular appeal. Some of the associations that fervently defended the Kemalist cause include *Atatürkçü düşünce derneği* (The Atatürk Thought Association), *Çağdaş Yaşamı Destekleme Derneği* (Association for the Support of Contemporary Living), "Daughters of Atatürk," "Sons of Atatürk," *Altıok Kemalizm* (Six-Arrow Kemalism), *Kemalist Izciler Forum* (Forum for Kemalist Scouts), *Atatürkçü düşünce topluluğu* (Society of Atatürkist Thought), *Genç Atatürkçüler* (Young Atatürkists), as well as other groups and NGOs. When discussing them, Zafer Toprak noted: "As a matter of fact, the army is not obsessed with a dogmatic interpretation of Kemalism; there are the NGOs in Turkey which are more dogmatic in terms of being obsessed with Kemalism."[82]

Contextualizing Popular Interpretations of Kemalism

As mentioned in the introduction, this study includes interviews, which were conducted in Turkey between 2004 and 2006. The interviews revealed historical continuities and patterns of interpretation that illumine popular intellectual approaches to Kemalism.

For instance, during the interview Melih Aşık, a columnist in the daily *Milliyet*, mentioned: "To be a Kemalist is something like being a Muslim in a secular Republic. For instance, we say that 99 percent of the Turkish population is Muslim, but not all of them are practicing Muslims; the same is true of Kemalism. Many people claim to be Kemalists, but not all of them are Kemalists."[83] He clarified: "When one says he/she is a Kemalist, he uses it as a mask. If there were too many Kemalists, we could not come to this point."[84] Professor Cüneyt Akalın, who was also a member of the radical leftist Worker's Party (*Işçi partisi*), underscored the need for Kemalism:

> Where is the French Revolution? Where is Marx in Germany? But the people carry those ideas that fueled the Revolution and Marxism. Kemalism is still an important ideology; it is a national ideology. We realize that we need it. If you do not have your own ideology, there are others' ideologies that can substitute for the gap, like the EU ideology. It's an anti-imperialistic ideology. Kemalism is the big heritage of the Turkish nation and state. After Atatürk, Turkey lost its ideological, political, cultural identity and dignity and became a semi-independent member of NATO.[85]

A veteran journalist and contributor to *Milliyet*, Sami Cohen, highlighted the complexity of the many identities, perceptions, and affiliations that were constructed around Kemalism: "Religious minded people in Turkey nowadays consider Kemalists ultra-Kemalists, whereas Kemalists consider even moderately religion-oriented people fundamentalists. But we have a lot of liberals in Turkey who think that Kemalism was imposed on people in a radical way, whom we call Kemalist-fundamentalists."[86] Cohen also outlined the dominant debate around Kemalism in the early 2000s, some of which could be applied to the 1930s, as well. "Today's debate is taking place on two levels—between Kemalists and non-Kemalists, and between the Kemalists themselves – liberals, progressives, western-oriented Kemalists, and ultra-Kemalists, who are more like near-xenophobic nationalists."[87] Professor Zafer Toprak of Boğazici University, also the director of the Atatürk Institute for Modern Turkish History, summarized his assessment: "There are so many Kemalisms in Turkey. To me what is left of Kemalism is laicism. It is the backbone of Kemalism. It is the only one left of six principles. All other principles have changed."[88] He described how his institute teaches Kemalism:

> We do teach Kemalism, as a separate, mandatory course, like Marxism-Leninism. It is some kind of anti-clerical course, it teaches to distant students from religious, fundamentalist trends. The same also concerns army officers, who are taught Kemalism with a heavy focus on laicism. It is done for two purposes: firstly, to raise the awareness of soldiers in order to enhance their vigilance; and secondly, to increase the awarenes of those soldiers who will carry their army service in Anatolia about religious sects, currents, etc.[89]

The next part of the interview covered the concepts of Kemalism vs. Atatürkism. Melih Aşık explained: "Kemalism is an ideology, whereas Atatürkçülük is different. I consider myself Atatürkçü because I support the right-wing principles introduced at that time."[90] Alin Taşçian's account differed:

> When you say Atatürkçü, that is O.K., but if you say Kemalist, it has negative connotations in Turkey, nowadays. This is important. When I see someone declaring himself a Kemalist, I do not see him/her as very progressive, very illumined. Instead, I see a true conformist, because they are more pro status quo people. People who really want to have a democratic state based on law and high moral principles of Atatürk, are mainly Atatürkçü-s. Because if some Kurdish nationalist calls himself a Kemalist,

it does not make sense. Atatürkçü-s are also not to be seen under a positive light, only. They are the ones who offered alternative interpretations to Kurds uprising and Kurdish nationalism with a hope to crush it down by all means.[91]

Since its inception, Kemalism has given way to many interpretations and perceptions. Scholars have approached it by examining its core principles and the values and ideas these principles entailed. Divergent approaches have underscored both the inclusive and exclusive nature of existing interpretations. Kemalism in the 1930s was a result of complex circumstances that bore the imprint of the era. For all practical purposes, it could not be too distant from Ottoman political and intellectual traditions, nor could it entirely neglect challenges arising from the social and political transformations specific to the republican era. Kemalism, therefore, served as an ideological device that consolidated society, according to the secular-nationalist-republican strategic goals of the new regime. In later decades, expectations of politicians, intellectuals, and various observers had visibly changed, even though Kemalism's key principles remained flexible enough to accommodate divergent social, ideological, and political transformations. These were clear indications that defining one correct "Kemalism" is virtually impossible, without understanding the longer historical perspective. This inference allows a space for the incorporation of transnational interpretations of Kemalism, which will be addressed in the next chapters.

NOTES

1. Dahl (1996, 24).
2. Carl Friedrich and Zbigniew Brzezinski. 1956. *Totalitarian Dictatorship and Autocracy.* Cambridge, MA: Harvard University Press, 89.
3. Ertan Aydın. 2004. "Pecularities of Turkish Revolutionary Ideology in the 1930s: The Ülku Version of Kemalism, 1933–1936." *Middle Eastern Studies* 40 (5): 55.
4. Nazım Irem. 2002. "Turkish Conservative Modernism: Birth of a Nationalist Quest for Cultural Reniewal." *International Journal of Middle East Studies* 34 (1): 96.
5. For the discussion of the Soviet influence on shaping the economic reforms in Turkey, see Mustafa Türkeş. 1999. "The Ideology of the *Kadro* [Cadre] Movement: A Patriotic Leftist Movement in Turkey," in *Turkey Before and After Atatürk: Internal and External Affairs,* edited by Sylvia Kedourie. London: Frank Cross, 92–119.

6. Özdalga (1978, 34–35).
7. George Harris. 1967. *The Origins of Communism in Turkey*. Stanford: Stanford University Press, 146.
8. Yakup Kadri Karaosmanoğlu. 1978. *Diplomat ponevole: Vospominanija i nabludenija* [A Dimplomat Against His Will: Recollections and Observations]. Moscow: Mezhdunarodnije otnoshenija, 20.
9. Zürcher (1993, 206).
10. Vedat Nedim, Devletin Yapıcılık ve Idarecilik Kudretine Inanmak Gerekid, *Kadro*, 1/12, aralık 1932, 43 cited in Hanioğlu, Şükrü. 2011. *Atatürk: An Intellectual Biography*. Princeton: Princeton University Press, 189.
11. Şevket Süreyya, Milli Kurtuluş Hareketleri Hakkında Bizim Tezimiz, *Kadro*, 2/15, mart 1933, 43 cited in Hanioğlu (2011, 189).
12. Hanioğlu (2011, 188).
13. Harris (1967, 146).
14. Harris (1967, 147).
15. Hanioğlu (2011, 190).
16. Hanioğlu (2011, 190–191).
17. Ahmet Yıldız. 2001. "Recep Peker." In *Kemalizm: Modern Türkiye'de Siyasi Düşünce*, edited by Murat Belge, 58–63. İstanbul: İletişim Yayınları.
18. Nusret Köymen. *Kemalizm ve Politika Bilgisi*, Ülkü 7/41, 1936, 323–324 cited in Hanioğlu (2011, 191).
19. Şevket Kansu. 1934. "Biyososyoloji." *Ülkü* 3/16. 253–262 cited in Hanioğlu (2011, 191).
20. İrem (2002, 88).
21. Peyami Safa. 1938. *Türk İnkılabına Bakışlar* [Reflections on the Turkish Revolution]. Ötüken Yayınları, 190–192.
22. Idem. "Inkılabın mektebi" [The school of the revolution], *Yeni Adam* (şubat 12, 1934), 5 and "Ahlak bunalimı" [The moral crisis], *Yeni Adam* 408 (ekim 22, 1942), 2; Peyami Safa, "Asıl Harp" [Real war], *Hafta*, (aralik 26, 1934), 2. cited in İrem (2002, 99).
23. Recep Peker. 1936. Inkilap Dersleri Notları. Ankara.
24. Şeref Aykut. 1936. Kemalizm. İstanbul: Muallim Ahmet Halit Kitap Evi.
25. Saffet Engin. 1939. *Kemalizm Inkılabının Prensepleri*, 3 cilt, Cumhuriyet Basımevi.
26. Mediha Muzaffer. 1933. *Inkilabın Ruhu*. Devlet Matbaası.
27. Halil Nimetullah Öztürk. 1930. *Halkçılık ve Cumhuriyet ve Türk Halkçılığı ve Cumhuriyeti*. Orhaniye Matbaası.
28. Weiker (1973, 219–220).
29. Tekin Alp. 1937. *Le Kemalisme*, Paris, 251.
30. Paul Dumont. 1984. "The Origins of Kemalist Ideology." in *Atatürk and the Modernization of Turkey*, edited by Jacob Landau. Boulder: Westview Press, 25.

31. Alp (1937, 13).
32. Alp (1937, 14).
33. Kolesnikov (1984, 71).
34. Falih Rıfkı Atay. 1931. *Faşist Roma, Kemalist Tiran ve Kaybolmuş Makidonya*, Hakimiyetti Milliye Matbaasi; *Zeytindağı*. İstanbul: Remzi Kitabevi, 1938.
35. Hande Özkan. 2001. "Falih Rıfkı Atay." In *Kemalizm, Modern Türkiye'de Siyasi Düşünce*, edited by Murat Belge. İstanbul: İletişim Yayınları, 66; Hakki Uyar. 2001. "Mahmut Esat Bozkurt." in *Kemalizm, Modern Türkiye'de Siyasi Düşünce*, edited by Murat Belge, 214–219. İstanbul: İletişim Yayınları.
36. Heper (1985, 71).
37. Taha Parla. 1985. *The Social and Political Thought of Ziya Gökalp*. Leiden: Brill, 77.
38. Kili (1969, 110).
39. Kili (1969, 297).
40. Shaw and Ezel (1977, 375).
41. Zürcher (2005, 14).
42. Özdalga (1978, 43).
43. Frank Tachau. 1984. *Turkey: The Politics of Authority, Democracy and Development*. New York: Praeger, 54.
44. Baskın Oran. 1981. "Altı Ok arasındaki ilişkiler ya da Milliyetçilik ekseni Çevresinda Kemalizm." [The Relations Among the Six Arrows or Kemalism Around the Axis of Nationalism.] In *International Atatürk Conference*, vol. 3, İstanbul: Boğaziçi Üniversitesi, 1–8.
45. Van der Lippe (2005, 18).
46. William Gilman. 1938. "Turkey with Western Dressing." *Current History* 49 (3): 38.
47. Darina Vasileva. 1986. "Forming the Kemalist Ideology and Its Influence on the Cultural Policy of Turkey Up the Second World War." *Études Balkaniques, Academie Bulgarie Des Sciences* 4: 17.
48. Ahmet Eskicumalı. 1994. *Ideology and Education: Reconstructing the Turkish Curriculum for Social and Cultural Change, 1923–1946*, Ph.D. dissertation, University of Wisconsin-Madison; Avonna Deanne Swartz. 1997. *Textbooks and National Ideology: A Content Analysis of the Secondary Turkish History Textbooks Used in the Republic of Turkey since 1929*, Ph.D. dissertation, University of Texas at Austin.
49. Fikret Adanır. 2001. "Kemalist Authoritarianism and Fascist Trends in Turkey During the Inter-War Period." in *Fascism Outside Europe*, edited by Stein Ugelvik Larsen, 313–361. Boulder: Social Science Monographs.
50. Adanır (2001, 359).
51. Adanır (2001, 360).

52. Taha Parla and Andrew Davison. 2004. *Corporatist Ideology in Kemalist Turkey: Progress or Order?* Syracuse: Syracuse University Press, 244.
53. Parla and Davison (2004, 247).
54. Parla and Davison (2004, 256).
55. Hamit Bozarslan. 2006. "Kemalism, Westernization and Anti-Liberalism." In *Turkey Beyond Nationalism*, edited by Hans-Lukas Kieser. London: I. B. Tauris, 29.
56. Özgür Gökmen. 2006. *Turkey*, Vols. 1: A-K, in *World Fascism: A Historical Encyclopedia*, edited by C. Blamires and P. Jackson. ABC Clio, 678.
57. Ibid.
58. Parker and Smith (1940, 75).
59. Dragos Mateescu. 2006. "Kemalism in the Era of Totalitarianism: A Conceptual Analysis." *Turkish Studies* 7 (2): 225–226, 238.
60. Eatwell (2001, 20).
61. Mann (2004, 5).
62. Friedrich and Brzezinski (1956, 9, 10).
63. Heather Rae. 2002. *State Identities and the Homogenisation of Peoples.* Cambridge: Cambridge University Press.
64. Karl Bracher. 1984. *The Age of Ideologies: A History of Political Thought in the Twentieth Century.* London: Weidenfeld, Ch. 1.
65. Eatwell (2001, 17–18).
66. Ibid., 23.
67. The detailed breakdown of the subordination tools as provided by Lee is helpful to lay down the cognitive map of the totalitarian ideologues—*coercion* (a system of physical and psychic terror, effected through party and secret police control), *propaganda and indoctrination* (complete monopoly of mass communication, manipulation of culture, history, a destruction of cultural pluralism and shaping of education, literature, art and music according to the political ideology) and *control* (terror, brutal forms of repression, purges and penal, labour or concentration camps, identification and elimination of all enemies (racial or class)).
68. Stephen Lee. 2005. *European Dictatorships, 1918–1945*, 2nd. ed. London: Routledge, 300, 305–307.
69. According to Lee, Stalinist Russia was a weak totalitarian model, Nazi Germany was an imperfect totalitarianism, Italian Fascism was on the borderline between the weak model of totalitarianism and authoritarianism, the Ustashi regime in Croatia and Szalasi's regime in Hungary were partially totalitarian.
70. Lee (2005, 301).
71. Larsen (2001, 717).
72. Ibid.

73. Roger Griffin. 2010. "Uniqueness and Family Resemblances in Generic Fascism." *East Central Europe* 37: 338–344.

74. *Fascism Outside Europe: The European Impusle Against Domestic Conditions in the Diffusion of Global Fascism*, edited by Stein Ugelvik Larsen. New York: Columbia University Press.

75. Roger Eatwell. 1992. "Towards a New Model of Generic Fascism." *Journal of Theoretical Politics* 4 (2): 161–194; Aristotle Kallis. 2003. "To Expand or Not to Expand? Territory, Generic Fascism and the Quest for an 'Ideal Fatherland'." *Journal of Contemporary History* 38 (2): 237–260; and Lorenzo Santoro. 2007. "Ideology and Political Religion: Towards a Conceptualization of Generic Fascism." *The European Legacy* 12 (6): 749–752.

76. Zeev Sternhell. 1987. "Fascism," in *Blackwell Encyclopaedia of Political Thought*, edited by D. Miller. Oxford: Basil Blackwell, 149.

77. Akçam (2006, 55).

78. Şükrü Hanıoğlu. 2001. *Preparation for a Revolution: The Young Turks 1902–1908*. Oxford: Oxford University Press, 308.

79. Kevorkian (2011, 190).

80. Kevorkian (2011, 191).

81. Vahram Ter-Matevosyan. 2009. "Kemalism as a Social Movement: Transforming Patterns of Collective Identities in Turkey." *Turkic and Ottoman Studies* 6: 86–104.

82. Interview with Zafer Toprak. May 10, 2005. Istanbul.

83. Interview with Melih Aşık. May 27, 2005. Istanbul.

84. Ibid.

85. Interview with Cüneyt Akalın. May 16, 2005. Istanbul.

86. Interview with Sami Cohen. May 12, 2005. Istanbul.

87. Ibid.

88. Interview with Zafer Toprak. May 10, 2005. Istanbul.

89. Ibid.

90. Interview with Melih Aşık. May 27, 2005. Istanbul.

91. Interview with Alin Taşçian. May 11, 2005. Istanbul.

REFERENCES

Adanır, Fikret. 2001. "Kemalist Authoritarianism and Fascist Trends in Turkey During the Inter-War Period." In *Fascism Outside Europe*, edited by Stein Ugelvik Larsen, 313–361. Boulder: Social Science Monographs.

Akçam, Taner. 2006. *A Shameful Act: The Armenian Genocide and the Question of Turkish Responsibility*. New York: Metropolitan Books.

Alp, Tekin. 1937. *Le Kemalisme*. Paris: F. Alcan.

Dahl, Ottar. 1996. "The Historical Study of Ideologies." In *Societies Made Up of History: Essays in Historiography, Intellectual History, Professionalization, Historical Social Theory and Proto-Industrialization*, edited by Björk Ragnar, Thorsten Nybom, and Rolf Torstendahl, 17–28. Stockholm: Edsbruk: Akademitryck AB.

Eatwell, Roger. 2001. "Universal Fascism? Approaches and Definitions." In *Fascism Outside Europe: The European Impulse Against Domestic Conditions in the Diffusion of Global Fascism*, edited by Stein Ugelvik Larsen, 15–45. Boulder: Social Science Monographs.

Friedrich, Carl, and Zbigniew Brzezinski. 1956. *Totalitarian Dictatorship and Autocracy*. Cambridge: Harvard University Press.

Hanioğlu, Şükrü. 2011. *Atatürk: An Intellectual Biography*. Princeton: Princeton University Press.

Harris, George. 1967. *The Origins of Communism in Turkey*. Stanford: Stanford University.

Heper, Metin. 1985. *The State Tradition in Turkey*. Beverley: Eothen Press.

İrem, Nazım. 2002. "Turkish Conservative Modernism: Birth of a Nationalist Quest for Cultural Renewal." *International Journal of Middle East Studies* 34 (1): 87–112.

Kevorkian, Raymond. 2011. *The Armenian Genocide: A Complete History*. London: I.B. Tauris.

Kili, Suna. 1969. *Kemalism*. İstanbul: School of Business Administration and Economics, Robert College.

Kolesnikov, Aleksandr. 1984. *Narodnye Doma v Obshhestvenno-politicheskoj i kul'turnoj zhizni Tureckoj Respubliki* [People's Houses in the Socio-Political and Cultural Life of the Turkish Republic]. Moscow: Nauka.

Larsen, Stein Ugelvik. 2001. "Was There Fascism Outside Europe? Diffusion from Europe and Domestic Impulses?" In *Fascism Outside Europe: The European Impulse Against Domestic Conditions in the Diffusion of Global Fascism*, edited by Stein Ugelvik Larsen. Boulder: Social Sciene Monographs.

Lee, Stephen. 2005. *European Dictatorships, 1918–1945*, 2nd. ed. London: Routledge.

Mann, Michael. 2004. *Fascists*. Cambridge: Cambridge University Press.

Özdalga, Elisabeth. 1978. *I Atatürks spår: Det Republikanska FolkPartiet och utvecklingsmobilisering I Turkiet från etatism till populism*. Lund: Dialog.

Parker, John, and Charles Smith. 1940. *Modern Turkey*. London: George Routledge and Sons.

Parla, Taha, and Andrew Davison. 2004. *Corporatist Ideology in Kemalist Turkey: Progress or Order?* Syracuse: Syracuse University Press.

Shaw, Stanford, and Shaw Kural Ezel. 1977. *History of the Ottoman Empire and Modern Turkey, Vol. II: Reform, Revolution, and Republic: The Rise of Modern Turkey, 1808–1975*. Cambridge: Cambridge University Press.

Van der Lippe, John. 2005. *The Politics of Turkish Democracy: İsmet İnönü and the Formation of the Multi-Party System, 1938–1950*. New York: State University of New York Press.

Weiker, Walter. 1973. *Political Tutelage and Democracy in Turkey: The Free Party and Its Aftermath*. Leiden: Brill.

Zürcher, Erik-Jan. 1993. *Turkey: A Modern History*. London: I.B. Tauris.

Zürcher, Erik-Jan. 2005. "Ottoman Sources of Kemalist Thought." In *Late Ottoman Society: The Intellectual Legacy*, edited by Elisabeth Özdalga, 13–26. London: Curzon.

Soviet Interpretations of Kemalism in the 1920s

Both founded in the wake of World War I, Turkey and the Soviet Union followed revolutionary modernizing pathways. After the consolidation of power, ruling regimes in both countries self-consciously set out to build something new and different, "national" in one case and "socialist" in the other. At the outset, it is easy to trace similarities in the two radical modernization paradigms. Their development models, however, and their political and social orders were radically distinct, which became more obvious with the passage of time. Despite their profound differences, both Turkey and the Soviet Union found rich opportunities for cooperation and convergence through economic, cultural, and diplomatic exchanges. This chapter discusses the first decade of Soviet perspectives on Kemalism, since the many interpretations and insights that emerged during the period would shape attitudes in later decades.

WHY BOTHER WITH SOVIET PERSPECTIVES ON KEMALISM?

While scholars have examined bilateral relations between Turkey and the Soviet Union, many aspects of the relationship have yet to be studied and contextualized. As contended in the introduction and the first chapter, scholars of Turkey's republican history have rarely examined Soviet historiography on Kemalism. Most analyses have focused on no less important problems: (a) bilateral relations between Turkey and the SU[1]; (b) domestic revolutionary transformations in Turkey[2]; (c) the Turkish

© The Author(s) 2019   173
V. Ter-Matevosyan, *Turkey, Kemalism and the Soviet Union,*
Modernity, Memory and Identity in South-East Europe,
https://doi.org/10.1007/978-3-319-97403-3_8

Communist Party and leftist movements[3]; and (d) the possible Russian influences on the Kemalist policy of étatism.[4] Since the beginning of the Kemalist movement in Turkey, however, Communist (Bolshevik) Party functionaries of Soviet Russia and the Caucasian Republics (Armenia, Georgia, and Azerbaijan[5]) closely followed developments there. In extensive discussions in the Soviet media and academic journals, these functionaries unearthed various aspects of the Kemalist transformation.

In the 1920s and 1930s, Western observers of Turkey shared insights about Kemalist transformations that were mainly descriptive and often sympathetic (marked by adjectives like *new*, *reborn*, and *ascending*). In contrast, the views and interpretations of Soviet commentators were noticeably different. They managed to analyze the Turkish transformation, despite the omnipotence of class analysis and Marxist methodology and vocabulary. Covering social and political processes, cultural and economic reforms, and ideological undertakings, they showed a degree of consistency in their writings that Western observations of the early Turkish Republic did not. Watching developments in Turkey, Soviet scholars were motivated by debates that emerged, the rise and fall of bilateral relations, and geopolitical rivalry. Their observations extended beyond mere reporting, and included nuanced discussions of the Kemalist transformation.

Soviet interest had multiple sources. Most of the SU's perspectives and perceptions of Kemalist Turkey were formed as a result of geopolitics and the world socialist revolution—the *idée fixe* of communist leaders. One significant reason had to do with Turkey's struggle against "imperialist France, Britain, and Greece," which rendered Ankara a natural ally of Soviet Russia, which fought "the same enemy"[6] and thus shared "the same kind of hostility."[7] The Kremlin also appreciated the Kemalist movement's ability to divert Entente resources, which otherwise would have been directed against the SU.[8] In 1934, Alimov admitted that the SU supported Turkey in the early 1920s because the latter played an "objectively revolutionary role by fighting against imperialism."[9] On the other hand, the SU, disappointed by the receding revolutionary tide in Europe, began paying more attention to radical nationalist movements in Asia. Soviet leaders hoped to see substantial prospects there and, deriving from that belief, argued that the East would play a more important role in the next phase of world revolution.[10] George Kennan noted that the Soviet attitude toward Turkey became a "forerunner of the tolerance" that Moscow showed to countries outside Europe that expressed anti-European sentiments and policies.[11]

The Communist regime had hoped to turn South Asia and the Near East into Soviet spheres of influence since the early 1920s, replacing Britain as the principal power in the region. O'Connor points to the important role played by Georgij Chicherin, Commissar of the PCFA from 1918 to 1930, in establishing Turkey, as well as Persia and Afghanistan, "as a potential bulwark of defence for Soviet Russia against the Western nations."[12] O'Connor argues that the Soviet Union planned a defensive alliance to create "a cordon of states" and buffer zone against renewed Western intervention. In February and March 1921, the SU signed treaties with three of these states. A few years later, these treaties were supplemented with additional treaties of neutrality, nonaggression, and nonparticipation in hostile associations and agreements directed against the third party.[13] While O'Connor observes clear patterns in Soviet policy vis-à-vis these states, his claim that the SU, and particularly Chicherin, successfully prevented Western influence is debatable. Stephen White notes expressions of solidarity and friendship in the face of a common enemy (British imperialism) accompanied the treaties. Yet Afghanistan, Iran, and Turkey stopped short of committing themselves to the Soviet social order.[14] The treaties did not contain explicit references to British imperialism. For example, the Moscow treaty between Russia and Turkey (March 16, 1921) noted that both states acknowledged "existing solidarity between them to fight against imperialism."[15]

In the 1920s and 1930s, the SU pursued its foreign policy objectives through a variety of institutions, among which the *Narodnij Kommissariat Inostrannikh Del* (People's Commissariat for Foreign Affairs—PCFA) and Comintern (Communist International) stood out. The PCFA underwent radical structural transformations in its early years that revised many of its approaches. The size and objectives of foreign missions also shifted. In the 1920s, the SU's mission abroad counted more diplomatic, commercial, and other personnel than other countries. In 1924, the SU's embassy in Ankara, for example, included eighty-four staff members, including forty-six diplomatic and consular employees, while thirty-eight individuals belonged to the trade delegation.[16] After England, Germany, and Latvia, it was the fourth largest Soviet mission abroad, its size signifying Turkey's importance for the Soviet government.

The Comintern, a new association of working-class parties, was tasked to spread socialist revolution to Europe and Asia. It soon became an important tool in the hands of Soviet leaders to internationalize revolutionary agitation and propaganda. Peoples of the East and West would inevitably look to the Soviet state, according to its leaders, for guidance and support in the quest to replace the imperialist state system. Chicherin was especially hopeful that the convergence of diplomacy, revolution, and financial and military support—vis-a-vis near Eastern, central Asian, and far Eastern nations—would lead to the spread of socialist revolution to the West.[17]

Bruce Hopper argued in 1940 that the PCFA was there "to placate other governments, and the Comintern to promote the overthrow of the same governments, the Bolsheviks were able over the years to create for themselves a position of special privilege in world politics, in which the right hand could deny responsibility for the left."[18] SU foreign missions abroad employed many Comintern field agents to offer cover and communication channels, given that the PCFA's diplomatic courier service was also at their disposal.[19] The Comintern's vast network of academic, research, propaganda, and mass media institutions shaped the SU's relations with other countries. Its publications closely followed decisions made by Comintern congresses and their resolutions as closely as possible.

These institutions often overlapped in their spheres of interest, by design, of course. In the early years, efforts to spread the revolution were clouded by uncertainty. Soviet diplomats saw the Comintern as "a great source of embarrassment for the Soviet diplomats," writes Uldricks, since it undermined the relationship between the mission and the host state. Uldricks claimed that diplomats grasped that world revolution was not imminent, which meant that the Soviet state was to be protected by diplomatic means.[20] For Chicherin, the overlap between institutions was especially troubling when it came to Germany and Turkey, which he regarded as "anchors of his foreign policy in Europe and Asia respectively." He vehemently objected to Comintern activities that might damage diplomatic relations with these countries.[21] The Comintern continued until 1943, although many like Chicherin and Litvinov were against it, according to Uldricks.

While the SU kept a close watch over radical domestic transformations in Turkey, some interpretations by those watching Kemalist transformations suggest that these authors were either ill-informed or pursuing divergent objectives. Shifts in Soviet approaches to Kemalism not only attested to the complexity of bilateral relations between Turkey and the SU, but also reflected the ambiguities and contradictions of Soviet foreign and domestic policies. Communist leaders supported Kemalist Turkey, despite the persistent persecution of communists there. During the 1923 Twelfth Congress of the Communist Party, Nikolay Bukharin, a leading party member and close confidant of Lenin, claimed that Turkey still played a "revolutionary role," by undermining the world imperialist system.[22] Yet, Soviet observers, especially in the post-1927 ideologically constrained environment, could not deviate from Soviet foreign policy or the objectives of the Communist International. Those who chose to do so paid a steep price.

Lenin's death in 1924 led to the resurgence of the left-right debate within the Communist Party on the future of world revolution. The main advocate of "permanent revolution," Lev Trotsky, argued that socialist survival required world revolution. But Stalin's wing of the party adopted the slogan "socialism in one country," acknowledging the unlikelihood of immanent world revolution, and argued for a focus on domestic social-political affairs.[23] The left wing was side-lined and defeated after 1927, when Stalin consolidated power and eliminated opponents.[24] These changes explain shifts in SU policy and rhetoric toward Turkey.

Closer analysis reveals that the SU hoped to see Kemalism both fail and succeed. Soviet leaders did not conceal their disappointment that Turkey neglected to show or express gratitude for Soviet assistance in the early days of the nationalist movement. Moreover, Turkey embarked on a path of development that diverged from what Soviet leaders wanted. However, by the end of the 1920s, SU leaders expected that strong anti-regime movements in Turkey would lead an agrarian revolution and topple the Kemalist government. Evidence suggests that the SU was motivated to closely monitor Kemalist transformations to achieve the following strategic goals: understanding the social and political implications of Kemalist reforms; seizing on potential opportunities; securing Turkey's neutrality; reducing anti-Soviet activities; and keeping Turkey in check by engaging with it. Efforts to meet these objectives changed often, in response to international and regional circumstances.

EARLY SOVIET APPROACHES TO KEMALISM

An early effort to trace the ideological bases of Kemalism took place in the Soviet Union. In 1921, Soviet diplomats, journalists, and politicians began using the term "Kemalism." A February 7, 1921 report, prepared by the head of the Information Department of the People's Commissariat for Foreign Affairs (PCFA) of Soviet Armenia, interpreted the foundation of Kemalism in the following way:

> After the General war armistice [Mudros] Turkish official intellectuals, army officers, and clergy were faced with the prospect of being left out on the streets. By being officials for generations, they were incapable of another job. Therefore, these layers, pursuing the intent of promoting their class interests, founded Kemalism – taking advantage of the discontent and hatred accumulated in the Turkish nation against the Entente. To deceive the Russian Revolution and national masses, they adopted the outer mask of the Bolshevism – red crescent, frontal part of the hat, red flag, and the title "minister" instead of the commissar.[25]

The report provided a vague, functionalist definition of Kemalism that ignored its ideological content. Still, it represented one of the earliest efforts to create a working definition for the emerging regime in Ankara. On February 13, 1921, the same department issued another report on Kemalists, referring to "nationalist" (milliyetçi), "national" (milliçi-s), "the government of Anadolu (Anatolia)," "the government of Angora (Ankara)," and "Milli (national) state."[26]

Georgij Astakhov, head of the Press Bureau of the Russian Soviet Federative Socialist Republic's (later, the SU's[27]) Plenipotentiary Representation in Turkey from March 1922 to November 1923, published a series on the transformation of Kemalist Turkey in the journal *Novij Vostok* and other Soviet periodicals. The articles would reappear in a State Publication (*Gosudarstvennoye Izdatelstvo*) book[28] in which Astakhov sought to generate knowledge on the Kemalist regime's domestic reforms and foreign policy problems between 1922 and 1924. Tasked with writing an account of "one of the defining periods of the Turkish revolution," he invoked "one of the greatest historical events of the contemporary period... having a revolutionary significance."[29] While, at the time, the objectives of the Kemalist movement were more practical (e.g., winning the war against the Greeks and overcoming domestic political cleavages), Astakhov tried to separate the system's ideological and political layers.

From a vague form with a chaotic content, the Anatolian national movement is gaining a more distinct appearance... If two-three years ago one could observe the synthesis of all possible tendencies – from vulgar Pan-Islamism to almost Communism, now from this chaos a new state with a democratic-Bonapartist political system was being crystalized.[30]

Astakhov failed to come up with a clear definition of Kemalism, but his efforts to describe its components is noteworthy. His view of the "ideology of Kemalism" suggested that there was "revolutionary energy" in Mustafa Kemal's speeches, a strong personality feature, economic ideals, and "theoretical foundations," promoted by various intellectuals of the day: Ahmet Ağaoğlu, Yusuf Akçura, and Ziya Gökalp.[31] Another two terms, employed by Astakhov, differed from what would follow in coming years. He referred to Kemalists as "liberals" and to the newly founded Turkey as a "democratic republic," drawing on the maxim: "The power belongs to the people without any conditions and any limitations."[32] He also described domestic transformations, which, years later, brought criticism: "Turkish revolution is the first successful... example of the colonial revolution. It proved that the backward semi-colonial nation ... is able not only to successfully complete its liberation from the imperialism but also to strengthen the economic independence, which is achieved by force, through feverish economic construction."[33]

Semyon Aralov was the SU's first plenipotentiary representative to Turkey (1922–1923). Decades after his tenure, he admitted that "the transfer of the Kars province along with the city of Kars and other regions to Turkey elevated the morale of the Turkish nation, instilled in it a sense of serenity for the eastern regions and trust in the Soviet Union as a kind neighbour of the revolutionary Turkey and its sincere friend."[34] His mission was to combat external and domestic reactionary forces that could undermine mutual trust between Turkey and the SU.[35] Recalling a conversation with Mustafa Kemal in 1923, Aralov expressed excitement: "Let's hope to join to our friendly family other Eastern nations too: Iran, Arab nations... It is my dream. I am not sure whether it is feasible or whether I would live up to it."[36] Aralov received assurances from Mustafa Kemal that Turkey's friendship with Soviet Russia was sustainable, robust, and that it formed "the foundation of Turkey's politics in international relations."[37] "We are not allowed to depart from each other," added Kemal. "This is my firm conviction and my maxim to the coming generations."[38] As it is apparent from the timing of the articles and reports, Aralov and Astakhov worked in Turkey during the same period. It is rather informative to observe how both diplomats described domestic transformations in Turkey and how they viewed the making of the Kemalist ideological project. They unequivocally supported the Kemalist cause and their diplomatic cables to Moscow were likely not different in content and approach. Hence, the PCFA relied on these reports when building its policy towards Turkey. During the 1920s, the PCFA and its leader, Chicherin, remained highly sympathetic to the Turkish government as opposed to the preferences of the party leadership.

Soviet observers of Turkey in the 1920s were adamant in tracing Soviet influences and implications on Turkey's transformations and political processes. It was common among Soviet historians to claim that the success of the Turkish National Revolution was, above all, conditioned by the October Revolution in Tsarist Russia. For instance, in 1921, referring to "dispatches of Entente agents" and reports in European newspapers, Pavlovich noted: "… all the Turks, starting from poor and ending with rich people, starting from illiterate ordinary people and ending with Professors, dream only of one thing, arrival of the Bolsheviks."[39] But a book by the same author published later in that year mentions that "extreme reactionary elements, i.e., representatives of the large landowners and high-ranking clergy" in the National Assembly and elements of society that endorsed Pan-Islamic and Pan-Turkic tendencies, "were not quite happy with the rapprochement with Soviet Russia."[40]

It was also common among Soviet observers to claim that without "the quiet (and secure) rear" of the Soviet Union, and without "the material and psychological-political assistance of the Soviet government," the Kemalist party could never win over internal and external foes and successfully finish "the first phase" of national revolution.[41] Along the same lines, Mel'nik argued that Mustafa Kemal was able to defeat the Sheikh Sait Rebellion in 1925 largely because the Kemalists had the backing of "friendly Soviet Republics," and therefore without any risk, Kemal could reposition military forces from the Caucasian border to face the insurgents. In the same vein, he saw similarities between Turkish independent courts created after the rebellion and Soviet revolutionary tribunals.[42]

In 1925, the "Association of Orientalists," which functioned under the auspices of the Central Executive Committee of the USSR, initiated a book series about the various struggles of people in the East. One covered Turkey, written by three prominent Turkologists of the day:

Pavlovich, Gurko-Kryazhin, and Raskol'nikov. However, these contributions were not new. The section by Pavlovich, for instance, was a reprint of his 1921 book, "Revolutionary Turkey."[43] Providing a detailed account of the rise of the Kemalist movement and its wars against Armenians and Greeks, Pavlovich expressed hopes that "the formation of a powerful, independent and democratic Turkey will deliver a crushing blow to the Entente." Further deciphering the ideological components of the Kemalist movement, he added: "… the triumph of the revolutionary-nationalist movement in Turkey, a country which enjoys a huge prestige in the entire Muslim world, will shake the foundations of the dominance of the capitalist powers in all Muslim colonies – Algeria, Morocco, Tunisia, Tripoli, Egypt, India, etc."[44] The latter was yet another confirmation of the long-nourished hope of Soviet leaders to use Turkey's influence in the Muslim world to "lead a large section of the East… at least into revolt against the Great Powers of Europe."[45]

Writing in 1926, Konstantin Youst (Feoktistov), head of the press bureau of the SU's Plenipotentiary Representation in Turkey (1925–1929), reported on the revolutionary deeds of Mustafa Kemal from Turkey. He described the atmosphere in the country and popular attitudes toward the Turkish leader. The mythical image of Kemal dominated the Turks. Kemal's personality was on par with "Christ, Mohammed, Buddha, Confucius, as well as with Washington, Lincoln, Luther, Peter the First, and Lenin."[46] Youst invoked "Kemalism" to capture to the counter-revolutionary zeal exhibited by the Kemalist elite's drive against Pan-Turkist circles.[47] Most likely, he used the term to evoke a general spirit of unity that was dominant among Kemalists.

EMERGENCE OF IDENTICAL INTERPRETATIONS: STALIN'S VIEW OF KEMALISM

1927 was a watershed for Soviet observers of Turkey, when their approaches and interpretations of Kemalism changed. Deepening polarization among observers of Turkey was also present between the "new" and "old" schools of Oriental Studies. Both Stalin's final consolidation of power and the growing role of the Bolshevik intelligentsia explain these shifts. Stalin's dictatorship began in 1927 as purges against "leftist opposition" strengthened his power.[48] As the Bolshevik intelligentsia worked to transform intellectual life, non-party, traditional, and bourgeois intelligentsia and specialists came under attack.[49] Increasingly rigid interpretations of party ideology emerged as party ideologues imposed strict interpretations of Marxist theory on the social sciences. Academia would not be unaffected. Michael David-Fox, who closely observed educational and academic reforms introduced by the Bolsheviks in the 1920s, points to three institutions that decisively shaped Marxist science: (a) Sverdlov Communist University, soon one of the party's key institutions for instilling in students a new communist lifestyle; (b) the Institute of Red Professors, which nurtured Communist professors; and (c) the Communist Academy, where Bolshevik scholars trained in Marxist methodology were made.[50]

The latter two led the assault against the old school. The "Red Professorship" and Bolshevik scholars stuck to the hard-line radicalism of Mikhail Pokrovskij, "head of the Marxist historical school of the USSR," David Riazanov, who led the Institute of Marx and Engels, Andrei Bubnov at the helm of the Agitation-Propaganda department, and other Bolshevik ideologues who made "… Marxism, Marxology a privileged discipline."[51] More than seventy research institutes were also established in the 1920s to advance this science. The prestigious 200-year-old Academy of Sciences, which enjoyed privileges from the Communist Party and government, made Bolshevik intellectuals at the Communist Academy especially uncomfortable. Until the late 1920s, many prominent "bourgeois academicians" managed to remain independent of the Communist Party.[52]

New research methods reshaped Oriental studies. By the mid-1920s, Oriental Studies centres in Leningrad, Moscow, Tashkent, and Baku published journals and books, addressing a wide range of problems. By the end of the decade, orthodox Marxism had arrived. The Scientific-Research Association was established in 1927 at the Stalin Communist University of the Toilers of the East, known either as KUTV, or Stalin School. It launched *Revoljutsionnyj Vostok* (Revolutionary East), soon the mouthpiece of the Marxist revisionist school of Soviet Orientalists, aspiring to dominance of the field. Writing in the pages of the "Revolutionary East," KUTV faculty fiercely criticized Soviet Orientalists who began their careers before the Bolsheviks. The old-timers were purported to deviate from Marxist research methods and to embrace bourgeois ideology.[53] "Revolutionary East" derided work published in *Novij Vostok* (New East), the journal of the (All) Russian Academic Association of Orientalists (RAAO), founded in 1921. Following the 1927 death of Mikhail Pavlovich, head of the RAAO, the Association's role in the

Soviet Orientalist school diminished. *Novij Vostok* closed in 1930, unable to counter criticism from party hardliners. *Novij Vostok* hardly ignored the Communist regime of the Soviet Union; rather, it was created by the regime and had to serve its members. As previously discussed, the journal used the prism of class analysis and Marxist methodology to study political transformations in the East and sometimes did ordinary reporting. While *Novij Vostok* attracted international attention, the new radical party mainstream condemned its insufficient loyalty and the inadequate attachment of "classical Orientalists" to Marxist methodology when it came to studying problems in the East.[54]

The RAAO ceased to exist in 1930, after its merger with the newly established Association of the Marxist Orientalists at the Communist Academy, which adopted a more radical stance towards Oriental Studies than the Academic Research Association of the KUTV. Dedicated to economics and politics in Eastern nations, the association examined new pathways of national-revolutionary movements and class struggle-related topics and published journals, including *Revoljutsija i Natsional'nosti* (Revolution and Nationalities), which covered Turkey. The new Orientalists' frontal attack not only marginalized the "old school" of Turkologists, but also affected the quality of new research and writing.

In 1927, Kitaygorodskij, a Soviet historian of the Middle East, coined the phrase "the kingdom of Kemalism"[55] to refer to Turkey, where Kemalist ideologues were doing their utmost to defend the rights of the new bourgeoisie. In Communist Party spirit, he urged "the red diplomacy" of the SU to take appropriate measures to ensure its friendly neutrality toward the SU both in word and deed.[56] In the conclusion, presumably speaking on behalf of other historians, he noted: "The aim of our notes is to draw the attention of the party and the Soviet society on contemporary Turkey, to identify the true face of this country, where the formerly national bourgeoisie became 'everything' from 'nothing.'"[57]

The same year, Lüfti noted that despite widely known achievements, failure defined the ruling party in Turkey. He pointed out that Kemalists had left the village untouched, aggravating social problems. He opined that the ruling party was not monolithic, and given that its social base was army vs. "what it was supposed to be–middle-layered villagers, landowners, craftsmen, petty and middle bourgeoisie and intelligentsia," "there is a danger that it may transform into a ruling clique." He also predicted that the RPP could merge with democratic and radical European parties with harmful implications for Turkey's political, social, and cultural domains. Therefore, he argued, Turkey should refrain from entering the League of Nations, "knowing that its political independence will be preserved only in the case of widening and deepening the friendship with the USSR."[58] In discerning the social bases of Kemalism, this observer foresaw deviations from what was supposed to be a predetermined path. These manifestations of concerns over Turkey's foreign policy orientations became more frequent and were reflected in scholarly journals associated with the Communist Party.

Vladimir Osetrov, the historian of Turkey and Iran who wrote under the pseudonym Irandoust, published "The Essence of Kemalism" in 1927 in the party's official press. Kemalism was an "authentic mass revolution," according to Irandoust, corresponding to a type of Eastern revolution that followed the bourgeois pathway. But Kemalism was "completely non applicable in those countries in the East," he claimed, "which entered the phase of the industrial revolution and possessed a sufficiently powerful and organized proletariat. We see that picture in China and India. Revolutionary developments in these countries, undoubtedly, will not follow the path of the Kemalist revolution."[59] Irandoust also defined the two characteristics of Kemalism that made it a unique case: its revolutionary and counter-revolutionary concepts.[60] For him, Kemalism retained its revolutionary significance since it was not operationalized with imperialism. Meanwhile, employing Marxian vocabulary, Irandoust envisioned the fate of Kemalism: "For Kemalism to survive, it needs to keep up its anti-imperialist positions because compromise to imperialism means a beginning of the failure of Kemalism and the collapse of its program."[61] His interpretations were in line with the period's orthodox views, but they placed Irandoust in the spotlight. His next book generated controversy, which will be discussed in greater detail below.

Bekar Ferdi, the pseudonym used by Turkish communist leader Şefik Hüsnü, published widely in the Communist Party press, working under close Soviet scrutiny. In 1927, he described Mustafa Kemal's Republican People's Party (RPP) as the party of the Kemalist cause. It had brought the national bourgeoisie to power at the expense of measures against possible opposition forces.[62] Writing the same year in the official mouthpiece of the Comintern, Ferdi argued that Kemalists erred in trusting the Western powers. While promising a rosy future for Turkey, they had placed the country on the "capitalist path."[63] Ferdi hoped that increasing Kemalist repression would allow "the Turkish working class to take advantage of the revolutionary propaganda" and, with Communist support, rise up against the bourgeoisie, which included both Kemalists and Unionists.[64]

In May 1927, Stalin met with faculty and students of the Sun Yat-Sen Communist University of the Toilers of China in Moscow. To attract and encourage Chinese Communists and revolutionaries, the Comintern had created the university in 1925. Stalin began the meeting noting that he had received only ten questions that would be answered in the designated two to three hours. The sixth query, "Is a Kemalist revolution possible in China?", launched a discussion in Soviet academia. Stalin's definition of Kemalism is relevant for this analysis: "The Kemalist revolution is a revolution from above, of the national mercantile bourgeoisie, which was created during the struggle against the foreign imperialists and, in its further development, was directed essentially against peasantry and workers, against the very possibilities of an agrarian revolution."[65] Stalin compared Turkey and China three months later, framing Kemalist revolution by its stage of development: "The characteristic feature … of the Turkish revolution (Kemalism), is that it is stuck in the 'first step', in the first phase of its development, the phase of the bourgeois-liberation movement, without even trying to proceed to the second phase of its development—the phase of the agrarian revolution."[66] In just a few months, Soviet historians were employing Stalin's definitions and ideas about Kemalism, apparent in a number of publications. Scholars used Stalin's formulations ("revolution from above," "bourgeois-revolution," and "against workers and peasants") to describe Kemalism, some of which persisted until the end of the Soviet Union.

Examining the main transformative features of Turkey in his 1928 book, Irandoust used simpler vocabulary to describe the agencies of the newly founded state, relying on terms such as "Kemalist Turkey" and "Kemalist movement" to convey the nature of the revolution carried out by "Kemalists," the rank-and-file of the ideological revolution, from 1918 to 1920.[67] The fashion among Soviet observers to ascribe revolutionary-theoretical dimensions to Kemalism, continued in Irandoust's book, sparking debate among Soviet scholars and Communist Party functionaries.

The trigger was a few terms, phrases, descriptions, and concepts used by Irandoust to analyse Kemalism. Based on the reviews and criticism the book received, one could easily observe that the emerging Marxist school of Oriental Studies in the Soviet Union deemed some parts of the book totally unacceptable and against the Marxist methodology for interpreting revolutions. This case revealed yet again the brutal face of Communist Party censorship, which would only grow more severe in coming years. Before entering into the details of Irandoust's analysis, which caused a fierce reaction among Marxists Orientalists, it is worth mentioning that Irandoust was accused of espionage activities and was executed in 1938.

In January 1929, a few months after the publication of Irandoust's book, A. Shneerson reviewed it in the bi-weekly "*Bol'shevik.*" Although he considered Irandoust's book "undoubtedly the best work on Kemalism" and "the first Marxist attempt to summarize the results of the development of Kemalism," he found "significant errors" in it.[68] He particularly criticized "comrade Irandoust" on the following grounds: (a) "overestimation of the revolutionism of the Kemalist bourgeoisie;" (b) failure to see that "in its fight against imperialism, the Turkish bourgeoisie is going backwards and losing its positions;" and (c) inability to see that the "bourgeoisie did not win over feudalism in Turkey, particularly in the Eastern part."[69] Irandoust was also criticized for not drawing necessary conclusions from Stalin's abovementioned definition of Kemalism. Along with criticism, Shneerson offered his own interpretation of the evolution of Kemalism, which followed Marxist terminology and phrasing:

> Kemalism once played the role of a revolutionary factor, because it led the mass movement against imperialism and succeeded in keeping the Turkish national-state intact... Kemalism became bourgeois-reformist, then, with the passage of events, it was transformed into counter-revolutionary factor, because the Kemalists eventually found a common language with the landowners and comprador bourgeoisie.[70]

He concluded his review: "Kemalism is not the path that ensures the preservation of the state's independence from the foreign capitalists. Ultimately, Kemalism is a pathway toward re-enslavement by the imperialists of their former colonies and semi-colonies."[71] A few months later, in a letter to the Executive Committee of the Comintern, Shneerson explained the roots of economic hardship in Turkey and blamed the government for it. He used the opportunity to re-convey his critical stance on "the revolutionary nature of Kemalism" because "in their statements, prominent Kemalists burst with joy and obeisance before Mussolini. This casts doubts on the USSR-oriented foreign policy of Turkey. For Kemalist Turkey, the USSR is more of a 'manoeuvring front.'"[72]

More criticism of Irandoust's book ensued. Following the philosophy and objectives of *"Revolutionary East,"* the journal of the Academic-Research Association of the KUTV, Ziya Feridov published an article that heavily criticized Irandoust (and Shneerson, too) for his ignorance of Marxist methodology and for using the "Marxist lexicon" without Marxism per se, which resulted in "confusion and distortion of clear concepts." In the 1928 book, Irandoust claimed that "Turkey has now finished the national-bourgeoisie revolution and is in the commencing stage of the bourgeois-democratic revolution."[73] This assertion became one reason for Feridov to accuse Irandoust of not being well-versed in Lenin's standpoint that "any nationalist movement can only be bourgeois-democratic."[74] While criticizing Irandoust, Feridov explained his position on the question of Kemalism. "Today's Kemalism has only little resemblance to what that term entailed during the struggle against the intervention. Currently, the social base of Kemalism is the Turkish bourgeoisie in tandem with landowners and kulaks [rich peasant farmers]. A pretty narrow base for the mass movement."[75] More probable was that Feridov used this argument about the social base of Kemalism to challenge Irandoust, who saw the Turkish peasantry as the main driving force of the Turkish revolution.[76] Feridov further criticized Irandoust's "revolutionary nature of Kemalism," seeing it as an "unsubstantiated claim," "babble," and "clear ridicule towards the revolution," because the revolutionary spirit of Kemalism has no meaning without "agrarian revolution" as "stated by Lenin and during the Sixth Comintern Congress."[77] Ridiculing Irandoust for describing Turkey as a "democratic secular republic," Feridov concludes that, in reality, Turkey had entered the stage of fascism, the final stage of the dictatorship of the bourgeoisie.[78] Feridov's conclusion was one of the first cases in Soviet historiography to draw parallels between the Kemalist regime and Italian or Spanish fascism.

Eight years after the publication of Astakhov's book, another Soviet observer of the "new school" of Orientalists and a diehard Communist, Abid Alimov, heavily criticized Astakhov on two grounds: (a) for presenting the "incomplete Turkish revolution as an example of a colonial revolution"; and (b) for arguing that Turkey achieved economic independence. He quoted Stalin's abovementioned claim[79] that Turkey was "stuck in the first phase," and argued that Turkey was still in the first phase of its revolution and that economic independence was only beginning.[80] What Alimov neglected to explain, however, was how in 1926,

Astakhov could foresee[81] Stalin's 1927 argument. In 1934, when Alimov published his criticism, Astakhov remained in the diplomatic service. After five years, he was fired, and one year later was accused of anti-Soviet activities and sentenced to fifteen years in prison. He died in a labour camp in 1942. Abid Alimov, however, died earlier than Astakhov, in January 1935, at the age of 35. He was killed in his house after being thrown down the stairwell. In spite of his age, since 1930, Alimov had held a number of key academic and teaching positions in Leningrad and Moscow, where he imposed heavy censorship on scholars working on Turkey and Iran.

Aleksandr Samojlovich, another prominent scholar of Turkey and Turkish language, visited Turkey in 1936. Since 1934, he had served as head of the Institute for Oriental Studies of the National Academy of Sciences, and in 1937 was arrested and executed the following year on charges of espionage (with Japan), terror (similar charges were presented to most of the scholars mentioned above), and for supporting Pan-Turkism.[82] There were other victims of Stalinist purges who had prior experience with Turkey. For instance, two former Soviet ambassadors to Turkey, Levon Karakhan (1934–1937) and Mikhail Karskii (1937), were executed in 1937. Because of the Great Purge,[83] which is also known as the Great Terror or *Yezhovshchina* (the "Yezhov affair/phenomenon"),[84] sixty-two percent of top-level diplomats and Commissariat officials became victims.[85]

While it is difficult to document how the works of Soviet scholars shaped their destiny, the Stalinist terror machine could not possibly exclude from official indictments the fact that some scholars had deviated from orthodox interpretations of Stalin, Lenin, and Marxism. Irandoust, Astakhov, and many others offer striking examples that help us observe how hundreds of Soviet scholars (in this case, Turkologists of the "old school") were persecuted for their views and opinions concerning social and political transformations taking place in foreign countries. The Stalinist machine did not tolerate scholars for "distorting the Marxist–Leninist determinism" of social transformations and for not being able to incorporate the Marxist methodology of studying historical processes, etc.

The terror against Soviet scholars, especially Orientalists, had irrefutable negative implications for the fate of Turkish Studies, too. Acute shortages of professionals made Anatolij Miller pen a note to the Department of Propaganda and Agitation of the CCCPSU in August 1945. This letter, which was first published in 2003, indicated the existence of "extremely serious shortcomings in Oriental Studies," which, according to him, had to be eliminated for Soviet science (*nauka*) to assist the Soviet state to achieve its specific role in the world and particularly in the East.[86] Miller also explained that the small number of scholars specializing in Turkey led to a dearth of comprehensive academic works on modern contemporary Turkish history and the struggle of democratic and reactionary forces there.[87] In addition to these problems, he pointed to the overlapping functions and research topics carried out by different research institutions, poor management and inadequate coordination of human resources, a lack of textbooks, underdeveloped post-graduate education, and a lack of Oriental Studies periodicals.[88] It bears mentioning that Miller sent this note to the Department of Propaganda and Agitation of the CCCPSU, and not the People's Commissariat for Enlightenment (a.k.a. Education), or the Union Committee on Questions of Higher Education existing at the Council of People's Commissars, which were in charge of higher education and research. It was yet another indication that Soviet authorities kept research on Oriental Studies under close supervision. Understandably, this letter did not contain criticism of the purges of the previous decade. Moreover, it occasionally praised new Bolshevik Orientalist scholars, "whose knowledge was based on the Marxist–Leninist understanding of history."[89]

In October 1928, when the Republic of Turkey celebrated its fifth anniversary, the journal, printed under the auspices of the PCFA, published an article by Anatolij Miller. As an author who was always sympathetic to Turkey and particularly to the Kemalist cause, he painted a positive picture of Turkey. In particular, Miller claimed that five years of the Republic had brought "major victories to the young Anatolian bourgeoisie" because Kemal and his party understood that they should not limit themselves to the experience of the Young Turks who "replaced only faces." Instead, Miller urged the Kemalists to implement "a complete restructuring of the entire political system of Turkey."[90] For him, Kemalist reforms were so radical that even the most courageous reform-oriented Ottoman sultan could not dream of implementing them.[91] Yet, following the reasoning of the day, Mel'nik urged readers not to deny that "Kemalist Turkey also had shadow sides," as it "exploits the working class, executes communist organizations, and there is a widespread corruption in the ruling circles." The article concluded on a hopeful note: "In the present moment, the Kemalists did not exhaust their revolutionary potential, as they did not solve those objectives, which, with the flow of events, were put before them as the avant-garde of the liberating bourgeoisie of the Eastern nations."[92]

Communism, Kemalism, and China

Irandoust's 1928 book also reflected a trend among Soviet Communist revolutionaries to project the Kemalist brand of revolution onto China. Pointing to social and political similarities between the two countries, Irandoust discussed how the term "Kemalism" was used to generalize counter-revolutionary movements backed by Chinese generals (Chiang Kai-shek and Phin Yui-sen) by international media, especially in Japan. Under the guise of anti-imperialism, these generals purportedly served the needs of the Chinese bourgeoisie.[93]

Prominent members of the Communist Party such as Grigory Zinovyev (Radomyslsky), who belonged to the Politburo (Political Bureau was the executive committee for the Communist Party), emphasized comparisons between China and Turkey in the 1920s. Looking at Turkey, they anticipated relative calm for China.[94] Ilan Butayev, an expert on Ottoman history, grouped together Turkey, Persia, and China, referring to "dependent but sovereign countries of the East."[95] In addition to Persia and China, Soviet observers at the time often mentioned Afghanistan. For Soviet analysts, deteriorating relations with the West were counterbalanced by Turkey's exemplary relations with Eastern nations. Mel'nik asserts: "it is difficult to refute, that for the Muslim nations, and first of all for Persia and Afghanistan, Turkey served as an example in the whole range of cultural and life affairs." He claimed that all significant reforms in Persia and Afghanistan, for instance—the emancipation of women, reform of attire, and secular education—were undoubtedly implemented under heavy influence from Turkey.[96]

During the May 1927 meeting with Sun Yat-Sen University students, Stalin put an end to these discussions, not only refusing to see any possibility of exporting the Kemalist revolution to China, but also arguing that this was impossible. According to Stalin, in addition to Turkey, only Persia and Afghanistan and countries that did not have an "industrial proletariat and a powerful agrarian-peasantry revolutionary" could possibly have a Kemalist revolution. The Kemalist revolution was therefore impossible in China because China possessed "(a) the known minimum of military and active industrial proletariat, which enjoys a tremendous authority among the peasants; and (b) there is a widespread agrarian revolution, which sweeps the remnants of feudalism from its way."[97]

Stalin also urged the audience to refrain from comparing the Kemalist party to the party of the left Kuomintang and finding parallels between Turkey and China. Turkey did not have centres like Shanghai, Wuhan, and Nanjing. International relations, he noted, were not identical because "imperialism" was able to wrest from Turkey most of what it demanded (Syria, Palestine, and Mesopotamia). Turkey was not interesting for the imperialists, either in terms of market size or assets. Stalin continued:

> The gravest mistake of the opposition (Zinovyev, Radek, and Trotsky) is that it doesn't notice all these differences between Turkey and China, as they confuse the Kemalist revolution with the agrarian revolution and lumps them into one pile without discrimination. I know there are people among the Chinese nationalists who cherish the idea of Kemalism. There are many pretenders out there to assume the role of Kemal. Chiang Kai-shek is number one among them. I know that some Japanese journalists are inclined to consider Chiang Kai-shek as a Chinese Kemal. But these are all dreams, illusions of the terrified bourgeois.[98]

Stalin's rather chaotic approach to Kemalism helps us understand not only Stalin's perspective on Turkey's transformations, but also what perceptive guidelines he provided to the party apparatus concerning the SU's future policy orientations regarding Turkey. One could argue that since members of the audience were Chinese students, he had to stress the importance of China and downplay the significance of Kemalism. However, this change in rhetoric was also indicative of a growing rift within the Communist Party.

Soon, Stalin's perspective started to have implications. As early as the following month, in June of 1927, Ferdi introduced policy proposals and analysis concerning the similarities and differences between the Turkish and Chinese revolutions. He expressed his belief that Chinese Communist leaders would draw necessary lessons from the mistakes of Kemalism, which had started as a national democratic revolution but was later hijacked by the ideas of the bourgeoisie and capitalism.[99] Mikhail Godes, who wrote on the history and economy of the Middle East, examined this view, offering strong support for Stalin's position. Comparisons between Chinese and Turkish revolutions were superficial, according to Godes; a Kemalist revolution in China was impossible.[100]

Yet, while criticizing artificial parallels between revolutions, he argued that when it came to social structure and international geopolitics, much of the Orient resembled pre-revolutionary Turkey. For Godes, Kemalism offered a model of revolutionary development, and Persia could import key features of the Kemalist revolution.[101]

In a May 6, 1927 letter to Nikolay Bukharin, Comintern leader, Chicherin, the top diplomat of the SU, pointed to the dangers of equating Chiang Kai-shek to Kemalism. "It is absolutely ridiculous and spoils our relations with Turkey," wrote Chicherin. "Isn't spoiling our relations with Germany enough for you?... and [now] you are spoiling our relations with Turkey!"[102] Yakov Sourits, Soviet Ambassador to Turkey, followed with a diplomatic cable to the PCFA of the SU, regarding a March 1928 visit to Ankara by the Chinese Nanjing government delegation. Chiang Kai-shek sent that delegation to "study Turkey and borrow the experience of Kemalism" (*opit Kemalizma*), reported the ambassador, while highlighting similarities between "Chiangkaishism" and Kemalism. The delegation left a "disgusting impression on İsmet-paşa [İnönü]" and an "unpleasant" one on Şükrü Kaya, Interior Minister, added the ambassador.[103] Yet, the Turkish government talked about how the Nanjing government should proceed: "Finish the capitulation regime, expel foreign armed forces and value the friendship with the SU."[104] The SU's general displeasure with the delegation was evident in the Soviet ambassador's cable. If the SU ever sought to export Kemalism to China, it was mainly concerned with the Nanjing government. In official Soviet communications, "Kemalism" was employed to describe social developments in Turkey.

It is clear from the preceding discussion that the SU's changing priorities toward Turkey and its regime also shaped its interpretations of Kemalism. The Soviets started to use the term with discernible ideological connotations long before it was done in Turkey and elsewhere. There was also a visible policy to constantly revisit Kemalism and adjust its interpretations according to changing circumstances. Until 1927, Soviet observers benefited from relatively limited freedom of research and relied on various approaches to conceptualize Kemalism. However, the rise of Bolshevik intellectuals and Stalin's interpretations of Kemalism were the defining factors that produced uniform interpretations. The censorship imposed on Soviet observers and the application of directed language and concepts questioned the validity of many interpretations that followed 1927.

NOTES

1. Kapur Harish. 1966. *Soviet Russia and Asia 1917–1927: A Study of Soviet Policy Towards Turkey, Iran and Afghanistan*. Geneva: Geneva Graduate Institute of International Studies. Chapters 4 and 5; S. Kuznetsova. 1961. *Ustanovlenie sovetsko-tureckih otnoshenij: K 40-letiju Moskovskogo dogovora mezhdu RSFSR i Turtsiej*. Moscow: Izdatel'stvo Vostochnoj Literatury; Pyotr Moiseyev and Rozaliyev Yurij. 1958. *K istorii sovetsko-tureckih otnoshenij* [The History of the Soviet-Turkish Relations]. Moscow: Gospolizdat.

2. Vladimir Danilov. 1997. "Kemalism and World Peace." In *Atatürk: A Founder of a Modern State*, 2nd ed., edited by Ergun Özbudun and Ali Kazancigil, 103–126. London: Hurst and Company; Anatolij Miller. 1948. *Kratkaja Istorija Turtsii* [Short History of Turkey]. Moscow: Gosudarstvennoe izdatel'stvo politicheskoj literatury; Emel Akal. 2012. *Mustafa Kemal, Ittihat Terakki ve Bolşevism Milli Mücadelenin Başlangıcında*. İstanbul: İletişim Yayıncılık.

3. George Harris. 1967. *The Origins of Communism in Turkey*. Stanford: Stanford University.

4. Bernard Lewis. 2002. *The Emergence of Modern Turkey*, 3rd ed. New York and Oxford: Oxford University Press, 283–286; Türkeş (1999, 92–119); and Özdalga (1978).

5. Before the formation of the Soviet Union in December 30, 1922, three South Caucasian Soviet Republics enjoyed some degree of formal freedom in conducting their foreign policies.

6. Vladimir Gurko-Kryazhin. 1923. *Istorija revolucii v Turtsii* [History of Revolution in Turkey]. Moscow: Mir. 126–127.

7. Danilov (1997, 117).

8. Harris (1967, 62).

9. Abid Alimov. 1934. "Turtsija." [Turkey.] In *Ocherki po istorii Vostoka v epokhu imperializa* [Outlines of the History of the East in the Age of Imperialism], edited by Abid Alimov and Mikhail Godes, 5–92. Moscow and Leningrad: Gosudarstvennoje social'no-ekonomicheskoje izdatel'stvo, 74.

10. Stephen White. 1984. "Soviet Russia and the Asian Revolution, 1917–1924." *Review of International Studies* 10 (3): 219.

11. George Kennan. 1960. Soviet Foreign Policy, 1917–1941. New York: D. Van Nostrand, 51.

12. Timothy Ed. O'Connor. 1988. *Diplomacy and Revolution: G. V. Chicherin and Soviet Foreign Policy Affairs, 1918–1930*. Ames: Iowa State University Press, 135, 142.

13. O'Connor (1988, 143, 145).

14. White (1984, 220).
15. Dogovor mezhdu Rossiej i Turtsiej, 16 marta, 1921 g. Dokumenty vneshnej politiki SSSR. Tom 3 [Treaty Between Russia and Turkey, March 16, 1921: USSR Documents on Foreign Policy]. 1959. Moscow: Gospolitzdat, 597–604.
16. Teddy Uldricks. 1979. *Diplomacy and Ideology: The Origins of Soviet Foreign Relations, 1917–1930.* London: Sage, 112.
17. O'Connor (1988, 144–149).
18. Bruce Hopper. 1940. "Narkomindel and Comintern: Instruments of World Revolution." *Foreign Affairs* 19 (1): 738.
19. Uldricks (1979, 157).
20. Uldricks (1979, 157–158).
21. Jon Jacobson. 1994. *When the Soviet Union Entered World Politics.* Berkeley: University of California Press, 50.
22. Twelfth congress of the RKP (b), Minutes. Moscow. 1968, 47–48. Cited in White (1984, 230).
23. David Priestland. 2007. *Stalinism and the Politics of Mobilization: Ideas, Power, the Terror in Inter-War Russia.* Oxford: Oxford University Press, 177–178.
24. Bülent Gökay. 2006. *Soviet Eastern Policy and Turkey, 1920–1991: Soviet Foreign Policy, Turkey, and Communism.* London and New York: Routledge, 36–37.
25. *Doklady Zavedujuschego Informacionnym Otdelom NKID SA o Turecko-armjanskikh otnoshenijah i o polozhenii v Turtsii posle peremirija i t.d.,* 1921 [Reports Prepared by the Head of Information Department of the PCFA of Soviet Armenia Concerning Turkish-Armenian Relations and About the Situation in Turkey After the Cease-Fire, 1921]. National Archives of Armenia. F. 114, L. 1, C. 225, 7.
26. "Dokladi zaveduyushevo," 1921, 225.
27. The Union of Soviet Socialist Republics was formally established on December 30, 1922.
28. Georgij Astakhov. 1926. *Ot Sultanata k Demokraticheskoj Turtsii: Ocherki iz Istorii Kemalizma* [From Sultanate Towards Democratic Turkey: Outlines of the History of Kemalism]. Moscow: Gosudarstvennoye Izdatelstvo.
29. Ibid., V, VI.
30. Ibid., 63.
31. Ibid., 65, 67, 73.
32. Ibid., IV, 63, 64, 69.
33. Astakhov (1926, 117–118).
34. Semyon Aralov. 1960. *Vospominaniya Sovetskogo Diplomata 1922–1923* [Memoirs of the Soviet Diplomat 1922–1923]. Moscow: Izdatel'stvo Instituta Mezhdunarodnykh Otnoshenii, 213.

35. Ibid., 214.
36. Ibid., 215.
37. Ibid., 217.
38. Ibid., 218.
39. Mikhail Pavlovich. 1921 [Republished in 1925]. *Revoljutsionnaja Turtsija* [Revolutionary Turkey]. Moscow. Pavlovich (1921, 220).
40. Pavlovich (1921, 5).
41. Mikhail Pavlovich. 1921. "Kemalistskoje Dvizhenie v Turtsii." [The Kemalist Movement in Turkey.] *Krasnaja Nov'* (1): 228; Kitaygorodskij, P. 1927. "Zametki o Kemalistskoj Turtsii: Prichini Pobedi Natsional'noj Revoljutsii v Turtsii." [Notes on the Kemalist Turkey: The Causes of the Victory of the National Revolution in Turkey] *Bol'shevik* (18): 41.
42. Anatolij Mel'nik. 1928. "Pjat' Let Respublikanskoj Turtsii." [Five Years of Republican Turkey.] *Mezhdunarodnaja zhizn'* (11): 6.
43. Pavlovich (1921).
44. Pavlovich (1925, 68).
45. Harris (1967, 62).
46. Konstantin Youst. 1926. "Pisma iz Turtsii: Novie puti i ikh smisl." [Letters from Turkey: New Paths and Their Meaning.] *Krasnaja Nov'*, 174.
47. Ibid., 184.
48. Bruce Pauley. 2015. *Hitler, Stalin, and Mussolini: Totalitarianism in the Twentieth Century.* Malden: Wiley Blackwell, 20.
49. Priestland (2007, 166–167, 177).
50. Michael David-Fox. 1997. *Revolution of the Mind: Higher Learning Among the Bolsheviks, 1918–1929.* Ithaca and London: Cornell University Press, 9.
51. Cited in David-Fox (1997, 205).
52. David-Fox (1997, 204). For a more detailed account of the difficult relations between the Soviet Academy of Sciences and the Communist party as well as on the purges and seizure of academic structure, see Loren Graham. 1967. *The Soviet Academy of Sciences and the Communist Party, 1927–1932.* Princeton: Princeton University Press.
53. Margarita Ivanova. 2006. *Introduction to the Regional Studies: From the History of the Soviet Oriental Studies.* Tomsk: Tomsk Pedagogical University, 13.
54. Ivanova (2006, 10–14).
55. Kitaygorodskij (1927, 50).
56. Ibid, 48, 50.
57. Ibid., 50.
58. Lüfti. 1927. "Turtsija Segodnya." [Turkey Today.] *Za Partiju* ("Pravdi Vostoka") (4): 76.

59. Ibid., 69.
60. Ibid., 63–64.
61. Ibid., 68.
62. Bekar Ferdi. 1927. "Evolucija Kemalizma: Ot Natsional'noj Revoljutsii k diktature burzhuazii." [Evolution of Kemalism: From National Revolution Towards the Bourgeoisie Dictatorship.] *Sputnik Kommunista* 4 (10 (43)): 30–38.
63. Ibid., 30–31.
64. Ibid., 39.
65. Iosif Stalin. *Beseda so Studentami Universiteta Imeni Sun Yat-Sena 13 maja, 1927 g.* [Discussion with the Students of the Sun Yat-Sen University, May 13, 1927], 559–581 was First Published in Iosif Stalin "Revolucija v Kitaje i oshibki oppozicii" [Revolution in China and the Mistakes of the Opposition]. Moscow-Leningrad: GosIzdat. 1927. It was published again in Iosif Stalin. *Ob oppozitsii: Stat'i i rechi 1921–1927* [About the Opposition: Articles and Speeches 1921–1927]. Moscow-Leningrad: GosIzdat, 1928, 273.
66. Iosif Stalin. *Mezhdunarodnoye Polozhenije i oborona SSSR (Rech' na Zasedanii Ob'edinennogo Plenuma CK i CKK 1 avgusta 1927 g.)* [International Situation and the Defence of the USSR (Speech at the United Session of the CC and CCC, August 1, 1927], 637–680 in Iosif Stalin. *Ob oppozitsii: Stat'i i rechi 1921–1927* [About the Opposition: Articles and Speeches 1921–1927]. Moscow-Leningrad: GosIzdat, 1928, 649.
67. Ibid., 5.
68. A. Shneerson. 1929. "Novaja Popitka Analiza Kemalizma." [A New Attempt to Analyse Kemalism.] *Bol'shevik* 1: 86.
69. Ibid., 86.
70. Ibid., 87.
71. Shneerson (1929, 90).
72. *Pis'mo A. Shneersona v Redizdat IKKI 09.05.1929* [Letter of A. Shneerson to Editorial and Publishing Department of the ECCI 09.05.1929], Russian State Archive of Social and Political History (RSASPH), F. 495, L. 78, C. 62, 4.
73. Irandoust (1928, 7).
74. Feridov (1929, 58).
75. Feridov (1929, 61).
76. Irandoust (1928, 21).
77. Feridov (1929, 63).
78. Feridov (1929, 69).
79. In the article Alimov provided a wrong page number to quote Stalin. Instead of page 649, he had page 273.

80. Alimov (1934, 92).
81. Although the book was published in 1926, Astakhov undersigned in the book's preface "June 1925, Tokyo", where he was posted after Turkey. That makes two years before Stalin's speech.
82. Fyodor Ashnin and Vladimir Alpatov. 1996. "Arkhivnie Dokumenti o Gibeli Akademika A. N. Samojlovicha." [Archival Documents on the Death of the Academic A. N. Samojlovich.] *Vostok* 5: 153–162.
83. Sheila Fitzpatrick. 1999. *Everyday Stalinism: Ordinary Life in Extraordinary Times: Soviet Russia in the 1930s.* Oxford: Oxford University Press, 190–217.
84. The secret police, the NKVD (The National Commissariat of Internal Affairs), headed by Nikolai Yezhov, carried out millions of arrests, interrogations, deportations, executions and imprisonments between 1936–1938.
85. More on this, see Uldricks (1979, 169–188).
86. Anatolij Miller. 2003. "Zapiska v upravlenie propagandy i agitacii CK BVP(b) 'O nedostatkah vostokovednoj raboty i o merah po ee uluch-sheniju'." [A Note to the Department of Propaganda and Agitation of the CCCPSU 'About the Lack of Research on Oriental Studies and Measures of Improvement'.] In *Sbornik statei v chest' 100-letija profesora A. F. Millera* [Collection of Articles Dedicated to the 100th Anniversary of A. F. Miller], edited by Mikhail Meier and S. F. Oreshkova, 337–343. Moscow: Muravej, 338.
87. Ibid., 338–339.
88. Ibid., 338–341.
89. Ibid., 337.
90. Mel'nik (1928, 4).
91. Ibid., 11.
92. Ibid., 10.
93. Irandoust (1928, 6).
94. Godes (1928, 4–5).
95. Butayev (1925, 202).
96. Mel'nik (1928, 9).
97. Stalin (1928, 256–258).
98. Ibid.
99. Bekar Ferdi. 1927. "Kitajskaya revolutsia ne dolzhna idti po puti kemalizma." [The Chinese Revolution Should Not Take the Road of Kemalism.] *Kommunisticheskij internatsional* (21 (98)): 33–37.
100. Mikhail Godes. 1928. *Chto Takoye Kemalist skij Put' i Vozmozhen li on v Kitae?* [What Is a Kemalist Pathway and Is It Possible in China?]. Leningrad: Priboj, 4–5, 109.
101. Ibid., 38.

102. This is quoted in an article published by the Foreign Minister of the USSR (1957–1985) Andrej Gromyko on the occasion of the 90th birth anniversary of Chicherin. Andrej Gromyko. 1963. *Diplomat Leninskoi shkoli: K 90-letiju so dnya rozhdenia G. V. Chicherina* [The Diplomat of the Leninist School: To the 90th Birth Anniversary of Chicherin] *Izvestia*". 1962 (288) 14142, December 4.

103. *Telegramma Polnomochnogo Predstavitelja SSSR v Turtsii v Narodnyj Komissariat Inostrannyh Del SSSR, March 25, 1928. 242–243. Ministerstvo Inostrannyh Del SSSR, Dokumenty Vneshnej Politiki SSSR* [Ministry for Foreign Affairs of the USSR—Documents of USSR Foreign Policy], Moskva, Izdatel'stvo Politicheskoj Nauki, 1966.

104. Ibid.

References

Alimov, Abid. 1934. "Turtsija." [Turkey.] In *Ocherki po Istorii Vostoka v Epokhu Imperializa* [Outlines of the History of the East in the Age of Imperialism], edited by Abid Alimov and Mikhail Godes, 5–92. Moscow-Leningrad: Gosudarstvennoe Social'no-Ekonomicheskoe Izdatel'stvo.

Astakhov, Georgij. 1926. *Ot Sultanata k Demokraticheskoj Turtsii: Ocherki iz Istorii Kemalizma* [From Sultanate Towards Democratic Turkey: Outlines of the History of Kemalism]. Moscow: Gosudarstvennoye Izdatelstvo.

Butayev, Inal. 1925. *Natsional'naja Revoljutsija na Vostoke: Problema Turtsii* [National Revolution in the Orient: The Problem of Turkey]. Leningrad: Priboj.

Danilov, Vladimir. 1997. "Kemalsm and World Peace." In *Atatürk: A Founder of a Modern State*, edited by Ergun Özbudun and Ali Kazancigil, 2nd ed., 103–126. London: Hurst and Company.

David-Fox, Michael. 1997. *Revolution of the Mind: Higher Learning Among the Bolsheviks, 1918–1929*. Ithaca and London: Cornell University Press.

Feridov, Ziya. 1929. "Kemalistskaya Turtsija i Fashizm." [The Kemalist Turkey and Fascism.] *Revolutsionnyi Vostok* (7): 56–69.

Godes, Mikhail. 1928. *Chto Takoye Kemalistskij Put' i Vozmozhen li on v Kitae?* [What is a Kemalist Pathway and Is It Possible in China?]. Leningrad: Priboj.

Harris, George. 1967. *The Origins of Communism in Turkey*. Stanford: Stanford University.

Irandoust. 1928. *Dvizhuschie Sily Kemalistskoj Revoljutsii* [The Driving Forces of the Kemalist Revolution]. Moscow-Leningrad: Gosizdat.

Ivanova, Margarita. 2006. *Introduction to the Regional Studies: From the History of the Soviet Oriental Studies*. Tomsk: Tomsk Pedagogical University.

Kitaygorodskij, P. 1927. "Zametki o Kemalistskoj Turtsii: Prichini Pobedi Natsional'noj Revoljutsii v Turtsii." [Notes on the Kemalist Turkey: The

Causes of the Victory of the National Revolution in Turkey.] *Bol'shevik* (18): 41–50.

Mel'nik, Anatolij. 1928. "Pjat' Let Respublikanskoj Turtsii." [Five Years of Republican Turkey.] *Mezhdunarodnaja zhizn'* (11): 3–11.

O'Connor, Timothy. 1988. *Diplomacy and Revolution: G. V. Chicherin and Soviet Foreign Policy Affairs, 1918–1930.* Ames: Iowa State University Press.

Özdalga, Elisabeth. 1978. *I Atatürks spår: Det Republikanska FolkPartiet och utvecklingsmobilisering I Turkiet från etatism till populism.* Lund: Dialog.

Pavlovich, Mikhail. 1921. "Kemalistskoje Dvizhenie v Turtsii." [The Kemalist Movement in Turkey.] *Krasnaja Nov'* (1): 218–228.

———. 1921 [Republished in 1925]. *Revoljutsionnaja Turtsija* [Revolutionary Turkey]. Moscow.

Priestland, David. 2007. *Stalinism and the Politics of Mobilization: Ideas, Power, the Terror in Inter-War Russia.* Oxford: Oxford University Press.

Shneerson, A. 1929. "Novaja Popitka Analiza Kemalizma." [A New Attempt to Analyse Kemalism.] *Bol'shevik* 1: 86–90.

Stalin, Iosif. 1928. *Ob Oppozitsii: Stat'i i Rechi 1921–1927* [About the opposition: Articles and Speeches 1921–1927]. Moscow-Leningrad: GosIzdat.

Türkeş, Mustafa. 1999. "The Ideology of the Kadro (Cadre) Movement: A Patriotic Leftist Movement in Turkey." In *Turkey Before and After Atatürk Internal and External Affairs*, edited by Sylvia Kedourie, 92–119. London: Frank Cass.

Uldricks, Teddy. 1979. *Diplomacy and Ideology: The Origins of Soviet Foreign Relations, 1917–1930.* London: Sage.

White, Stephen. 1984. "Soviet Russia and the Asian Revolution, 1917–1924." *Review of International Studies* 10 (3): 219–232.

Geopolitics and Complexities of Soviet Interpretations

This chapter discusses major changes that occurred in Soviet interpretations of Kemalism from the end of the 1920s to the 1970s. During this relatively long period, Soviet perspectives of domestic ideological transformations in Turkey made a few radical turns, which reflected new complexities in bilateral relations and the polarizing nature of the international order. Developments after WWII put the Soviet Union and Turkey on opposite sides of the Cold War, significantly affecting relations between the two countries. Yet in the 1960s, while inhabiting opposite geopolitical camps, the two countries could find ways to cooperate, which in turn positively affected Soviet perspectives of Kemalism.

EXPANDING TIDE OF CRITICISM

Between 1928 and 1930, some Soviet observers became outspokenly critical of Turkey and its Kemalist principles. Their articles, containing strikingly repetitive arguments, data, and claims, showed less pluralism and creativity and a greater desire to follow the emerging definition of Kemalism, given by Stalin in 1927. Publications that were associated with the Comintern, which coordinated official Communist Party propaganda, were especially consistent in their descriptions of domestic developments in Turkey. In Turkey, the Communist Party journals, *Kommunist* and *Inkilap Yolu*, published articles in 1929 describing the Kemalist regime as "bourgeois-feudal" which had abandoned its

© The Author(s) 2019   201
V. Ter-Matevosyan, *Turkey, Kemalism and the Soviet Union,*
Modernity, Memory and Identity in South-East Europe,
https://doi.org/10.1007/978-3-319-97403-3_9

"anti-imperialist" claims. These articles also depicted the oppressive nature of the Kemalist regime.[1] That year, on August 5, Mustafa Kemal equated communism with treason.[2] The timing of critical articles published in Turkey and Russia in 1929 and later suggests that some authors were likely responding to Kemal's statement.

Forty days after his statement equating Communism with treason, *Kommunisticheskij Internatsional,* "the militant weekly organ of the Executive Committee of the Communist International,"[3] published a critical article written by a certain P. K. After analysing the economic state of affairs and the anti-Soviet pronouncements of the Turkish government, P. K. argues that "Kemalism has completed its circle" and "was regenerated into 'Young-Turkism.'"[4] The author further defined Kemalism "as a revolutionary anti-imperialist current in the milieu of the Turkish national bourgeoisie" and argued that it is "already an anachronism." "Unprecedented anti-Soviet campaign signals to the West the preparedness of the Kemalists to attack the USSR by including themselves in the anti-Soviet front"… "Just like the 'Young Turks,' they dream of seizing Azerbaijan and strengthening the Pan-Turkic domination over the Soviet Orient." With these remarks, P. K. joined other critical voices of the day, like Feridov and Kitaygorodskij, questioning the dominant assertion in the Soviet Orientalist school that Kemalist Turkey was "an anti-imperialist state," since its position on the question of disarmament (1928) and the Friendship Treaty with Italy (1928) were viewed as anti-Soviet positions aimed at aligning Turkey with the West.[5]

The author also rationalized the position of Turkish Communists between 1920 and 1925, when they helped Kemalists fight "imperialists and the remnants of the ancient regime." Yet the same author adds that since the Kemalists had deviated from their social base and merged with the "comprador bourgeoisie" by taking the road of "Young-Turkism," the Turkish Communist Party could push the counter-revolutionary "People's Party" [i.e., RPP] into the abyss.[6] The author then gives the major phases of the evolution of Kemalism:

> We will not concentrate on all the phases of the evolution of Kemalism from peoples, peasant ideology towards pure-bourgeoisie. At the dawn of its youth, Kemalism was revolutionary; however, it did not want to deepen the national revolution, let alone push it into the road of non-capitalist development. The formula of "neither capitalism, nor Communism" was obviously vague and utopian. Soon Kemalism turned toward capitalism by declaring a relentless struggle against Communism. However, with that, it

[i.e., Kemalism], predetermined its own fatal road of capitulation in front of imperialism as fighting the latter it solidified… Only a non-capitalist road to development can ensure the political and economic sovereignty of the state.[7]

This critical and essentially unusual article by P. K. is noteworthy for several reasons. First, it reiterates the turbulent nature of Turkish–Soviet relations in the second half of the 1920s. Each time there was an outburst of tension in bilateral relations, Soviet observers were quick to produce negative descriptions of Kemalism and its development. More interestingly, being critical helped P. K. lay out the ideological evolutionary phases of Kemalism and depict the characteristic features of each stage. Only a close observer who followed developments in Turkey consistently could have done this. Although ideological-doctrinal conceptual approaches prevailed, periodization and an analytical approach help understand the Kemalism of the 1920s. It needs to be stressed again that orthodox Kemalism had yet to be firmly conceptualized in Turkey, whereas Soviet Communist observers were already contemplating its demise.

In 1929, the "International Red Aid" (known in Russian as *Mezhdunarodnaja Organizatsija Pomoshi Bortsam Revoljutsii—MOPR*), an international organization established by the Communist International, published a brochure penned by Kitaygorodskij. It reiterated a commonly held argument among Communists: "The young Turkish bourgeoisie and its leader, Mustafa-Kemal, created a new Kemalist Turkey on the ruins of the sultanic Turkey, which turned out to be a spiteful stepmother towards the class of workers and the peasantry."[8]

Some Soviet orientalists hewed to the party line of the late 1920s, even decades later. Nor could they hide their dissatisfaction with unexpected events in Turkey. Dmitrij Yeremeyev, a renowned scholar in the Soviet Orientalist school, explained in 1963 that the Kemalist movement was initially viewed as "progressive and democratic" since it included "large masses of the Turkish nation and was under the influence of the October revolution." It excluded chauvinistic and reactionary forces, but once "the Kemalist revolutionary war was over," the spirit of Kemalism was distorted by Pan-Turkic movements, namely chauvinistic and reactionary forces that were tolerated by Mustafa Kemal. The SU interpreted this shift as an aggressive one.[9] Discussing Turkish–Soviet relations at the end of the 1920s, Sahakyan noted in 1960 that Turkey was carrying out an "inconsistent and contradictory policy. The bourgeoisie-nationalist government of the Kemalists… hated the country of the Soviets."[10]

Another reason for growing criticism in the late 1920s was the new Comintern program, which was adopted at its Sixth Congress in 1929. The program claimed that the capitalist system was approaching its final collapse, and stressed the dangers of the national bourgeoisie, which had betrayed the national-revolutionary movement, opting for rapprochement with imperialist powers.[11] The rise of aggressive rhetoric in Turkey, from radical nationalists, racists, and Pan-Turkists, was another source of anti-Turkish sentiment. For Soviet observers, this irredentism posed a threat to Turkic nations living in its territory.

Party functionaries, leaders, and scholars examined the ideological bases of these developments, referring to "Kemalism" long before the term was circulated in official circles in Turkey. The spread of the term in the 1920s can also be explained by Turkism, Pan-Turkism, and Turanism—concepts that were familiar in the late imperial and early Soviet periods. The Soviets were also keen to apply a conceptual and ideological lens to change, tacking on an "ism" to the end of many processes. Kemalism was therefore the continuation of some of these political and ideological trends. Soviet leaders also regarded the Turkish political and intellectual elite as possessing the skills and experience to produce a new ideological framework for the development of the newly formed Turkish nation-state.

Beyond Moscow, officials in Soviet Republics that had historical grievances against Turkey monitored developments there. While Soviet Armenian Communist functionaries followed changes in Turkey in the early 1920s, following the consolidation of the Soviet system, they could not pursue an agenda independent of Moscow. Still, Armenian intellectuals and former members of the Armenian Revolutionary Federation (ARF) (which ruled the short-lived Republic of Armenia during 1918–1920), who left Armenia after its Sovietization, had their own interpretations of Kemalist Turkey. They hoped to better understand Turkish–Armenian relations and post-war transformations in Turkey.

Rouben (Rouben Ter-Minassian), a prominent member of the ARF and former Minister of Defence of the Republic of Armenia, published a two-part article in 1928 that offered a comprehensive account of Kemalism and the Kemalist transformation of the 1920s. Going against the common view that Turkey was undergoing a revolution, Rouben argued that true revolutions require resistance.

The Angora [Ankara] government adopts one revolutionary law after another … without facing a real resistance. Therefore, it is not a Turkish revolution, but a coup carried out by Kemal and the Kemalists. That is why it is accurate that what happened is named either "Kemalist" or "Kemalist movement," which is dear to Kemal himself, but not to Turks and Turkey.[12]

Rouben was understandably sceptical of the future of Kemal's reforms. "An empty word and insubstantial box… which probably will serve as a coffin both for Kemalism and Turanism" was how he described reality in Kemalist Turkey.[13] Shahan Natali (Hakob Ter-Hakobyan), a prominent member of the ARF, went against most Armenian émigré intellectuals and former leaders of the ARF who questioned the viability of Kemalist Turkey. Disagreeing with Rouben's claim, Natali wrote:

… the Turkish national ideology is not a novice enterprise; it is fifty years old and is in a stage of maturity. It is not the making of a few minds, but the life of a few generations. That is why Mustafa Kemal is not an ordinary man, but represents the entire collective and a forty-twenty years old young nation. It is not an academic exercise, but a marching labor with checked and balanced steps.[14]

CONVERGENCE OF MODERATION AND CRITICISM

Kemalist Turkey and the SU signed several treaties, conventions, protocols, and agreements[15] between 1921 and 1935 that proved mutually beneficial and mutually legitimizing. Scepticism flowed both ways, but the period between 1929 and 1935 was "revealing," as the two states intensified their political, economic, and cultural exchange.[16]

Soviet observers of Turkey closely followed socio-economic transformations and the effects of the Great Depression in that country. However, comparison of arguments and positions reveals logical inconsistencies and continuations. For instance, in 1927, in the monthly of the Central Asian Bureau of CCCPSU (B.) *Za Partiju* (For the party), published in Tashkent, Lüfti praised Turkey for getting rid of "quasi-feudal colonial status," and implementing reforms that aimed to "emancipate the Turkish national economy from the control of the West-European capital and achieving complete economic independence."[17] Only two years later, in 1929, Soviet writer P. K. noted: "The Kemalist party of the Turkish national bourgeoisie is rolling downward towards the capit-ulation in front of the foreign capital, by yielding to it one position after another."[18] The author further noted: "... after a few years of various experiments exemplified in the politics of 'étatism,' after imposing state monopolies, after imitating our system of VneshTorg [Foreign Trade], they had to push the brakes while rolling downward in its [i.e. Turkey's] cooperation with comprador bourgeoisie and foreign capital." P. K. listed other examples of state mishandling of the economy (abusing state subsi-dies and open and covert monopolies, embezzlement, misappropriation, and bribery) and cynically claimed that "Kemalist Turkey was becoming a 'normal' bourgeoisie state."[19] In contrast, Alimov dated the consoli-dation of the Anatolian bourgeoisie, what he called, "first-class" bour-geoisie, to 1922–1923, when Turkey was negotiating in Lausanne.[20] He defined the étatism of the Kemalists as "a distinct mercantilism of the twentieth century."[21] Reflecting on Kemalist economic policies, Boris Potskhveria, another Soviet Turkologist, whose academic supervisor was Anatolij Miller, explained étatism's rationalization: "The economic policy of Kemal Atatürk was based on the principles of protection of the weak national economy from the imperialist monopolies... Atatürk's proposed economic policy of étatism provoked harsh discontent from the interna-tional monopolists and Turkish comprador circles associated with them. Turkey was exposed, in essence, to a financial blockade. It was refused of loans and credits, its foreign trade positions were shattered, hoping to bring it to a monetary bankruptcy."[22] For Nikolay Kireev, who has writ-ten extensively on economic development and the history of the Turkish Republic, étatism was not about state interference into the economy. He interpreted it from an "opposite dimension"—"étatism [is] a specific social-economic form of societal existence, which necessitated the expan-sion of interference of the private entrepreneurs into the existing system, by granting them more space for activities and providing them direct - without bureaucratic bourgeoisie—leadership over the capitalist develop-ment of the state."[23]

In 1931, Boris Platonov, another observer of Turkish political and economic affairs, authored a study in the pages of a monthly published by the Oriental Department of the State Academic-Research Institute of Azerbaijan. The global economic crisis acutely exacerbated the sit-uation, he wrote, "as if a surgeon's knife helped to unveil those pro-cesses, which accrued in Kemalist Turkey for the past years. It was the natural result of economic policies of Kemalism."[24] Platonov argued that in the face of "structural economic crisis," "the social base of Kemalism was rapidly strained," which "ripened the political crisis."[25] By opposing the dominant Soviet interpretation that anti-government rebellions (Kurdish rebellions of the 1920s and the Menemen incident) were organized by Western powers, Platonov argues that the real reasons were class contradictions and discontent surrounding Kemalism's economic and nationalist policies. He also criticized Soviet scholars who failed to see it, labelling them "rightist opportunists or bourgeoisie orientalists from the little schools of Gurko-Kryazhin and Iranskij."[26] He uses the word "*shkolki*" (little schools) to belittle and disparage two leading Soviet scholars of the previous decade. This open criticism towards the old school of orientalists was yet another manifestation (Irandoust and Astakhov were already being criticized) that rigid Marxist-Leninist ideological principles required for academic research. Scholars who failed to follow new research methodologies and objectives were publicly discredited.[27] The case between Platonov and Gurko-Kryazhin once again attested to the existence of this conflict.

After criticizing those who failed to see the domestic root causes of the Kurdish rebellions, Platonov admitted that Britain and France should be interested in the uprisings because an independent Kurdistan would create a platform to attack the SU.[28] At the same time, Platonov also praised Turkish leaders for mitigating the pressure of "imperialist states" to pay the Ottoman debt.[29] Platonov argued that with the firm, friendly backing of the SU, Turkey had ably manoeuvred through the disagreements between Western powers and did not concede to ultimatums.[30] Ottoman debt was a serious concern for Soviet observers, who considered it against Turkish interest and economic realities. Months after the 1928 deal to repay the debt, Feridov noted: "In spite of self-confidence, the Kemalists cannot stand against the unified Anglo-French capital without trembling. In good old times, they could struggle against them with arms in their hands; those were heroic times... Kemalists themselves are not the same anymore... The late-born baby grew old without being able to reach the blossoming age of adolescence."[31] Reflecting official and popular convictions and repeating what Mel'nik and Astakhov mentioned in the 1920s, Platonov went a step further and claimed that Turkey's friendly relations with the SU formed a foundation for Turkish state sovereignty.[32] Thus, Platonov was rather critical about the economic and political dimensions of Kemalist reforms. In his analysis, however, the mutual importance of Turkey and the SU stood out.

On January 21, 1934, after two years of negotiations, Turkey signed the protocol with the SU to receive a non-interest twenty-year credit of eight million USD (16.5 million Turkish lira) in order to acquire Soviet-produced machinery and build two textile factories in Kayseri and Nazilli. In addition to building two textile factories, the SU also built auto-repair workshops in Ankara, and supplied 100 buses and trucks to develop the transportation system. Soviet specialists also helped to build a number of commercial facilities and irrigation systems.[33] The SU, thus, not only extended economic aid to Turkey but also provided loans to implement the Turkish Five-Year Development Plan, which started in 1934, and was designed in consultation with Soviet experts.[34] Yurij Rozaliev argues that by supporting Turkey the SU aimed to decrease its economic and political dependence from foreign states, which has been the official policy since the early 1920s.[35] That policy objective of the SU, however, did not work out as Turkey continued to transfer much-needed technology from Europe and the United States via direct foreign investments, joint ventures, licensing, and build-operate-transfer arrangements. Foreign companies (for instance, *Ford, H. A. Brassert, Siemens*) continued to build factories and industrial enterprises by bringing their own people to train the citizens of Turkey on how to manage and operate these enterprises.[36]

Until 1937, Turkey and the SU exchanged official visits that were widely covered in reports on bilateral relations.[37] The Turkish PM was the first to visit the SU in 1932, which was reciprocated by the SU's Defence Commissar Clement Voroshilov's visit to Turkey to participate in the tenth anniversary of the Turkish Republic in 1933.[38] The daily *Izvestija*, the official mouthpiece of the Central Executive Committee of the USSR, dedicated most of the front page of its April 28, 1932 issue to Turkish PM İnönü's official visit to the SU. On April 26, 1932, the Turkish delegation arrived in Odessa on the streamer *Gruzija* and was warmly received by the SU, first by the cruiser "Profintern" on Soviet territorial waters, which gave "the salute of the Nation, twenty-one shots," then in the harbor, where the Turkish official anthem and the *Internationale* were both played. A large sign, announcing "*Sefa geldiniz*" (Welcome) was displayed in the harbor, while Turkish flags decorated the streets of Odessa.[39] During the banquet given in his honor, İnönü spoke as "a representative of the national and revolutionary Turkey," and admitted that he was impressed by the warm welcome. For İnönü, the friendship between the two nations was only twelve years old and was not based on "an artificial combination ... but derived from mutual interests."[40] After fourteen hours, he continued his trip to Moscow via Kiev. On April 27, he visited the laboratories of the National Academy of Science of Ukraine and the "Anti-religious Museum" in Kiev.[41] Writing in the same issue of *Izvestija*, Anatolij Mel'nik once again stressed that the different pathways of the two countries should not hinder cooperation. He also provided examples of similar challenges facing the two nations. For the SU, it was more important to keep a close watch on Turkey, while hoping that Ankara's changing relations with the West could make it turn toward the SU once again.

Following the emerging positive mode, Avel' Yenukidze, Secretary of the Central Executive Committee of the USSR and a prominent politician and science administrator, published an article in "*Mirovoje Khoziaestvo i Mirovaya Politika*" ("World Economy and World Politics"), the journal of the Communist Academy, on the occasion of the tenth anniversary of the Turkish Republic. Unlike the works of previous authors who were critical of important questions regarding Turkish domestic and foreign policy issues, Yenukidze's article hardly contained any criticism. In fact, he claimed that the tenth anniversary was a big celebration, not only for the Turkish nation but also for "the nations of the Soviet Republics, which are tied to the Turkish nation with the links of friendship and cooperation." He called Turkey "a friendly power" and "a capitalist state of a different nature," and praised its leaders for protecting its economic independence.[42] While interpreting the 1931 RPP program and its six principles, Yenukidze also mentioned "the inviolability of private property" as another principle. He did not elaborate on the reasons for this addition. He also referred to "*halkçılık*" (populism) principles of Kemalism as "*demokratism*" (democracy (ism)), as Feridov had in 1928.[43]

Technical and financial assistance to Turkey diminished in the mid-1930s, and a new interpretation of Kemalist Turkey emerged as Soviet criticism of Kemalism grew louder. Officials portrayed Kemal as a "reactionary tyrant... who ruled by means of a unique mixture of terror and social demagogy, a special Turkish brand of 'national fascism' or 'agrarian Bonapartism.'"[44] But Soviet historiography, in general, depicted Kemal in a positive light, as an experienced statesman. Chernikov claimed that even though "Atatürk expressed the interests of Turkish national bourgeoisie," he was a "talented leader and a true patriot who led the Turkish state ship for two decades."[45] He claimed that his death in 1938 had negative implications for Turkish–Soviet relations, because, "in contrast to other Turkish political leaders, only he could stop those erroneous steps, which resulted in pernicious consequences."[46]

Another factor that complicated relations between the two countries was the Soviet government's concerns with Germany's increased presence in Turkey. In a diplomatic communication with Moscow, the Soviet Ambassador to Ankara noted that "Germans were profitable buyers and sellers whom Kemal does not want to lose."[47] Aron Novichev argues that Turkish–German relations were particularly good after Bayar, whom he called a "Germanophile,"[48] became PM. Amid tense relations, the SU closed down its consulates in Izmir and Kars. Turkey reciprocated by shuttering its consulates in Odessa, Baku, Leninakan (current Gyumri), and Yerevan.[49]

İnönü, Atatürk's replacement, had travelled to the SU twice in the 1930s, and often reassured Soviet leaders of Turkey's commitment to friendship between the two nations. After 1938, his policy line towards the SU took a different turn. "A struggle was unleashed against the friendship between Turkey and the USSR," wrote Aralov, "after Kâzim Karabekir, Rauf Orbay, and Ali Fuat Cebesoy—former opponents of Atatürk—came to power and assumed responsible positions."[50] Aralov was critical of Turkey, especially after 1941, when Turkey concentrated its armed forces near the Caucasian border with the SU. "This was a disgraceful and perfidious response of the Turkish government to the frank assistance of the USSR during the most difficult and dangerous times for Turkey," wrote Aralov in his memoirs. "Simultaneously, it was also a shabby desecration upon the memory of Mustafa Kemal Atatürk."[51]

IRREDENTIST TRENDS, PAN-TURKISM, AND SOVIET RESPONSES

With growing cooperation between Germany and Turkey, the SU began treating the Kemalist regime with outright suspicion and increasing hostility. A Soviet commentator even called Turkey "an appendage of German fascism."[52] During World War II, the SU was openly critical of rising irredentism in radical circles of the Turkish government and among the intellectual elite. The Turkish Republic, according to its leaders, was not interested in adventurism in foreign policy, let alone in pursuing expansionist goals. Examining Soviet and Armenian sources, however, tells a somewhat different story and highlights other aspects of

Turkish–Soviet geopolitics and ideological antagonism during and after WWII.

The Kemalist leadership was mostly satisfied with the results of the nationalist movement. Most of its territorial demands were met in the Moscow, Kars, and Lausanne treaties.[53] Relations with the Soviet Union were particularly important for Mustafa Kemal as he did not want to endanger the new Republic's achievements by pursuing irredentist dreams.[54] However, nostalgia among some members of the Kemalist regime toward former Ottoman territories, the irredentism and eventual annexation of Hatay to Turkey, and incessant ambitions toward Mosul, Batumi, Northern Iran, some parts of the Balkans, and other minor and major ambitions significantly throw into question the argument about the lack of territorial expansionist trends of the Kemalist regime. This is consistent with Ilker Aytürk's claims that the swift recovery of devastated German lands and the ease with which the Nazis transgressed boundaries imposed on Germany at Versailles "mesmerized the leading Kemalist cabinet ministers, politicians, and intellectuals."[55]

Vladimir Gordlevskij, Professor at the Moscow Institute of Oriental Studies, noted that the main feature of Kemalist domestic politics was the "strengthening and recovery of the Turkish nation" through "creation of a powerful Turkish nucleus." He goes on: "… however, Turks, impoverished by the war, experience a sharp outburst of chauvinism and are intolerant towards indigenous Christians, who are blamed for all the tragedies which befall the country." Gordlevskij interprets these policies as the "implementation of theoretical presuppositions of nationalists (Pan-Turkists–Turanists), who dream of cultural unification of 'Turanic' nations, in order to create a federal state."[56] Zarevand has argued that the early republican political and intellectual elite was largely composed of former supporters of Pan-Turanism, which meant lasting irredentist ambitions.[57] The same author claimed that in the 1920s, hundreds of Turkish teachers in the Soviet schools of Azerbaijan, Dagestan, Turkestan, the Volga Region, and the Crimea used Turkish textbooks printed in Turkey. He confirmed that Pan-Turkist propaganda was visible among Russian Turkic-Tatars, and therefore: "Turkey is seen as a true political Mecca for all of them, and Mustafa Kemal is seen as a genuine Prophet. His portraits hang in every Turkic house and the personality cult of the Turkish dictator made the Soviet authorities initiate special measures to stop it."[58] In June 1923, a special four-day meeting of national communists was held in Moscow to discuss disloyalty and nationalism observed among Soviet Muslim Communists in Tatarstan and the Caucasus. Key members of the Communist Party, including Stalin, Kamenev, Trotsky, Ordzhonikidze, Zinovyev, and others, attended. Valerian Kuibishev, chair of the Communist Party Central Control Commission, reported: "Students in the Azerbaijan Muslim-teachers school wore badges featuring Turkey's Mustafa Kemal."[59]

Some Soviet scholars criticized Pan-Turkic émigré ideologues who lived and published in Turkey. For instance, Arshaluys Arsharouni, a Soviet journalist covering the developments in the East, criticized the ideas and visions of the Istanbul-based theoreticians of Pan-Turkism: A. Validov, Mustafa Chokayev, and M. Rasul-Zade in a 1928 *Novij Vostok* (New Orient) article. He was particularly critical of them for supporting the worn-out idea of uniting all the Turkic nations of the SU into a "Turkish Federal Republic."[60] He condemned Pan-Turkist ideologues for promoting the Soviet policy of dividing the Turkic nation into Tatars, Kyrgyz-Kazakhs, Bashkirs, Uzbeks, etc. He concluded by denouncing these ideas as marginal, and the ideologues as weak and impotent, with no appeal to Central Asian Republics and "Communist Youth."[61] Decades later, Raffi Kondakchyan, another prominent Soviet Turkologist who studied Pan-Turkist propaganda in Turkey, noted that Crimean Tatars, Caucasian Tatars (whom he referred to as Azerbaijanis), people from the North Caucasus, the Volga region, and Central Asia were able to establish territorial-friendly associations ("Turkish Cultural Union" and the "Union of the Youth of Turkestan") in Turkey and carry out their activities unhindered by Turkish authorities. He added that periodicals published by these organizations preached the ideas of Pan-Turkism and unification with Muslims living in the SU, the "New Caucasus," "New Turkestan," and "Azeri Turks."[62] This suggests that even though Mustafa Kemal condemned all previous instances of Pan-Turkic policies, after the establishment of the Republic, some political circles in Turkey maintained contacts with Turkic ethnicities in the newly formed Soviet Union. This process began in the 1920s but was subdued by heavy Soviet criticism and punitive action. It continued in the 1940s—a process that is discussed, below.

The official journal of the Armenian Revolutionary Federation (Dashnaktsutyun), *Droshak*, contended that Turkey's intentions toward some Persian territories defied Ankara's denunciations of "Pan-Islamic and Pan-Turanic dreams." *Droshak* cited the Ararat rebellion of Kurds in 1929, when the Turkish government used the uprising as a pretext to "carry out visible policies of conquering Maku (a city and a county in northern Iran) and, even farther, Atrpatakan (a region in northern Iran)." The same journal also referred to Turkish policies that created harsh conditions for Kurds, keeping more than one million Turkish Armenians away, and the fierce assimilation of Circassians, Laz, and other nationalities.[63] George Bournoutian's recent study of the 1932 border agreement between Iran and Turkey partially supports the argument that Turkey intended to modify parts of its borders in the 1920s and 1930s. He argues that because of territorial exchanges and the final demarcations of 1934, Iran obtained some eighty square miles near its north-western border, south of Bayazid, while Turkey obtained disproportionately more territory, some of which had both symbolic and strategic importance. In particular, Turkey received ninety square miles east of Qotur, northeast of Lake Urmia and Lesser Ararat (or Sis), and the plain of Ağrı Dağı (Mount Ararat) around it, which had belonged to Iran since 1639. Bournoutian asserts: "Turkey, which had taken over Greater Ararat in the 1921 treaties of Moscow and Kars, ended up controlling both peaks."[64]

The revival of the irredentism among some of the Turkish political elite had different manifestations. The successful *Anschluss* of Aleksandretta Sanjak (Hatay province) strengthened the confidence of the Turkish political elite. Hanioğlu cites popular beliefs of the 1930s, which included the identification of the Alexendretta Sanjak as part of the old Hittite empire, and that a Turkic people, the Hurrians, had settled there long before Semite Arabs. He also referred to Atatürk's statement that it was "the Turkish homeland of four thousand years."[65] In speeches, Atatürk famously referred to the Hatay issue (Iskenderun) as the "greatest national problem," which had to be resolved with all seriousness and determination to return Hatay "to Turks, who are the true owners of it."[66]

Furthermore, during WWII, with many influential Young Turks back in Turkey, Pan-Turkist ambitions were revitalized in intellectual and social discourses, and some government officials (including PM Saracoğlu) were even sympathetic to Pan-Turkism. Journals of Pan-Turkist orientation (*Bozkurt, Çınaraltı,* and *Türk Amacı,* etc.) proliferated, openly discussing the possibility of attacking the Soviet Union to restore "the Turkish fatherland," composed of seventeen state entities.[67] In February 1943, the remains of Talat Paşa, one of the masterminds of the Armenian Genocide, who was gunned down by Soghomon

Tehleryan in March 1921 in Berlin, were reburied in Istanbul at Hürriyet Tepesi, site of the Young Turk victory in 1908. President İnönü and PM Saracoğlu, leading civil and military officers, and the ambassador of Germany (Franz von Papen) were present at the ceremony of reburial.[68]

Communist Party functionaries in the SU were very critical in their remarks about anti-Soviet statements and the irredentist ambitions of Pan-Turkist circles. The CPSU official journal labelled them "Turkish-fascists" who were funded and supported by Nazi Germany and dreamed of establishing "Greater Turkey" with a population of sixty-five-million at the expense of the territories of the SU.[69] The same journal also reported that a few months after the German invasion of the SU in 1941, the German embassy in Ankara and consulate in Istanbul financed Turkish and German scholarly expeditions to Turkey's eastern regions. Their aim was "to prepare the local Pan-Turkists to carry out their job... when Germany invades the Caucasus in six weeks."[70]

An important episode during WWII was the ascent of Pan-Turkist (ethnic expansionism), Pan-Turanist (cultural expansionist) elements, and irredentist opinions inside and outside the Turkish government. In this process, former members and sympathizers of the Turkish Hearths played no minor role.[71] A number of high-ranking officials (PM Saracoğlu, Secretary General of the Foreign Ministry and Foreign Minister after 1942, Numan Menemencioğlu, Chief of General Staff Fevzi Çakmak, and many others) held strong Pan-Turkist sympathies and sought to revive hopes of unity with the Turkic peoples of the Caucasus and Central Asia. The Pan-Turkist current was a mixture of racism and fascism, Nazi myths and slogans, social arch-conservatism, a romantic passion for the past (antedating the Ottoman history), and an irrational belief in and exaltation of personal valor and of war, purity of blood, and discrimination against all groups considered non-Turkish.[72] Although Pan-Turkism did not bring any significant changes to the government's foreign policy, since many of its proponents left their official positions, they did influence political discourse within Turkey by offering alternative foreign policy models.

V. Krimskij, a contributor to the journal *Bol'shevik*, defied Soviet orthodoxy in 1944. Any displays of Turkish expansionism were to be identified as Pan-Turkism, but Krimskij saw in Turkey's Pan-Turkic organizations "unrestricted fascist-Nazi intelligence in Turkey, which Hitlerists created long before WWII."[73] Drawing comparisons between Nazi Germany and Turkey, he pointed to parallels between the two countries, including incitement to ethnic cleansing, the persecution of ethnic minorities, irredentism, nationalist radicalism, ethnic supremacist propaganda, anti-communist campaigns, and the burning of the books of progressive Turkish writers.[74]

Krimskij's reflections are also important for the study of Soviet popular interpretations of the 1944 "Racism-Turanism Trials." The trials of Nihal Atsız and his supporters, which Aytürk considers a turning point in the history of Turkish nationalism,[75] was indeed a significant moment during WWII. In May 1944, the Turkish government took forty-seven prominent racist Turanists and sympathizers into custody and began a trial process that lasted three years. It is widely believed that this was done to appease the Soviets. However, İnönü himself was not happy with the rising popularity of Atsız, who, for a decade or so, had openly challenged and criticized the Kemalist notion of nationalism. On May 19, 1944, or "*Youth Day*," İnönü urged young people to stay vigilant against the proliferation of the dangerous ideology of Turanism and racism. In his commentary, Krimskij was particularly critical of the Turkish government media reporting on the Turkish racists who were taken into custody. He defied the wording by the "Anadolu news agency," which claimed that the Turkish government unveiled a secret organization of Pan-Turkists. He claimed the investigators were not courageous enough to accept that the "secret" organization was not secret at all, since it was widely known by certain groups, particularly students and youth.[76] Krimskij further analyzed the history of "the newly unveiled secret organization" and the activities of some prominent Pan-Turkists (he used the terms Pan-Turkism and Turanism interchangeably). He identified dozens of names, among them retired general Hüseyin Erkilet, Ali Ihsan Sabis, Nihal Atsız, journalist Yunus Nadi and his son Nadir Nadi, Yusuf Ziya Ortaç, Orhan Sayfi Orhon, and many others. He coined them "lackeys of Hitler," "Turkish Quislings," and "the agents of Goebbel's ministry."[77] Krimskij ridiculed the expansionist ambitions of Pan-Turkists:

> Following the example of German-Italian fascists, who dreamed of world domination... Turkish fascists raved about creating the "Great Turkey" with a population of 65 million. Of course they turned out to be more modest than their Berlin bosses as they are not intending to conquer the entire world; instead they are satisfied with seizing only those foreign

territories where Turkic nations live (Soviet Caucasus, Central Asia, Iran, and other states in the vicinity of Turkey).[78]

He also added that although the current Pan-Turkists identified themselves as followers of Ziya Gökalp, "the latter would congratulate his students for adding a new chapter in his theory of racism."[79] He concluded by noting: "The activities of Pan-Turkists contradict the main principle of Kemalism, the 'National Pact' …, which denied the Sultan's predatory policy. However, with the anti-Soviet activities, the Pan-Turkists defy the principles and achievements of Kemalism." He also expressed hope that Turkish authorities would be determined to finish the investigation and stop the Pan-Turkists from "spread[ing] the fascist plague in Kemalist Turkey."[80]

The Armenian daily, *Paikar*, published in Boston, reported that during WWII, Pan-Turanism was a vibrant movement among Turkish political and intellectual elites. In particular, it referred to efforts by prominent nationalists (Nihal Atsız, Tahsin Demiray, and Nurullah Parıman) to establish a political party based on "racist and Turanist principles," which would include "particularly the racists and Turanists as its members."[81] Another instance of awakening Pan-Turanist tendencies was related to the Korean War. The Armenian daily, *Arev*, published in Cairo, referred to existing Pan-Turkic tendencies among Turkey's ruling elite. It also printed excerpts from the February 1951 *Orkun* periodical, the voice of an increasingly popular Pan-Turkic movement, which was edited by Atsız. Known for its aggressive and adventurist stance, the daily had claimed the Turkish ruling elite was of the view that the Korean War would expand to China, Mongolia, Kazan, Ural, Central Asia, and the Caucasus. This new movement would make Turkic nations take up arms, and with the help of "UN armies," unite all Turks under one flag.[82]

INTERPRETATIONS OF KEMALISM IN THE POST-WWII DECADE

Soviet-Turkish relations were particularly tense between 1945 and 1953. In 1945, the Soviets refused to renew the 1925 agreement and presented territorial demands to Turkey, hoping to acquire a base at the Straits and return Kars and the Ardahan regions to Armenia and Georgia, respectively. The Soviet government also reinforced troops stationed in Bulgaria, and along Armenian and Georgian borders with Turkey. With these steps, the SU initiated "a war of nerves" with Turkey that had domestic implications.[83] Behlül Özkan suggests that it is misleading to name Soviet territorial ambitions *demands*, and prefers to use *proposals*. Relying on various statements by members of the political leadership and elites in Turkey, including İnönü, Bayar, Aras, Çakmak, and Köprülü, he claims that SU declarations were greatly exaggerated by right-wing and conservative-nationalist movements in Turkey. The common belief was that the SU was weak and not ready to wage a new war against Turkey.[84]

The Soviet Embassy in Ankara likely overreacted to certain assignments and again played the fascism card. For instance, in December 1945, students and nationalist groups in Istanbul organized protests to frighten leftist movements and the press. Recently, Jamil Gasanly, an Azerbaijani historian, unveiled correspondence between the Soviet Ambassador to Turkey, S. Vinogradov, and the PCFA. His study shows that the Soviet envoy likely suggested that Moscow call the December protests in Istanbul manifestations of fascism, and on this basis, discontinue contacts with Ankara and reinforce garrisons along the Soviet-Turkish border. The PCFA responded promptly, referring to the ambassador's suggestion as "ill-advised and unacceptable:" "You should bear in mind that we cannot make official statements to the Turkish government about the rise of fascism in Turkey because this is the Turks' internal affair... You should ... not forward hasty suggestions that might cause political complications for our state. Think it over and try to be more reasonable next time—your responsible position and your post oblige you to do this."[85] The response from the SU Politburo did not deny or refute the existence of fascism in Turkey.

Until the late 1950s, continued tension characterized relations between the two countries. In the post-WWII period, as American influence in Turkey visibly increased, with the Truman Doctrine, Marshall Plan, and Turkey's NATO membership, the Soviets directed their criticism at Turkey.[86] Soviet suspicions that intensifying American pressure weakened Turkish sovereignty led Soviet party functionaries and scholars to censure the ruling Turkish regime and its ideology. For instance, Andrej Zhdanov, a Politburo member and Secretariat of the CCCPSU, who was responsible for ideology, propaganda, and foreign policy, characterized the ruling regime in Turkey as "reactionary anti-democratic" and "a dictatorship of the fascist minority over the nation," in a famous speech delivered in Poland in September 1947.[87] Even though the PCFA disagreed with Vinogradov's description of Turkey, the political leadership of the SU kept using the term fascism in different statements.

Anna Tveritinova, a renowned expert who published extensively on Turkish history, viewed the ruling Kemalist elite as "a coalition of bourgeoisie and landlords which completely impoverished the nation because of its reactionary nature." "As a result," she argued, "the ideology of Kemalism was transformed from national-chauvinism towards national treachery because of its anti-popular and anti-national character."[88] She saw no difference between the RPP and the DP. For her, both parties "appear to be advocates of the predatory ideology of Pan-Turkism, misanthropic racism, and chauvinism; they implement a policy of national treason and act as agents of imperialism."[89]

Career diplomat Ivan Samilovskij, once Soviet ambassador to Afghanistan, a radiobroadcast editor and head of the Department of Broadcasting to the Middle East for the Soviet State Radio Committee, described Kemalist ideology as expansionist.[90] The United States had encouraged "cranky aspirations of Turkish rulers to restore the former Turkish Empire," wrote Samilovskij. They had received "a green light" from "US imperialists" to control parts of the territories of Lebanon, Syria, and its city of Aleppo.[91] Given his outsized role in the Soviet propaganda machine, Samilovskij toed the official policy line. Using his critical approach, Samilovskij was continuing the dominant trend of his day. For instance, he had used the same terms as Akopyan two years earlier to describe Turkey and its ruling regime. They both used expressions such as "Turkey became the patrimony of Wall Street," or "Turkey is a patrimony of American imperialism."[92]

In 1952, the High Party School at the CCCPSU published a book by N. Lavrov that included lectures the author delivered between 1939 and 1951 to important cadres of the Communist Party about Turkey. Utterly critical of Turkey's position during and after WWII, the author described the Kemalism of earlier decades in harsh terms. He argued that "chauvinism and nationalism cultivated by the Kemalists over the course of many years" had its roots in the 1931 program, which gave special status to the Turkish nation.[93] He presented the plans of the Kemalists to conquer the Soviet Caucasus and the Crimea "as anti-Soviet policy implemented under the cloak of neutrality," in violation of the 1929 Soviet-Turkish Treaty. He employed the term "Turkish-fascists" and the phrase "fascist terror in Turkey against progressive forces" when talking both about government policy against the SU and ultra-nationalist organizations with a Pan-Turkist agenda. He used the phrase "fascistizing Pan-Turkists" to explain the plans of Pan-Turkic groups who were active not only during the war but also after.[94] Like Anna Tveritinova, he also saw no difference between the RPP and the DP, describing both as parties of "bourgeois-landowners." He wanted future leaders of the Communist Party apparatus and bureaucracy to believe that the 1950 change in power was "the manoeuvre of the ruling classes in Turkey aiming to mitigate the eruption of the popular hatred, which accumulated against the Peoples' Republican Party of the Kemalists for the twenty-seven years it was in power."[95]

Aralov interpreted Turkey's choice of the US and NATO as "a breach of the National Pact and the legacy of Mustafa Kemal Atatürk. The independence of Turkey... was lost and trampled."[96] Miller claimed that during the difficult moments of WWII and the post-war period, the Turkish nation felt the absence of Atatürk in particular. As a result, "his successors adopted an 'anti-national position,' resulting in 'the reactionary clique of Bayar-Menderes' remaining at the helm of government for an entire decade and bringing the country to the edge of the abyss."[97] These authors used identical terms and descriptions to convey their criticisms of Turkey.

Soviet observers in the 1950s attacked Kemalism's nationalism and populism above all else, just like they had in previous decades. The former promoted "specific national characters" that lacked a historical foundation. Its nature was racist; nationalism was deployed to forcefully Turkify national minorities.[98] It promoted fashionable tendencies of expansionism and Pan-Turkism and empowered fascism in Turkey.[99] The latter principle, populism, offered an unpersuasive argument about "absolute equality" within Turkey that was unattainable, given the country's deeply rooted social inequality, according to Tveritinova.[100] This is the context in which Samilovskij argued that the Turkish working class was slowly shedding "the poison of Kemalism and chauvinism and of the influence of the DP and RPP."[101]

Back to Normalization: Revised Interest Towards Kemalism

Although Stalin died in 1953, relations between his country and Turkey did not improve for some time. Writing to General Cemal Gürsel, head of the first military intervention in Turkey, on June 28, 1960, Soviet leader Nikita Khrushchev expressed his hope that Turkey's new government would maintain its commitments, staying loyal to the principles of Atatürk. If Turkey's new government followed through on its post-intervention promises, said Khrushchev, "we all will see how the Soviet-Turkish relations will return back to the level of genuine good neighbourly relations and true friendship" that Lenin and Atatürk had established.[102] Upset with the DP government, Soviet leaders wanted to restore relations with Turkey following the military ouster. Days after Khrushchev's letter, Soviet media started to spread its positive expectations of military leaders. For instance, ten days after the letter was sent to Gürsel, the July 8 issue of the foreign policy weekly *Novoje Vremya* (New Time) published a short piece by Yuri Plotnikov, reminding the Soviet reader that even though Atatürk's successors had neglected and betrayed his principles with dire consequences for state sovereignty, the new government headed by Gürsel "declared its return to the principles and ideals of Atatürk."[103]

A few months after Khrushchev's statement, the memoirs of Semyon Aralov, former Soviet ambassador to Turkey, whose writings were discussed in previous chapters, were published by the Institute of International Relations. In the forward to the book, chief editor D. Yuditskij expressed Soviet expectations of Turkey's new government, confirmed once again that previous governments had distorted "the progressive reforms of Atatürk" and "turned them towards the path of reaction." The "people of Washington" such as Bayar, Menderes, Zorlu, and Polatkan had "betrayed the legacy of Atatürk … causing huge damage to the Turkish nation."[104]

Despite continued mutual distrust, relations between the two countries improved starting only from the mid-1960s, resulting in reciprocal visits by high-ranking officials. The Chairman of the Council of Ministers of the SU, Alexei Kosygin, visited Turkey twice in the 1960s and 1970s. In turn, Ürgüplü, Demirel, and Ecevit visited the Soviet Union during their tenure as prime ministers. The President of Turkey Cevdet Sunay paid an official visit to the SU in 1969.[105] Soviet scholars interpreted the shift in the foreign policy of Turkey a result of intensive policy efforts of Soviet diplomacy. They even argued: "establishing of relations with the USSR was inevitable," because of the increasing international isolation of Turkey.[106] Improvement of Turkish–Soviet relations was marked by agreements and extensive Soviet economic and technical aid. By the end of the 1970s, the Soviet Union assisted Turkey in the implementation of more than forty development projects. As a result,

Turkey became the largest recipient of Soviet economic assistance, receiving more "than any country in the Third World," which included credits of over three billion USD between 1965 and 1979.[107] One explanation for the rapprochement was the emerging contradictions between Turkey and the West over the Cyprus conflict. The expanding Turkish economy and industrialization projects needed strong external assistance, while the decline of US economic assistance in the 1960s and 1970s could have dire consequences. Hence, Soviet assistance was timely and well received in Turkey.

The Soviet leadership, in particular, PM Aleksei Kosygin, nurtured hopes that the leader of the RPP, Bülent Ecevit, after shifting the ideological focus of the party toward the centre-left, would be particularly interested in closer relations with the Soviets. Ecevit also viewed cooperation with the SU in a positive light. Gasimli even argued that in 1977–1978 Turkish–Soviet relations were on "the edge of a qualitatively new phase of collaboration."[108] As a leader of the RPP, Ecevit visited the SU in June 1976, then again in June 1978, when he visited the SU in the capacity of Turkish PM. In the run-up to the Moscow trip, Ecevit told Edward Boghosian, editor of New York's *Armenian Reporter*: "We [i.e. Turkey and the SU] have cooperated in many areas. In fact, Turkey has been lagging behind many of her allies in establishing closer relations with the Soviet Union after the Cold War period ended. We are trying to make up for lost time."[109]

Soviet observers also hoped that "the Soviet nation" could "return to the times of friendship, the foundations of which were laid by Lenin and Atatürk" through the normalization of relations between Turkey and the USSR.[110] The approach of Soviet scholars to Kemalism and its legacy also shifted. During the 1960s, one could observe a slightly modified Soviet approach toward ideological developments in Turkey. For instance, Miller argued that the principles of Atatürk were still useful for the gradual development of Turkish society.[111] The interpretations of other Soviet scholars about the diversification of Kemalist discourse differed slightly. Some even claimed that the existing need for the metamorphosing of Kemalism was more widely demanded than ever before.

New expectations from Turkey's growing leftist movements replaced harsh criticisms of Kemalism that had dominated previous decades. The proliferation of these movements invigorated Soviet observers who began redefining the key principles of Kemalism, often in ways that paralleled Soviet ideological views. The 1961 "Manifesto of 150," or

"*Yön Manifestosu*,"[112] which brought together more than 1000 Turkish intellectuals, teachers, journalists, writers, officers, and students, proved especially encouraging. It was translated and published in the journal *Za Rubezhom* (Abroad).[113] The proposal to introduce the "new étatism" garnered praise from Soviet pundits, who hoped that it would serve as the foundation of a newly emerging social and political order.[114] The manifesto derided the newly formed government for distorting the social order and failing to address deep-rooted social problems.[115] It represented the outright rejection of Kemalist claims of the "classless nature" of Turkish society, according to Gasanova, and challenged the Kemalist principle of populism.[116] All "leftist" movements acknowledged Atatürk's authority, wrote Gasanova, in calling themselves Atatürkists. Leftist movements wanted "an updated Kemalism" and a more developed version of it—Atatürkism—she noted, urging observers to differentiate between the two.[117]

In the 1960s, Soviet Turkologists studied the mixed terminology used to discuss domestic ideological developments in Turkey in the 1920s. In 1968, Gasanova, for example, conceded that Soviet scholarship had failed to agree on a precise definition of Kemalism.[118] When Soviet functionaries invoked "Kemalism" in the 1920s, she added, they referred to the Kemalist revolution's socio-economic content. Terms like "Kemalists," "Kemalist movements," and "Kemalist Turkey" amounted to empirical descriptions of developments in Turkey.[119] Gasanova downplayed the expectations—political and ideological—that Soviet Communist Party leaders had of Turkey.

Revisiting previous approaches, Dmitrij Yeremeyev provided another internal differentiation of Kemalism by presenting two alternative versions of it. He proposed "ideological Kemalism" and "political Kemalism," albeit without further elaboration.[120] These two terms, it can be interpreted, went hand-in-hand with the course of republican history. Political Kemalism had distinct manifestations and a difficult pathway, while ideological Kemalism had been transformed into a guidebook for various political parties, movements, and organizations.

This chapter considered the ways in which, during certain periods of mutual animosity, the SU regarded Kemalism and the Turkish development model as "an extension of fascism," or "the patrimony of the imperialist West." The SU was especially critical of Turkish leadership and the ideological shift it undertook from the mid-1930s to the 1960s. While interpreting domestic ideological transformations in Turkey, Communist

Party functionaries and scholars parroted the official state line. Most condemned Turkish leadership and its alleged distortion of the Kemalist legacy; but after 1960, when the first military intervention took place, and as the leftist movement grew in Turkey that decade, Soviet attitudes shifted, and scholars began to revisit earlier analyses of Kemalism.

NOTES

1. Gökay (2006, 46–47).
2. Ibid., 46.
3. It is worth noting that, in addition to this and other self-descriptions and objectives, the backside of the journal's cover mentioned that it "reflects ideological and tactical lines of the Executive Committee and the entire experience of international Communism" and "pays particular attention to the national-liberation struggle of oppressed people."
4. P. K. 1929. "Imperialisticheskoye pererozhdenie kemalizma." [The Imperialist Rebirth of Kemalism.] *The Communist International*, 53–54.
5. P. K. (1929, 52); Feridov (1929, 60); Kitaygorodskij (1929, 32); R. Sahakyan. 1960. "Iz Istorii Sovettsko-Tureckikh otnoshenii (1928–1929)." [From the History of Soviet-Turkish Relations.] *Digest of the National Academy of Sciences of Armenian SSR, Social Sciences* (2): 18–20.
6. P. K. (1929, 53).
7. P. K. (1929, 54).
8. P. Kitaygorodskij. 1929. *Turtsija* [Turkey]. Moscow: CC MOPR USSR, 8.
9. Dmitrij Yeremeyev. 1963. "Kemalizm i Pantjurkizm." [Kemalism and Pan-Turkism.] *Narody Azii i Afriki* 3: 62–63.
10. Sahakyan (1960, 19).
11. The Programme of the Communist International. Comintern Sixth Congress 1929. https://www.marxists.org/history/international/comintern/6th-congress/ch01.htm (accessed on January 12, 2016).
12. Rouben. 1926. "Noraguyn Turkian yev ir tsevapokhumnery." [Modern Turkey and Its Transformations.] *Hayrenik*, April, 156.
13. Ibid., 166.
14. Shahan Natali. 1992. "Turkismy Angorayen Paku yev trkakan orientasion (qnnadatakan haj qakhaqakan mtki)." [Turkism from Angora to Baku and the Turkish Orientation (Critique of Armenian Political Thought).] In *Turks and Us*, by Shahan Natali, 25–181. Yerevan: Shoushan, 33.
15. "Treaty of Friendship" or "Moscow treaty" signed on March 16, 1921; "Friendship and Neutrality Treaty" signed in 1925; "Protocol on the

Option of Soviet and Turkish Citizens in the Frontier Area" signed in May 1926; "Convention with Turkey for the Regulation of the Use of Frontier waters, and Protocol" signed in January 1927; "Trade and Navigation Agreement with Turkey" signed in March 1927; "Convention with Turkey on the Investigation and Settlement of Frontier Disputes" singed in August 1928; "Convention with Turkey on the Crossing of the Soviet-Turkish Frontier by Inhabitants of the Frontier Zone" signed in August 1928; "Naval agreement" signed on March 8, 1931; and "Treaty on economic cooperation" in 1932.

16. Samuel Hirst. 2013. "Anti-Westernism on the European Periphery: The Meaning of Soviet-Turkish Convergence in the 1930s." *Slavic Review* 72 (1): 37.
17. Lüfti (1927, 71).
18. P. K. (1929, 49).
19. Ibid., (1929, 51, 52).
20. Alimov (1934, 80).
21. Alimov (1934, 82).
22. Boris Potskhveria. 1963. "Mustafa Kemal Ataturk: K 25-letiju so dnja smerti." [Mustafa Kemal Atatürk: To the 25th Anniversary of His Death.] *Azija i Afrika Segodnja* (12): 48.
23. Nikolay Kireev. 1991. *Istorija Etatizma v Turtsii* [History of Etatism in Turkey]. Moscow: Nauka.
24. Boris Platonov. 1931. "Kemalizm segodnya." [Kemalism Today.] *Blizhnij Vostok* (2–3): 31.
25. Ibid., 36.
26. Platonov (1931, 33). When mentioning Iranskij, Platonov most probably was referring to Irandoust, whose works have already been discussed above.
27. Ivanova (2006, Ch. 2).
28. Ibid., 33.
29. In 1928, the Turkish government agreed to the bondholders' representatives of the Council of the Ottoman Public Debt to resume the payment.
30. Ibid., 31–32.
31. Feridov (1928, 39).
32. Platonov (1931, 34–35).
33. Jurij Rozaliev. 1980. *Ekonomicheskaja Istorija Turetskoj Respubliki* [Economic History of Turkish Republic]. Moscow: Nauka, 126–139.
34. Hirst (2013, 38, 43).
35. Rozaliev (1980, 127, 134).
36. Arnold Reisman. 2006. *Turkey's Modernization: Refugees from Nazism and Atatürk's Vision*. Washington: New Academia Publishing, 441

37. Kurbanbayev (1932, 9–19); Chernikov (1977). V Interesakh Mira. 33–59. Mel'nik (1936, 48–49); Potskhveria, (1963, 48).

38. Anatolij Mel'nik. 1936. "Chto predstavyayet soboj sovremennaja Turtsija?" [What Is Contemporary Turkey?] *Sputnik Agitatora* [The Sputnik of the Agitator] 13 (2): 48.

39. *Izvestija*, 1932, April 28.

40. Ibid.

41. Anatolij Mel'nik. 1932. Sovetskij Soyuz i Turtsija, [The Soviet Union and Turkey] *Izvestija*, April 28.

42. Avel' Yenukidze. 1933. "Desat' let Turetskoj Respubliki." [Ten Years of Turkish Republic.] *Mirovoje Khozayestvo i Mirovaya Politika* (10): 86–93.

43. Ibid., 89.

44. Laqueur (1959, 105).

45. Chernikov (1977, 31).

46. Chernikov (1977, 30).

47. The Telegraph of the Plenipotentiary Representative of the USSR in Turkey, Lev Karakhan to the People's Commissary of Foreign Affairs of the USSR, March 14, 1935, 177. *Dokumenty Vneshnej Politiki* [Foreign Policy Documents—USSR MFA]. 1963. Ministerstvo Inostrannyh Del SSSR. Moskva: Gosudarstvennoe izdatel'stvo politicheskoj literatury.

48. Aron Novichev. 1942. *Turtsija: Gosudarstvennyj Stroj. Ekonomika. Eetnografija* [Turkey: Political Structure, Economy and Ethnography]. Tbilisi: Politicheskoe Upravlenie Zakavkazskogo Fronta, 125–126.

49. Aleksei Radionov. 2006. *Turtsija: Perekrestok Sudeb* [Turkey: Crossroad of Destinies]. Moskva: Mezhdunarodnye otnoshenija, 19–24.

50. Aralov (1960, 219).

51. Ibid.

52. Anna Tveritinova. 1953. "Ot Natsional-shovinizma k Natsional-predatel'stvu." [From National-Chauvinism to National Treachery.] *Zvezda Vostoka* 8 (79): 79.

53. Interview with Zafer Toprak. May 10, 2005. Istanbul.

54. Landau (2004, 48).

55. Aytürk (2011, 334).

56. This work was published decades later. Vladimir Gordlevskij. 1962. "Ideologija Novoj Turtsii." [Ideology of New Turkey.] In *Izbrannije Sochinenije* [Selected Works] by Gordlevskij Vladimir, 3rd vol., 492–506. Moscow: Oriental Literature Press.

57. Zarevand. 1930. *Turtsija i Panturanizm (vvedenie A. N. Mandel'shtama)* [Turkey and Pan-Turkism with a Foreword of Mandelstam]. Paris. 147. In the Preface to the 1971 publication of another book, Vahagn Dadrian notes: "Zarevand was the penname of a man and wife team, Zaven

and Vartouhie Nalbandian, who have co-authored the book as well as a number of politico-historical essays and articles dealing with Turks, Armenia, their relations through the ages" (Zarevand. 1971. *United and Independent Turania: Aims and Designs of the Turks*, translated from the Armenian by V. N. Dadrian. Leiden: Brill).

58. Ibid., 154.
59. Stephen Kotkin. 2015. *Stalin: Paradoxes of Power, 1878–1928*, vol. 1. New York: Pinguin Books, 502–503.
60. Arshaluys Arsharouni. 1928. "Krizis Tyurskoj ideologii." [Crisis of Turkic Ideology.] *Novij Vostok* 22: 249–253.
61. Ibid., 253
62. Raffi Kondakchyan. 1974. "Propaganda Pantyurkizma v Turtsii v Gody Vtoroj Mirovoj Voyni." [Propaganda of Pan-Turkism in Turkey during WWII.] *Herald of the Yerevan University: Social Sciences* 1 (22): 199.
63. "Droshak". 1931. July–August.
64. George Bournoutian. 2015. "The Iran-Turkey-Armenia Borders as Depicted in Various Maps." *Iran and the Caucasus* 19 (1): 97–107.
65. Nurreddin Ardıç. 1937. *Antakya-Iskenderun Etrefındakı Türk Davasınün Tarihi Esasları*. İstanbul: Tecelli Matbassi; Tayfur Sökmen. 1978. *Hatayın Kurtuluşu İçin Harcanan Çabalar*. Ankara: Türk Tarih Kurumu Yayınları, Ankara. as cited in Hanioğlu (2011, 166).
66. Kemal Atatürk. 1966. *Izbrannye Rechi i Vystuplenija* [Selected Speeches and Statements]. Moscow: Progress, 394–402.
67. Tveritinova (1953, 83, 85) and Yeremeyev (1963, 67–68).
68. Robert W. Olson. 1986. "The Remains of Talat: A Dialectic Between Republic and Empire." *Die Welt des Islams* XXVI: 46–56. The remains of Enver Paşa, the next mastermind of the Armenian Genocide who was killed in Central Asia, were returned to Turkey and reburried in August 1996. The president of Turkey, Süleyman Demirel, led the military and religious funeral. See Muammar Kaylan. 2005. *The Kemalists: Islamic Revival and the Fate of Secular Turkey*. New York: Prometheus Books, 82.
69. V. Krimskij. 1944. "Panturkisti—fashistskaja agentura." [Pan-Turkists: Fascists Agents in Turkey.] *Bol'shevik* (10–11): 81–82.
70. Ibid., 83.
71. Kolesnikov (1984, 74–75).
72. Kemal Karpat. 1959. *Turkish Politics*. Princeton: Princeton University Press, 266.
73. Krimskij (1944, 79).
74. Ibid., 80.
75. Aytürk (2011, 318, 335).
76. Krimskij (1944, 79).

77. Ibid., 80–81.
78. Krimskij (1944, 81).
79. Ibid.
80. Krimskij (1944, 85).
81. "*Paikar*". 1947. Thursday, July 10.
82. "*Arev*". 1954. September 13 and 17.
83. Bruce Kuniholm. 1996. "Turkey and the West Since World War I I." In *Turkey Between East and West: New Challenges for a Rising Regional Power*, by Vojtech Mastny and Craig Nation, 45. Boulder: Westview Press.
84. Özkan (2012, 165–181).
85. Ankara, Vinogradovu. Priniato po VCh. 07.12.1945 g., RSASPH, Record group 558, Inventory 11, File 99, sheet 117 quoted in Jamil Gasanly. 2008. "The "Turkish Crisis" of the Cold War Period and The South Caucasian Republic." *The Caucasus and Globalization* 2 (4): 126.
86. *SSSR I Turtsija*. 1981. 187–194.
87. Doklad A. A. Zhdanova [Report of Zhdanov]. 1947. *Pravda*, October 25.
88. Tveritinova (1953, 79).
89. Ibid., 79.
90. Ivan Samilovskij. 1952. *Turtsija—Votchina Wall-Strita* [Turkey—Patrimony of the Wall Street]. Moscow: GosPolitIzdat.
91. Ibid., 12.
92. Samilovskij (1952); G. Akopyan. 1951. "Turtsija—votchina amerikanskogo imperializma." [Turkey—A Patrimony of American Imperialism.] *Propanagist i Agitator* 14: 23–31; N. Lavrov, 1952. *Turtsija v 1939–1951 Godah (Lektsii Pprochitannie v Visshoj Partijnoj Shkole pri CK VKP (b))* [Turkey Between 1939 and 1951 (Lectures Given in the High Party School at the CC CPSU)]. Moscow.
93. Lavrov (1952, 6).
94. Ibid., 20.
95. Ibid., 21.
96. Aralov (1960, 220).
97. Anatolij Miller. 1963. "Formirovanije Politicheskikh Vzglyadov Kemal'a Ataturka (K 25-letiju so dnja ego smerti)." [Formation of Political Ideas of Kemal Atatürk (25th Year Since His Death).] *Azija i Afrika Segodnya* (5): 65, 84.
98. Tveritinova (1953, 80–81).
99. Samilovskij (1952, 67).
100. Tveritinova (1953, 81–82).
101. Samilovskij (1952, 68).
102. *Izvestiya*. 1.9.1960.

103. Yurij Plotnikov. 1960. "Printsipi Kemaliza." [Principles of Kemalism.] *Novoje Vremja* (28): 29–30.
104. Aralov. 1960. 11. Foreword by Yuditskij.
105. *SSSR i Turtsija* (1981).
106. *SSSR i Turtsija* (1981, 216–218).
107. Bruce Kuniholm. 1983. "Turkey and Nato: Past, Present and Future." *Orbis: A Journal of World Affairs* 27 (2): 425, 427; Duygu Sezer. 1985. "Peaceful Coexistence: Turkey and the Near East in Soviet Foriegn Policy." *The Annals of the American Academy of Political and Social Sciences* 481: 121.
108. Musa Gasimli. 2008. *SSSR-Turtsija: Ot Normalizatsii otnoshenij do novoj kholodnoj voijni, 1960–1979* [USSR-Turkey: From Normalization of Relations to New Cold War, 1960–1979]. Moscow: Insan, 468.
109. Interview with Prime Minister Bülent Ecevit. 1978. The Armenian Reporter. Transcripts of the highlights of the interview, 12–13.
110. Potskhveria (1963, 49).
111. Miller (1963, 84).
112. "Aydınların ortak bildirisi". Yön. 1961. aralık 20.
113. "Po Kakoi put'i Poidiot Turtsija? Manifest 150 predstavitelej turetskoj inteligentsii." [What Road Will Turkey Take? The Manifesto of 150 Representatives of the Turkish Intelligentsia.] 1962. *Za Rubezhom* 4: 18–19.
114. V. Vasiljev. 1962. "Manifest 150-i." [The Manifesto of 150.] *Za Rubezhom* 4: 18.
115. "Aydınların ortak bildirisi" (1961).
116. Esmeralda Gasanova. 1968. "Ob ideologicheskih osnovah kemalizma i ih sovremennom tolkovanii v Turtsii." [On the Ideological Foundations of Kemalism and Their Contemporary Interpretations in Turkey.] *Narody Azii i Afriki* (3): 33
117. Ibid., 25, 33.
118. Ibid., 25.
119. Ibid., 25. Esmeralda Gasanova (1968, 33).
120. Yeremeyev (1963, 66).

REFERENCES

Alimov, Abid. 1934. "Turtsija [Turkey]." In *Ocherki po Istorii Vostoka v Epokhu Imperializa* [Outlines of the History of the East in the Age of Imperialism], edited by Abid Alimov and Mikhail Godes, 5–92. Moscow-Leningrad: Gosudarstvennoe Social'no-Ekonomicheskoe Izdatel'stvo.

Aralov, Semyon. 1960. *Vospominaniya sovetskogo diplomata 1922–1923* [Memoirs of the Soviet diplomat 1922–1923]. Moscow: Izdatel'stvo Instituta Mezhdunarodnyh Otnoshenii.

Aydınların ortak bildirisi. 1961. *Yön*. aralık 20.

Aytürk, Ilker. 2011. "The Racist Critics of Atatürk and Kemalism: From the 1930s to the 1960s." *Journal of Contemporary History* 46 (2): 308–335.

Chernikov, Igor'. 1977. *V Interesakh Mira i Dobrososedstva: (O Sovetsko-Turetskikh Otnoshenijakh v 1935–1970 gg)* [In the Interest of Peace and Friendly-Neighboring Relations: About Soviet-Turkish Relations 1935–1970]. Kiev: Naukova Dumka.

Feridov, Ziya. 1928. "Nekotorie Voprosi Sovremennoj Turtsii." [Some Questions of Contemporary Turkey.] *Revolutsionnyi Vostok* (6): 24–41.

———. 1929. "Kemalistskaya Turtsija i Fashizm." [The Kemalist Turkey and Fascism.] *Revolutsionnyi Vostok* (7): 56–69.

Gasanova, Esmeralda. 1968. "Ob Ideologicheskih Osnovah Kemalizma i ih Sovremennom Tolkovanii v Turtsii." [On the Ideological Foundations of Kemalism and their Contemporary Interpretations in Turkey.] *Narody Azii i Afriki* (3): 24–35.

Gökay, Bülent. 2006. *Soviet Eastern Policy and Turkey, 1920–1991: Soviet Foreign Policy, Turkey and Communism*. London and New York: Routledge.

Hanioğlu, Şükrü. 2011. *Atatürk: An Intellectual Biography*. Princeton: Princeton University Press.

Hirst, Samuel. 2013. "Anti-Westernism on the European Periphery: The Meaning of Soviet-Turkish Convergence in the 1930s." *Slavic Review* 72 (1): 32–53.

Ivanova, Margarita. 2006. *Introduction to the Regional Studies: From the History of the Soviet Oriental Studies*. Tomsk: Tomsk Pedagogical University.

Kitaygorodskij, P. 1929. *Turtsija* [Turkey]. Moscow: CC MOPR USSR.

Kolesnikov, Aleksandr. 1984. *Narodnye Doma v Obshhestvenno-politicheskoj i kul'turnoj zhizni Tureckoj Respubliki* [People's Houses in the Socio-Political and Cultural Life of the Turkish Republic]. Moscow: Nauka.

K., P. 1929. "Imperialisticheskoye Pererozhdenie Kemalizma." [The Imperialist Rebirth of Kemalism.] *Kommunisticheskij Internatsional*, 46–54.

Krimskij, V. 1944. "Panturkisti—Fashistskaja Agentura." [Pan-Turkists: Fascists Agents in Turkey.] *Bol'shevik* (10–11): 79–85.

Kurbanbayev, S. 1932. "Ot Rezhima Kapituljatsii—K Nezavisimosti. K poseshen-iju Sovetskogo Sojuza Turetskoj Delegatsii." [From the Regime of the Capitulation to Independence: About the Visit of Turkish Delegation to the Soviet Union.] *Revolyutsia i Natsionalnost'* (6): 9–19.

Landau, Jacob. 2004. *Exploring Ottoman and Turkish History*. London: Hurst & Company.

Laqueur, Walter. 1959. *The Soviet Union and the Middle East*. New York: Frederick A. Praeger.

Lavrov, N. 1952. *Turtsija v 1939–1951 Godah (Lektsii Prochitannie v Visshoj Partijnoj Shkole pri CK VKP (b))* [Turkey Between 1939 and 1951 (Lectures given in the High Party School at the CC CPSU)]. Moscow.

Lüfti. 1927. "Turtsija Segodnya." [Turkey Today.] *Za Partiju* ("Pravdi Vostoka") (4): 66–76.

Mel'nik, Anatolij. 1936. "Chto Predstavyayet Soboj Sovremennaja Turtsija." [What is Contemorary Turkey?] *Sputnik Agitatora* 13 (2): 35–50.

Miller, Anatolij. 1963. "Formirovanije Politicheskikh Vzglyadov Kemal'a Atatürka (K 25-letiju so dnja ego smerti)." [Formation of Political Ideas of Kemal Ataturk (25th Year Since His Death).] *Azija i Afrika Segodnya* (5): 65–85.

Özkan, Behlül. 2012. *From the Abode of Islam to the Turkish Vatan: The Making of a National Homeland in Turkey.* New Haven and London: Yale University Press.

Platonov, Boris. 1931. "Kemalizm Segodnya." [Kemalism Today.] *Blizhnij Vostok* (2–3): 30–36.

Potskhveria, Boris. 1963. "Mustafa Kemal Atatürk: K 25-letiju so dnja smerti." [Mustafa Kemal Ataturk: To the 25th Anniversary of His Death.] *Azija i Afrika Segodnja* (12): 31–33, 48–49.

Rozaliev, Yurij. 1980. *Ekonomicheskaja Istorija Turetskoj Respubliki* [Economic History of the Turkish Republic]. Moscow: Nauka.

Sahakyan, Rouben. 1960. "Iz Istorii Sovetsko-Turetskikh otnoshenii (1928–1929)." [From the History of Soviet-Turkish Relations.] *Digest of the National Academy of Sciences of Armenian SSR, Social Sciences* (2): 17–26.

Samilovskij, Ivan. 1952. *Turtsija—Votchina Wall-Strita* [Turkey—Patrimony of the Wall Street]. Moscow: GosPolitIzdat.

SSSR i Turtsija. 1917–1979. [USSR and Turkey. 1917–1979]. 1981. Edited by M. Gastrasyan and P. Moiseyev. Moscow: "Nauka" Press.

Tveritinova, Anna. 1953. "Ot Natsional-Shovinizma k Natsional-Predatel'stvu." [From National-Chauvinism to National Treachery.] *Zvezda Vostoka* 8 (79): 70–87.

Yeremeyev, Dmitrij. 1963. "Kemalizm i Pantjurkizm." [Kemalism and Pan-Turkism.] *Narody Azii i Afriki* 3: 58–70.

CONCLUSION

The evidence presented and analyzed in this study allows us to make a few generalizations and conclusions. Kemalism should be seen as a system of principles, ideas, and visions that sought to conceptualize strategies for development and modernization, initially expounded by Turkey's founding leader, Mustafa Kemal. As this protean "system of principles" developed and was continuously transformed, it served as a source of legitimacy for the ruling elite (which sought to survive and sustain its power while indoctrinating society at large) and those who challenged it. In doing so, Kemalism reflected rival domestic and external influences that included ethnic nationalism (Turkish and Kurdish) and a broad spectrum of political/religious ideologies (from radical nationalism, conservatism, and political Islam to democratic capitalism, secularism, and socialism).

As a result, interpretations of Kemalism were shifting, contradictory, and contested. As discussed, the RPP had to constantly renew itself and its party ideology by seeking new directions. In some cases, radical turns were undertaken, as they were at the 1931, 1935, 1947, and 1966 RPP Congresses. In many instances, members of the ruling political elite and opposition, army, or intellectuals adopted unique and peculiar interpretations of Kemalism, which, in turn, produced constant disagreement among them over interpretations of Kemalism's core meaning.

This work also examined the continuity of intellectual currents and movements from the late Ottoman Empire to the republican era. Some fashionable ideas and ideologies of previous decades were adjusted

© The Editor(s) (if applicable) and The Author(s) 2019   231
V. Ter-Matevosyan, *Turkey, Kemalism and the Soviet Union,*
Modernity, Memory and Identity in South-East Europe,
https://doi.org/10.1007/978-3-319-97403-3

according to the needs and policy priorities of Republican Turkey, while others were excluded or ignored. In general, the early Kemalist era witnessed profound efforts to conceptualize different development strategies. Since the 1920s, the Kemalist elite tried to reach out to society with concise conceptual packaging. This study observed the same tendency both at the beginning of the nationalist movement and during the formative years of the Republic. The power of conceptualized and systemized political ideology (or system of thought), however, was initially downplayed. On the other hand, large-scale social and cultural reforms failed to generate the necessary level of support that the Kemalist regime needed in order to sustain its power. It required a better framework and more practical guidelines. The heavy reliance on party programs and People's Houses were aimed at producing a conceptualized system of thought and at indoctrinating society, further. On the other hand, since its very inception, Kemalism as an official ideology was diversified, with varying interpretations even within the Kemalist elite. Hence, Kemalism was born with many faces, each looking in different directions.

After Atatürk's death, a bureaucratic interpretation of Kemalism followed, which coincided with the outbreak of WWII. The next three decades were a period of survival and adjustment for Kemalism. As indicated, the 1950 elections and major political developments that followed came to be seen as a watershed between the authoritarian-totalitarian past and a contested democratic future. For the Kemalist elite, the 1950s was a decade of retreat and rethinking. In the following decades, the social and ideological landscapes changed beyond recognition. Kemalist ideology, with its radical modernization strategies and top-down development models, faced increasing challenges. It ceased to be the monopoly of the Kemalist era ruling elite and affiliated bureaucratic circles. It was instilled in the popular mind as a flexible and convenient source of legitimacy for political undertakings. The 1960s–1970s were replete with such examples. Only critical ideological repositioning could expand Kemalism's room for action. Until 1980, major developments indicated that contested democracy imposed visible constraints on Kemalist development models. Various interpretations of Kemalism in the last two decades under consideration confirmed that it became increasingly difficult for ardent supporters of Kemalism to promote a system of principles as consistently and vigorously as before. In an atmosphere of intense and even violent ideological polarization in the 1960s–1970s, Kemalism confronted serious challenges. The RPP had to transform and rebrand it by giving it new meaning and appeal to survive and remain relevant in highly competitive Turkish politics. Concurrently, a number of ideological movements on the left and right and various political parties faced a need to elaborate their stance vis-à-vis Kemalism to meet their objectives. On the whole, these decades also saw the evolution of the Kemalist system of thought, although many scholars have argued the opposite. To them, Kemalism became irrelevant, weak, and obsolete.

This study also discussed Soviet insights into the Turkish ideological transformation. Soviet analysts of Turkey produced commentary that shared some distinctive features, even while interpretations of Kemalism in the Soviet Union and the West reflected the ideologies of these Cold War rivals and the state of relations with Turkey. From the outset, Soviet Russia, and then the Soviet Union, hoped that it had won a loyal ally in Kemalist Turkey to fight the West and export Communism to the Muslim world. Disappointed with the outcomes of both of these tasks, the Soviet Union continued to carefully watch Turkey's ideological evolution. Significantly, analysts there began to conceptualize Kemalism earlier than the Kemalist elite did. Soviet literature on Turkey reflected a deep desire to understand the Turkish development model within the framework of Kemalism. As a result of this close examination of Turkey—its power relations, internal debates, and discussions—Soviet observers and society were well versed in Turkey's social, cultural, and political transformations. Employing the Marxist vocabulary of history, capitalism, class struggle, and revolution did not impede Soviet observers from identifying inherent problems in the Kemalist development model. Soviet observers were the first foreigners to note that among many policy deficiencies, the modernizing reforms of Kemalism failed to penetrate rural Turkey and engage with the population there. As a result, Kemalism remained elitist and urban-centred, according to Soviet analysts, creating a gap that impoverished the village by precluding its cultural and social development. Based on this assumption, Soviet observers noticed early on that Kemalism did not enjoy grassroots support, since rural Turkey remained conservative and entrenched in feudal or outdated social structures. They also accurately noted the merger of the party and the State much earlier than the scholarly literature. By the same token, studying Soviet sources helps us understand that in the 1920s, the ruling RPP of Mustafa Kemal was poorly institutionalized and had a weak organizational capacity. Although the observations of Soviet scholars were based on multiple sources and motivations, they could glean

Kemalism's implications for society. At the same time, the Communist regime and Soviet scholars failed to influence the Kemalist regime to the extent they had anticipated.

It is noteworthy that Soviet interpretations of Kemalism were shaped not only by the changing nature of Communist Party policies toward a world socialist revolution, but also by the turbulent nature of Turkish–Soviet relations and global and regional policy dynamics. In other words, geopolitics heavily influenced the nature of Soviet perspectives on Kemalism. In times of crisis, Soviet observers were quick with negative descriptions of Kemalism and its development model. When relations between two countries were normal, Soviet criticism waned and observers tended to be rather supportive. Since the mid-1920s, when Turkey's position vis-à-vis the West was solidified, the Soviet Union started to look at Kemalism with a mixture of suspicion and criticism. From the mid-1930s to the mid-1960s, when Soviet–Turkish relations were at their nadir, the SU was unequivocally critical of Kemalism and the Turkish development model, seeing "an extension of fascism." Reports and articles produced in the SU were also concerned with Pan-Turkic movements in Turkey as well as Soviet Muslim sympathy for Mustafa Kemal. These negative manifestations were more vivid in the 1940s and 1950s when Soviet observers spared no criticism in their discussions of domestic power relations and ideological shifts in Turkey. In the 1960s, after the ouster of the Democrat Party and with the rise of Ecevit and leftist politics in Turkey, the SU noticeably revised its position toward Turkey. This revision affected interpretations of Kemalism, too. Soviet analysts used less ideologically driven and more rigorous methodologies. But this does not imply that the approaches that existed since the 1920s had completely disappeared; on the contrary, certain formulations of earlier decades endured until the 1980s.

How "the West" perceived Turkey has always been a matter of scholarly debate both inside and outside the country. Undoubtedly, "the West" was mostly restricted to Europe and North America. That is why the Soviet historiography of Kemalism was not a matter of interest. Western academics were poorly motivated to study "northern" or Soviet perspectives on Kemalism. Although the SU has attracted more attention for numerous reasons, due to the popularity of leftist views among Turkish intellectuals, the study of Soviet perspectives of Kemalism remains sparse. This work has underscored the importance of incorporating the Soviet perspective into Turkish Studies.

BIBLIOGRAPHY

PRIMARY SOURCES

"10 ans de République: Résumé du guide, publié, par le Parti Républicain du Peuple, à l'occasion du X. anniversaire de la République: 1923–1933." Ankara. 1933.

Ataturk, Kemal. 1966. *Izbrannye rechi i vystuplenija* [Selected speeches and statements], ed. A. Miller. Moscow: Progress.

Atatürk'ün Söylev ve Demeçleri, I–III. 2006. Atatürk Kültür, Dil ve Tarih Yüksek Kurumu, Atatürk Araştırma Merkezi.

Ak Günlere: Cumhuriyet Halk Partisi 1973 Seçim Bildirgesi. 1973. Ankara: Ajans-Türk Matbaacılık Sanayi.

Bulletin of the Turkish Press. The Ministry for Foreign Affairs of the USSR.

Cümhuriyet Halk Fırkası Nizamnamesi. 1927. Ankara.

C.H.F. Nizamnamesi ve Programı. 1931. Ankara, T. B. M. M. Matbaası.

C.H.P. Dördüncü Büyük Kurultayı Görüşmeleri Tutulgasi. 1935. Ankara.

C.H.P. Dördüncü Büyük Kurultayının Görüşmeleri Tutulgasi. 1935. Ankara: Ulus Basımevi.

C.H.P. Programı. 1935. Mayis. Ankara: Ulus Basımevi.

C.H.P. Programı. 1939. Ankara: Ulus Basımevi.

C.H.P. Programı. 1943. Ankara: Zerbamat Basımevi.

C.H.P. Programı. 1976. Ankara: Ajans-Türk Matbaacılık Sanayi.

C.H.P. Genel Sektreteri R. Peker'in Söylevleri. 1935. Ankara: Ulus Basımevi.

C.H.P. Yedinci Büyük Kurultayı. 1947. Ankara, TBMM.

Constitution of the Turkish Republic. Translated for the Committee of National Unity by Sadık Balkan, Ahmet Uysal and Kemal Karpat, Ankara 1961.

© The Editor(s) (if applicable) and The Author(s) 2019
V. Ter-Matevosyan, *Turkey, Kemalism and the Soviet Union*,
Modernity, Memory and Identity in South-East Europe,
https://doi.org/10.1007/978-3-319-97403-3

Documents on International Affairs 1938, v. 1. 1942. Oxford: Oxford University Press.

Doklady Zavedujuschego Informacionnym Otdelom NKID SA o Turetsko-Armjanskikh Otnoshenijah i o Polozhenii v Turtsii Posle Peremirije i t.d., 1921 [Reports prepared by the Head of Information department of the PCFA of Soviet Armenia concerning Turkish-Armenian relations and about the situation in Turkey after the cease-fire, 1921]. National Archives of Armenia, Fond 114, L. 1, c. 225.

Dokumenty Vneshnej Politiki [Foreign Policy Documents—USSR MFA]. 1959, 1960, 1961, 1962, 1963. Ministerstvo Inostrannyh Del SSSR. Moscow: Gosudarstvennoe Izdatel'stvo politicheskoj literatury.

Declaration of the 18th congress of the RPP. Translated by Yunus Emre, see Emre. 2014. 234–236. *Halkevleri Hakkında Genel idare Kurulunun Açıkması*. 1951. Ankara.

Gökman, Muzaffer. 1981–1983. Atatürk ve Devrimleri Tarihi Bibliyografyası (Bibliography of the History of Atatürk and His Reforms), cilt 3. Istanbul: Milli Eğitimi Basımevi.

Howland Shaw's Strictly Confidential Memorandum to the Secretary of State in State Secretary Records, Decimal File 867.000/3006. From: Howland Shaw to Secretary of State. *Strictly Confidential*, September 1, 1934, Cited in Criss.

Kemal, Ghazi Mustafa. 2008. *The Great Speech (Nutuk)*, 2nd ed. Ankara: Atatürk Research Center.

Kemal, Mustafa. 1929a. *Put' Novoj Turtsii* [The Road of the New Turkey]. vol. 1. Moscow: Litizdat, NKID.

———. 1929b. *A Speech*. Leipzig: K. F. Keohler.

National Archives of Armenia. Fond 114. L. 1.

Pis'mo A. Shneersona v Redizdat IKKI 09.05.1929 [Letter of A. Shneerson to Editorial and Publishing Department of the ECCI 09.05.1929], Russian State Archive of Social and Political History (RSASPH), F. 495, L. 78, C. 62.

Soviet Documents on Foreign Policy. 1952. Selected and edited by Jane Degras, vol. II 1925–1932. London: Oxford University Press.

Stalin, Iosif. 1928. *Ob Oppozitsii: Stat'i i Rechi 1921–1927* [About the opposition: Articles and Speeches 1921–1927]. Moscow-Leningrad, GosIzdat.

Turkey. Background Notes. 1988. The United States Department of State Bureau of Public Affairs.

Memoirs

Aralov, Semyon. 1960. *Vospominaniya sovetskogo diplomata 1922–1923* [Memoirs of the Soviet diplomat 1922–1923]. Moscow: Izdatel'stvo Instituta Mezhdunarodnyh Otnoshenii.

Atay, Falih Rıfkı. 1931. *Faşist Roma, Kemalist Tiran ve Kaybolmuş Makidonya*. Istanbul: Istanbul Hakimiyeti Milliye Matbaasi.

———. 1932. *Moskova Roma*. Istanbul: Muallim Ahmet Halit Kitaphanesi.

———. 1938. *Zeytindağı*. Istanbul: Remzi Kitabevi.

Cebesoy, Ali Fuat. 1960. Siyasi Hatıralar, 2 kısım. Istanbul: Doğan Kardeş.

Karabekir, Kâzım. 1960. *Istiklâl Harbimiz*. Istanbul: Türkiye Yayınevi.

Karaosmanoğlu, Yakup Kadri. 1978. *Diplomat Ponevole: Vospominanija i nabljudenija* [A Diplomat Against his Will: Recollections and Observations]. Moscow: Mezhdunarodnye Otnoshenija.

Orbay, Hüseyin Rauf. 1962–1963. Hatıraları, *Yakın Tarihimiz*, cilt 2, 4, İstanbul.

Peker, Recep. 1931. *RPP Programinin Izahi* [Explanation of RPP's program]. Ankara: Ulus Matbaasi.

———. 1935. *Inkilap Dersleri* [Lectures on Revolution]. Ankara: Ulus Basımevi.

Radionov, Aleksey. 2006. *Turtsia: Perekrestok Sudeb* [Turkey: Crossroad of Destinies]. Moscow: Mezhdunarodnye otnoshenija.

Tengirşek, Yusuf Kemal. 1935. *Türk İnkilâbı Dersleri—Ekonomik Değişmeler* [Lectures on Turkish Revolutioin—Economic changes]. Istanbul.

PERIODICALS

"*Azija i Afrika Segodnya*" (Asia and Africa Today)

"Arev" Journal Armenien

"*Blizhnij Vostok*" (Near East)

"*Bol'shevik*" (Bolshevik)

"Droshak" (Flag)

"Forum"

"Hayrenik" (Fatherland)

"Hareket"

"Istanbul"

"Izvestija"

"Milliyet"

"*Narody Aziji I Afriki*" (People of Asia and Africa)

"Novij Vostok" (New Orient)

"*Kommunisticheskij Internatsional*" (Communist International)

"*Krasnaja Nov'*" (Red New)

"*Mezhdunarodnaja zhizn*" (International Life)

"Paikar" (Struggle)

"Propanagist i Agitator" (Propagandist and Agitator)

"*Revolyucija I nasional'nost'*" (Revolution and Nationality)

"*Revolyucionij Vostok*" (Revolutionary East)

"Special'nyj Bjulleten'" (Special bulletin)

"*Sputnik Komunista*" (Companion of the Communist)

"T.C. Resmi gazette"

"Türk Yurdu"
"Ulus"
"Yeni Istanbul"
"*Za Partiju*" (For the party)
"Zvezda" (Star)
"*Zvezda Vostoka*" (Star of the East)

INTERVIEWS

Interview with Emre Nuhoğlu. August 18. 2004. Istanbul.
Interview with Alin Taşçian. May 11. 2005. Istanbul.
Interview with Melih Aşık. May 27. 2005. Istanbul.
Interview with Zafer Toprak. May 10. 2005, Istanbul.
Interview with Cüneyt Akalın. May 16. 2005. Istanbul.
Interview with Etyen Mahçupian. May 18, 2005, Istanbul.
Interview with Sami Cohen. May 12. 2005. Istanbul.
Interviews with members of Turkey's National Unity Committee. 1960. Edited by Cevat Baskut, Yaşar Kemal, Ecvet Guresin. U.S. Joint Publications Research Service.

Adak, Hülya. 2003. "National Myths and Self-Na(rra)tions: Mustafa Kemal's Nutuk and Halide Edib's Memoirs and The Turkish Ordeal." *The South Atlantic Quarterly* 102 (2/3): 509–527.
Adanır, Fikret. 2001. "Kemalist Authoritarianism and Fascist Trends in Turkey During the Inter-War Period." In *Fascism Outside Europe*, edited by Stein Ugelvik Larsen, 313–361. Boulder: Social Science Monographs.
Ağaoğlu, Ahmet. 1927. *Üç Medeniyet*. Ankara: Türk Oçakları Merkez Heyeti Turkish Experiment inMatbaası.
Ahmad, Feroz. 1977. *The Turkish Experiment in Democracy 1950–1975*. London: C. Hurst & Company.
———. 1993. *The Making of Modern Turkey*. London & New York: Routledge.
Akal, Emel. 2012. *Mustafa Kemal, Ittihat Terakki ve Bolşevism Milli Mücadelenin Başlangıcında*. İstanbul: Iletişim Yayıncılık.
Akçalı, Emel, and Mehmet Perinçek. 2009. "Kemalist Eurasianism: An Emerging Geopolitical Discourse in Turkey." *Geopolitics* 14 (3): 550–569.
Akçam, Taner. 2006. *A Shameful Act: The Armenian Genocide and the Question of Turkish Responsibility*. New York: Metropolitan Books.
Akçura, Yusuf. 1976. *Üç Tarz-i Siyaset*. Ankara: Türk Tarihi Kurumu Basimevi.
Akopyan, G. 1951. "Turtsija - Votchina Amerikanskogo Imperializma." [Turkey—A Patrimony of the American Imperialism.] *Propagandist i Agitator* 14: 23–31.
Akşin, Sina. 1999. "The Nature of the Kemalist Revolution." In *The Turkish Republic at Seventy-Five Years*, edited by David Shankland, 14–28. Cambridgeshire: The Eothen Press.

Akural, Sabri. 1984. "Kemalist Views on Social Change." In *Atatürk and the Modernization of Turkey*, edited by Jacob Landau, 125–152. Boulder, CO: Westview Press.

Akyol, Mustafa. 2007. "The Gospel According to Atatürk." *Turkish Daily News*, November 10, Saturday.

Alaranta, Toni. 2008. "Mustafa Kemal Atatürk's Six-Day Speech of 1927: Defining of Official Historical View of the Foundation of Turkish Republic." *Turkish Studies* 9 (1): 115–129.

———. 2011. *Kemalism, Enlightenment, and Legitimacy: The Reproduction of Secularist National Identity in Turkey (1930–1980)*. Saarbrücken: Lambert Academic Publishing.

———. 2014. *Contemporary Kemalism: From Universal Secular-Humanism to Extreme Turkish Nationalism*. Oxon: Routledge.

Alibekov, Ingilab. 1966. *Gosudarstvennyi Kapitalizm v Turtsii* [State Capitalism in Turkey]. Moscow: Nauka Press.

Alimov, Abid. 1934. "Turtsija." [Turkey.] In *Ocherki po Istorii Vostoka v Epokhu Imperializa* [Outlines of the History of the East in the Age of Imperialism], edited by Abid Alimov and Mikhail Godes, 5–92. Moscow-Leningrad: Gosudarstvennoe Social'no-Ekonomicheskoe Izdatel'stvo.

Alkan, Türker. 1980. "Turkey: Rise and Decline of Political Legitimacy in a Revolutionary Regime." *Journal of South Asian and Middle Eastern Studies* (4) 2: 37–48.

Allen, Henry Elisha. 1935. *The Turkish Transformation: A Study in Social and Religious Development*. Chicago: University of Chicago Press.

Alp, Tekin. 1937. *Le Kemalisme*. Paris: F. Alcan.

Althusser, Louis. 1971. "Ideology and Ideological State Apparatuses." In *Lenin and Philosophy and Other Essays*, edited by Louis Althusser. New York: Monthly Review Press.

Araji, Masami. 1992. *Turkish Nationalism in the Young Turk Era*. Leiden: Brill.

Arsharouni, Arshaluys. 1928. "Krizis Tyurskoj Ideologii." [The Crisis of Turkic Ideology.] *Novij Vostok* (22): 249–253.

Ashnin, Fyodor, and Vladimir Alpatov. 1996. "Arkhivnie Dokumenti o Gibeli Akademika A. N. Samojlovicha." [Archival Documents on the Death of the Academic A. N. Samojlovich.] *Vostok* 5: 153–162.

Aslan, Senem. 2007. "'Citizen, Speak Turkish!': A Nation in the Making." *Nationalism and Ethnic Politics* 13 (2): 245–272.

Astakhov, Georgij. 1926. *Ot Sultanata k Demokraticheskoj Turtsii: Ocherki iz Istorii Kemalizma* [From Sultanate Towards Democratic Turkey: Outlines of the History of Kemalism]. Moscow: Gosudarstvennoye Izdatelstvo.

Atay, Falih Rıfkı. 1966. *Atatürkçülük Nedir?* Istanbul: Baha Matbaası.

Avcıoğlu, Doğan. 1963. "Sosyalizme Giden Yollar: Sosyalizmden once Atatürkçülük." *Yön* 69: 8–9.

Aybay, Rona. 1978. *Milli Güvenlik Kavramı ve Milli Güvenlik Kurulu*, vol. 33, 59–82. Ankara: Ankara Universitesi Siyasal Bilgiler Fakültesi.

Aydemir, Şevket Süreyya. 1964. "Atatürk ve Atatürk Ideolojisi." In *Çeşitli Cepheleriyle Atatürk*, edited by Nusret Kurosman, 8–22. İstanbul: İstanbul Matbaası.

———. 1999. *Tek Adam: Mustafa Kemal, cilt 3.* Istanbul: Remzi kitabevi.

Aydin, Ertan. 2004. "Pecularities of Turkish Revolutionary Ideology in the 1930s: The Ülku Version of Kemalism, 1933–1936." *Middle Eastern Studies* 40 (5): 55–82.

Aydınların ortak bildirisi. 1961. *Yön*, aralık 20.

Aykut, Şeref. 1936. *Kemalizm.* İstanbul: Muallim Ahmet Halit Kitap Evi.

Aytürk, Ilker. 2004. "Turkish Linguists Against the West: The Origins of Linguistic Nationalism in Atatürk's Turkey." *Middle Eastern Studies* 40 (6): 1–25.

———. 2011. "The Racist Critics of Atatürk and Kemalism: From the 1930s to the 1960s." *Journal of Contemporary History* 46 (2): 308–335.

Azak, Umut. 2010. *Islam and Secularism in Turkey: Kemalism, Religion and the Nation State.* London: I.B. Tauris.

B., D. 1931. "Turtsija v Krizise." [Turkey in Crisis.] *Bulletin of the Middle East's Press* (12): 7–29.

Bagdonas, Özlem Demirtaş. 2008. "The Clash of Kemalisms? Reflections on the Past and Present Politics of Kemalism in Turkish Political Discourse." *Turkish Studies* 9 (1): 99–114.

Baghdasaryan, Suren. 2001. *Turkiaji Qaghaqakan hamakargy, 1920–1930-akan tt.* [Turkey's Political System, 1920–1930s]. Yerevan: Institute of Oriental Studies, NAARA.

Bahattin, Akşit. 1991. "Islamic Education in Turkey: Medrese Reforms in Late Ottoman Times and Imam-Hatip Schools in the Republic." In *Islam in Modern Turkey*, edited by Richard Tapper, 145–170. London: I.B. Tauris.

Baker, Robert. 1935. "Turkey's Nationalist Creed." *Current History* 42 (4): 409–415.

Baldwin, Elbert Francis. 1922. "The Turco-Bolshevist Menace: Editorial Correspondence from the Lausanne Conference." *The Outlook*, December 20: 698.

Barlas, Dilek. 1998. *Etatism and Diplomacy in Turkey: Economic and Foreign Policy Strategies in an Uncertain World, 1929–1939.* Leiden: Brill.

———. 2004. "Friends or Foes? Diplomatic Relations Between Italy and Turkey, 1922–1936." *International Journal of Middle East Studies* 36 (2): 231–252.

Başar, Ahmet Hamdi. 1962. "Ne Liberalizm, ne Sosyalizm, fakat Kemalizm." [What Liberalism, What Sosialism, Only Kemalism.] *Barış Dünyası*, nisan: 4–8.

Baudner, Joerg. 2014. "The Domestic Effects of Turkey's EU Accession Negotiations: A Missed Opportunity for Europe?" In *Turkey and the European Union: Facing New Challenges and Opportunities*, edited by Firat Cengiz and Lars Hoffmann, 178–194. London and New York: Routledge.

Belge, Murat, ed. 2001. *Kemalizm: Modern Turkiye'de Siyasi Düşünce. cilt 2.* İstanbul: İletişim Yayınları.

Bell, James. 1952. "Turkey: Strategic and Tough." *Readers Digest [Condensed from Time] National Archives of Armenia, F. 412, L. 1, case 1958,* February.

Berkes, Niyazi. 1964. *The Development of Secularism in Turkey.* Montreal: McGill University Press.

Beşikçi, İsmail. 1977. *Türk-tarih Tezi ve Kürt Sorunu* [Turkish History Thesis and the Kurdish Question]. İstanbul: Komal.

Bibliografija Turtsii (1917–1975) [Bibliography of Turkey 1917–1975]. 1982. *Collected by Sverchevskaja A., and Cherman T.* Edited by A. Shamsutdinov. Moscow: Nauka.

Birand, Ali Mehmet. 1991. *Shirts of Steel: An Anatomy of the Turkish Armed Forces.* London: I.B. Tauris.

Bisbee, Eleanor. 1951. *The New Turks: Pioneers of the Republic.* Philadelphia: University of Pennsylvania Press.

Bodurgil, Abraham. 1974. *Atatürk and Turkey: A Bibliography, 1919–1938.* Washington: Library of Congress, Near East Section, Orientalia Division.

Bora, Tanıl, and Taşkın Yüksel. 2009. "Sağ Kemalizm." In *Kemalizm, Modern Türkiye'de Siyasi Düşünce, cilt 2,* edited by Murat Belge, 529–554. Istanbul: İletişim Yayınları.

Borovali, Ali Fuat. 1985. "Kemalist Tradition, Political Change and the Turkish Military." Unpublished dissertation, Queen's University.

Bournoutian, George. 2015. "The Iran-Turkey-Armenia Borders as Depicted in Various Maps." *Iran and the Caucasus* 19 (1): 97–107.

Bozarslan, Hamit. 2006. "Kemalism, Westernization and Anti-Liberalism." In *Turkey Beyond Nationalism,* edited by Hans-Lukas Kieser, 28–34. London: I.B. Tauris.

Bracher, Karl. 1984. *The Age of Ideologies: A History of Political Thought in the Twentieth Century.* London: Weidenfeld.

Burke, Peter. 2005. *History and Social Theory,* 2nd ed. Cambridge: Polity Press.

Butayev, Inal. 1925. *Natsional'naja Revoljutsija na Vostoke: Problema Turtsii* [National Revolution in the Orient: The Problem of Turkey]. Leningrad: Priboj.

Buzan, Barry. 1998. *People, States and Fear: An Agenda for International Security Studies in the Post-Cold War Era,* 2nd ed. Boulder: Lynne Rienner.

Buzan, Barry, Ole Waever, and Jaap de Wilde. 1998. *Security: A New Framework for Analysis.* Boulder: Lynne Rienner.

Çağaptay, Soner. 2002. "Reconfiguring the Turkish Nation in the 1930s." *Nationalism and Ethnic Politics* (8) 2: 67–82.

———. 2003. "Crafting the Turkish Nation: Kemalism and Turkish Nationalism in the 1930s." Unpublished PhD dissertation, Yale University.

———. 2004. "Race, Assimilation and Kemalism: Turkish Nationalism and the Minorities in the 1930s." *Middle Eastern Studies* 40 (3): 86–101.

————. 2006. *Islam, Secularism and Nationalism in Modern Turkey: Who is a Turk?* London: Routledge.

Caliş, Şaban. 1997. "Pan-Turkism and Europeanism: A Note on Turkey's 'Pro-German Neutrality' During the Second World War." *Central Asian Survey* 16 (1): 103–114.

Çambel, Hasan Cemil. 1939. http://www.kultur.gov.tr/TR,25417/tarih.html. Accessed May 12, 2012.

Çamuroglu, Reha. 1998. "Alevi Revival in Turkey." In *Alevi Identity: Cultural, Religious and Social Perspectives*, edited by T. Olson, E. Özdalga, and Catherine Raudvere, 93–99. İstanbul: Swedish Research Institute in Istanbul.

Casier, Marlies, and Joost Jongerden, eds. 2010. "Nationalism and Politics in Turkey: Political Islam, Kemalism and the Kurdish Issues." London: Routledge.

Chernikov, Igor'. 1977. *V Interesakh Mira i Dobrososedstva: (O Sovetsko-Turetskikh Otnoshenijakh v 1935-1970 gg.)* [In the Interest of Peace and Friendly-Neighboring Relations: About Soviet-Turkish Relations 1935–1970]. Kiev: Naukova Dumka.

Childress, Faith J. 2001. *Republican Lessons: Education and the Making of Modern Turkey.* Unpublished PhD dissertation, University of Utah.

Ciddi, Sinan. 2009. *Kemalism in Turkish Politics: The Republican People's Party: Secularism and Nationalism.* London: Routledge.

Cindoglu, Dilek, and Gizem Zencirci. 2008. "The Headscarf in Turkey in the Public and State Spheres." *Middle Eastern Studies* 44 (5): 791–806.

Comintern Sixth Congress, The Programme of the Communist International. 1929. https://www.marxists.org/history/international/comintern/6th-congress/ch01.htm. Accessed January 12, 2016.

Creel, Frank. 1980. "Abdullah Cevdet: A Father of Kemalism." *Journal of Turkish Studies* 4 (9): 9–26.

Criss, Nur Bilgi. 2009. "Shades of Diplomatic Recognition: American Encounters with Turkey (1923–1937)." In *Studies in Atatürk's Turkey: The American Dimension*, edited by George Harris and Nur Bilgi Criss, 97–144. Leiden: Brill.

Cumhuriyet. 1962. December 10.

Dahl, Ottar. 1996. "The Historical Study of Ideologies." In *Societies Made Up of History: Essays in Historiography, Intellectual History, Professionalization, Historical Social Theory and Proto-Industrialization*, edited by Björk Ragnar, Thorsten Nybom, and Rolf Torstendahl, 17–28. Stockholm: Edsbruk: Akademitryck AB.

Danilov, Vladimir. 1997. "Kemalsm and World Peace." In *Atatürk: A Founder of a Modern State*, edited by Ergun Özbudun and Ali Kazancigil, 2nd ed., 103–126. London: Hurst and Company.

David-Fox, Michael. 1997. *Revolution of the Mind: Higher Learning Among the Bolsheviks, 1918–1929.* Ithaca and London: Cornell University Press.

Deringil, Selim. 1989. *Turkish Foreign Policy During the Second World War: An "Active" Neutrality.* Cambridge: Cambridge University Press.

Dodd, Clement. 1979. *Democracy and Development in Turkey.* Beverley: The Eothen Press.

———. 1983. *The Crisis of Turkish Democracy.* Beverley: The Eothen Press.

Doğan, Akyaz. 2001. "Ordu ve Resmi Atatürkçülük." In *Kemalizm: Modern Türkiye'de Siyasi Düşünce, cilt 2*, edited by Murat Belge, 180–191. İstanbul: İletişim Yayınları.

Doklad A. A. Zhdanova [Report of Zhdanov]. 1947. *Pravda*, October 25.

Dost-Niyego, Pınar. 2014. *Le Bon Dictateur: L'image de Mustafa Kemal Atatürk en France (1923–1938).* İstanbul: Libra Yayınevi.

Dumont, Paul. 1984. "The Origins of Kemalist Ideology." In *Atatürk and the Modernization of Turkey*, edited by Jacob Landau, 25–44. Boulder: Westview Press.

Eatwell, Roger. 1992. "Towards a New Model of Generic Fascism." *Journal of Theoretical Politics* 4 (2): 161–194.

———. 2001. "Universal Fascism? Approaches and Definitions." In *Fascism Outside Europe: The European Impulse Against Domestic Conditions in the Diffusion of Global Fascism*, edited by Stein Ugelvik Larsen, 15–45. Boulder: Social Science Monographs.

Ecevit, Bülent. 1968a. *Bu Düzen Değişmelidir.* Ankara: Tekin Yayınevi.

———. 1968b. *Ortanın Solu.* Ankara: Tekin Yayinevi.

———. 1969. *Atatürk ve Devrimcilik.* Ankara: Tekin Yayınevi.

Edib, Halide. 1930. *Turkey Faces West: A Turkish View on Recent Changes and Their Origin.* New Haven: Yale University Press.

Elibal, Gültekin. 1973. *Atatürk ve Resim-heykel.* İstanbul: Türkiye İş bankası Kültür Yayınları.

Ellison, Grace. 1928. *Turkey To-Day.* London: Hutchinson.

Emre, Yunus. 2014. *The Emergence of Social Democracy in Turkey: The Left and the Transformation of the Republican People's Party.* London: I.B. Tauris.

Engin, Saffet. 1938. *Kemalizm Inkılabının Prensipleri, 2 cilt.* İstanbul: Cumhuriyet Matbaasi.

Eren, Nuri. 1963. *Turkey Today and Tomorrow: An Experiment in Westernization.* London: Frederick A. Praeger.

Erkanlı, Orhan. 1972. *Anılar, Sorular, Sorumlular.* İstanbul: Baha Matbassi.

Ersanlı, Büşra. 2002. "History Textbooks as Reflections of the Politicsl Self: Turkey (1930s and 1990s) and Uzbekistan (1990s)." *International Journal of Middle East Studies* 34 (2): 337–349.

Esen, Berk. 2014. "Nation-Building, Party-Strength and Regime Consolidation: Kemalism in Comparative Perspective." *Turkish Studies* 15 (4): 600–620.

Eskicumalı, Ahmet. 1994. *Ideology and Education: Reconstructing the Turkish Curriculum for Social and Cultural Change, 1923–1946*. PhD dissertation, University of Wisconsin-Madison.

Esra, Özyürek. 2005. "Miniaturizing Atatürk: Privatization of State Imagery and Ideology in Turkey." *American Ethnologist* 31 (3): 374–391.

Ferdi, Bekar. 1927a. "Evolutsija Kemalizma: Ot Natsional'noj Revoljutsii k Diktature Burzhuazii." [Evolution of Kemalism: From National Revolution Towards the Bourgeoisie Dictatorship.] *Sputnik Kommunista* 4 (10 (43)): 30–38.

———. 1927b. "Kemalizm na Rel'sah Kapitalisticheskogo Razvitija." [Kemalism on the Capitalist Track of Development.] *Kommunisticheskij Internatsional* (21 (95)): 30–35.

———. 1927c. "Kitajskaya Revolutsia ne Dolzhna Idti po Puti Kemalizma." [The Chinese Revolution Should Not Take the Road of Kemalism.] *Kommunisticheskij Internatsional* (21 (98)): 33–37.

Feridov, Ziya. 1928. "Nekotorie Voprosi Sovremennoj Turtsii." [Some Questions of Contemporary Turkey.] *Revolutsionnyi Vostok* (6): 24–41.

———. 1929. "Kemalistskaya Turtsija i Fashizm." [The Kemalist Turkey and Fascism.] *Revolutsionnyi Vostok* (7): 56–69.

Feroz, Ahmad. 1977. *The Turkish Experiment in Democracy 1950–1975*. London: C. Hurst & Company.

Feroze, Muhammad Rashid. 1976. *Islam and Secularism in Post-Kemalist Turkey*. Islamabad: Islamic Research Institute.

Feyzioğlu, Turhan. 1975. *Millet yonunda*. İstanbul: Dergah Yayınları.

———. 1987. *Atatürk ve milliyetçilik*. Ankara: Atatürk Araştırma Merkezi.

Film Censorship in Turkey, August 1936, National Archives of Armenia, F. 412, L. 1, Case 2025, (Articles on Turkey's Domestic and Foreign Policies), p. 64.

Findley, Carter. 2010. *Turkey, Islam, Nationalism, and Modernity: A History, 1789–2007*. New Haven: Yale University Press.

Fine, Gary Alan, and Kent Sandstrom. 1993. "Ideology in Action: A Pragmatic Approach to a Contested Concept." *Sociological Theory* 11 (1): 21–38.

Fitzpatrick, Sheila. 1999. *Everyday Stalinism: Ordinary Life in Extraordinary Times: Soviet Russia in the 1930s*. Oxford: Oxford University Press.

Frey, Frederick. 1963. "Surveying Peasant Attitudes in Turkey." *Public Opinion Quarterly* 27 (3): 335–355.

———. 1965. *The Turkish Political Elite*. Cambridge: Massachusetts Institute of Technology.

———. 1968. "Socialization of National Identification of Among Turkish Peasants." *The Journal of Politics* 30 (4): 934–965.

———. 1975. "Patterns of Elite Politics in Turkey." In *Political Elites in the Middle East*, edited by George Lenczowski, 41–82. Washington, DC: American Enterprize Institute for Public Policy Research.

Friedrich, Carl, and Zbigniew Brzezinski. 1956. *Totalitarian Dictatorship and Autocracy.* Cambridge: Harvard University Press.

Gasanly, Jamil. 2008. "The 'Turkish Crisis' of the Cold War Period and The South Caucasian Republic." *The Caucasus and Globalization* 2 (4): 114–127.

Gasanova, Esmeralda. 1959. "K Istorii Zhurnala "Türk Yurdu"." [On the History of the Journal "Türk Yurdu".] *Izvestija Akademii Nauk Azerbajdzhanskoj SSR, Serija Obshhestvennyh nauk* (6): 127–135.

———. 1966. *Ideologija Burzhuaznogo Natsionalizma v Turtsii v Period Mladoturok (1908–1914)* [Ideology of Bourgeoisie-Nationalism in Turkey in the Era of Young Turks (1908–1914)]. Baku: Publication of National Academy of Sciences of Azerbaijani SSR.

———. 1968. "Ob Ideologicheskih Osnovah Kemalizma i ih Sovremennom Tolkovanii v Turtsii." [On the Ideological Foundations of Kemalism and Their Contemporary Interpretations in Turkey.] *Narody Azii i Afriki* (3): 24–35.

———. 1974. "Voprosy Ideologii Kemalizma v Trudakh Sovestkih Uchenykh." [Questions of the Ideology of Kemalism in the Works of the Soviet Scholars.] In *Doklady i Soobshhenija Sovetskoj Delegatsii. III Mezhdunar. s"ezd po izuchen-iju stran Jugo-Vostochnoj Evropy, Buharest, 4-10 sentjabrja,* 9 p. Moscow.

Gasimli, Musa. 2008. *SSSR-Turtsija: Ot Normalizatsii Otnoshenij do Novoj Kholodnoj Voijni, 1960-1979* [USSR-Turkey: From Normalization of Relations to New Cold War, 1960–1979]. Moscow: Insan.

Gates, Caleb. June 1931. "The New Turkey Under Mustafa Kemal." *Current History* 34 (3): 390–394.

Gellner, Ernest. 1994. *Encounters with Nationalism.* Cambridge: Blackwell.

Georges-Gaulis, Berthe. 1924. *La Nouvelle Turquie.* Paris: A. Colin.

Geyikdaği, Mehmet Yaşar. 1984. *Political Parties in Turkey: The Role of Islam.* New York: Praeger Publishers.

Gilman, William. 1938. "Turkey with Western Dressing." *Current History* 49 (3): 37–39.

Giritli, İsmet. 1984. "Kemalism as an Ideology of Modernization." In *Atatürk and the Modernization of Turkey,* edited by Jacob Landau. Boulder: Westview Press.

———. 2001. "The Superiority of the Kemalist Ideology Over Dogmatic Ideologies." In *A Handbook of Kemalist Thought,* translated by Ayşegül Amanda Yeşilbursa, 125–136. Ankara: Atatürk Research Center.

Göçek, Fatma Müğe. 1996. *Rise of the Bourgeoisie, Demise of Empire: Ottoman Westernization and Social Change.* Oxford: Oxford University Press.

———. 2011. *The Transformation of Turkey: Redefining State and Society from the Ottoman Empire to the Modern Era.* London: I.B. Tauris.

Godes, Mikhail. 1928. *Chto Takoye Kemalistskij Put' i Vozmozhen li on v Kitae?* [What is a Kemalist Pathway and Is It Possible in China?]. Leningrad: Priboj.

Gökay, Bülent. 2006. *Soviet Eastern Policy and Turkey, 1920–1991: Soviet Foreign Policy, Turkey and Communism.* London and New York: Routledge.

Gökman, Muzaffer. 1981–1983. *Atatürk ve Devrimleri Tarihi Bibliyografyası* [Bibliography of the History of Atatürk and His Reforms], *cilt 3*. İstanbul: Milli Eğitimi Basımevi.

Gökmen, Özgür. 2006. *Turkey*. Vols. Vol 1: A-K, in *World Fascism: A Historical Encyclopedia*, edited by C. Blamires and P. Jackson. ABC Clio.

Göle, Nilüfer. 1996. *Forbidden Modern: Civilization and Veiling*. Ann Arbor: University of Michigan Press.

Goloğlu, Mahmut. 1970. *Üçüncü Meşrutiyet, 1920* [The Third Constitutionalism, 1920]. Ankara: Başnur Matbaası.

———. 1974. *Tek Partili Cumhuriyet (1931–1938)* [The Republic of One Party (1931–1938)]. Ankara: Goloğlu Yayınları.

Gordlevskij, Vladimir. 1962. "Ideologija Novoj Turtsii." [Ideology of New Turkey.] In *Izbrannije Sochinenije* [Selected Works], edited by Vladimir Gordlevskij, vol. 3, 492–506. Moscow: Oriental Literature Press.

———. 1968. "Izuchenije Turtsii v SSSR." [Research on Turkey in the USSR.] In *Izbrannije Sochinenie* [Selected Writings], edited by Vladimir Gordlevskij, vol. 4, 356–359. Moscow: Nauka.

Graham, Loren. 1967. *The Soviet Academy of Sciences and the Communist Party, 1927–1932*. Princeton: Princeton University Press.

Griffin, Roger. 2010. "Uniqueness and Family Resemblances in Generic Fascism." *East Central Europe* 37: 338–344.

Grigoriadis, Ioannis. 2007. "Türk or Türkiyeli? The Reform of Turkey's Minority Legislation and the Rediscovery of Ottomanism." *Middle Eastern Studies* 43 (3): 423–438.

Grigoriadis, Ioannis, and Irmak Özer. 2010. "Mutations of Turkish Nationalism: From Neo-Nationalism to the Ergenekon Affair." *Middle East Policy* 17 (4): 101–113.

Gromyko, Andrej. 1962. "Diplomat Leninskoj Shkoli: K 90-letiju so Dnya rozhdenia G. V. Chicherina." [The Diplomat of the Leninist School: To the Chicherin's 90th Birth Anniversary.] *Izvestija*, December 4, 288.

Guclu, Yucel. 1999. "Fascist Italy's 'Mare Nostrum' Policy and Turkey." *Belleten* LXIII 238: 813–845.

Gündüz, Mustafa. 2009. "Sociocultural Origins of Turkish Educational Reforms and Ideological Origins of Late Ottoman Intellectuals (1908–1930)." *History of Education* 38 (2): 191–216.

Gurko-Kryazhin, Vladimir. 1923. *Istorija Revolucii v Turtsii* [History of Revolution in Turkey]. Moscow: Mir.

———. 1928. "Vozniknovenie Natsional'no-osvoboditel'nogo Dvizhenija v Turtsii." [The Origins of the National-Liberation Movement in Turkey.] *Novyj Vostok* (23–24): 268–275.

Gürpınar, Doğan. 2013. "The Reinvention of Kemalism: Between Elitism, Anti-Elitism and Anti-Intellectualism." *Middle Eastern Studies* 49 (3): 454–476.

———. 2015. "Turkish Radicalism and Its Images of the Ottoman Ancien Régime (1923–38)." *Middle Eastern Studies* 51 (3): 395–415.

Güventürk, Faruk. 1964. *Gerçek Kemalizm.* İstanbul: Okat Yayınevi.

Hagopian, Mark. 1984. *Regimes, Movements and Ideologies.* London: Longman.

Hakkı, Murat Metin. 2006. "Turkey and the EU: Past Challenges and Important Issues Lying Ahead." *Turkish Studies* 7 (3): 451–471.

Hall, Josef Washington. 1930. *Eminent Asians: Six Great Personalities of the New East.* New York and London: D. Appleton and Company.

Hamdullah Suphi Tanrıöver. 1931. *Dağyolu*, 2nd ed. Ankara: Türk Ocakları İlim ve San'at Hey'eti.

Hanioğlu, Şükrü. 1997. "Garbcılar: Their Attitudes Toward Religion and Their Impact on the Official Ideology of The Turkish Republic." *Studia Islamica* 86 (2): 133–158.

———. 2001. *Preparation for a Revolution: The Young Turks, 1902–1908.* Oxford: Oxford University Press.

———. 2006. "Turkism and the Young Turks, 1889–1908." In *Turkey Beyond Nationalism: Towards Post-Nationalist Identities*, edited by Hans-Lukas Kieser, 3–19. London: I.B. Tauris.

———. 2011. *Atatürk: An Intellectual Biography.* Princeton: Princeton University Press.

Harish, Kapur. 1966. *Soviet Russia and Asia 1917–1927: A Study of Soviet Policy Towards Turkey, Iran and Afghanistan.* Geneva: Geneva Graduate Institute of International Studies.

Harper, W. A. 1933. "The Gazi of Turkey." *The Journal of Religion* 13 (1): 1–17.

Harris, George. 1967. *The Origins of Communism in Turkey.* Stanford: Stanford University.

———. 1972. *Troubled Alliance: Turkish-American Problems in Historical Perspective.* Washington, DC: American Enterprise Institute for Public Policy Research.

Harris, George, and Criss Bilgi Nur. 2009. *Studies in Atatürk's Turkey: The American Dimension.* Leiden: Brill.

Heper, Metin. 1979. "Recent Instability in Turkish Politics: End of Monocentrist Polity." *International Journal of Turkish Studies* 1: 102–113.

———. 1985. *The State Tradition in Turkey.* Beverley: Eothen Press.

———. 1988. "State and Society in Turkish Political Experience." In *State, Democracy and the Military.* Berlin: Walter de Gruyter.

———. 1998. *İsmet İnönü: The Making of a Turkish Statesman.* London: Brill.

Hirst, Samuel. 2013. "Anti-Westernism on the European Periphery: The Meaning of Soviet-Turkish Convergence in the 1930s." *Slavic Review* 72 (1): 32–53.

Hopper, Bruce. 1940. "Narkomindel and Comintern: Intruments of World Revolution." *Foreign Affairs* 19 (1): 737–750.

Hotham, David. 1972. *The Turks*. London: John Murray.

Hovhannisyan, Anush. 1989. "Turkiajum «Nor Patmakan Kontseptsiayi» Mshakman Hartsi Shurdj, XX d. 30-akan tt.." [About the Elaboration of the 'New Historical Concepts' in Turkey, 1930s.] *Merstavor yev Mijin Arevelki Yerkrner yev Zhoghovurdner* [States and Nations of the Middle and Near East], 5–13.

Huntington, Samuel. 1968. *Political Order in Changing Societies*. New Haven: Yale University Press.

Huntington, Samuel, and Clement Moore. 1970. *Authoritarian Politics in Modern Society: The Dynamics of Established One-Party Systems*. New York, London: Basic Books, Inc.

Ince, Başak. 2012. *Citizenship and Identity in Turkey: From Atatürk's Republic to the Present Day*. New York: I.B. Tauris.

Ince, Nurhan, and Robert Olson. 1980. "Yön and Its Influence on the Leftist Movement in Turkey and on Foreign and Domestic Policy: 1960–1964." *Turcica: Revue d'Etudes Turques* Tome XII: 174–186.

Interview with Prime Minister Bülent Ecevit. 1978. The Armenian Reporter (Transcripts of the Highlights of the Interview).

Irandoust. 1927. "Sushnost' Kemalizma." [The Essence of Kemalism.] *Za partiju* (2): 62–69.

Irandoust. 1928. *Dvizhuschie Sily Kemalistskoj Revoljutsii* [The Driving Forces of the Kemalist Revolution]. Moscow-Leningrad: Gosizdat.

İrem, Nazım. 2002. "Turkish Conservative Modernism: Birth of a Nationalist Quest for Cultural Renewal." *International Journal of Middle East Studies* 34 (1): 87–112.

———. 2004. "Undercurrents of European Modernity and the Foundations of Modern Turkish Conservatism: Bergsonism in Retrospect." *Middle Eastern Studies* 40 (4): 79–112.

Ivanova, Margarita. 2006. *Introduction to the Regional Studies: From the History of the Soviet Oriental Studies*. Tomsk: Tomsk Pedagogical University.

Jacobson, Jon. 1994. *When the Soviet Union Entered World Politics*. Berkeley: University of California Press.

Jameson, Samuel Haig. May 1936. "Social Mutation in Turkey." *Social Forces* 14 (4): 482–496.

K., P. 1929. "Imperialisticheskoye Pererozhdenie Kemalizma." [The Imperialist Rebirth of Kemalism.] *Kommunisticheskij Internatsional*, 46–54.

Kadıoğlu, Ayşe. 1998. "Republican Epistemology and Islamic Discourse in Turkey in the 1990s." *The Muslim World* 88 (1).

Kallis, Aristotle. 2003. "To Expand or Not to Expand? Territory, Generic Fascism and the Quest for an 'Ideal Fatherland'." *Journal of Contemporary History* 38 (2): 237–260.

Kansu, Şevket. 1934. "Biyososyoloji." *Ülkü*, 253–262.

Karabelias, Gerassimos. 2008. "Dictating the Upper Tide: Civil–Military Relations in the Post-Özal Decade, 1993–2003." *Turkish Studies* (9) 3: 457–473.

Karal, Enver Ziya. 1945. *Türkiye Cumhuriyeti Tarihi* [History of Turkish Republic], 1st ed. İstanbul.

———. 1997. "The Principles of Kemalism." In *Ataturk: Founder of a Modern State*, edited by Ergun Özbudun and Ali Kazancigil, 2nd ed., 11–36. London: Hurst and Company.

———. n.d. *Türkiye'de Siyasal Partiler (1859–1952)* [Turkey's Political Parties (1859–1952)]. Istanbul: Arba yayınları.

Karan, Muzaffer. 1970. "Bağımsız Türkiye mi, Kemalist Türkiye mi?" *Devrim*.

Karasipahi, Sena. 2009. *Muslims in Modern Turkey: Kemalism, Modernism and the Revold of the Islamic Intellectuals*. London: I.B. Tauris.

Kardeş, Doğan. 1963–1965. *Tek Adam, cilt 3*. Istanbul: Remzi kitabevi.

Karpat, Kemal. 1959. *Turkish Politics*. Princeton: Princeton University Press.

———. 1963. "The People's Houses in Turkey: Establishment and Growth." *Middle East Journal* 17 (1).

———. 1973a. "Ideology in Turkey After the Revolution of 1960." In *Social Change and Politics in Turkey: A Structural-Historical Analsysis*, edited by Kemal Karpat, 317–366. Leiden: E. J. Brill.

———. 1973b. *Social Change and Politics in Turkey: A Structural-Historical Analysis*. Leiden: Brill.

———. 1981. "Turkish Democracy at Impasse: Ideology, Party Politics and the Third Military Intervention." *International Journal of Turkish Studies* 2 (1): 1–43.

———. 1982. "Introduction to Political and Social Thought in Turkey." In *Political and Social Thought in the Contemporary Middle East*, edited by Kemal Karpat, 365–377. New York: Praeger.

———. 1985. "'The Personality of Atatürk' (Review of *The Immortal Atatürk: A Psychobiography* by Vamik D. Volkan and Norman Itzkowitz)." *The American Historical Review* 90 (4): 893–899.

———. 1988. "Military Interventions: Army-Civilian Relations in Turkey Before and After 1980." In *State, Democracy and the Military*, edited by Metin Heper and Ahmet Evin, 137–158. Berlin: Walter de Gruyter.

———. 2004. *Studies on Turkish Politics and Society: Selected Articles and Essays*. Leiden and Boston: Brill.

Kautsky, John. 1994. *Marxism and Leninism, Not Marxism-Leninism: An Essay in the Sociology of Knowledge*. London: Greenwood Press.

Kavakçı, Merve. 2010. *Headscarf Politics in Turkey: A Postcolonial Reading*. New York: Palgrave Macmillan.

Kaylan, Muammar. 2005. *The Kemalists: Islamic Revival and the Fate of Secular Turkey*. New York: Prometheus Books.

Kaynar, Erdal. 2015. "Review of Stefan Ihrig's '*Atatürk in the Nazi Imagination*,' The Belknap Press of Harvard University Press, Massachusetts." *International Journal of Turkish Studies* 21 (1–2): 227–229.

Kazancığil, Ali. 2001. "Anti-emperialist Bağimsızlık Ideologisi ve Üçüncü Dünya Ulusçuluğu Olarak Kemalizm." In *Kemalizm: Modern Turkiye'de Siyasi Düşünce. cilt 2*, edited by Murat Belge, 235–246. İstanbul: İletişim Yayınları.

Kazimirskij, K. 1927. "Sovremennaja Evropejskaja Turtsija." [Contemporary European Turkey.] *Novyj Vostok* (16–17): 178–189.

Kennan, George. 1960. *Soviet Foreign Policy, 1917–1941*. New York: D. Van Nostrand.

Kevorkian, Raymond. 2011. *The Armenian Genocide: A Complete History*. London: I.B. Tauris.

Khalid, Detlev. 1975. *The Kemalist Attitude Towards Muslim Unity: Islam and the Modern Age*. New Delhi.

Kieser, Hans-Lukas. 2006. "An Ethno-Nationalist Revolutionary and Theorist of Kemalism: Dr. Mahmut Esat Bozkurt (1892–1943)." In *Turkey Beyond Nationalism*, edited by Hans-Lukas Kieser. London: I.B. Tauris.

———. 2008. *Türklüğe İhtida: 1830–1939 İsviçre'sinde Yeni Türkiye'nin Öncüleri*. İstanbul: İletişim.

———. 2011a. "From "Patiotism" to Mass Murder: Dr. Mehmed Reşid (1873–1919)." In *A Question of Genocide: Armenians and Turks at the End of the Ottoman Empire*, edited by Ronald Suny, Fatma Müge Göçek and Norman Naimark, 126–150. Oxford: Oxford University Press.

———. 2011b. "World War and World Revolution: Alexander Helphand-Parvus in Germany and Turkey." *Kritika: Explorations in Russia and Eurasian History* 12 (2): 387–410.

Kili, Suna. 1969. *Kemalism*. İstanbul: School of Business Administration and Economics, Robert College.

———. 1971. *Turkish Constitutional Developments and Assembly Debates on the Constitutions of 1924 and 1961*. Istanbul: Robert College Research Centre.

———. 1980. "Kemalism in Contemporary Turkey." *International Political Science Review* 1 (3): 380–404.

———. 2003. *The Atatürk Revolution: A Paradigm of Modernization*. İstanbul: Türk Iş Bankası, Kültür Yayınları.

Kinross, Lord. 1964. *Atatürk: The Rebirth of a Nation*. London: Weidenfeld and Nicolson.

Kireev, Nikolay. 1991. *Istorija Etatizma v Turtsii* [History of Etatism in Turkey]. Moscow: Nauka.

Kitaygorodskij, P. 1927. "Zametki o Kemalistskoj Turtsii: Prichini Pobedi Natsional'noj Revoljutsii v Turtsii." [Notes on the Kemalist Turkey: The Causes of the Victory of the National Revolution in Turkey.] *Bol'shevik* (18): 41–50.

Kitaygorodskij, P. 1929. *Turtsija* [Turkey]. Moscow: CC MOPR USSR.

Kızılay, Naşit. 1955. *Atatürk (Felsefe gözüyle)*. Ankara.

Koçak, Cemil. 2004. "Some Views on the Turkish Single-Party Regime During the Inönü Period (1938–1945)." In *Men of Order: Authoritarian*

Modernization Under Atatürk and Reza Shah, edited by Touraj Atabaki and Erik-Jan Zürcher, 113–129. London and New York: I.B. Tauris.

Kohn, Hans. 1933. "10 Years of Turkish Republic." *Foreign Affairs* 12 (1): 141–155.

———. 1943. *Revolutions and Dictatorship,* 3rd ed. Cambridge: Harvard University Printing Office.

Köker, Levent. 2001. "Kemalism/Atatürkçülük: Modernleşme, Devlet ve Demokrasi." In *Kemalizm: Modern Turkiye'de Siyasi Düşünce,* edited by Murat Belge, 97–112. İstanbul: İletişim Yayınları.

Kolesnikov, Aleksandr. 1984. *Narodnye Doma v Obshhestvenno-politicheskoj i kul'turnoj zhizni Tureckoj Respubliki* [People's Houses in the Socio-Political and Cultural Life of the Turkish Republic]. Moscow: Nauka.

Kondakchyan, Raffi. 1974. "Propaganda Pantyurkizma v Turtsii v Gody Vtoroj Mirovoj Voyni." [Propaganda of Pan-Turkism in Turkey During WWII.] *Herald of the Yerevan University: Social Sciences* 1 (22): 198–205.

Korkhmazyan, Rita. 1977. *Turetsko-Germanskije Otnoshenije v Gody Vtoroj Mirovoj Voiny* [Turkish-German Relations During the Second World War]. Yerevan: NAS Armenia SSR Press.

Kotkin, Stephen. 2015. *Stalin: Paradoxes of Power, 1878–1928,* vol. 1. New York: Pinguin Books.

Köymen, Nusret. 1936. "Kemalizm ve Politika Bilgisi." *Ülkü.*

Krimskij, V. 1944. "Panturkisti – Fashistskaja Agentura." [Pan-Turkists: Fascists Agents in Turkey.] *Bol'shevik* (10–11): 79–85.

Kross, T. 1930. "Vnutrennee Polozhenie Turtsii." [The Domestic Situation in Turkey.] *Mezhdunarodnaja Zhizn'* (NKID) (7–8): 57–66.

Kubicek, Paul. 2005. "Turkey's Accession to the European Union." *World Affairs* 168 (2): 67–78.

Kuniholm, Bruce. 1983. "Turkey and NATO: Past, Present and Future." *Orbis: A Journal of World Affairs* 27 (2): 421–445.

———. 1996. "Turkey and the West Since World War II." In *Turkey Between East and West: New Challenges for a Rising Regional Power,* edited by Vojtech Mastny and Craig Nation, 45–69. Boulder: Westview Press.

Kurbanbayev, S. 1932. "Ot Rezhima Kapituljatsii—K Nezavisimosti. K posesheniju Sovetskogo Sojuza Turetskoj Delegatsii." [From the Regime of the Capitulation to Independence: About the Visit of Turkish Delegation to the Soviet Union.] *Revolyutsia i Natsionalnost'* (6): 9–19.

Kuru, Ahmet. 2007. "Passive and Assertive Secularism: Historical Conditions, Ideological Struggles, and State Politicies toward Religion." *World Politics* 59 (4): 568–594.

Kuznetsova, S. 1961. *Ustanovlenie Sovetsko-Turetskikh Otnoshenii: K 40-letiju Moskovskogo Dogovora Mezhdu RSFSR i Turtsiej* [Establishment of Soviet-Turkish Relations: To the 40th Anniversary of the Moscow Treaty Between the RSFSR and Turkey]. Moscow: Izdatel'stvo Vostochnoj Literatury.

Landau, Jacob. 1974. *Radical Politics in Turkey*, vol. 14. Leiden: Brill.
———. 2004. *Exploring Ottoman and Turkish History*. London: Hurst & Company.
———. 2018. "A Note on Kemalizm in the Hebrew Press of Palestine." *Middle Eastern Studies* 54 (4): 723–728.
Landau, Rum. 1938. *Search for Tomorrow: The Things Which Are and the Things Which Shall Be Hereafter*. London: Nicolson and Watson Limited.
Laqueur, Walter. 1959. *The Soviet Union and the Middle East*. New York: Frederick A. Praeger.
Larsen, Stein Ugelvik. 2001. "Was There Fascism Outside Europe? Diffusion from Europe and Domestic Impulses?" In *Fascism Outside Europe: The European Impulse Against Domestic Conditions in the Diffusion of Global Fascism*, edited by Stein Ugelvik Larsen. Boulder: Social Sciene Monographs.
Lavrov, N. 1952. *Turtsija v 1939-1951 Godah (Lektsii Prochitannie v Visshoj Partijnoj Shkole pri CK VKP (b))* [Turkey Between 1939 and 1951 (Lectures Given in the High Party School at the CC CPSU)]. Moscow.
Lee, Stephen. 2005. *European Dictatorships, 1918–1945*, 2nd. ed. London: Routledge.
Lewis, Bernard. 1952. "Islamic Revival in Turkey." *International Affairs* 28 (1): 38–48.
———. 1968. *The Emergence of Modern Turkey*. London: Oxford University Press.
———. 2002. *The Emergence of Modern Turkey*, 3rd ed. New York and Oxford: Oxford University Press.
Lewis, Geoffrey. 1977. "Political Change in Turkey Since 1960." In *Aspects of Modern Turkey*, edited by William Hale, 9–20. London: Bowker in Association with the Centre for Middle Eastern and Islamic Studies of the University of Durham.
Linke, Lilo. 1937. *Allah Dethroned: A Journey Through Modern Turkey*. London: Constable & Co. Ltd.
Ludwig, Emil. 1930. "Kemal: a Vivid Portrait of a Dictator." *New York Times*, March 9.
Lüfti. 1927. "Turtsija Segodnya." [Turkey Today.] *Za Partiju* ("Pravdi Vostoka") (4): 66–76.
Luke, Sir Harry. 1936. *The Making of Modern Turkey: From Byzantium to Angora*. London: Macmillan.
Macfie, Alec. 1994. *Atatürk*. London and New York: Longman.
Mango, Andrew. 1976. "Turkey: Emergence of a Modern Problem." In *Aspects of Modern Turkey*, edited by William Hale, 9–14. London: Bowker in Association with the Centre for Middle Eastern and Islamic Studies of the University of Durham.
———. 1999. *Atatürk*. New York: The Overlook Press.

————. 2002. "Kemalism in a New Century." In *Turkish Transformation: New Century, New Challenges*, edited by Beeley Brian, 22–36. Tallahassee: The Eothen Press.

Mann, Michael. 2004. *Fascists.* Cambridge: Cambridge University Press.

Mantran, Robert. 2005. "Mustafa Kemal Atatürk." In *Turkey Today—A European Country?*, edited by Olivier Roy, 119–130. London: Anthem Press.

Mardin, Şerif. 1973. "Centre-Periphery Relations: A Key to Turkish Politics?" *Daedalus: Journal of the American Academy of Arts and Sciences* 102 (1): 169–190.

————. 1978. "Youth and Violence in Turkey." *European Journal of Sociology* 19 (2): 229–254.

————. 2006. *Religion, Society, and Modernity in Turkey.* Syracuse: Syracuse University Press.

Marmorstein, Emile. 1952. "Religious Opposition to Nationalism in the Middle East." *International Affairs* 28 (3): 344–359.

Marwick, Arthur. 2001. *The New Nature of History: Knowledge, Evidence, Language.* Basingstoke: Palgrave Macmillan.

Mateescu, Dragos. 2006. "Kemalism in the Era of Totalitarianism: A Conceptual Analysis." *Turkish Studies* 7 (2): 225–241.

McCullagh, Behan. 2004. *The Logic of History: Putting Postmodernism in Perspective.* London: Routledge.

McFadden, John. 1985. "Civil-Military Relations in the Third Turkish Republic." *The Middle East Journal* 39 (1): 69–85.

McMeekin, Sean. 2014. *The Ottoman Endgame: War, Revolution, and the Making of the Modern Middle East, 1908–1923.* New York: Penguin Press.

Mediha, Muzaffer. 1933. *Inkilabın Ruhu.* İstanbul: Devlet Matbaası.

Mel'nik, Anatolij. 1928. "Pjat' Let Respublikanskoj Turtsii." [Five Years of Republican Turkey.] *Mezhdunarodnaja zhizn'* (11): 3–11.

————. 1932. "Sovetskij Soyuz i Turtsija." [The Soviet Union and Turkey.] *Izvestija*, April 28: 1.

Mel'nik, Anatolij. 1936. "Chto Predstavyayet Soboj Sovremennaja Turtsija." [What Is Contemorary Turkey?] *Sputnik Agitatora* 13 (2): 35–50.

————. 1937. *Turtsija* [Turkey]. Moscow: Gosudarstvennoe Social'no-jekonomicheskoe Izdatel'stvo.

Menderes, Cınar. 2006. "Turkey's Transformation Under the AKP Rule." *The Muslim World* 96 (3): 469–486.

Merriam, Charles. 1934. *Political Power, Its Composition and Incidence.* New York: Whittlesey House.

Miller, Anatolij. 1948. *Kratkaja Istorija Turtsii* [Short History of Turkey]. Moscow: Gosudarstvennoe izdatel'stvo politicheskoj literatury.

————. 1963. "Formirovanije Politicheskikh Vzglyadov Kemal'a Atatürka (K 25-letiju so dnja ego smerti)." [Formation of Political Ideas of Kemal Ataturk (25th year since his death).] *Azija i Afrika Segodnya* (5): 65–85.

———. 2003. "Zapiska v upravlenie propagandy i agitacii CK BVP(b) "O nedostatkah vostokovednoj raboty i o merah po ee uluchsheniju"." [A Note to the Department of Propaganda and Agitation of the CCCPSU "About the Lack of Research on Oriental Studies and Measures of Im".] In *Ot Stambula do Moskvi: Sbornik statei v chest' 100-letija profesora A. F. Millera* [From Istanbul to Moscow: Collection of Articles Dedicated to the 100th Anniversary of A. F. Miller], edited by Mikhail Meier and S. F. Oreshkova, 337–343. Moscow: Muravej.

Miller, William. 1913. *The Ottoman Empire 1801–1913.* Cambridge: University Press.

Moiseyev, Pyotr and Rozaliyev Yurij. 1958. *K Istorii Sovetsko-turetskih Otnoshenii* [The History of the Soviet-Turkish Relations]. Moscow: Gospolizdat.

Naimark, Norman. 2011. "Preface." In *A Question of Genocide: Armenians and Turks at the End of the Ottoman Empire,* edited by Ronald Grigor Suny, Fatma Müğe Göçek, and Norman Naimark, xiii–xix. Oxford: Oxford University Press.

Narli, Nilüfer. 2000. "Civil-Military Relations in Turkey." *Turkish Studies* 1 (1): 107–127.

Natali, Shahan. 1992. "Turkismy Angorayen Baku yev trkakan orientasion (qnna-datakan haj qakhaqakan mtki)." [Turkism from Angora to Baku and the Turkish Orientation (Critique of Armenian Political Thought).] In *Turks and us,* edited by Shahan Natali, 25–181. Yerevan: Shoushan.

National Archives of Archive, Record group 412, L. 1, Case file 2025, p. 38. 1931. "The Triumvirate in Turkey: Soldiers All." September: An Excerpt from an Unspecified British Newspaper, Arshak Safrastian Unit (Articles on Turkey's Domestic and Foreign Policies).

Nedim, Vedat. 1933. "Develetin Yapıcılık ve İdarecilik Kudretine İnanmak Gerekir." *Kadri* 2/15: 13–19.

Nolte, Ernst. 1965. *Three Faces of Fascism.* London: Weidenfeld and Nicolson.

Novichev, Aron. 1942. *Turtsija: Gosudarstvennyj Stroj. Ekonomika. Ehtnografija* [Turkey: Political Structure, Economy and Ethnography]. Tbilisi: Politicheskoe Upravlenie Zakavkazskogo Fronta.

Nyrop, Richard F. 1973. *Area Handbook for the Republic of Turkey.* Washington: U.S. Govt. Print. Office.

O'Connor, Timothy. 1988. *Diplomacy and Revolution: G. V. Chicherin and Soviet Foreign Policy Affairs, 1918–1930.* Ames: Iowa State University Press.

Olson, W. Robert. 1986. "The Remains of Talat: A Dialectic Between Republic and Empire." *Die Welt des Islams* XXVI: 46–56.

Oran, Baskın. 1981. "Altı Ok arasındaki ilişkiler ya da Milliyetçilik ekseni Çevresinda Kemalizm." [The Relations Among the Six Arrows or Kemalism Around the Axis of Nationalism.] *International Atatürk Conference,* 1–8. İstanbul: Boğaziçi Üniversitesi.

Orga, Irfan. 1958. *Phoenix Ascendant: The Rise of Modern Turkey.* London: Hale.

Örs, Rasim Dirsehan. 2010. *Rus Basınında Kurtuluş Savaşı ve Atatürk. Devrim Yılları.* İstanbul: Cumhuriyet Kitapları.

Overy, Richard. 2004. *The Dictators: Hitler's Germany and Stalin's Russia.* Allen Lake: Penguin Books.

Ozankaya, Özer. 1971. *Köyde Toplumsal yapi ve siyasal kultur; iki grup köyde yapılan karşılaştırmalı bir araştırma.* Ankara: Sevinç Matbaası.

Ozavci, Hilmi Ozan. 2015. *Intellectual Origins of the Republic: Ahmet Ağaoğlu and the Genealogy of Liberalism in Turkey.* Leiden: Brill.

Özbudun, Ergun, and Ömer Faruk Gençkaya. 2009. *Democratization and the Politics of Constitution-Making in Turkey.* Budapest: Central European University Press.

Özdalga, Elisabeth. 1978. *I Atatürks spår: Det Republikanska FolkPartiet och utvecklingsmobilisering I Turkiet från etatism till populism.* Lund: Dialog.

———. 1998. *The Veiling Issue. Official Secularism and Popular Islam in Modern Turkey.* Richmond: Curzon Press.

Özel, Sevgi, ed. 1988. *Baba Inönü'den Erdal Inönü'ye Mektuplar* [Letters from Father Inönü to Erdal Inönü]. Ankara: Bilgi Yayınevi.

Ozherel'eva, Z. (compiler). 1979. *Kemalizm (Ukazatel' Inostrannih knig 1930–1976 gg. (Po fondam bibliotek Moskvi, Leningrada i Baku))* [Kemalism (Index of Foreign Books 1930–1976 (Based on the Fonds of Libraries of Moscow, Leningrad and Baku)]. Moscow: Institute of Scientific Information for Social Sciences, National Academy of Sciences.

Özkan, Behlül. 2012. *From the Abode of Islam to the Turkish Vatan: The Making of a National Homeland in Turkey.* New Haven and London: Yale University Press.

Özkan, Hande. 2000. "Falih Rıfkı Atay." In *Kemalizm: Modern Türkiye'de Siyasi Düşünce,* edited by Murat Belge, 64–74. İstanbul: İletişim Yayınları.

Öztürk, Halil Nimetullah. 1930. *Halkçılık ve Cumhuriyet ve Türk Halkçılığı ve Cumhuriyeti.* Istanbul: Orhaniye Matbaası.

Paillarès, Michel. 1922. *Le Kemalisme: Devant Les Alliès.* Constantinople, Paris: Bosphore.

Parker, John, and Charles Smith. 1940. *Modern Turkey.* London: George Routledge and Sons.

Parla, Taha. 1985. *The Social and Political Thought of Ziya Gökalp, 1876–1924.* Leiden: Brill.

Parla, Taha, and Andrew Davison. 2004. *Corporatist Ideology in Kemalist Turkey: Progress or Order?* Syracuse: Syracuse University Press.

Pauley, Bruce. 2015. *Hitler, Stalin, and Mussolini: Totalitarianism in the Twentieth Century,* 4th ed. Malden: Wiley Blackwell.

Pavlovich, Mikhail. 1921. "Kemalistskoje Dvizhenie v Turtsii." [The Kemalist Movement in Turkey.] *Krasnaja Nov'* (1): 218–228.

———. 1921 [Republished in 1925]. *Revoljutsionnaja Turtsija* [Revolutionary Turkey]. Moscow.

Payne, Stanley. 1995. *A History of Fascism, 1941–1945*. Madison: University of Wisconsin Press.

———. 1980. *Fascism: Definition and Comparison*. Madison: University of Wisconsin Press.

Platonov, Boris. 1931. "Kemalizm Segodnya." [Kemalism Today.] *Blizhnij Vostok* (2–3): 30–36.

Plotnikov, Yurij. 1960. "Printsipi Kemalizma." [Principles of Kemalism.] *Novoje Vremja* (28): 29–30.

Po kakoi put'i poidiot Turtsija? Manifest 150 predstavitelej turetskoj inteligentsii [What Road Will Turkey Take? The Manifesto of 150 Representatives of the Turkish Intelligentsia]. 1962. *Za Rubezhom* (4): 18–19.

Potskhveria, Boris. 1963. "Mustafa Kemal Atatürk: K 25-letiju so dnja smerti." [Mustafa Kemal Ataturk: To the 25th Anniversary of His Death.] *Azija i Afrika Segodnja* (12): 31–33, 48–49.

———. 2003. "Chornije dni A. F. Millera." [Black Days of A. F. Miller.] In *Ot Stambula do Moskvi: Sbornik statei v Chest' 100-letija profesora A. F. Millera* [From Istanbul to Moscow: Collection of Articles Dedicated to the 100th Anniversary of Professor A. F. Miller], 23–30. Moscow: Muravej.

Poulton, Hugh. 1997. *Top Hat, Grey Wolf and Crescent: Turkish Nationalism and the Turkish Republic*. New York: New York University Press.

Priestland, David. 2007. *Stalinism and the Politics of Mobilization: Ideas, Power, the Terror in Inter-War Russia*. Oxford: Oxford University Press.

Qureshi, Naeem. 2014. *Ottoman Turkey, Atatürk, and Muslim South Asia: Perspectives, Perceptions, and Responses*. Karachi: Oxford University Press.

Radionov, Aleksej. 2006. *Turtsija: Perekrestok Sudeb* [Turkey: Crossroad of Destinies]. Moskva: Mezhdunarodnye otnoshenija.

Rae, Heather. 2002. *State Identities and the Homogenisation of Peoples*. Cambridge: Cambridge University Press.

Reed, Howard. 1954. "Revival of Islam in Secular Turkey." *The Middle East Journal* 8 (3): 267–282.

———. 2009. "Turkey and Her Nationalist Leaders as Seen in the 1923 Reports of Louise Bryant." In *Studies in Ataturk's Turkey: The American Dimension*, edited by George Harris and Nur Bilge Criss, 83–96. Leiden: Brill.

Reginbogin, Herbert R. 2009. *Faces of Neutrality: A Comparative Analysis of the Neutrality of Switzerland and Other Neutral Nations During WWII*. Berlin: Lit Verlag.

Reisman, Arnold. 2006. *Turkey's Modernization: Refugees from Nazism and Atatürk's Vision*. Washington: New Academia Publishing.

Rejai, Mostafa. 1991. *Political Ideologies: A Comparative Approach*. London: M. E. Sharpe.

Rıfat, Bali. 2008a. *1934 Trakya Olayları*. Istanbul: Kitabevi.

———. 2008b. "The 1934 Thrace Events. Continuity and Change Within Turkish State Policies Regarding Non-Muslim Minorities. Interview with Rıfat Bali." *European Journal of Turkish Studies (Online), Thematic Issue* 7 (7).

Rıfat, Bali, ed. 2012. *Wealth Tax. The (Varlik Vergisi) Affair: Documents from the British National Archives*. Istanbul: Libra Kitapçılık ve Yayıncılık.

Rouben. 1926. "Noraguyn Turkian yev ir Tsevapokhumnery." [Modern Turkey and Its Transformations.] *Hayrenik*, April: 153–167.

Roucek, Joseph. 1947. *Governments and Politics Abroad*. New York: Funk & Wagnalls Company.

Rozaliev, Yurij. 1980. *Ekonomicheskaja Istorija Turetskoj Respubliki* [Economic History of the Turkish Republic]. Moscow: Nauka.

Rustow, Dankwart. 1966. "Development of Political Parties in Turkey." In *Political Parties and Political Development*, edited by Joseph. La Palombara and Myron Weiner, 107–133. Princeton: Princeton University Press.

Safa, Peyami. 1938. *Türk İnkılabına Bakışlar* [Reflections on the Turkish Revolution]. İstanbul: Kanaat Kitabevi.

Sahakyan, Rouben. 1960. "Iz Istorii Sovetsko-Turetskikh otnoshenii (1928-1929)." [From the History of Soviet-Turkish Relations.] *Digest of the National Academy of Sciences of Armenian SSR, Social Sciences* (2): 17–26.

Saikal, Amin. 1982. "Kemalism: Its Influences on Iran and Afghanistan." *International Journal of Turkish Studies* 2 (2): 25–32.

Salamone, Stephen. 1989a. "The Dialectics of Turkish National Identity: Ethnic Boundary Maitenance and State Ideology." *East European Quarterly* 23 (1 (Spring)): 33–61.

———. 1989b. "The Dialectics of Turkish National Identity: Ethnic Boundary Maintenance and State Ideology (Part Two)." *East European Quarterly* 23 (2 (July)): 225–248.

Samilovskij, Ivan. 1952. *Turtsija – Votchina Wall-Strita* [Turkey—Patrimony of the *Wall Street*]. Moscow: GosPolitIzdat.

Samojlovich, Alexander. 1936. "Stambul'skie Vpechetlenija." [Impressions from Istanbul.] *Zvezda* 12: 161–168.

Santoro, Lorenzo. 2007. "Ideology and Political Religion: Towards a Conceptualization of Generic Fascism." *The European Legacy* 12 (6): 749–752.

Sayari, Sabri. 1990. "Bülent Ecevit." In *Political Leaders of the Contemporary Middle East and Africa*, edited by Bernard Reich, 159–166. Westport, CT: Greenwood.

———. 2010. "Political Violence and Terrorism in Turkey, 1976–80: A Retrospective Analysis" *Terrorism and Political Violence* 22 (2): 198–215.

Selçuk, Ilhan. 1966. "Atatürkçü Antiimperyalist Cephe Kurulamadıkça." *Yön*, November 11.

Sezer, Duygu. 1985. "Peaceful Coexistence: Turkey and the Near East in Soviet Foreign Policy." *The Annals of the American Academy of Political and Social Sciences* 481: 117–126.

Shaw, Stanford, and Shaw Kural Ezel. 1977. *History of the Ottoman Empire and Modern Turkey, Vol. II: Reform, Revolution, and Republic: The Rise of Modern Turkey, 1808–1975.* Cambridge: Cambridge University Press.

Shissler, Holly. 2002. *Between Two Empires: Ahmet Ağaoğlu and the New Turkey.* London: I.B. Tauris.

Shneerson, A. 1929. "Novaja Popitka Analiza Kemalizma." [A New Attempt to Analyse Kemalism.] *Bol'shevik* 1: 86–90.

Şimşek, Sefa. 2005. "'People's Houses' as a Nationwide Project for Ideological Mobilization in Early Republican Turkey." *Turkish Studies* 6 (1): 71–91.

Smith, Anthony. 1997. "The 'Golden Age' and National Renewal." In *Myths and Nationhood*, edited by G Hosking and G. Schopfin. London: Hurst.

Smogorzewski, K. 1954. "Democracy in Turkey." *The Contemporary Review* 186: 80–85.

Spencer, Robert. 1958. "Cultural Process and Intellectual Current: Durkheim and Atatürk." *American Anthropologist* 60 (4): 640–657.

SSSR i Turtsija. 1917–1979 [USSR and Turkey. 1917–1979]. 1981. Edited by M. Gastrasyan and P. Moiseyev. Moscow: "Nauka" Press.

Steinbach, Udo. 1984. "Atatürk's Impact on Turkey's Political Culture Since World War II." In *Atatürk and The Modernization of Turkey*, 78–88. Boulder: Westview Press.

Sternhell, Zeev. 1998. "The Crisis of fin-de-sciecle Thought." In *International Fascism: Theories, Causes and the New Consensus*, edited by Roger Griffin, 169–174. London: Arnold.

———. 1987. "Fascism." In *The Blackwell Encyclopedia of Political Thought*, edited by D. Miller. Oxford: Basil Blackwell.

Süleyman, İnan. 2007. "The First 'History of the Turkish Revolution' Lectures and Courses in Turkish Universities (1934–1942)." *Middle Eastern Studies* 43 (4): 593–609.

Sunar, İlkay. 2004. *State, Society and Democracy in Turkey.* İstanbul: Bahçeşehir University Publication.

Süreyya, Şevket. 1933. "Milli Kurtuluş Hareketleri Hakkında Bizim Tezimiz." *Kadro*, mart.

Sverchevskaia, Antonina. 1983. *Sovetsko-Turetskie Kul'turnye Sviazi 1925–1981.* [Soviet-Turkish Cultural Relations 1925–1981]. Moscow: Nauka.

Swartz, Avonna Deanne. 1997. *Textbooks and National Ideology: A Content Analysis of the Secondary Turkish History Textbooks Used in the Republic of Turkey Since 1929.* PhD dissertation, University of Texas at Austin.

Tachau, Frank. 1984. *Turkey: The Politics of Authority, Democracy and Development.* New York: Praeger.

Tamkoç, Metin. 1976. *The Warrior Diplomats: Guardians of the National Security and Modernization of Turkey*. Salt lake City: University of Utah Press.

Tepe, Sultan. 2000. "A Kemalist-Islamist Movement? The Nationalist Action Party." *Turkish Studies* 1 (2): 59–72.

Ter-Matevosyan, Vahram. 2008. *Islamy Turkiayi Hasarakakan-Qakhaqakan Kyankum Islam, 1970–2001* [Islam in the Social and Political Life of Turkey, 1970–2001]. Yerevan: Limush Publication.

———. 2009. "Kemalism as a Social Movement: Transforming Patterns of Collective Identities in Turkey." *Turkic and Ottoman Studies* 6: 86–104.

———. 2015. "Review of Stefan Ihrig's Atatürk in the Nazi Imagination, The Belknap Press of Harvard University Press, Cambridge." *International Journal of Armenian Genocide Studies* 2 (1): 87–92.

The General Secretatiat of the National Security Council. 1982. *12 September in Turkey: Before and After*. Ankara: The General Secretatiat of the National Security Council.

Toker, Metin. 1990. *DP'in Altın Yılları, 1950–1954* [Golden Years of the DP]. Ankara: Bilge.

———. 1991. *Demokrasimizin İsmet Paşalı yılları 1944–1973*. Ankara: Bilgi Yayınevi.

Toktaş, Şule, and Bülent Aras. 2009. "The EU and Minority Rights in Turkey." *Political Science Quarterly* 124 (4): 697–720.

Tolz, Vera. 2008. "European, National, and (Anti-)Imperial: The Formation of Academic Oriental Studies in Late Tsarist and Early Soviet Russia." *Kritika: Explorations in Russian and Eurasian History* 9 (1): 53–81.

———. 2011. *Russia's Own Orient: The Politics of Identity and Oriental Studies in the Late Imperial and Early Soviet Periods*. Oxford and New York: Oxford University Press.

Tongas, Gerard. 1939. *Atatürk and the True Nature of Modern Turkey*. London: Luzac & Co.

Toprak, Binnaz. 1981. *Islam and Political Development in Turkey*. Leiden: Brill.

Toynbee, Arnold J., and Kenneth P. Kirkwood. 1926. *Turkey*. London: Benn.

Trask, Roger. 1971. *The United States Response to Turkish Nationalism and Reform, 1914–1939*. Minneapolis: The University of Minnesota Press.

Tunaya, Tarık Zafer. 1952. *Türkiye'de Siyasi Partiler (1859–1952)* [Political Parties in Turkey (1859–1952)]. İstanbul: Doğan Kardeş.

Tunçay, Mete. 1981. *Türkiye Cumhuriyet'nde Tek Parti Yonetimi'nin Kurulmasi (1923–1931)* [The Founding of the Single Party Regime in the Turkish Republic (1923–1931)]. İstanbul: Cem Yayınevi.

Türkeş, Mustafa. 1999. "The Ideology of the *Kadro* (Cadre) Movement: A Patriotic Leftist Movement in Turkey." In *Turkey Before and After Atatürk Internal and External Affairs*, edited by Sylvia Kedourie, 92–119. London: Frank Cass.

Turkey's Future. 1928. *Arev, Journal Armenien*, April 25: 3.

Tveritinova, Anna. 1953. "Ot Natsional-Shovinizma k Natsional-Predatel'stvu." [From National-Chauvinism to National Treachery.] *Zvezda Vostoka* 8 (79): 70–87.

Uldricks, Teddy. 1979. *Diplomacy and Ideology: The Origins of Soviet Foreign Relations, 1917–1930*. London: Sage.

Ulus, Özgür Mutlu. 2011. *The Army and Radical Left in Turkey: Military Coups, Social Revolution and Kemalism*. London: I.B. Tauris.

Uyar, Hakkı. 2001a. "Necmettin Sadık Sadak." In *Kemalizm: Modern Türkiye'de Siyasi Düşünce*, edited by Murat Belge, 102–112. İstanbul: İletişim Yayınları.

———. 2001b. "Mahmut Esat Bozkurt." In *Kemalizm, Modern Türkiye'de Siyasi Düşünce*, edited by Murat Belge, 214–219. Istanbul: İletişim Yayınları.

VanderLippe, John. 2005. *The Politics of Turkish Democracy: İsmet İnönü and the Formation of the Multi-Party System, 1938–1950*. New York: State University of New York Press.

Vasileva, Darina. 1986. "Forming the Kemalist Ideology and Its Influence on the Cultural Policy of Turkey Up the Second World War." *Études balkaniques, Academie Bulgarie Des Sciences* (4): 3–17.

Vasiljev, V. 1962. "Manifest 150-i." [The Manifesto of 150.] *Za Rubezhom* (4): 18.

Vdovichenko, Dmitrij. 1967. *Bor'ba Politicheskih Partii v Turtsii (1944–1965)* [The Struggle of Political Parties in Turkey (1944–1965)]. Moscow: Nauka.

Verba, Sidney. 1965. "Conclusion: Comparative Political Culture." In *Political Culture and Political Development, Studies in Political Development*, edited by Lucian W. Pye and Sidney Verba, 512–560. Princeton: Princeton University Press.

Vygodskii, S. 1963. *Vneshnaia politika SSSR* [Foreign Policy of the USSR]. Moscow: Gosudarstvennoje Izdatel'stvo Politicheskoj Literatury.

Walter, Denny. 1982. "Atatürk and Political Art in Turkey." *Bulletin of the Turkish Studies Association* (Turkish Studies Association) 6 (2): 17–24.

Walton, J. 1932. "Was Adam a Turk?: Angora's Historian's New Claim." *The Daily Telegraph*, September 9.

Webster, Donald E. 1939. *The Turkey of Atatürk*. Philadelphia: The American Academy of Political and Social Science.

Weiker, Walter. 1963. *The Turkish Revolution 1960–1961: Aspects of Military Politics*. Washington, DC: The Brookings Institution.

———. 1973. *Political Tutelage and Democracy in Turkey: The Free Party and Its Aftermath*. Leiden: Brill.

———. 1981. *The Modernization of Turkey: From Atatürk to the Present Day*. New York: Holmes and Meier.

White, Stephen. 1984. "Soviet Russia and the Asian Revolution, 1917–1924." *Review of International Studies* 10 (3): 219–232.

Wilson, Christopher Samuel. 2007. *Remembering and Forgetting in the Funerary Architecture of Mustafa Kemal Atatürk: The Construction and Maintenance of National Memory*. Unpublished dissertation, Middle East Technical University, Ankara.

———. 2011. "The Persistence of the Turkish Nation in the Mausoleum of Mustafa Kemal Atatürk." In *Nationalism in a Global Era: The Persistence of Nations*, edited by Mitchell Young, Andreas Sturm, and Eric Zuelow, 93–114. London: Routledge Press.

Yavuz, Hakan. 1997. "Political Islam and the Welfare (Refah) Party in Turkey." *Comparative Politics* 30 (1): 63–82.

———. 2003. *Islamic Political Identity in Turkey*. Oxford: Oxford University Press.

Yavuz, Hakan, and Mujeeb R. Khan. 2000. "Turkey's Fault Lines and the Crisis of Kemalism." *Current History* 99 (633): 33–38.

Yenukidze, Avel'. 1933. "Desat' let Tureckoj Respubliki." [Ten Years of Turkish Republic.] *Mirovoje Khozayestvo i Mirovaya Politika* (10): 86–93.

Yeremeyev, Dmitrij. 1963. "Kemalizm i Pantjurkizm." [Kemalism and Pan-Turkism.] *Narody Azii i Afriki* 3: 58–70.

Yıldız, Ahmet. 2001. "Recep Peker." In *Kemalizm: Modern Türkiye'de Siyasi Düşünce*, edited by Murat Belge, 58–63. İstanbul: İletişim Yayınları.

Yılmız, Hale. 2013. *Becoming Turkish: Nationalist Reforms and Cultural Negotiations in Early Republican Turkey, 1923–1945*. New York: Syracuse University Press.

Yön. 1960. "Feyzioğlunun Görüşleri." *ağustos* 22: 4.

Yörük, Zafer. 1997. "Turkish Identity from Genesis to the Day of Judgment." In *Politics and the Ends of Identity*, edited by Kathryn Dean, 103–134. Vermont: Ashgate.

Youst, Konstantin. 1926. "Pisma iz Turtsii: Novie Puti i Ikh Smisl." [Letters from Turkey: New Paths and Their Meaning.] *Krasnaja Nov'*, 174–186.

Zara, Phillippe De. 1936. *Mustaptha Kemal: Dictateur*. Paris: Fernand Sorlot.

Zarevand. 1930. *Turtsija i Panturanizm [vvedenie A. N. Mandel'shtama]* [Turkey and Pan-Turkism: Foreword by Mandelshtam]. Paris.

Zürcher, Erik-Jan. 1984. *The Unionist Factor: The Role of the Committee of Union and Progress in the Turkish National Movement 1905—1926*. Leiden: Brill.

———. 1991. *Political Opposition in the Early Turkish Republic: The Progressive Republican Party 1924–1925*. Leiden: Brill.

———. 1992. "The Ottoman Legacy of the Turkish Republic: An Attempt at a New Periodization." *Die Welt des Islams* 32: 237–253.

———. 1993. *Turkey: A Modern History*. London: I.B. Tauris.

———. 2005. "Ottoman Sources of Kemalist Thought." In *Late Ottoman Society: The Intellectual Legacy*, edited by Elisabeth Özdalga, 13–26. London: Curzon.

———. 2010. *The Young Turk Legacy and Nation Building: From the Ottoman Empire to Atatürk's Turkey*. London: I.B. Tauris.

———. 2017. *Turkey: A Modern History*, 4th ed. London: I.B. Tauris.

Index

© The Editor(s) (if applicable) and The Author(s) 2019
V. Ter-Matevosyan, *Turkey, Kemalism and the Soviet Union*,
Modernity, Memory and Identity in South-East Europe,
https://doi.org/10.1007/978-3-319-97403-3

Printed by Printforce, the Netherlands